ELEMENTS

Literature

FIFTH COURSE

The Holt Reader
An Interactive WorkText

Instruction in Reading Literature and Related Materials

Standardized Test Practice

HOLT, RINEHART AND WINSTON
A Harcourt Education Company
Austin • Orlando • Chicago • New York • Toronto • London • San Diego

CREDITS

Supervisory Editors: Juliana Koenig, Fannie Safier

Managing Editor: Mike Topp

Administrative Managing Editor: Michael Neibergall

Senior Product Manager: Don Wulbrecht

Editors: Terence J. Fitzgerald, Michael Fleming, Carroll Moulton, Alan Shaw

Copyediting Supervisor: Mary Malone

Copyeditors: Elizabeth Dickson, *Senior Copyeditor;* Christine Altgelt, Joel Bourgeois, Emily Force, Julie A. Hill, Julia Thomas Hu, Jennifer Kirkland, Millicent Ondras, Dennis Scharnberg

Project Administration: Elizabeth LaManna

Editorial Support: Bret Isaacs, Brian Kachmar, Mark Koenig, Erik Netcher

Editorial Permissions: Ann B. Farrar, Carrie Jones, David Smith

Design: Bruce Bond, *Design Director, Book Design*

Electronic Publishing: Nanda Patel, JoAnn Stringer, *Project Coordinators;* Sally Dewhirst, *Quality Control Team Leader;* Angela Priddy, Barry Bishop, Becky Golden-Harrell, Ellen Rees, *Quality Control;* Juan Baquera, *Electronic Publishing Technology Services Team Leader;* Christopher Lucas, *Team Leader;* Lana Kaupp, Kim Orne, Susan Savkov, *Senior Production Artists;* Ellen Kennedy, Patricia Zepeda, *Production Artists;* Heather Jernt, *Electronic Publishing Supervisor;* Robert Franklin, *Electronic Publishing Director*

Production/Manufacturing: Belinda Barbosa Lopez, Michael Roche, *Senior Production Coordinators;* Carol Trammel, *Production Manager;* Beth Prevelige, *Senior Production Manager*

For acknowledgments, see pages 472–73, which are an extension of the copyright page.

Printed in the United States of America

5 179 05

Contents

PART 2 Standardized Test Practice

Literary Period Tests

Comparing Literature

Skills Table of Contents

Literary Skills

Vocabulary Skills

To the Student

A Book for You

The Holt Reader: An Interactive WorkText is a book created especially for you. It is a size that's easy to carry around. This book actually tells you to write in it, circling, underlining, jotting down responses to the literature and related materials. In addition to outstanding selections and background information providing the context for these selections, you'll find graphic organizers that encourage you to think a different way.

The Holt Reader: An Interactive WorkText is designed to accompany *Elements of Literature*. Like *Elements of Literature*, it helps you interact with the literature and background materials. The chart below shows you what's in the book and how it's organized.

PART 1 Reading Literature and Related Materials	PART 2 Standardized Test Practice
Introductions to Literary Periods Literary Selections from *Elements of Literature*	Literary Period Tests Comparing Literature

Reading Literature and Related Materials

When you read a historical essay, you read mainly to get information that is stated directly on the page. When you read literature, you need to go beyond understanding what the words mean and getting the facts straight. You need to read between the lines of a poem or story to discover the writer's meaning. No matter what kind of reading you do, *The Holt Reader: An Interactive WorkText* will help you practice the skills and strategies you need to become an active and successful reader.

A Walk Through PART 1 Reading Literature and Related Materials

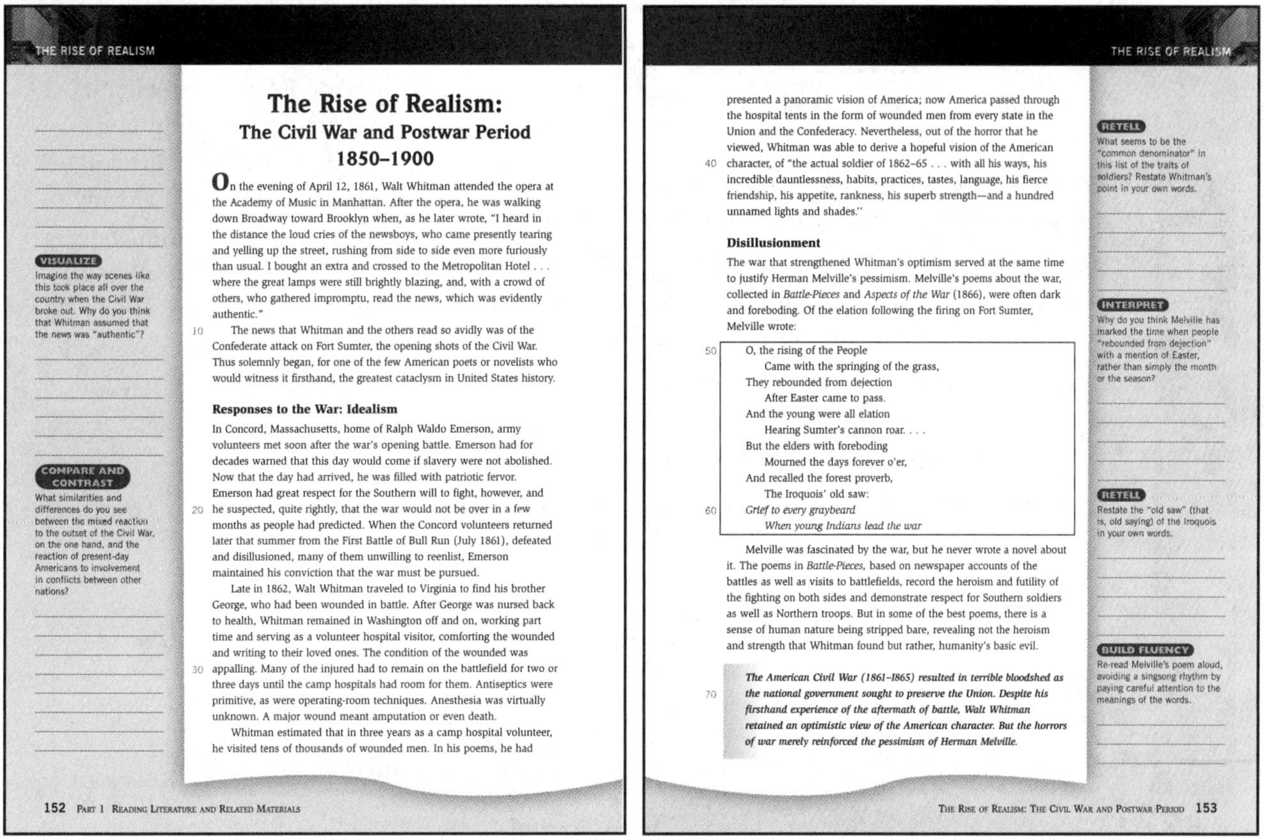
THE RISE OF REALISM

VISUALIZE
Imagine the way scenes like this took place all over the country when the Civil War broke out. Why do you think that Whitman assumed that the news was "authentic"?

COMPARE AND CONTRAST
What similarities and differences do you see between the mixed reaction to the outset of the Civil War, on the one hand, and the reaction of present-day Americans to involvement in conflicts between other nations?

The Rise of Realism:
The Civil War and Postwar Period
1850–1900

On the evening of April 12, 1861, Walt Whitman attended the opera at the Academy of Music in Manhattan. After the opera, he was walking down Broadway toward Brooklyn when, as he later wrote, "I heard in the distance the loud cries of the newsboys, who came presently tearing and yelling up the street, rushing from side to side even more furiously than usual. I bought an extra and crossed to the Metropolitan Hotel . . . where the great lamps were still brightly blazing, and, with a crowd of others, who gathered impromptu, read the news, which was evidently authentic."

The news that Whitman and the others read so avidly was of the Confederate attack on Fort Sumter, the opening shots of the Civil War. Thus solemnly began, for one of the few American poets or novelists who would witness it firsthand, the greatest cataclysm in United States history.

Responses to the War: Idealism

In Concord, Massachusetts, home of Ralph Waldo Emerson, army volunteers met soon after the war's opening battle. Emerson had for decades warned that this day would come if slavery were not abolished. Now that the day had arrived, he was filled with patriotic fervor. Emerson had great respect for the Southern will to fight, however, and he suspected, quite rightly, that the war would not be over in a few months as people had predicted. When the Concord volunteers returned later that summer from the First Battle of Bull Run (July 1861), defeated and disillusioned, many of them unwilling to reenlist, Emerson maintained his conviction that the war must be pursued.

Late in 1862, Walt Whitman traveled to Virginia to find his brother George, who had been wounded in battle. After George was nursed back to health, Whitman remained in Washington off and on, working part time and serving as a volunteer hospital visitor, comforting the wounded and writing to their loved ones. The condition of the wounded was appalling. Many of the injured had to remain on the battlefield for two or three days until the camp hospitals had room for them. Antiseptics were primitive, as were operating-room techniques. Anesthesia was virtually unknown. A major wound meant amputation or even death.

Whitman estimated that in three years as a camp hospital volunteer, he visited tens of thousands of wounded men. In his poems, he had presented a panoramic vision of America; now America passed through the hospital tents in the form of wounded men from every state in the Union and the Confederacy. Nevertheless, out of the horror that he viewed, Whitman was able to derive a hopeful vision of the American character, of "the actual soldier of 1862–65 . . . with all his ways, his incredible dauntlessness, habits, practices, tastes, language, his fierce friendship, his appetite, rankness, his superb strength—and a hundred unnamed lights and shades."

Disillusionment

The war that strengthened Whitman's optimism served at the same time to justify Herman Melville's pessimism. Melville's poems about the war, collected in *Battle-Pieces* and *Aspects of the War* (1866), were often dark and foreboding. Of the elation following the firing on Fort Sumter, Melville wrote:

O, the rising of the People
  Came with the springing of the grass,
They rebounded from dejection
  After Easter came to pass.
And the young were all elation
  Hearing Sumter's cannon roar. . . .
But the elders with foreboding
  Mourned the days forever o'er,
And recalled the forest proverb,
  The Iroquois' old saw:
Grief to every graybeard
  When young Indians lead the war

Melville was fascinated by the war, but he never wrote a novel about it. The poems in *Battle-Pieces*, based on newspaper accounts of the battles as well as visits to battlefields, record the heroism and futility of the fighting on both sides and demonstrate respect for Southern soldiers as well as Northern troops. But in some of the best poems, there is a sense of human nature being stripped bare, revealing not the heroism and strength that Whitman found but rather, humanity's basic evil.

The American Civil War (1861–1865) resulted in terrible bloodshed as the national government sought to preserve the Union. Despite his firsthand experience of the aftermath of battle, Walt Whitman retained an optimistic view of the American character. But the horrors of war merely reinforced the pessimism of Herman Melville.

RETELL
What seems to be the "common denominator" in this list of the traits of soldiers? Restate Whitman's point in your own words.

INTERPRET
Why do you think Melville has marked the time when people "rebounded from dejection" with a mention of Easter, rather than simply the month or the season?

RETELL
Restate the "old saw" (that is, old saying) of the Iroquois in your own words.

BUILD FLUENCY
Re-read Melville's poem aloud, avoiding a singsong rhythm by paying careful attention to the meanings of the words.

152 PART 1 READING LITERATURE AND RELATED MATERIALS

THE RISE OF REALISM: THE CIVIL WAR AND POSTWAR PERIOD 153

Historical Introductions

An introduction is provided for each literary period covered: Beginnings to 1800, American Romanticism, the American Renaissance, a New American Poetry, The Rise of Realism, The Moderns, American Drama, and Contemporary Literature. Side notes focus on important figures and events. Brief medial summaries and lists of characteristics help to reinforce content.

A Walk Through PART 1 Reading Literature and Related Materials

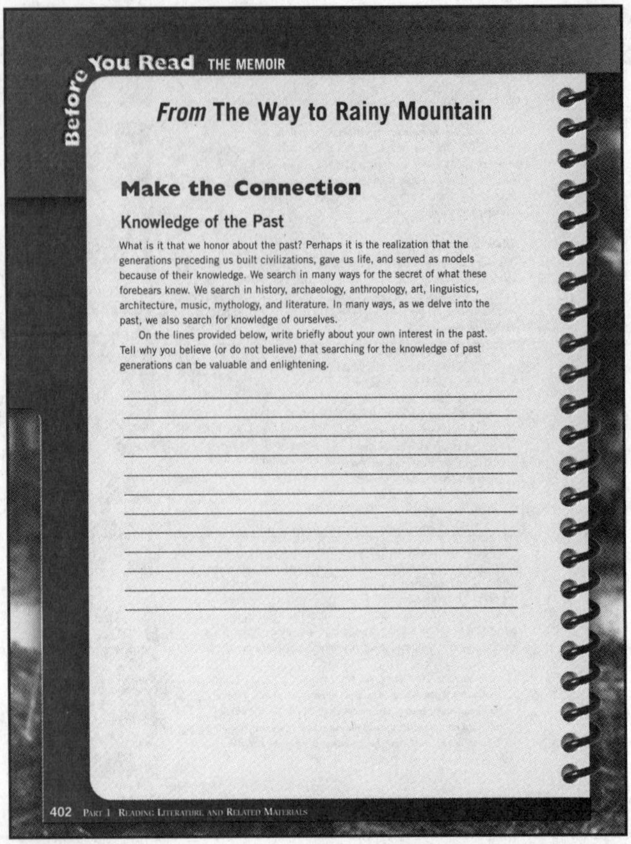

Before You Read THE MEMOIR

From The Way to Rainy Mountain

Make the Connection

Knowledge of the Past

What is it that we honor about the past? Perhaps it is the realization that the generations preceding us built civilizations, gave us life, and served as models because of their knowledge. We search in many ways for the secret of what these forebears knew. We search in history, archaeology, anthropology, art, linguistics, architecture, music, mythology, and literature. In many ways, as we delve into the past, we also search for knowledge of ourselves.

On the lines provided below, write briefly about your own interest in the past. Tell why you believe (or do not believe) that searching for the knowledge of past generations can be valuable and enlightening.

402 PART 1 READING LITERATURE AND RELATED MATERIALS

Before You Read

In Part 1, the Before-You-Read activity helps you make a personal connection with the selection you are about to read. It helps you sharpen your awareness of what you already know by asking you to think and write about a topic before you read. The more you know about the topic of a text, the easier it is to understand the text. Sometimes this page will provide background information you need to know before you read the text.

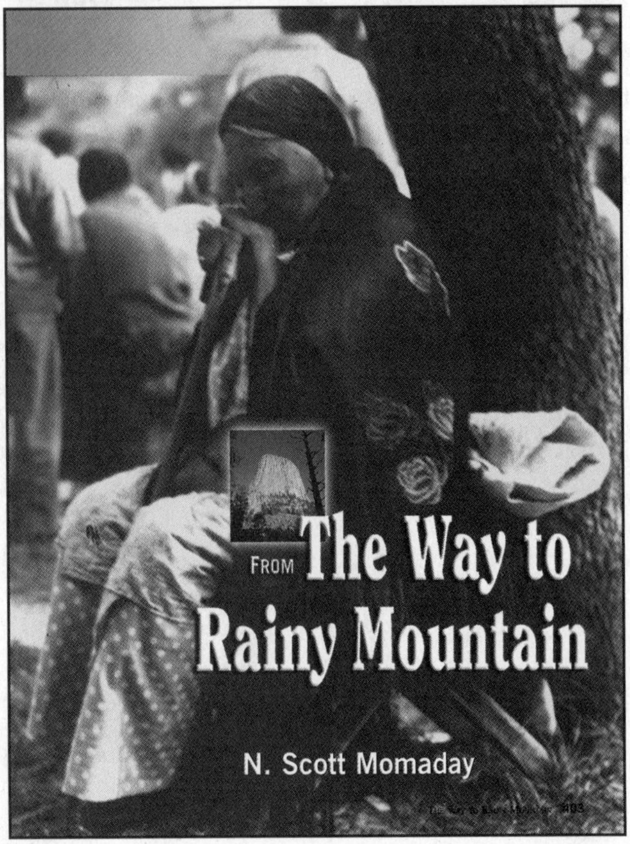

Interactive Selections from *Elements of Literature*

The literary selections in Part 1 are from *Elements of Literature,* Fifth Course. The selections are reprinted in a single column and in larger type to give you the room you need to mark up the text.

PART 1 Reading Literature and Related Materials

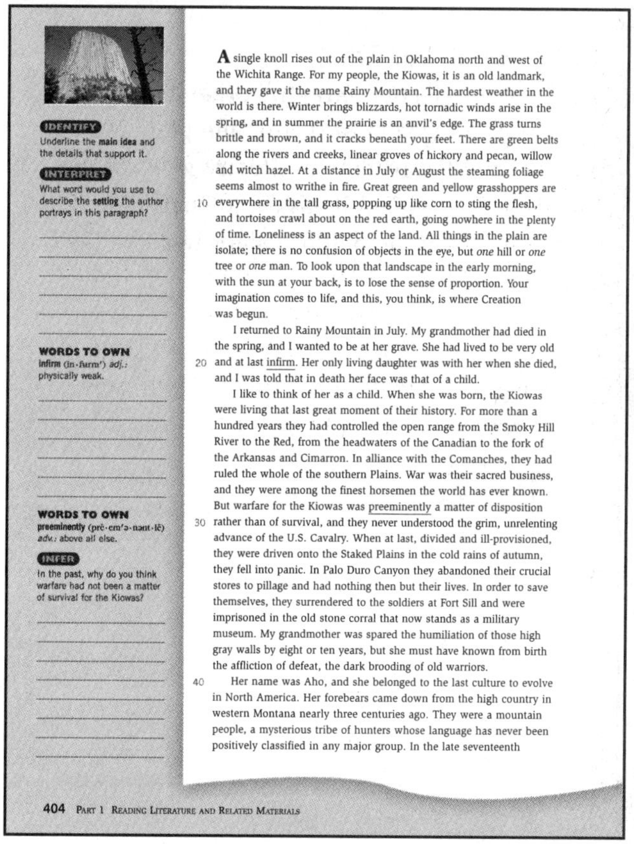

IDENTIFY
Underline the **main idea** and the details that support it.

INTERPRET
What word would you use to describe the **setting** the author portrays in this paragraph?

A single knoll rises out of the plain in Oklahoma north and west of the Wichita Range. For my people, the Kiowas, it is an old landmark, and they gave it the name Rainy Mountain. The hardest weather in the world is there. Winter brings blizzards, hot tornadic winds arise in the spring, and in summer the prairie is an anvil's edge. The grass turns brittle and brown, and it cracks beneath your feet. There are green belts along the rivers and creeks, linear groves of hickory and pecan, willow and witch hazel. At a distance in July or August the steaming foliage seems almost to writhe in fire. Great green and yellow grasshoppers are everywhere in the tall grass, popping up like corn to sting the flesh, and tortoises crawl about on the red earth, going nowhere in the plenty of time. Loneliness is an aspect of the land. All things in the plain are isolate; there is no confusion of objects in the eye, but *one* hill or *one* tree or *one* man. To look upon that landscape in the early morning, with the sun at your back, is to lose the sense of proportion. Your imagination comes to life, and this, you think, is where Creation was begun.

I returned to Rainy Mountain in July. My grandmother had died in the spring, and I wanted to be at her grave. She had lived to be very old and at last infirm. Her only living daughter was with her when she died, and I was told that in death her face was that of a child.

WORDS TO OWN
infirm (in·furm') *adj.:* physically weak.

I like to think of her as a child. When she was born, the Kiowas were living that last great moment of their history. For more than a hundred years they had controlled the open range from the Smoky Hill River to the Red, from the headwaters of the Canadian to the fork of the Arkansas and Cimarron. In alliance with the Comanches, they had ruled the whole of the southern Plains. War was their sacred business, and they were among the finest horsemen the world has ever known. But warfare for the Kiowas was preeminently a matter of disposition rather than of survival, and they never understood the grim, unrelenting advance of the U.S. Cavalry. When at last, divided and ill-provisioned, they were driven onto the Staked Plains in the cold rains of autumn, they fell into panic. In Palo Duro Canyon they abandoned their crucial stores to pillage and had nothing then but their lives. In order to save themselves, they surrendered to the soldiers at Fort Sill and were imprisoned in the old stone corral that now stands as a military museum. My grandmother was spared the humiliation of those high gray walls by eight or ten years, but she must have known from birth the affliction of defeat, the dark brooding of old warriors.

WORDS TO OWN
preeminently (prē·em'ə·nənt·lē) *adv.:* above all else.

INFER
In the past, why do you think warfare had not been a matter of survival for the Kiowas?

Her name was Aho, and she belonged to the last culture to evolve in North America. Her forebears came down from the high country in western Montana nearly three centuries ago. They were a mountain people, a mysterious tribe of hunters whose language has never been positively classified in any major group. In the late seventeenth

404 PART 1 READING LITERATURE AND RELATED MATERIALS

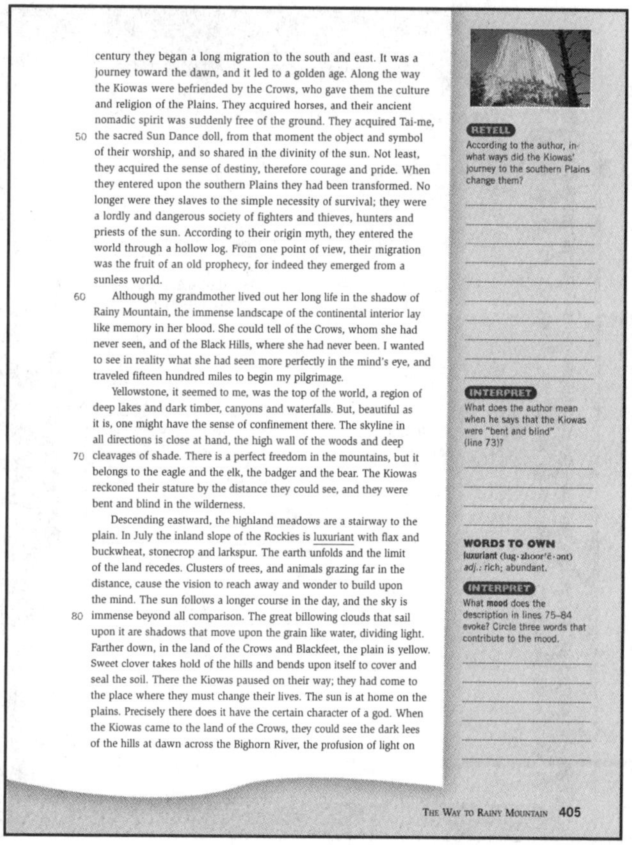

century they began a long migration to the south and east. It was a journey toward the dawn, and it led to a golden age. Along the way the Kiowas were befriended by the Crows, who gave them the culture and religion of the Plains. They acquired horses, and their ancient nomadic spirit was suddenly free of the ground. They acquired Tai-me, the sacred Sun Dance doll, from that moment the object and symbol of their worship, and so shared in the divinity of the sun. Not least, they acquired the sense of destiny, therefore courage and pride. When they entered upon the southern Plains they had been transformed. No longer were they slaves to the simple necessity of survival; they were a lordly and dangerous society of fighters and thieves, hunters and priests of the sun. According to their origin myth, they entered the world through a hollow log. From one point of view, their migration was the fruit of an old prophecy, for indeed they emerged from a sunless world.

RETELL
According to the author, in what ways did the Kiowas' journey to the southern Plains change them?

Although my grandmother lived out her long life in the shadow of Rainy Mountain, the immense landscape of the continental interior lay like memory in her blood. She could tell of the Crows, whom she had never seen, and of the Black Hills, where she had never been. I wanted to see in reality what she had seen more perfectly in the mind's eye, and traveled fifteen hundred miles to begin my pilgrimage.

Yellowstone, it seemed to me, was the top of the world, a region of deep lakes and dark timber, canyons and waterfalls. But, beautiful as it is, one might have the sense of confinement there. The skyline in all directions is close at hand, the high wall of the woods and deep cleavages of shade. There is a perfect freedom in the mountains, but it belongs to the eagle and the elk, the badger and the bear. The Kiowas reckoned their stature by the distance they could see, and they were bent and blind in the wilderness.

INTERPRET
What does the author mean when he says that the Kiowas were "bent and blind" (line 73)?

Descending eastward, the highland meadows are a stairway to the plain. In July the inland slope of the Rockies is luxuriant with flax and buckwheat, stonecrop and larkspur. The earth unfolds and the limit of the land recedes. Clusters of trees, and animals grazing far in the distance, cause the vision to reach away and wonder to build upon the mind. The sun follows a longer course in the day, and the sky is immense beyond all comparison. The great billowing clouds that sail upon it are shadows that move upon the grain like water, dividing light. Farther down, in the land of the Crows and Blackfeet, the plain is yellow. Sweet clover takes hold of the hills and bends upon itself to cover and seal the soil. There the Kiowas paused on their way; they had come to the place where they must change their lives. The sun is at home on the plains. Precisely there does it have the certain character of a god. When the Kiowas came to the land of the Crows, they could see the dark lees of the hills at dawn across the Bighorn River, the profusion of light on

WORDS TO OWN
luxuriant (lug·zhoor'ē·ənt) *adj.:* rich; abundant.

INTERPRET
What **mood** does the description in lines 75–84 evoke? Circle three words that contribute to the mood.

THE WAY TO RAINY MOUNTAIN 405

Strategies to Guide Your Reading: Side Notes

Notes in the side column accompany each selection. They guide your interaction with the text and help you unlock meaning. Many notes ask you to circle or underline in the text itself. Others provide lines on which you can write.

Identify asks you to find information that is stated directly in the text. You will often be asked to circle or underline the information in the text.

Retell asks you to restate or explain in your own words something that appears in the text.

Infer asks you to make an **inference,** or an educated guess. You make inferences on the basis of clues writers give you and on experiences from your own life. When you make an inference, you read between the lines to figure out what the writer suggests but does not say directly.

Predict asks you to figure out what will happen next. Making predictions as you read helps you think about and understand what you are reading. To make predictions, look for clues that the writer gives you. You'll probably find yourself adjusting predictions as you read.

Interpret asks you to explain the meaning of something. When you make an interpretation of a character, for example, you look at what the character says or does, and then you think about what the character's words and actions mean. Interpretations help you get at the main idea of a selection, the discovery about life you take away from it.

Evaluate asks you to form opinions about what you read. For example, you might see the following note at the end of a story: "How satisfying is the ending of this story? Give two reasons for your answer."

Visualize asks you to picture the characters, settings, and events being described in a selection. As you read, look for details that help you make a mental picture.

Compare and Contrast asks you to find similarities or differences in the text.

Connect asks you to explore the relationship between some event or idea in literature and your own experience.

Build Fluency asks you to read aloud a poem or passage from a story. It lets you practice phrasing, expression, and reading in meaningful chunks. Sometimes hearing text read aloud makes the text easier to understand.

Words to Own lists words for you to learn and own. These words are underlined in the selection, letting you see the words in context. The words are defined for you right in the side column.

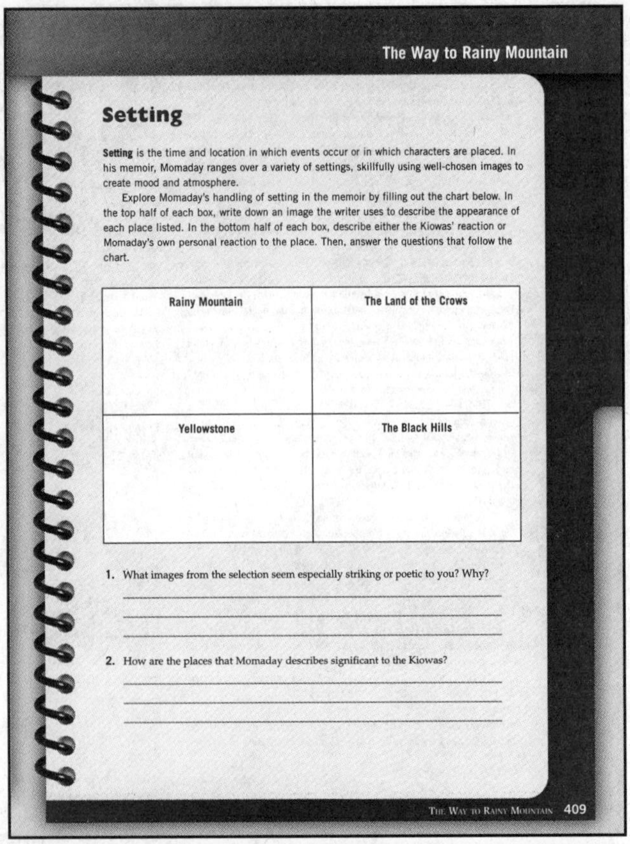

The Way to Rainy Mountain

Setting

Setting is the time and location in which events occur or in which characters are placed. In his memoir, Momaday ranges over a variety of settings, skillfully using well-chosen images to create mood and atmosphere.

Explore Momaday's handling of setting in the memoir by filling out the chart below. In the top half of each box, write down an image the writer uses to describe the appearance of each place listed. In the bottom half of each box, describe either the Kiowas' reaction or Momaday's own personal reaction to the place. Then, answer the questions that follow the chart.

Rainy Mountain	The Land of the Crows
Yellowstone	The Black Hills

1. What images from the selection seem especially striking or poetic to you? Why?

2. How are the places that Momaday describes significant to the Kiowas?

THE WAY TO RAINY MOUNTAIN 409

After You Read: Graphic Organizers

After each selection, **graphic organizers** give you a visual way to organize, interpret, and understand the reading or literary focus of the selection. You might be asked to chart the main events of the plot or complete a cause-and-effect chain.

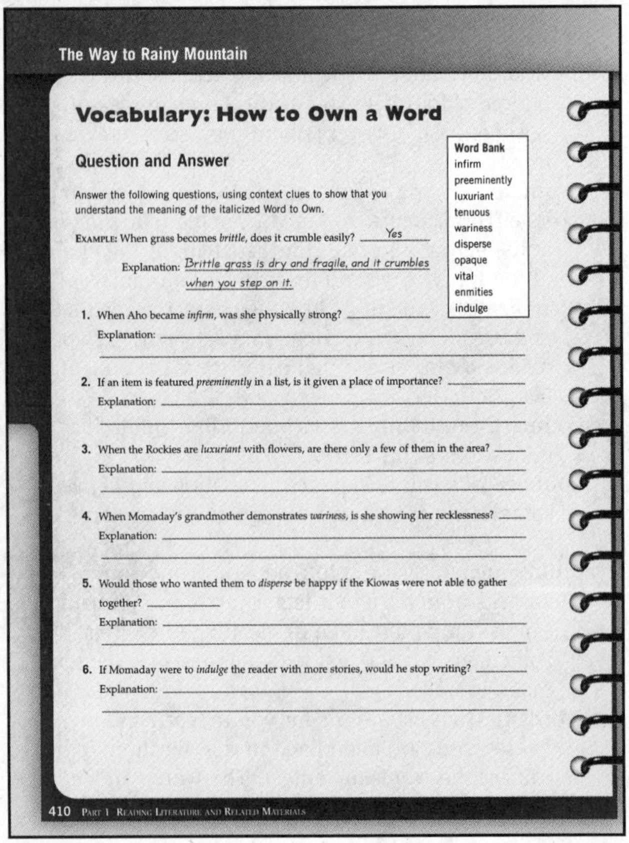

The Way to Rainy Mountain

Vocabulary: How to Own a Word

Question and Answer

Answer the following questions, using context clues to show that you understand the meaning of the italicized Word to Own.

Word Bank
infirm
preeminently
luxuriant
tenuous
wariness
disperse
opaque
vital
enmities
indulge

EXAMPLE: When grass becomes *brittle*, does it crumble easily? Yes

Explanation: *Brittle grass is dry and fragile, and it crumbles when you step on it.*

1. When Aho became *infirm*, was she physically strong?
   Explanation:
2. If an item is featured *preeminently* in a list, is it given a place of importance?
   Explanation:
3. When the Rockies are *luxuriant* with flowers, are there only a few of them in the area?
   Explanation:
4. When Momaday's grandmother demonstrates *wariness*, is she showing her recklessness?
   Explanation:
5. Would those who wanted them to *disperse* be happy if the Kiowas were not able to gather together?
   Explanation:
6. If Momaday were to *indulge* the reader with more stories, would he stop writing?
   Explanation:

410 PART 1 READING LITERATURE AND RELATED MATERIALS

After You Read: Vocabulary: How to Own a Word

Vocabulary: How to Own a Word worksheets at the end of literary selections check your knowledge of the Words to Own and help you develop skills for vocabulary building.

Part 2 Standardized Test Practice

STANDARDIZED TEST PRACTICE

LITERARY PERIOD TEST
BEGINNINGS TO 1800

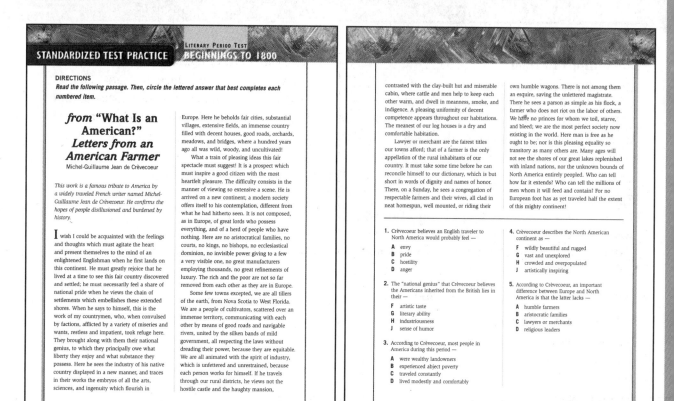

DIRECTIONS
Read the following passage. Then, circle the lettered answer that best completes each numbered item.

from "What Is an American?" *Letters from an American Farmer*

Michel-Guillaume Jean de Crèvecoeur

This work is a famous tribute to America by a widely traveled French writer named Michel-Guillaume Jean de Crèvecoeur. He confirms the hopes of people disillusioned and burdened by history.

I wish I could be acquainted with the feelings and thoughts which must agitate the heart and present themselves to the mind of an enlightened Englishman when he first lands on this continent. He must greatly rejoice that he lived at a time to see this fair country discovered and settled; he must necessarily feel a share of national pride when he views the chain of settlements which embellishes these extended shores. When he says to himself, this is the work of my countrymen, who, when convulsed by factions, afflicted by a variety of miseries and wants, restless and impatient, took refuge here. They brought along with them their national genius, to which they principally owe what liberty they enjoy and what substance they possess. Here he sees the industry of his native country displayed in a new manner, and traces in their works the embryos of all the arts, sciences, and ingenuity which flourish in Europe. Here he beholds fair cities, substantial villages, extensive fields, an immense country filled with decent houses, good roads, orchards, meadows, and bridges, where a hundred years ago all was wild, woody, and uncultivated!

What a train of pleasing ideas this fair spectacle must suggest! It is a prospect which must inspire a good citizen with the most heartfelt pleasure. The difficulty consists in the manner of viewing so extensive a scene. He is arrived on a new continent; a modern society offers itself to his contemplation, different from what he had hitherto seen. It is not composed, as in Europe, of great lords who possess everything, and of a herd of people who have nothing. Here are no aristocratical families, no courts, no kings, no bishops, no ecclesiastical dominion, no invisible power giving to a few a very visible one, no great manufacturers employing thousands, no great refinements of luxury. The rich and the poor are not so far removed from each other as they are in Europe.

Some few towns excepted, we are all tillers of the earth, from Nova Scotia to West Florida. We are a people of cultivators, scattered over an immense territory, communicating with each other by means of good roads and navigable rivers, united by the silken bands of mild government, all respecting the laws without dreading their power, because they are equitable. We are all animated with the spirit of industry, which is unfettered and unrestrained, because each person works for himself. If he travels through our rural districts, he views not the hostile castle and the haughty mansion, contrasted with the clay-built hut and miserable cabin, where cattle and men help to keep each other warm, and dwell in meanness, smoke, and indigence. A pleasing uniformity of decent competence appears throughout our habitations. The meanest of our log houses is a dry and comfortable habitation.

Lawyer or merchant are the fairest titles our towns afford; that of a farmer is the only appellation of the rural inhabitants of our country. It must take some time before he can reconcile himself to our dictionary, which is but short in words of dignity and names of honor. There, on a Sunday, he sees a congregation of respectable farmers and their wives, all clad in neat homespun, well mounted, or riding their own humble wagons. There is not among them an esquire, saving the unlettered magistrate. There he sees a parson as simple as his flock, a farmer who does not riot on the labor of others. We have no princes for whom we toil, starve, and bleed; we are the most perfect society now existing in the world. Here man is free as he ought to be; nor is this pleasing equality so transitory as many others are. Many ages will not see the shores of our great lakes replenished with inland nations, nor the unknown bounds of North America entirely peopled. Who can tell how far it extends? Who can tell the millions of men whom it will feed and contain? For no European foot has as yet traveled half the extent of this mighty continent!

1. Crèvecoeur believes an English traveler to North America would probably feel —
   - **A** envy
   - **B** pride
   - **C** hostility
   - **D** anger

2. The "national genius" that Crèvecoeur believes the Americans inherited from the British lies in their —
   - **F** artistic taste
   - **G** literary ability
   - **H** industriousness
   - **J** sense of humor

3. According to Crèvecoeur, most people in America during this period —
   - **A** were wealthy landowners
   - **B** experienced abject poverty
   - **C** traveled constantly
   - **D** lived modestly and comfortably

4. Crèvecoeur describes the North American continent as —
   - **F** wildly beautiful and rugged
   - **G** vast and unexplored
   - **H** crowded and overpopulated
   - **J** artistically inspiring

5. According to Crèvecoeur, an important difference between Europe and North America is that the latter lacks —
   - **A** humble farmers
   - **B** aristocratic families
   - **C** lawyers or merchants
   - **D** religious leaders

Part 2 of this book consists of literary period tests and selections for comparison. The selections and multiple-choice questions are similar to the ones you'll see on state and national standardized tests.

PART 1 Reading Literature and Related Materials

Beginnings to 1800

The United States is a land of immigrants. The first people began entering North America on foot many thousands of years ago. Then came people in wooden sailing ships. Later, millions came against their will in the stifling holds of slave ships. Millions of others endured weeks of discomfort in cramped, uncomfortable steerage sections of steamships. The latest immigrants are arriving by plane or even on flimsy rafts. Most likely you, your relatives, or some of your classmates immigrated to this country.

The First Migration: Ice Age Travelers

Archaeological evidence tells us that anywhere from twenty to over forty thousand years ago, Ice Age hunters traveling with dogs crossed the Bering land bridge (now submerged under the Bering Strait) from Siberia to what is now Alaska. Slowly, these people and their descendants, known today as American Indians, migrated south. By the 1490s, when the great wave of European exploration of the Americas started, numerous groups of Native Americans were scattered across the continent. Societies populating what is now the United States and Canada were relatively small; most were made up of only a few thousand people.

What's important to remember is that there were people here when the Europeans arrived in the fifteenth century; descendants of those people are still here, and their traditions remain.

People first migrated to North America from twenty to over forty thousand years ago. When the first Europeans arrived in the fifteenth century, American Indians were living in diverse societies spread across the continent.

The Europeans Arrive: The Explorers

The first written observations of life in this vast continent were recorded in Spanish and French by the European explorers of the fifteenth and sixteenth centuries. These writings open a window to a tumultuous time when the so-called New World was the heady focus of the dreams and desires of an entire era. Christopher Columbus (1451–1506) and many others described the Americas in a flurry of eagerly read letters, journals, and books. Hoping to fund further expeditions, the explorers emphasized the Americas' abundant resources, the peacefulness and hospitality of the inhabitants, and the promise of the unlimited wealth to be gained from fantastic treasuries of gold.

DENTIFY

nderline the words and nrases that indicate the arious ways people have ome to America.

CONNECT

ame any Native American eoples that live (or have ved) in your area.

CONNECT

ist any place names in your rea that have American ndian origins.

Naturally, then, it was greed that brought many of the first Europeans to the Americas. Bartolomé de Las Casas, a Spanish missionary, was horrified by the behavior of some of his countrymen. In his *Very Brief Account of the Destruction of the Indies* (1542), de Las Casas decried the treatment of the Native Americans.

> *The reason why the [Europeans] have killed and destroyed such infinite numbers of souls is solely because they have made gold their ultimate aim, seeking to load themselves with riches in the shortest time . . . These lands, being so happy and so rich, and the people so humble, so patient, and so easily subjugated, they have . . . taken no more account of them . . . than—I will not say of animals, for would to God they had considered and treated them as animals—but as even less than the dung in the streets.*

The first Europeans to visit the Americas were the explorers. Their enthusiastic accounts of the beauty and wealth of the Americas drew further expeditions to what Renaissance Europeans saw as the New World—and also, at times, encouraged greed for gold and cruelty toward the Native Americans.

The Puritan Legacy

Interesting and valuable as the explorers' writings are, they are not central to the development of the American literary tradition in the way the writings of the Puritans of New England are. In many respects, the American character has been shaped by the moral, ethical, and religious convictions of the Puritans.

Puritan is a broad term, referring to a number of Protestant groups that, beginning about 1560, sought to "purify" the Church of England, which since the time of Henry VIII (who reigned from 1509 to 1547) had been virtually inseparable from the country's government. Like other Protestant reformers on the European continent, English Puritans wished to return to the simpler forms of worship and church organization described in the New Testament. For them, religion was first of all a personal, inner experience. They did not believe that the clergy or the government should or could act as an intermediary between the individual and God.

Many Puritans suffered persecution in England. Some were put in jail and whipped, their noses slit and their ears lopped off. Some fled England for Holland and later for what was advertised as the New World. The first and most famous group of these Puritans—known to us as the Pilgrims—set sail in 1620 aboard the *Mayflower* and landed on the tip of Cape Cod, just before Christmas. They were followed, ten years

INTERPRET
Who might be Las Casas's intended audience for this condemnation of those who mistreated the Native Americans?

CONNECT
Name the first European explorers or settlers in your area.

IDENTIFY
What is the origin of the term *Puritan*? Underline the answer.

later, by seven hundred more Puritan settlers. By 1640, as many as twenty thousand English Puritans had sailed to what they called New England. There they hoped to build a new society patterned after God's word. For the Puritans, the everyday world and the spiritual world were closely intertwined.

The Puritans were single-minded visionaries convinced of the rightness of their beliefs, but they were also practical and businesslike. They felt that Christian worship and church organization should be simplified in order to more closely resemble Biblical models. Many Puritans were persecuted for their beliefs and fled England for Holland and, ultimately, for North America.

Puritan Beliefs: Sinners All?

At the center of Puritan theology was an uneasy mixture of certainty and doubt. The certainty was that because of Adam and Eve's sin of disobedience, most of humanity would be damned for all eternity. But the Puritans were also certain that God in his mercy had sent his son Jesus Christ to earth to save particular people. The doubt centered on whether a particular individual was one of the saved (the "elect") or one of the damned (the "unregenerate"). How did you know if you were saved or damned?

As it turns out, you did not know. There were two principal indications of the state of your soul, neither of them completely certain. You were saved by the grace of God, and you could *feel* this grace arriving, in an intensely emotional fashion. The inner arrival of God's grace was demonstrated by your outward behavior. After receiving grace, you were "reborn" as a member of the community of saints, and you behaved like a saint. People hoping to be among the saved examined their inner lives closely for signs of grace, and they tried to live exemplary lives. So American Puritans came to value self-reliance, industriousness, temperance, and simplicity. These were, coincidentally, the ideal qualities needed to carve out a new society in a strange land.

Puritans believed that Adam and Eve's sin had damned most people for all eternity. They also believed that Jesus Christ had been sent to earth to save particular people, known as the "elect." It was difficult to know for certain if one was saved or damned, so the Puritans tried to behave in as exemplary a manner as possible.

IDENTIFY

List the qualities that were valued by the Puritans.

Puritan Politics: Government by Contract

In the Puritan view, a covenant, or contract, existed between God and humanity. This spiritual covenant was a useful model for worldly social organization as well: Puritans believed that people should enter freely into agreements concerning their government. On the *Mayflower,* for example, the Puritans composed and signed the Mayflower Compact, outlining how they would be governed once they landed. In this use of a contractual agreement, they prepared the ground for American constitutional democracy.

On the other hand, because the Puritans believed the saintly "elect" should exert great influence on government, their political views tended to be undemocratic. There was little room for compromise. The witchcraft hysteria in Salem, Massachusetts, in 1692, resulted in part from fear that the community's moral foundation was threatened, and therefore its political cohesion was also in danger.

The Bible in America

The Puritans read the Bible as the story of the creation, fall, wanderings, and rescue of the human race. Within this long and complex narrative, each Puritan could see connections to events in his or her own life or to events in the life of the community. Each Puritan was trained to see life as a pilgrimage, or journey, to salvation.

The Puritans believed that the Bible was the literal word of God. Reading the Bible was a necessity for all Puritans, as was the ability to understand theological debates. For these reasons, the Puritans placed great emphasis on education. Thus, Harvard College, originally intended to train Puritan ministers for the rapidly expanding Colony, was founded in 1636, only sixteen years after the first Pilgrims had landed. And, just three years later, the first printing press in the American Colonies was set up. Not surprisingly, one of the most popular Puritan literary forms was the sermon; "Sinners in the Hands of an Angry God" by Jonathan Edwards (1703–1758) is a classic example.

Their beliefs required the Puritans to keep a close watch on both the inner and outer events of their lives. This central aspect of the Puritan mind greatly affected their writings. Diaries and histories were important forms of Puritan literature because they were records of the workings of God. We see this in Puritan poetry as well; even the terrifying loss of her house to fire prompted Anne Bradstreet (1612–1672), the American colonies' first published poet, to remind herself that "My hope and treasure lies above."

INFER

What does the title of Edwards's sermon suggest about Puritan ideas of human nature?

Puritan belief in a spiritual compact between God and humanity paved the way for American constitutional democracy. The Puritans emphasized education so that people could read and understand the Bible and follow religious debates. Diaries and histories were important forms of Puritan literature.

Characteristics of Puritan Writing

- The Bible provided a model for Puritan writing: a conception of each individual life as a journey to salvation. Puritans saw direct connections between Biblical events and their own lives.
- Puritans used writing to explore their inner and outer lives for signs of the workings of God.
- Diaries and histories were the most common forms of expression in Puritan society; in them writers described the workings of God.
- Puritans favored a plain style that stressed clarity of expression and avoided complicated figures of speech.

The Age of Reason: Tinkerers and Experimenters

By the end of the seventeenth century, new ideas that had been fermenting in Europe began to present a challenge to the unshakable faith of the Puritans.

The Age of Reason, or the Enlightenment, began in Europe with the philosophers and scientists of the seventeenth and eighteenth centuries who called themselves rationalists. **Rationalism** is the belief that human beings can arrive at truth by using reason, rather than by relying on the authority of the past, on religious faith, or on intuition.

The Puritans saw God as actively and mysteriously involved in the workings of the universe. The rationalists saw God differently; the great English rationalist Sir Isaac Newton (1642–1727), who devised the laws of gravity and motion, compared God to a clockmaker. Having created the perfect mechanism of this universe, God then left his creation to run on its own, like a clock. The rationalists believed that God's special gift to humanity was reason—the ability to think in an ordered, logical manner. This gift of reason enabled people to discover both scientific and spiritual truth. Everyone, then, had the capacity to regulate and improve his or her own life.

While the theoretical background for the Age of Reason took shape in Europe, a homegrown practicality and interest in scientific tinkering or experimenting already thrived in the American Colonies. From the earliest Colonial days, Americans had to be generalists and tinkerers; they had to make do with what they had, and they had to

NTERPRET

ny might the Age of ason also be known the Enlightenment?

achieve results. The frontier farmer with little access to tools shared a problem with the scientist who had few books and a whole new world of plants and animals to catalog. American thought had to be thought in action: an urge to improve the public welfare by being willing to experiment, to try things out, no matter what the authorities might say.

> *What then is . . . this new man? . . . He is an American, who, leaving behind him all his ancient prejudices and manners, receives new ones from the new mode of life he has embraced, the new government he obeys, and the new rank he holds. . . . [In America] individuals of all nations are melted into a new race of men, whose labors . . . will one day cause great changes in the world.*

—Michel-Guillaume Jean de Crèvecoeur,
Letters from an American Farmer (1782)

BUILD FLUENCY
Re-read this passage aloud, carefully pronouncing each word.

The Smallpox Plague

In April 1721, a ship from the West Indies docked in Boston Harbor. In addition to its cargo of sugar and molasses, this ship carried smallpox.

In the seventeenth and eighteenth centuries, smallpox was one of the scourges of life, as the AIDS virus is today. The disease spread rapidly, disfigured its victims, and was often fatal. The outbreak in Boston in 1721 was a major public-health problem.

The Puritan minister Cotton Mather (1663–1728) was interested in natural science and medicine. He had heard of a method for dealing with smallpox devised by a Turkish physician. This method was called inoculation. In June 1721, as the smallpox epidemic spread throughout Boston, Mather began a public campaign for inoculation.

Boston's medical community violently opposed such an experiment, especially one borrowed from the Muslims. A debate raged all summer and into the fall. Controversy developed into violence. In November, Mather's house was bombed.

Despite such fierce opposition, Mather succeeded in inoculating nearly three hundred people. By the time the epidemic was over, in March of the following year, only six of these had died. Of the almost six thousand other people who contracted the disease, about eight hundred fifty had died. The evidence, according to Mather's figures, was clear: Inoculation worked.

The smallpox controversy illustrates that contradictory qualities of the American character often existed side by side. A devout Puritan like Mather could also be a practical scientist.

Mather's experiment also reveals that a practical approach to social change and scientific research was necessary in America. American thought had to be thought in action: an urge to improve the public welfare by being willing to experiment, to try things out.

Deism: Are People Basically Good?

Like the Puritans, the rationalists discovered God through the medium of the natural world, but in a different way. Rationalists thought it unlikely that God would choose to reveal himself only at particular times to particular people. It seemed much more reasonable to believe that God had made it possible for *all* people at *all* times to discover natural laws through their God-given power of reason.

This outlook, called **deism** (dē′iz′əm), was shared by many eighteenth-century thinkers, including many founders of the American nation. American deists came from different religious backgrounds. But the deists avoided supporting specific religious groups. They sought, instead, the principles that united all religions.

IDENTIFY

Vhat were three beliefs held
›y the deists?

Deists believed that the universe was orderly and good. In contrast to the Puritans, deists stressed humanity's goodness. They believed in the perfectibility of every individual through the use of reason. God's objective, in the deist view, was the happiness of his creatures. Therefore, the best form of worship was to do good for others. There already existed in America an impulse to improve people's lives. Deism elevated this impulse to one of the nation's highest goals. To this day, social welfare is still a political priority and still the subject of fierce debate.

The American struggle for independence was justified largely by appeals to rationalist principles. The Declaration of Independence bases its arguments on rationalist assumptions about the relations between people, God, and natural law.

In contrast to Puritans, deists believed that God was available to all people all of the time. Deists believed that people were inherently good, that every individual had the gift of reason and with that gift could perfect himself or herself and society.

The Rationalist Worldview

- People arrive at truth by using reason rather than by relying on the authority of the past, on religion, or on nonrational mental processes like intuition.
- God created the universe but does not interfere in its workings.

- The world operates according to God's rules, and through the use of reason we can discover those rules.
- People are basically good and perfectible.
- Since God wants people to be happy, they worship God best by helping other people.
- Human history is marked by progress toward a more perfect existence.

Self-Made Americans

Most of the literature written in the American Colonies during the Age of Reason was, understandably, rooted in reality. This was an age of pamphlets, since most literature was intended to serve practical or political ends. Following the Revolutionary War (1775–1783), the problems of organizing and governing the new nation were of the highest importance.

The unquestioned masterpiece of the American Age of Reason is Benjamin Franklin's *Autobiography*. Franklin (1706–1790) used the autobiographical narrative, a form common in Puritan writing, and took out its religious justification. Written in clear, witty prose, this account of the development of the self-made American provided the model for a story that would be told again and again. In the twentieth century, it appears in F. Scott Fitzgerald's novel *The Great Gatsby* (1925), as well as in the countless biographies and autobiographies of self-made men and women on the best-seller lists today.

The masterpiece of the Revolutionary era is Franklin's* Autobiography. *Franklin took the Puritan impulse toward self-examination and molded it into the classic American rags-to-riches story—the triumph of the self-made person.

EVALUATE

Does rationalism represent an optimistic or a pessimistic view of human nature? Suppo your opinion.

IDENTIFY

Where does the idea of the self-made man or woman come from?

Here Follow Some Verses upon the Burning of Our House, July 10, 1666

Make the Connection

Tests of Strength

How we deal with losses in life is perhaps the greatest test of our inner strength. Some losses are so enormous that they shake us to our core and challenge our very sense of self. Response to such a loss is the topic of this poem: It portrays an internal debate, a kind of dialogue between self and soul. The poet struggles against despair with a determination to make the loss of her house and all her belongings strengthen her faith in God's goodness, not destroy it.

In his play *As You Like It,* Shakespeare wrote, "Sweet are the uses of adversity." That is, misfortune can provide new opportunities for improvement and even happiness. To explore the ways that we make "sweet use of adversity," complete this chart.

Misfortune	Danger	Opportunity
Examination failure	Discouragement, loss of motivation	"Wake-up call" to study harder
Auto accident		
Athletic injury		
Lost political election		
House damaged by storm		

Here Follow Some Verses upon the Burning of Our House, July 10, 1666

Anne Bradstreet

ISUALIZE

s poem tells a story. How
es this story begin? Visualize
scene suggested by
es 1–4.

NTERPRET

w is Bradstreet able to
im that the loss of her
use was "just"?

DENTIFY

rcle words in lines 25–34
at indicate some of the
ssessions destroyed in the
e.

NTERPRET

hy might Bradstreet have
sed the word *ever* in its
sual form in line 35 but the
ntracted form *e'er* in
nes 31 and 33?

In silent night when rest I took
For sorrow near I did not look
I wakened was with thund'ring noise
And piteous shrieks of dreadful voice.
That fearful sound of "Fire!" and "Fire!"
Let no man know is my desire.
I, starting up, the light did spy,
And to my God my heart did cry
To strengthen me in my distress
And not to leave me succorless.[1]
Then, coming out, beheld a space
The flame consume my dwelling place.
And when I could no longer look,
I blest His name that gave and took,[2]
That laid my goods now in the dust.
Yea, so it was, and so 'twas just.
It was His own, it was not mine,
Far be it that I should repine;
He might of all justly bereft
But yet sufficient for us left.
When by the ruins oft I past
My sorrowing eyes aside did cast,
And here and there the places spy
Where oft I sat and long did lie:
Here stood that trunk, and there that chest,
There lay that store I counted best.
My pleasant things in ashes lie,
And them behold no more shall I.
Under thy roof no guest shall sit,
Nor at thy table eat a bit.
No pleasant tale shall e'er be told,
Nor things recounted done of old.
No candle e'er shall shine in thee,
Nor bridegroom's voice e'er heard shall be.
In silence ever shall thou lie,
Adieu, Adieu,[3] all's vanity.
Then straight I 'gin my heart to chide,
And did thy wealth on earth abide?
Didst fix thy hope on mold'ring dust?
The arm of flesh didst make thy trust?

---

1. **succorless** (suk′ər·lis): without aid or assistance; helpless.
2. **that gave and took:** allusion to Job 1:21: "The Lord gave, and the Lord hath taken away; blessed be the name of the Lord."
3. **Adieu** (à·dyö′): French for "goodbye."

Raise up thy thoughts above the sky
That dunghill mists away may fly.
Thou hast an house on high erect,
Framed by that mighty Architect,
With glory richly furnished,
Stands permanent though this be fled.
It's purchased and paid for too
By Him who hath enough to do.
A price so vast as is unknown
Yet by His gift is made thine own;
There's wealth enough, I need no more,
Farewell, my pelf,[4] farewell my store.
The world no longer let me love,
My hope and treasure lies above.

INTERPRET

Whom does Bradstreet mean by the **metaphor** "mighty Architect"?

BUILD FLUENCY

Beginning with line 43, read the conclusion of the poem aloud. Read expressively. Avoid falling into a singsong rhythm by carefully attending to the real meaning of the words.

4. **pelf:** wealth or worldly goods; sometimes used as a term of contempt.

Poetic Inversion

The Puritans prized simple, plain expression and straightforward sentiments. Still, Bradstreet's work displays techniques used by virtually all seventeenth-century poets. Because poets of this period adhered to strictly regular patterns of **rhyme** and **meter,** they often allowed themselves a grammatical flexibility called **inversion,** in which word order is reversed (that is, *inverted*) in order to accommodate the demands of sound. For example, in the poem you have read, the first line ends "when rest I took"—not "when I took rest," because that would miss the rhyme with "look" in the next line.

Consider the examples of poetic inversion shown in the chart below, and then "translate" each phrase into its ordinary, natural order.

Inverted Form in Poem	Normal Order
EXAMPLE: "when rest I took" (line 1)	*when I took rest*
"I wakened was" (line 3)	
"I, starting up, the light did spy" (line 7)	
"When by the ruins oft I past" (line 21)	
"My pleasant things in ashes lie" (line 27)	
"at thy table eat a bit" (line 30)	

Inverted Form in Poem	Normal Order
"voice e'er heard shall be" (line 34)	
"In silence ever shall thou lie" (line 35)	
"And did thy wealth on earth abide?" (line 38)	
"mists away may fly" (line 42)	
"The world no longer let me love" (line 53)	

From Sinners in the Hands of an Angry God

Make the Connection

The Great Motivator

Most religious people today think of their faith as a source of comfort. The Puritans, though, believed that comfort led to complacency and complacency led to sin and damnation. They placed their hopes for salvation in *discomfort,* especially a terror of hell, as the pathway to heaven. "The fear of the Lord," reads one of the Psalms, "is the beginning of wisdom." When Puritan minister Jonathan Edwards delivered his most famous sermon, "Sinners in the Hands of an Angry God," he repeatedly had to ask for quiet because so many in the congregation were shrieking with fear.

Religious styles may have changed since Edwards's fire-and-brimstone sermon of 1741, but we still seek sensations of terror—just look at the popularity of today's horror movies. Why is this so? Partly, of course, we try to scare ourselves into behaving better. Fear of injury makes us buckle our seat belts. Fear of failure makes some of us study or work harder. But fear seems to stir something deeper in us—a profound feeling of being alive.

Complete the chart below to explore the fears we seek.

Frightening Stimulus	Root Source of Fear	Reason for Popularity
Television Crime Dramas	fear of becoming a crime victim, mistrust of strangers	satisfaction of seeing "the bad guys lose and the good guys win"
Horror Movies		
Extreme Sports (Snowboarding, Bungee Jumping, etc.)		
Thrill Rides (Roller Coasters, etc.)		

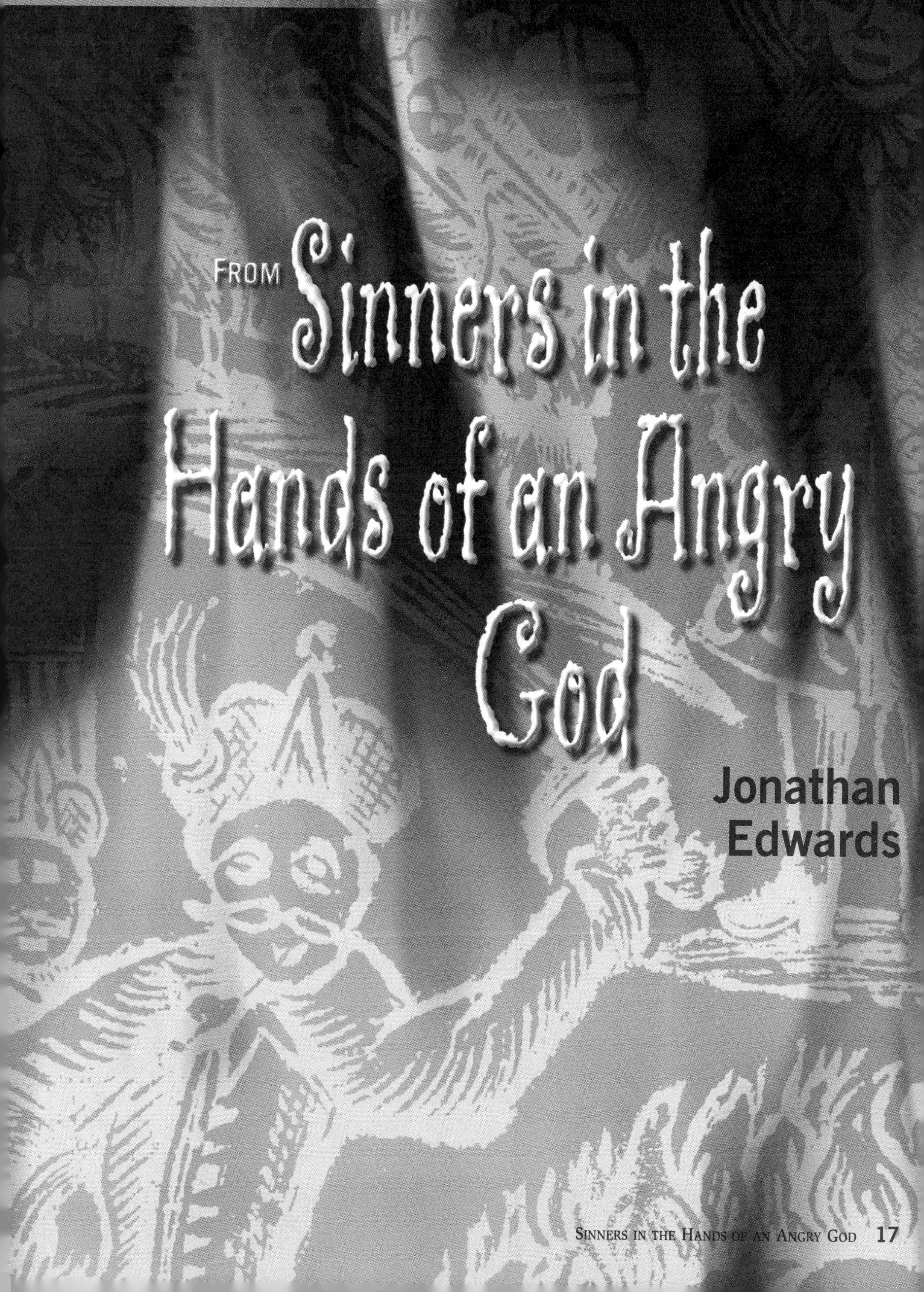

FROM *Sinners in the Hands of an Angry God*

Jonathan Edwards

So that, thus it is that natural men are held in the hand of God, over the pit of hell; they have deserved the fiery pit, and are already sentenced to it; and God is dreadfully provoked, His anger is as great toward them as to those that are actually suffering the executions of the fierceness of His wrath in hell, and they have done nothing in the least to appease or abate that anger, neither is God in the least bound by any promise to hold them up one moment: The devil is waiting for them, hell is gaping for them, the flames gather and flash about them, and would fain lay hold on them, and swallow them up; the fire pent up in their own hearts is struggling to break out: And they have no interest in any Mediator, there are no means within reach that can be any security to them.

In short, they have no refuge, nothing to take hold of; all that preserves them every moment is the mere arbitrary will, and uncovenanted, unobliged forbearance of an incensed God.

The use of this awful subject may be for awakening unconverted persons in this congregation. This that you have heard is the case of every one of you that are out of Christ. That world of misery, that lake of burning brimstone, is extended abroad under you. There is the dreadful pit of the glowing flames of the wrath of God; there is hell's wide gaping mouth open; and you have nothing to stand upon, nor anything to take hold of; there is nothing between you and hell but the air; it is only the power and mere pleasure of God that holds you up.

You probably are not sensible of this; you find you are kept out of hell, but do not see the hand of God in it; but look at other things, as the good state of your bodily constitution, your care of your own life, and the means you use for your own preservation. But indeed these things are nothing; if God should withdraw His hand, they would avail no more to keep you from falling, than the thin air to hold up a person that is suspended in it.

Your wickedness makes you as it were heavy as lead, and to tend downward with great weight and pressure toward hell; and if God should let you go, you would immediately sink and swiftly descend and plunge into the bottomless gulf, and your healthy constitution, and your own care and prudence, and best contrivance, and all your righteousness, would have no more influence to uphold you and keep you out of hell, than a spider's web would have to stop a fallen rock. . . .

The wrath of God is like great waters that are dammed for the present; they increase more and more, and rise higher and higher, till an outlet is given; and the longer the stream is stopped, the more rapid and mighty is its course, when once it is let loose. It is true, that judgment against your evil works has not been executed hitherto; the floods of God's vengeance have been withheld; but your guilt in the meantime is constantly increasing, and you are every day treasuring up more wrath; the waters are constantly rising, and waxing more and more mighty; and

VORDS TO OWN

rovoked (prō·vōkt′) *adj.:* nraged; angered.

ppease (ə·pēz′) *v.:* to calm; atisfy.

IDENTIFY

Circle words in the first paragraph that Edwards uses to portray God's anger at sinners.

VISUALIZE

Picture the lake of burning brimstone (that is, sulphur); magine being suspended precariously above the flames.

WORDS TO OWN

constitution (kän′stə·to͞o′shən) *n.:* physical condition.

PREDICT

If Edwards is trying so deliberately to frighten his hearers early in the sermon, what hope might he offer them later?

WORDS TO OWN

contrivance (kən·trī′vəns) *n.:* scheme; plan.

VISUALIZE

Picture the rising water and the buildup of pressure.

there is nothing but the mere pleasure of God that holds the waters back, that are unwilling to be stopped, and press hard to go forward. If God should only withdraw His hand from the floodgate, it would immediately fly open, and the fiery floods of the fierceness and wrath of God, would rush forth with inconceivable fury, and would come upon you with omnipotent power; and if your strength were ten thousand times greater than it is, yea, ten thousand times greater than the strength of the stoutest, sturdiest devil in hell, it would be nothing to withstand or endure it.

The bow of God's wrath is bent, and the arrow made ready on the string, and justice bends the arrow at your heart, and strains the bow, and it is nothing but the mere pleasure of God, and that of an angry God, without any promise or obligation at all, that keeps the arrow one moment from being made drunk with your blood. Thus all you that never passed under a great change of heart, by the mighty power of the Spirit of God upon your souls; all you that were never born again, and made new creatures, and raised from being dead in sin, to a state of new, and before altogether unexperienced light and life, are in the hands of an angry God. However you may have reformed your life in many things, and may have had religious affections,[1] and may keep up a form of religion in your families and closets,[2] and in the house of God, it is nothing but His mere pleasure that keeps you from being this moment swallowed up in everlasting destruction. However unconvinced you may now be of the truth of what you hear, by and by you will be fully convinced of it. Those that are gone from being in the like circumstances with you, see that it was so with them; for destruction came suddenly upon most of them; when they expected nothing of it, and while they were saying, peace and safety: Now they see, that those things on which they depended for peace and safety, were nothing but thin air and empty shadows.

The God that holds you over the pit of hell, much as one holds a spider, or some loathsome insect over the fire, abhors you, and is dreadfully provoked: His wrath toward you burns like fire; He looks upon you as worthy of nothing else but to be cast into the fire; He is of purer eyes than to bear to have you in His sight; you are ten thousand times more abominable in His eyes than the most hateful venomous serpent is in ours. You have offended Him infinitely more than ever a stubborn rebel did his prince; and yet it is nothing but His hand that holds you from falling into the fire every moment. It is to be ascribed to nothing else, that you did not go to hell the last night; that you was suffered to awake again in this world, after you closed your eyes to sleep. And there is no other reason to be given, why you have not dropped into hell since

1. **affections:** feelings.
2. **closets:** rooms for prayer and meditation.

WORDS TO OWN

inconceivable (in'kən·sēv'ə·bəl *adj.:* unimaginable; beyond understanding.

omnipotent (äm·nip'ə·tənt) *adj.:* all-powerful.

INTERPRET

What does Edwards mean by the phrase "by and by you will be fully convinced of it"?

WORDS TO OWN

abhors (ab·hôrz') *v.:* scorns; hates.

abominable (ə·bäm'ə·nə·bəl) *adj.:* disgusting; loathsome.

ascribed (ə·skrībd') *v.:* attributed to a certain cause.

INFER

Vhy do you think Edwards ddresses this sermon to you"?

EVALUATE

f indeed there is "nothing that ou can do" to save yourself, hen what good does it do Edwards's listeners to be told of God's wrath against them?

WORDS TO OWN

induce (in·do͞os′) *v.:* to persuade; force; cause.

BUILD FLUENCY

Re-read the last paragraph aloud in the expressive manner that a preacher like Edwards might have used to terrify his congregation.

you arose in the morning, but that God's hand has held you up. There is no other reason to be given why you have not gone to hell, since you have sat here in the house of God, provoking His pure eyes by your sinful wicked manner of attending His solemn worship. Yea, there is nothing else that is to be given as a reason why you do not this very moment drop down into hell.

O sinner! Consider the fearful danger you are in: It is a great furnace of wrath, a wide and bottomless pit, full of the fire of wrath, that you are held over in the hand of that God, whose wrath is provoked and incensed as much against you, as against many of the damned in hell. You hang by a slender thread, with the flames of divine wrath flashing about it, and ready every moment to singe it, and burn it asunder; and you have no interest in any Mediator, and nothing to lay hold of to save yourself, nothing to keep off the flames of wrath, nothing of your own, nothing that you ever have done, nothing that you can do, to induce God to spare you one moment. . . .

Figures of Speech

Figures of speech describe one thing in terms of another, very different thing. Writers often use comparisons when discussing concepts such as *love* or *liberty* or *happiness;* these abstractions might be better understood in terms of concrete images like a rose, an open cage, or a smiling face. Although Edwards's belief in damnation for the wicked and heaven for the righteous is very real, he makes extensive use of figures of speech to compare God's wrath to ordinary, everyday things that his listeners could relate to and understand.

Explore Edwards's figures of speech by completing the chart below.

Edwards's Figure of Speech	Literal Meaning	Point of Similarity
"There is the dreadful pit of the glowing flames of the wrath of God. . . ." (lines 18–19)	God's wrath is terrible.	The torment of a soul in hell is like the pain of a body in fire.
"The wrath of God is like great waters that are dammed for the present. . . ." (lines 37–38)		
"The bow of God's wrath is bent, and the arrow made ready on the string, and justice bends the arrow at your heart. . . ." (lines 54–55)		
"The God that holds you over the pit of hell, much as one holds a spider, or some loathsome insect over the fire, abhors you. . . ." (lines 75–76)		

Vocabulary: How to Own a Word

Context Clues

Word Bank
provoked
appease
constitution
contrivance
inconceivable
omnipotent
abhors
abominable
ascribed
induce

Read the sentences below. Using context clues and definitions of your Words to Own to guide you, circle the word that correctly completes the sentence. Underline any context clues that helped you arrive at the answer.

EXAMPLE: Edwards preaches that God is (*provoked*, *ascribed*) by sin, and if angered, God will cast human beings into hell.

1. Is there a (*constitution, contrivance*) that can help one avoid eternal damnation? According to Edwards, no such human plan exists.

2. Edwards attempts to (*induce, appease*) his congregation to follow his advice by using his power of persuasion.

3. An individual may take care of her or his (*constitution, contrivance*), but, Edwards asserts, attention to one's physical condition will not keep one out of hell.

4. Edwards evidently (*appeases, abhors*) "sinners." His fiery words communicate this hatred.

5. Edwards believes that God is an (*inconceivable, omnipotent*), or all-powerful, being who can bring about catastrophe at any time.

6. According to Edwards, God can be (*induced, provoked*) by anyone. An angry God has prepared eternal punishment for all.

7. The ways of humans, says Edwards, are mostly (*abominable, inconceivable*) to God, who is displeased by our loathsome behavior.

8. Is it (*inconceivable, omnipotent*) for people to find salvation outside the Puritan church?

9. According to Edwards, one cannot simply (*induce, appease*) God with good works or other calming actions.

10. Edwards (*ascribed, provoked*) God's wrath to people reluctant to accept Christ as their Savior, who are an affront to God.

From The Autobiography

Make the Connection

The Road to Success

"Rags to riches" is the success story that drives so much of American life and culture. Ever since the California Gold Rush of 1849, Americans have dreamed of "striking it rich," more by some stroke of luck than by any particular merit or virtue.

Before the Gold Rush, though, the classic rags-to-riches story was that of Benjamin Franklin—the poor boy who rose to prominence through hard work, an instinct for opportunity, and the determined cultivation of moral virtue. Franklin was justly proud of exemplifying this older vision of the American dream, and the *Autobiography* he began writing when he was sixty-five was intended as a kind of guidebook to success that any American could follow.

Which version of the rags-to-riches story do you find more compelling—"striking it rich" all at once like a lucky gambler, or steadily improving your condition like a clever, hardworking Benjamin Franklin? Complete the following chart to consider the many faces of the American dream.

Who dreams of success?	How might such a person define "success"?	How might this success be achieved?	How realistic is this dream?
Medical student	thriving clinical practice	long years of study and training	possible only for very serious student
High school basketball player			
Immigrant taxi driver			
Singer in a "garage band"			
Apprentice carpenter			

Benjamin Franklin

FROM The Autobiography

Leaving Boston

At length, a fresh difference arising between my brother and me, I took upon me to assert my freedom, presuming that he would not venture to produce the new indentures. It was not fair in me to take this advantage, and this I therefore reckon one of the first errata[1] of my life; but the unfairness of it weighed little with me, when under the impressions of resentment for the blows his passion too often urged him to bestow upon me, though he was otherwise not an ill-natured man: Perhaps I was too saucy and provoking.

When he found I would leave him, he took care to prevent my getting employment in any other printing house of the town, by going round and speaking to every master, who accordingly refused to give me work. I then thought of going to New York, as the nearest place where there was a printer; and I was rather inclined to leave Boston when I reflected that I had already made myself a little obnoxious to the governing party, and, from the arbitrary proceedings of the Assembly in my brother's case, it was likely I might, if I stayed, soon bring myself into scrapes; and farther, that my indiscreet disputations about religion began to make me pointed at with horror by good people as an infidel or atheist. I determined on the point, but my father now siding with my brother, I was sensible that, if I attempted to go openly, means would be used to prevent me. My friend Collins, therefore, undertook to manage a little for me. He agreed with the captain of a New York sloop for my passage, under the notion of my being a young acquaintance of his, that had got a naughty girl with child, whose friends would compel me to marry her, and therefore I could not appear or come away publicly. So I sold some of my books to raise a little money, was taken on board privately, and as we had a fair wind, in three days I found myself in New York, near 300 miles from home, a boy of but 17, without the least recommendation to, or knowledge of any person in the place, and with very little money in my pocket.

My inclinations for the sea were by this time worn out, or I might now have gratified them. But, having a trade, and supposing myself a pretty good workman, I offered my service to the printer in the place, old Mr. William Bradford,[2] who had been the first printer in Pennsylvania, but removed from thence upon the quarrel of George Keith. He could give me no employment, having little to do, and help enough already; but says he, "My son at Philadelphia has lately lost his principal hand,[3] Aquila Rose, by death; if you go thither, I believe he may employ you."

1. **errata** (er·rät′ə): Latin for "errors"; a printer's term.
2. **William Bradford:** one of the first American printers; not to be confused with *Of Plymouth Plantation* author William Bradford. Bradford (1663–1752) set up the first printing presses in Philadelphia (1685) and New York (1693).
3. **principal hand:** best employee.

WORDS TO OWN

assert (ə·sʉrt′) *v.:* to declare; claim.

IDENTIFY

Underline two phrases that indicate Franklin's attempt to present a fair, balanced account of his dispute with his brother.

WORDS TO OWN

arbitrary (är′bə·trer′ē) *adj.:* based on whims or individual preferences.

indiscreet (in′di·skrēt′) *adj.:* careless in speech or action.

IDENTIFY

Circle a word in this paragraph that indicates the kind of small sailing ship that took Franklin away from Boston.

IDENTIFY

Circle a word in this paragraph that means "that place"; underline a word in this paragraph that means "to there."

Philadelphia was 100 miles further; I set out, however, in a boat for Amboy,[4] leaving my chest and things to follow me round by sea.

In crossing the bay, we met with a squall that tore our rotten sails to pieces, prevented our getting into the Kill,[5] and drove us upon Long Island. In our way, a drunken Dutchman, who was a passenger too, fell overboard; when he was sinking, I reached through the water to his shock pate,[6] and drew him up, so that we got him in again. His ducking sobered him a little, and he went to sleep, taking first out of his pocket a book, which he desired I would dry for him. It proved to be my old favorite author, Bunyan's *Pilgrim's Progress,*[7] in Dutch, finely printed on good paper, with copper cuts,[8] a dress better than I had ever seen it wear in its own language. I have since found that it has been translated into most of the languages of Europe, and suppose it has been more generally read than any other book, except perhaps the Bible. Honest John was the first that I know of who mixed narration and dialogue; a method of writing very engaging to the reader, who in the most interesting parts finds himself, as it were, brought into the company and present at the discourse. . . .

When we drew near the island, we found it was at a place where there could be no landing, there being a great surf on the stony beach. So we dropped anchor, and swung round toward the shore. Some people came down to the water edge and hallooed to us, as we did to them; but the wind was so high, and the surf so loud, that we could not hear so as to understand each other. There were canoes on the shore, and we made signs, and hallooed that they should fetch us; but they either did not understand us, or thought it impracticable, so they went away, and night coming on, we had no remedy but to wait till the wind should abate; and, in the meantime, the boatman and I concluded to sleep, if we could; and so crowded into the scuttle,[9] with the Dutchman, who was still wet, and the spray beating over the head of our boat, leaked through to us, so that we were soon almost as wet as he. In this manner we lay all night, with very little rest; but, the wind abating the next day, we made a shift to reach Amboy before night, having been thirty hours on the water, without victuals,[10] or any drink but a bottle of filthy rum, and the water we sailed on being salt.

---

4. **Amboy:** Perth Amboy, New Jersey.
5. **Kill:** channel (from the Dutch *kil*). Based on the explorations of Henry Hudson in 1609, the Dutch claimed land in the Middle Colonies and gave Dutch names to some of its geographic features.
6. **shock pate** (pāt): shaggy head.
7. ***Pilgrim's Progress:*** religious allegory by the Puritan writer John Bunyan (1628–1688), first published in 1678. It tells how the hero, Christian, makes his journey to salvation. Notice that Franklin admires the book for literary and historical, rather than religious, reasons.
8. **copper cuts:** engravings.
9. **scuttle:** covered opening in hull or deck of a ship.
10. **victuals** (vit′'lz): food; sometimes spelled "vittles."

INFER

Why do you think Franklin makes a point of praising a style that "mixed narration and dialogue"?

VISUALIZE

Picture the scene of the boat forced to ride out the storm near the shore. Underline vivid details.

WORDS TO OWN

abate (ə·bāt′) *v.:* lessen.

IDENTIFY

How do lines 75–81 show Franklin's self-reliance?

WORDS TO OWN

itinerant (ī·tin′ər·ənt) *adj.:* traveling.

INTERPRET

How seriously do you think Franklin disapproves of Dr. Brown's literary endeavor? Explain.

In the evening I found myself very feverish, and went in to bed; but, having read somewhere that cold water drank plentifully was good for a fever, I followed the prescription, sweat plentiful most of the night, my fever left me, and in the morning, crossing the ferry, I proceeded on my journey on foot, having fifty miles to Burlington,[11] where I was told I should find boats that would carry me the rest of the way to Philadelphia.

It rained very hard all the day; I was thoroughly soaked, and by noon a good deal tired; so I stopped at a poor inn, where I stayed all night, beginning now to wish that I had never left home. I cut so miserable a figure, too, that I found, by the questions asked me, I was suspected to be some runaway servant, and in danger of being taken up on that suspicion. However, I proceeded the next day, and got in the evening to an inn, within eight or ten miles of Burlington, kept by one Dr. Brown. He entered into conversation with me while I took some refreshment, and, finding I had read a little, became very sociable and friendly. Our acquaintance continued as long as he lived. He had been, I imagine, an itinerant doctor, for there was no town in England, or country in Europe, of which he could not give a very particular account. He had some letters,[12] and was ingenious, but much of an unbeliever, and wickedly undertook, some years after, to travesty the Bible in doggerel verse, as Cotton had done Virgil.[13] By this means he set many of the facts in a very ridiculous light, and might have hurt weak minds if his work had been published; but it never was.

At his house I lay that night, and the next morning reached Burlington, but had the mortification to find that the regular boats were gone a little before my coming, and no other expected to go before Tuesday, this being Saturday; wherefore I returned to an old woman in the town, of whom I had bought gingerbread to eat on the water, and asked her advice. She invited me to lodge at her house till a passage by water should offer; and being tired with my foot traveling, I accepted the invitation. She understanding I was a printer, would have had me stay at that town and follow my business, being ignorant of the stock necessary to begin with. She was very hospitable, gave me a dinner of oxcheek with great goodwill, accepting only of a pot of ale in return; and I thought myself fixed till Tuesday should come. However, walking in the evening by the side of the river, a boat came by, which I found was going toward Philadelphia, with several people in her. They took me in, and, as there was no wind, we rowed all the way; and about midnight, not having yet seen the city, some of the company were confident we

11. **Burlington:** Burlington, New Jersey; about eighteen miles from Philadelphia.
12. **letters:** education.
13. **doggerel . . . Virgil:** Doggerel is irregularly constructed comical verse, often used for satirical purposes. In 1664, Charles Cotton (1630–1687) published a doggerel version, or a parody, of the *Aeneid,* an epic poem by the Roman poet Virgil (70–19 B.C.).

must have passed it, and would row no farther; the others knew not where we were; so we put toward the shore, got into a creek, landed near an old fence, with the rails of which we made a fire, the night being cold, in October, and there we remained till daylight. Then one of the company knew the place to be Cooper's Creek, a little above Philadelphia, which we saw as soon as we got out of the creek, and arrived there about eight or nine o'clock on the Sunday morning, and landed at the Market Street wharf.

Arrival in Philadelphia

I have been the more particular in this description of my journey, and shall be so of my first entry into that city, that you may in your mind compare such unlikely beginnings with the figure I have since made there. I was in my working dress, my best clothes being to come round by sea. I was dirty from my journey; my pockets were stuffed out with shirts and stockings, and I knew no soul nor where to look for lodging. I was fatigued with traveling, rowing, and want of rest, I was very hungry; and my whole stock of cash consisted of a Dutch dollar, and about a shilling in copper. The latter I gave the people of the boat for my passage, who at first refused it, on account of my rowing; but I insisted on their taking it. A man being sometimes more generous when he has but a little money than when he has plenty, perhaps through fear of being thought to have but little.

Then I walked up the street, gazing about till near the market house I met a boy with bread. I had made many a meal on bread, and, inquiring where he got it, I went immediately to the baker's he directed me to, in Second Street, and asked for biscuit, intending such as we had in Boston; but they, it seems, were not made in Philadelphia. Then I asked for a three-penny loaf, and was told they had none such. So not considering or knowing the difference of money, and the greater cheapness nor the names of his bread, I bade him give me three-penny worth of any sort. He gave me, accordingly, three great puffy rolls. I was surprised at the quantity, but took it, and, having no room in my pockets, walked off with a roll under each arm, and eating the other. Thus I went up Market Street as far as Fourth Street, passing by the door of Mr. Read, my future wife's father; when she, standing at the door, saw me, and thought I made, as I certainly did, a most awkward, ridiculous appearance. Then I turned and went down Chestnut Street and part of Walnut Street, eating my roll all the way, and, coming round, found myself again at Market Street wharf, near the boat I came in, to which I went for a draft of the river water; and, being filled with one of my rolls, gave the other two to a woman and her child that came down the river in the boat with us, and were waiting to go farther.

INTERPRET

What impression does Franklin make by including such specific factual details as the time of day and the name of the wharf?

BUILD FLUENCY

Read this paragraph aloud, taking care to pronounce each word clearly and distinctly.

VISUALIZE

Imagine Franklin's appearance as he walked down the street with pockets stuffed with extra clothing and the big bread rolls under his arms. Underline the visual details.

IDENTIFY

Underline a phrase that means "took a drink."

Thus refreshed, I walked again up the street, which by this time had many clean-dressed people in it, who were all walking the same way. I joined them, and thereby was led into the great meetinghouse of the Quakers near the market. I sat down among them, and, after looking round awhile and hearing nothing said, being very drowsy through labor and want of rest the preceding night, I fell fast asleep, and continued so till the meeting broke up, when one was kind enough to rouse me. This was, therefore, the first house I was in, or slept in, in Philadelphia. . . .

Arriving at Moral Perfection

It was about this time I conceived the bold and arduous project of arriving at moral perfection. I wished to live without committing any fault at any time; I would conquer all that either natural inclination, custom, or company might lead me into. As I knew, or thought I knew, what was right and wrong, I did not see why I might not always do the one and avoid the other. But I soon found I had undertaken a task of more difficulty than I had imagined. While my care was employed in guarding against one fault, I was often surprised by another; habit took the advantage of inattention; inclination was sometimes too strong for reason. I concluded, at length, that the mere speculative conviction that it was our interest to be completely virtuous, was not sufficient to prevent our slipping; and that the contrary habits must be broken, and good ones acquired and established, before we can have any dependence on a steady, uniform rectitude of conduct. For this purpose I therefore contrived the following method.

In the various enumerations of the moral virtues I had met with in my reading, I found the catalog more or less numerous, as different writers included more or fewer ideas under the same name. Temperance, for example, was by some confined to eating and drinking, while by others it was extended to mean the moderating every other pleasure, appetite, inclination, or passion, bodily or mental, even to our avarice and ambition. I proposed to myself, for the sake of clearness, to use rather more names, with fewer ideas annexed to each, than a few names with more ideas; and I included under thirteen names of virtues all that at that time occurred to me as necessary or desirable, and annexed to each a short precept, which fully expressed the extent I gave to its meaning.

These names of virtues, with their precepts, were:

1. **Temperance.** Eat not to dullness; drink not to elevation.
2. **Silence.** Speak not but what may benefit others or yourself; avoid trifling conversation.
3. **Order.** Let all your things have their places; let each part of your business have its time.

VORDS TO OWN
rduous (är′jo͞o·əs) *adj.:* ifficult.

PREDICT
low successfully do you xpect the young Franklin to chieve his goal of "moral erfection"?

WORDS TO OWN
ectitude (rek′tə·to͞od′) *n.:* correctness.

IDENTIFY
Circle a word meaning 'greed"; underline a word neaning "commandment" or "principle."

BUILD FLUENCY
Read Franklin's list of virtues and their associated precepts, taking care to pronounce each word clearly and correctly.

4. **Resolution.** Resolve to perform what you ought; perform without fail what you resolve.
5. **Frugality.** Make no expense but to do good to others or yourself; i.e., waste nothing.
6. **Industry.** Lose no time; be always employed in something useful; cut off all unnecessary actions.
7. **Sincerity.** Use no hurtful deceit; think innocently and justly, and, if you speak, speak accordingly.
8. **Justice.** Wrong none by doing injuries, or omitting the benefits that are your duty.
9. **Moderation.** Avoid extremes; forbear resenting injuries so much as you think they deserve.
10. **Cleanliness.** Tolerate no uncleanliness in body, clothes, or habitation.
11. **Tranquility.** Be not disturbed at trifles, or at accidents common or unavoidable.
12. **Chastity.** Rarely use venery[14] but for health or offspring, never to dullness, weakness, or the injury of your own or another's peace or reputation.
13. **Humility.** Imitate Jesus and Socrates.[15]

My intention being to acquire the *habitude* of all these virtues, I judged it would be well not to distract my attention by attempting the whole at once, but to fix it on one of them at a time; and, when I should be master of that, then to proceed to another, and so on, till I should have gone through the thirteen; and, as the previous acquisition of some might facilitate the acquisition of certain others, I arranged them with that view, as they stand above. *Temperance* first, as it tends to procure that coolness and clearness of head, which is so necessary where constant vigilance was to be kept up, and guard maintained against the unremitting attraction of ancient habits, and the force of perpetual temptations. This being acquired and established, *silence* would be more easy; and my desire being to gain knowledge at the same time that I improved in virtue, and considering that in conversation it was obtained rather by the use of the ears than of the tongue, and therefore wishing to break a habit I was getting into of prattling, punning, and joking, which only made me acceptable to trifling company, I gave *silence* the second place. This and the next, *order,* I expected would allow me more time for attending to my project and my studies. *Resolution,* once become habitual, would keep me firm in my endeavors to obtain all the subsequent virtues; *frugality* and *industry* freeing me from my remaining

14. **venery** (ven′ər·ē): sex.
15. **Socrates** (säk′rə·tēz′) (470–399 B.C.): Greek philosopher. He is said to have lived a simple, virtuous life.

EVALUATE

Would a person possessing each of the virtues on this list truly represent the "moral perfection" that Franklin desired? Explain.

WORDS TO OWN

facilitate (fə·sil′ə·tāt′) *v.:* simplify.

WORDS TO OWN

subsequent (sub′si·kwənt) *adj.:* following.

debt, and producing affluence and independence, would make more easy the practice of *sincerity* and *justice,* etc., etc. Conceiving then, that, agreeably to the advice of Pythagoras[16] in his Golden Verses, daily examination would be necessary, I contrived the following method for conducting that examination.

I made a little book, in which I allotted a page for each of the virtues. I ruled each page with red ink, so as to have seven columns, one for each day of the week, marking each column with a letter for the day. I crossed these columns with thirteen red lines, marking the beginning of each line with the first letter of one of the virtues, on which line, and in its proper column, I might mark, by a little black spot, every fault I found upon examination to have been committed respecting that virtue upon that day.

PREDICT

How successfully do you think young Franklin will be able to keep up with this method of moral bookkeeping?

Form of the Pages

Temperance							
Eat not to dullness. Drink not to elevation.							
	S	M	T	W	T	F	S
T							
S							
O							
R							
F							
I							
S							
J							
M							
Cl							
T							
Ch							
H							

16. **Pythagoras** (pi·thag′ə·rəs): Greek philosopher and mathematician of the sixth century B.C.

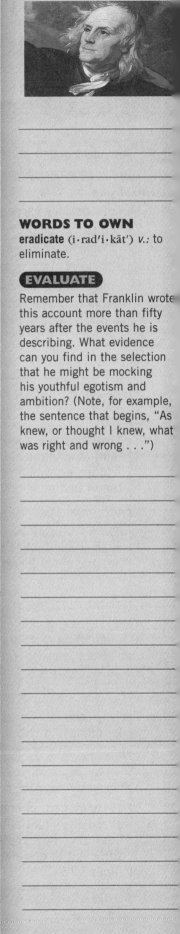

I determined to give a week's strict attention to each of the virtues successively. Thus, in the first week, my great guard was to avoid every[17] the least offense against *temperance,* leaving the other virtues to their ordinary chance, only marking every evening the faults of the day. Thus, if in the first week I could keep my first line, marked T, clear of spots, I supposed the habit of that virtue so much strengthened, and its opposite weakened, that I might venture extending my attention to include the next, and for the following week keep both lines clear of spots. Proceeding thus to the last, I could go through a course complete in thirteen weeks, and four courses in a year. And like him who, having a garden to weed, does not attempt to eradicate all the bad herbs at once, which would exceed his reach and his strength, but works on one of the beds at a time, and, having accomplished the first, proceeds to a second, so I should have, I hoped, the encouraging pleasure of seeing on my pages the progress I made in virtue, by clearing successively my lines of their spots, till in the end, by a number of courses, I should be happy in viewing a clean book, after a thirteen weeks' daily examination. . . .

17. every: archaic for "even."

WORDS TO OWN

eradicate (i·rad′i·kāt′) *v.:* to eliminate.

EVALUATE

Remember that Franklin wrote this account more than fifty years after the events he is describing. What evidence can you find in the selection that he might be mocking his youthful egotism and ambition? (Note, for example, the sentence that begins, "As knew, or thought I knew, what was right and wrong . . .")

First-Person Point of View

An **autobiography** presents the writer's life as a continuous narrative, a sort of story. Like most autobiographers, Franklin tells his life story in the first person, writing as "I." The **first-person point of view** can give writing immediacy and intimacy. The writer speaks as the person to whom the events actually happened. The writer can also speak to the reader confidentially, person to person. The first-person point of view has some disadvantages as well. The writer cannot speak with firsthand knowledge about events he or she did not witness, even when they may be important to the story. And the writer's viewpoint colors and may distort the entire account.

In order to explore Franklin's autobiographical style, complete the following chart by paraphrasing Franklin's words into sentences that a modern biographer might write. Note that the first-person "I," "me," and "my" become, in the third person, "he" (or "Franklin"), "him," and "his."

Franklin's Original First-Person Narrative	Modern Third-Person Narrative
"I wished to live without committing any fault at any time. . . . But I soon found I had undertaken a task of more difficulty than I had imagined." (lines 168–173)	Although he wanted to live faultlessly, Franklin soon found this was more difficult than he had thought.
"While my care was employed in guarding against one fault, I was often surprised by another. . . ." (lines 173–174)	
". . . habit took the advantage of inattention. . . ." (lines 174–175)	
". . . inclination was sometimes too strong for reason." (lines 175–176)	
"I concluded, at length, that the mere speculative conviction that it was our interest to be completely virtuous, was not sufficient to prevent our slipping. . . ." (lines 176–178)	

Vocabulary: How to Own a Word

Context

Word Bank
assert
arbitrary
indiscreet
abate
itinerant
arduous
rectitude
facilitate
subsequent
eradicate

Using context clues, determine which Word to Own best completes each sentence and write the word on the line provided.

Example: Dr. Brown, an erudite physician who was quite knowledgeable, became Franklin's lifelong friend.

1. Who knows what ______________ words passed between Franklin and his brother? Franklin may have been careless.

2. Franklin's father could have done something to simplify his son's search for a job, but he decided not to ______________ this quest.

3. Franklin's journey to Philadelphia was long and ______________, but these difficulties taught him a lot about himself.

4. As he traveled about, Franklin tried to be correct in his manners. The ______________ of his behavior impressed others.

5. With the few pennies he had, Franklin bought some rolls. They seemed to ______________ his hunger, for he gave two of them away.

6. Franklin seems to disapprove of ______________ actions. Rather than follow his whims, he tries to think before acting.

7. Franklin believed that it was possible to eliminate nonproductive ways of thinking and behaving. To help ______________ undesirable behavior, he made a "little book" to track the development of his virtues.

8. Franklin declared that his "little book" made him more virtuous. To ______________ this was to claim success.

9. Franklin called Dr. Brown ______________, because the physician had traveled widely and had lived in many places.

10. Following the fight with his brother, Franklin tried to make his way on his own. These ______________ efforts were largely successful.

Speech to the Virginia Convention

Make the Connection

Words into Actions

The American Revolution was fought not only with muskets but also with thousands of pamphlets, essays, songs, and speeches. Patrick Henry delivered the speech you are about to read at a historical moment when the angry passions between Britain and the American Colonies had reached the boiling point. Leading Revolutionary radicals were crowded into a small church in Richmond, Virginia, to debate an agonizing question—should the American Colonists declare themselves independent of the mother country, Great Britain? Henry's words electrified those present; one clergyman who was there recalled that the speech left him "sick with excitement." At the climactic moment, Henry is said to have grabbed an ivory letter opener and plunged it toward his chest at the final word, *death*.

Like almost any persuasive speaker or writer, Patrick Henry used two modes of **persuasion:** appeals to **logic** and appeals to **emotions** or values. In the following chart you'll find, in the left-hand column, a number of claims intended to be persuasive. Decide whether each one is an appeal to logic or to emotion (or both), and then decide whether or not you find it genuinely persuasive.

Claim	Appeal to Logic?	Appeal to Emotion?	Persuasive?
"America should support nations that have demonstrated a real commitment to democracy and freedom."	✔		✔
"You're either with us or against us—which will it be?"			
"Since all citizens share equally in the benefits of government services, all citizens should shoulder the tax burden equally."			
"Another reason to support our schools is that increases in education spending per capita often lead to decreases in the rate of crime."			

Speech to the Virginia Convention

Patrick Henry

/ISUALIZE

cture the scene: a small urch crowded with evolutionary leaders like eorge Washington and homas Jefferson. Amid the amor of heated debate, atrick Henry rises to speak—portedly without a text or en notes. The "President" e is addressing here is the eeting's chairman.

NTERPRET

hat "earthly king" in articular might Henry be ferring to?

EVALUATE

ow effectively does Henry ake his point that the past guide to the future?

VORDS TO OWN

olace (säl′is) *v.:* to comfort.
nsidious (in·sid′ē·əs) *adj.:* sly; neaky.

IDENTIFY

Jnderline the phrases or entences in lines 25–39 hat are **figures of speech**—hat is, implied comparisons etween Henry's actual subject nd images he has chosen for llustration.

Mr. President: No man thinks more highly than I do of the patriotism, as well as abilities, of the very worthy gentlemen who have just addressed the House. But different men often see the same subject in different lights; and, therefore, I hope that it will not be thought disrespectful to those gentlemen, if, entertaining as I do, opinions of a character very opposite to theirs, I shall speak forth my sentiments freely and without reserve. This is no time for ceremony. The question before the House is one of awful moment[1] to this country. For my own part I consider it as nothing less than a question of freedom or slavery; and in proportion to the magnitude of the subject ought to be the freedom of the debate. It is only in this way that we can hope to arrive at truth, and fulfill the great responsibility which we hold to God and our country. Should I keep back my opinions at such a time, through fear of giving offense, I should consider myself as guilty of treason toward my country, and of an act of disloyalty toward the majesty of heaven, which I revere above all earthly kings.

Mr. President, it is natural to man to indulge in the illusions of hope. We are apt to shut our eyes against a painful truth, and listen to the song of that siren, till she transforms us into beasts.[2] Is this the part of wise men, engaged in a great and arduous struggle for liberty? Are we disposed to be of the number of those who, having eyes, see not, and having ears, hear not, the things which so nearly concern their temporal salvation? For my part, whatever anguish of spirit it may cost, I am willing to know the whole truth; to know the worst and to provide for it.

I have but one lamp by which my feet are guided; and that is the lamp of experience. I know of no way of judging of the future but by the past. And judging by the past, I wish to know what there has been in the conduct of the British ministry for the last ten years, to justify those hopes with which gentlemen have been pleased to solace themselves and the House? Is it that insidious smile with which our petition[3] has been lately received? Trust it not, sir; it will prove a snare to your feet. Suffer not yourselves to be betrayed with a kiss. Ask yourselves how this gracious reception of our petition comports[4] with these warlike preparations which cover our waters and darken our land. Are fleets and armies necessary to a work of love and reconciliation? Have we shown ourselves so unwilling to be reconciled, that force must be called in to win back our love? Let us not deceive ourselves, sir.

1. **awful moment:** great importance.
2. **listen . . . beasts:** In Greek mythology, the sirens are sea maidens whose seductive singing lures men to wreck their boats on coastal rocks. In the *Odyssey,* an epic by the Greek poet Homer (c. eighth century B.C.), Circe, an enchanter, transforms Odysseus' men into swine after they arrive at her island home. Henry's allusion combines these two stories.
3. **our petition:** The First Continental Congress had recently protested against new tax laws. King George III had withdrawn the laws conditionally, but the colonists were unwilling to accept his conditions.
4. **comports:** agrees.

These are the implements of war and subjugation; the last arguments to which kings resort.

I ask gentlemen, sir, what means this martial array, if its purpose be not to force us to submission? Can gentlemen assign any other possible motives for it? Has Great Britain any enemy, in this quarter of the world, to call for all this accumulation of navies and armies? No, sir, she has none. They are meant for us; they can be meant for no other. They are sent over to bind and rivet upon us those chains which the British ministry have been so long forging. And what have we to oppose to them? Shall we try argument? Sir, we have been trying that for the last ten years. Have we anything new to offer on the subject? Nothing. We have held the subject up in every light of which it is capable; but it has been all in vain. Shall we resort to entreaty and humble supplication? What terms shall we find which have not been already exhausted? Let us not, I beseech you, sir, deceive ourselves longer. Sir, we have done everything that could be done, to avert the storm which is now coming on. We have petitioned; we have remonstrated; we have supplicated; we have prostrated ourselves before the throne, and have implored its interposition[5] to arrest the tyrannical hands of the ministry and Parliament. Our petitions have been slighted; our remonstrances have produced additional violence and insult; our supplications have been disregarded; and we have been spurned, with contempt, from the foot of the throne. In vain, after these things, may we indulge the fond[6] hope of peace and reconciliation. There is no longer any room for hope. If we wish to be free—if we mean to preserve inviolate those inestimable privileges for which we have been so long contending—if we mean not basely to abandon the noble struggle in which we have been so long engaged, and which we have pledged ourselves never to abandon until the glorious object of our contest shall be obtained, we must fight! I repeat it, sir, we must fight! An appeal to arms and to the God of Hosts is all that is left us!

They tell us, sir, that we are weak; unable to cope with so formidable an adversary. But when shall we be stronger? Will it be the next week, or the next year? Will it be when we are totally disarmed, and when a British guard shall be stationed in every house? Shall we gather strength by irresolution and inaction? Shall we acquire the means of effectual resistance, by lying supinely on our backs, and hugging the delusive phantom of hope, until our enemies shall have bound us hand and foot? Sir, we are not weak, if we make a proper use of the means which the God of nature hath placed in our power. Three millions of people, armed in the holy cause of liberty, and in such a country as that which we possess, are invincible by any force which our enemy can send against

5. **interposition:** intervention; stepping in to try to solve the problem.
6. **fond:** foolishly optimistic.

WORDS TO OWN
martial (mär′shəl) *adj.:* warlike

IDENTIFY

A **rhetorical question** is a question asked not to elicit information but to make a point. Underline the rhetorical questions Henry asks in this paragraph. How many are there?

WORDS TO OWN
supplication (sup′lə·kā′shən) *n.:* earnest plea.
avert (ə·vurt′) *v.:* to prevent; turn away.
spurned (spurnd) *v.:* rejected.
inviolate (in·vī′ə·lit) *adj.:* uncorrupted.

EVALUATE

What do you consider Henry's strongest argument in this paragraph?

WORDS TO OWN
adversary (ad′vər·ser′ē) *n.:* opponent.

VORDS TO OWN

gilant (vij′ə·lənt) *adj.* used as
.: watchful.

evitable (in·ev′i·tə·bəl) *adj.*:
ot avoidable.

BUILD FLUENCY

e-read this paragraph aloud ith the expressive passion f a man urging his country war.

us. Besides, sir, we shall not fight our battles alone. There is a just God who presides over the destinies of nations; and who will raise up friends to fight our battles for us. The battle, sir, is not to the strong alone; it is to the vigilant, the active, the brave. Besides, sir, we have no election.[7] If we were base enough to desire it, it is now too late to retire from the contest. There is no retreat, but in submission and slavery! Our chains are forged! Their clanking may be heard on the plains of Boston! The war is inevitable—and let it come! I repeat it, sir, let it come!

It is in vain, sir, to extenuate the matter. Gentlemen may cry peace, peace—but there is no peace. The war is actually begun! The next gale that sweeps from the north will bring to our ears the clash of resounding arms! Our brethren are already in the field! Why stand we here idle? What is it that gentlemen wish? What would they have? Is life so dear, or peace so sweet, as to be purchased at the price of chains and slavery? Forbid it, Almighty God! I know not what course others may take; but as for me, give me liberty, or give me death!

7. **election:** choice.

Persuasion

Persuasion is a form of speaking or writing that aims to move an audience to take a specific action. A good persuasive speaker or writer uses both head and heart—reasons and feelings, or logic and emotion—to win over an audience. To be successful, a writer or speaker must provide reasons to support a particular opinion or course of action. In the final analysis, though, audiences are often won over not only by the force of the speaker's arguments but also by the power of his or her personality.

Patrick Henry's oratory made masterful use of **rhetorical devices**—that is, modes of expression that enabled him to argue his points effectively. Complete the following table to explore Henry's use of the techniques of persuasion.

Rhetorical Device	Example from Henry's Speech	Appeal to Logic or Emotion?
Rhetorical question	"Shall we gather strength by irresolution and inaction?"	logic
Repetition of key word or phrase		
Allusion		
Analogy		
Metaphor		
Hyperbole (Exaggeration)		
Understatement		
Personification		

Vocabulary: How to Own a Word

Analogies

Word Bank
solace
insidious
martial
supplication
avert
spurned
inviolate
adversary
vigilant
inevitable

An **analogy** expresses a relationship between two things. Many standardized tests include an "Analogies" section that calls for you to determine the relationship between words.

Analogies are often presented in this form: "A : B : : C : D," which is read, "A is to B as C is to D." The words in the first pair have the same relationship to each other as do those in the second pair. For example, "house : dwelling : : road : lane" ("house is to dwelling as road is to lane") is a valid analogy because the words in each pair are synonyms.

Many relationships between words are possible; here are a few common types:

Example	Relationship
catastrophe : disaster	synonym
innocent : guilty	antonym
eloquent : speaker	description

Fill in the blanks below to complete the analogies, and then identify the relationship between the word pairs. A dictionary and a thesaurus will be helpful in finding words.

EXAMPLE: arduous : easy : : ethereal : earthly Relationship: antonym

1. **inviolate** : corrupted : :
   despairing : ______________
   Relationship: ______________

2. **solace** : comfort : :
   calm : ______________
   Relationship: ______________

3. loyal : patriot : :
   insidious : ______________
   Relationship: ______________

4. fight : battle : :
   supplication : ______________
   Relationship: ______________

5. **spurned** : welcomed : :
hindered : ______________________
Relationship: ______________________

6. prevent : **avert** : :
warn : ______________________
Relationship: ______________________

7. conciliatory : mediator : :
martial : ______________________
Relationship: ______________________

8. ally : **adversary** : :
coward : ______________________
Relationship: ______________________

9. generous : selfish : :
inevitable : ______________________
Relationship: ______________________

10. **vigilant** : shepherd : :
hostile : ______________________
Relationship: ______________________

From The Autobiography: The Declaration of Independence

Make the Connection

The Burden of Freedom

Without a doubt, the cornerstone of the "American dream" is the ideal of freedom. The words of the Declaration of Independence are a ringing affirmation of freedom. Yet Jefferson knew well that freedom's twin is responsibility—every kind of liberty we enjoy has to be balanced by an equal amount of personal responsibility.

What was true in Jefferson's day is still very much true today. We have the freedom to elect anyone we want to represent us in Congress, for example—but this comes with the responsibility to vote. Complete the chart below to examine the balance of freedoms and responsibilities that constitute American citizenship.

Freedom	Responsibility
Elect representatives to Congress	Vote in primary and general elections
Attend government-supported schools	
Express political opinions openly	
Own property, such as a house	
Drive vehicles on public roadways	

The Declaration of Independence

Thomas Jefferson

FROM The Autobiography

IN CONGRESS.
The unanimous Declaration

VORDS TO OWN

ensures (sen′shərz) *n. pl.:* trong, disapproving criticisms.

INTERPRET

Vhat is Jefferson implying bout the involvement of ortherners in the institution f slavery?

VISUALIZE

The following text of the Declaration shows not only Jefferson's original draft, but also the words deleted by Congress (underlined) and the words inserted by Congress (in the margin at right).

BUILD FLUENCY

Re-read this opening paragraph aloud, pronouncing each word clearly and following the punctuation to produce a natural, even cadence.

Congress proceeded the same day to consider the Declaration of Independence, which had been reported and lain on the table the Friday preceding, and on Monday referred to a committee of the whole. The pusillanimous[1] idea that we had friends in England worth keeping terms with, still haunted the minds of many. For this reason, those passages which conveyed censures on the people of England were struck out, lest they should give them offense. The clause too, reprobating the enslaving the inhabitants of Africa, was struck out in complaisance to South Carolina and Georgia, who had never attempted to restrain the importation of slaves, and who, on the contrary, still wished to continue it. Our northern brethren also, I believe, felt a little tender under those censures; for though their people had very few slaves themselves, yet they had been pretty considerable carriers of them to others. The debates, having taken up the greater parts of the 2d, 3d, and 4th days of July, were, on the evening of the last, closed; the Declaration was reported by the committee, agreed to by the House, and signed by every member present, except Mr. Dickinson.[2] As the sentiments of men are known not only by what they receive, but what they reject also, I will state the form of the Declaration as originally reported. The parts struck out by Congress shall be distinguished by a black line drawn under them; and those inserted by them shall be placed in the margin, or in a concurrent column.

A Declaration by the Representatives of the United States of America, in General Congress Assembled

When, in the course of human events, it becomes necessary for one people to dissolve the political bands which have connected them with another, and to assume among the powers of the earth the separate and equal station to which the laws of nature and of nature's God entitle them, a decent respect to the opinions of mankind requires that they should declare the causes which impel them to the separation.

1. **pusillanimous** (pyo͞o′si·lan′ə·məs): cowardly; lacking courage.
2. **Mr. Dickinson:** John Dickinson (1732–1808), one of Pennsylvania's representatives to the Second Continental Congress, led the conservative opposition to the Declaration and refused to sign the document.

We hold these truths to be self-evident: that all men are created equal; that they are endowed by their creator with inherent and inalienable rights;[3] that among these are life, liberty, and the pursuit of happiness; that to secure these rights, governments are instituted among men, deriving their just powers from the consent of the governed; that whenever any form of government becomes destructive of these ends, it is the right of the people to alter or to abolish it, and to institute new government, laying its foundation on such principles, and organizing its powers in such form, as to them shall seem most likely to effect their safety and happiness. Prudence, indeed, will dictate that governments long established should not be changed for light and transient causes; and accordingly all experience hath shown that mankind are more disposed to suffer while evils are sufferable, than to right themselves by abolishing the forms to which they are accustomed. But when a long train of abuses and usurpations,[4] begun at a distinguished[5] period and pursuing invariably the same object, evinces a design to reduce them under absolute despotism, it is their right, it is their duty to throw off such government, and to provide new guards for their future security. Such has been the patient sufferance of these colonies; and such is now the necessity which constrains them to expunge their former systems of government. The history of the present king of Great Britain is a history of unremitting injuries and usurpations, among which appears no solitary fact to contradict the uniform tenor of the rest, but all have in direct object the establishment of an absolute tyranny over these states. To prove this, let facts be submitted to a candid world for the truth of which we pledge a faith yet unsullied by falsehood.

He has refused his assent to laws the most wholesome and necessary for the public good.

certain

alter

repeated

all having

IDENTIFY

Circle the words in this long sentence that identify the specific rights that Jefferson believed "inalienable" to all human beings.

WORDS TO OWN

transient (tran′shənt) *adj.:* temporary; passing.

RETELL

Paraphrase Jefferson's assertion about "mankind" in lines 48–51.

WORDS TO OWN

constrains (kən·strānz′) *v.:* forces.

expunge (ek·spunj′) *v.:* to erase; remove.

candid (kan′did) *adj.:* unbiased; fair.

---

3. **inalienable** (in·āl′yən·ə·bəl) **rights:** rights that cannot be taken away.
4. **usurpations** (yo͞o′sər·pā′shənz): acts of unlawful or forceful seizure of property, power, rights, and the like.
5. **distinguished** (di·stiŋ′gwisht): clearly defined.

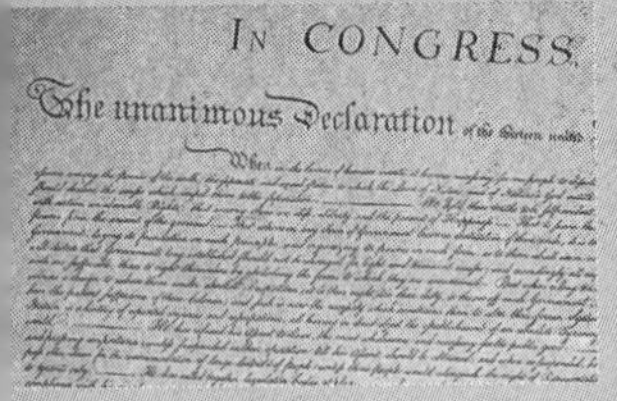

INTERPRET

'araphrase Jefferson's charge gainst King George in lines 33–87.

He has forbidden his governors to pass laws of immediate and pressing importance, unless suspended in their operation till his assent should be obtained; and, when so suspended, he has utterly neglected to attend to them.

He has refused to pass other laws for the accommodation of large districts of people, unless those people would relinquish the right of representation in the legislature, a right inestimable to them, and formidable to tyrants only.[6]

He has called together legislative bodies at places unusual, uncomfortable, and distant from the depository of their public records, for the sole purpose of fatiguing them into compliance with his measures.

He has dissolved representative houses repeatedly and continually for opposing with manly firmness his invasions on the rights of the people.

He has refused for a long time after such dissolutions to cause others to be elected, whereby the legislative powers, incapable of annihilation, have returned to the people at large for their exercise, the state remaining, in the meantime, exposed to all the dangers of invasion from without and convulsions within.

He has endeavored to prevent the population of these states; for that purpose obstructing the laws for naturalization of foreigners, refusing to pass others to encourage their migrations hither, and raising the conditions of new appropriations of lands.

He has suffered the administration of justice totally to cease in some of these states refusing his assent to laws for establishing judiciary powers.

obstructed by

He has made our judges dependent on his will alone for the tenure of their offices, and the amount and payment of their salaries.

He has erected a multitude of new offices, by a self-assumed power and sent hither swarms of

6. **formidable . . . only:** causing fear only to tyrants.

new officers to harass our people and eat out their substance.

He has kept among us in times of peace standing armies and ships of war without the consent of our legislatures.

He has affected to render the military independent of, and superior to, the civil power.

He has combined with others[7] to subject us to a jurisdiction foreign to our constitutions and unacknowledged by our laws, giving his assent to their acts of pretended legislation for quartering large bodies of armed troops among us; for protecting them by a mock trial from punishment for any murders which they should commit on the inhabitants of these states; for cutting off our trade with all parts of the world; for imposing taxes on us without our consent; for depriving us [ ] of the benefits of trial by jury; for transporting us beyond seas to be tried for pretended offenses; for abolishing the free system of English laws in a neighboring province,[8] establishing therein an arbitrary government, and enlarging its boundaries, so as to render it at once an example and fit instrument for introducing the same absolute rule into these states; for taking away our charters, abolishing our most valuable laws, and altering fundamentally the forms of our governments; for suspending our own legislatures, and declaring themselves invested with power to legislate for us in all cases whatsoever.

in many cases

colonies

He has abdicated government here withdrawing his governors, and declaring us out of his allegiance and protection.

by declaring us out of his protection, and waging war against us.

He has plundered our seas, ravaged our coasts, burnt our towns, and destroyed the lives of our people.

He is at this time transporting large armies of foreign mercenaries to complete the works of death, desolation, and tyranny already begun

WORDS TO OWN
abdicated (ab′di·kāt′id) *v.:* given up responsibility for.

7. **others:** members of British Parliament and their supporters and agents.
8. **neighboring province:** Québec in Canada.

EVALUATE

he brackets in line 155 ndicate a passage, shown at ght, that was added by ongress. Does this change om Jefferson's original text nake the final version more or ess effective? Explain.

WORDS TO OWN

confiscation (kän′fis·kā′shən) n.: seizure of property by authority.

INTERPRET

Why might Congress have deleted this entire paragraph on the subject of slavery?

with circumstances of cruelty and perfidy [ ] unworthy the head of a civilized nation.

scarcely paralleled in the most barbarous ages, and totally

He has constrained our fellow citizens taken captive on the high seas, to bear arms against their country, to become the executioners of their friends and brethren, or to fall themselves by their hands.

He has [ ] endeavored to bring on the inhabitants of our frontiers, the merciless Indian savages, whose known rule of warfare is an undistinguished destruction of all ages, sexes, and conditions of existence.

excited domestic insurrection among us, and has

He has incited treasonable insurrections of our fellow citizens, with the allurements of forfeiture and confiscation of our property.

He has waged cruel war against human nature itself, violating its most sacred rights of life and liberty in the persons of a distant people who never offended him, captivating and carrying them into slavery in another hemisphere, or to incur miserable death in their transportation thither. This piratical warfare, the opprobrium[9] of INFIDEL powers, is the warfare of the CHRISTIAN king of Great Britain. Determined to keep open a market where MEN should be bought and sold, he has prostituted his negative[10] for suppressing every legislative attempt to prohibit or to restrain this execrable commerce. And that this assemblage of horrors might want no fact of distinguished die,[11] he is now exciting those very people to rise in arms among us, and to purchase that liberty of which he has deprived them, by murdering the people on whom he also obtruded them: thus paying off former crimes committed against the LIBERTIES of one people, with crimes which he urges them to commit against the LIVES of another.

In every stage of these oppressions we have petitioned for redress in the most humble terms: Our repeated petitions have been answered only by repeated injuries.

---

9. **opprobrium** (ə·prō′brē·əm): shameful conduct.
10. **negative:** veto.
11. **fact of distinguished die:** clear stamp or mark of distinction. Jefferson is being sarcastic here.

A prince whose character is thus marked by every act which may define a tyrant is unfit to be the ruler of a [ ] people who mean to be free. Future ages will scarcely believe that the hardiness of one man adventured, within the short compass of twelve years only, to lay a foundation so broad and so undisguised for tyranny over a people fostered and fixed in principles of freedom.

free

Nor have we been wanting in attentions to our British brethren. We have warned them from time to time of attempts by their legislature to extend a jurisdiction over these our states. We have reminded them of the circumstances of our emigration and settlement here, no one of which could warrant so strange a pretension: that these were effected at the expense of our own blood and treasure, unassisted by the wealth or the strength of Great Britain: that in constituting indeed our several forms of government, we had adopted one common king, thereby laying a foundation for perpetual league and amity with them: but that submission to their parliament was no part of our constitution, nor ever in idea, if history may be credited: and, we [ ] appealed to their native justice and magnanimity as well as to the ties of our common kindred to disavow these usurpations which were likely to interrupt our connection and correspondence. They too have been deaf to the voice of justice and of consanguinity,[13] and when occasions have been given them, by the regular course of their laws, of removing from their councils the disturbers of our harmony, they have, by their free election, re-established them in power. At this very time too, they are permitting their chief magistrate to send over not only soldiers of our common blood, but Scotch and foreign mercenaries to invade and destroy us. These facts have given the last stab to agonizing affection, and manly spirit bids us to renounce forever these unfeeling brethren. We must endeavor to forget our former

an unwarrantable / us

have

and we have conjured[12] them by

would inevitably

We must therefore

WORDS TO OWN
magnanimity (mag'nə·nim'ə·tē) *n.:* nobility of spirit.

WORDS TO OWN
renounce (ri·nouns') *v.:* to give up.

12. **conjured** (kən·jo͞ord'): solemnly called upon.
13. **consanguinity** (kän'saŋ·gwin'ə·tē): kinship; family relationship.

VORDS TO OWN

cquiesce (ak′wē·es′) *v.:* agree r accept quietly.

IDENTIFY

Jnderline the phrase, added to his paragraph by Congress, hat invokes the aid of God.

EVALUATE

Whom do you think Jefferson had in mind as the real audience, besides King George and his ministers, for the Declaration of Independence?

love for them, and hold them as we hold the rest of mankind, enemies in war, in peace friends. We might have been a free and a great people together; but a communication of grandeur and of freedom, it seems, is below their dignity. Be it so, since they will have it. The road to happiness and to glory is open to us too. We will tread it apart from them and acquiesce in the necessity which denounces[14] our eternal separation [ ]!

We, therefore, the representatives of the United States of America in General Congress assembled, [ ] do in the name, and by the authority of the good people of these states reject and renounce all allegiance and subjection to the kings of Great Britain and all others who may hereafter claim by, through or under them; we utterly dissolve all political connection which may heretofore have subsisted between us and the people or parliament of Great Britain: And finally we do assert and declare these colonies to be free and independent states, and that as free and independent states, they have full power to levy war, conclude peace, contract alliances, establish commerce, and to do all other acts and things which independent states may of right do.

And for the support of this declaration, [ ] we mutually pledge to each other our lives, our fortunes, and our sacred honor.

and hold them as we hold the rest of mankind, enemies in war, in peace friends.

appealing to the supreme judge of the world for the rectitude of our intentions,

colonies, solemnly publish and declare, that these united colonies are, and of right ought to be free and independent states; that they are absolved from all allegiance to the British crown, and that all political connection between them and the state of Great Britain is, and ought to be, totally dissolved;

with a firm reliance on the protection of divine providence,

The Declaration thus signed on the 4th, on paper, was engrossed on parchment, and signed again on the 2d of August.

14. **denounces** (dē·nouns′iz): archaic for "announces, proclaims."

Parallelism

Parallelism is the repeated use of sentences, clauses, or phrases with identical or similar structure. For example, when Jefferson cites the truths that are "self-evident," he begins each clause with *that.* He also begins a long series of paragraphs with the words "He has . . ." Jefferson's use of parallelism emphasizes his view that all the truths he represents are of equal importance. The parallel structure also creates a stately **rhythm** or cadence in the Declaration—a cadence that may be quite formal, but is also a very natural expression of the way people speak and think.

Complete the chart below by finding additional examples of Jefferson's use of parallelism in the Declaration. Note that in parallel constructions the specific *words* are not necessarily the same, but grammatical *forms* are the same. *I am studying literature,* therefore, is parallel to *she is learning French,* but it is **not** parallel with *I am a student,* because the verb form is different.

First Item in Series	Grammatically Parallel Item in Same Series
"We hold these truths to be self-evident: that all men are created equal. . . ." (lines 31–32)	". . . that among these are life, liberty, and the pursuit of happiness . . ."
". . . it is their right. . . ." (line 55)	
"He has refused his assent to laws. . . ." (line 70)	
". . . for quartering large bodies of armed troops . . ." (lines 124–125)	

Vocabulary: How to Own a Word

Etymologies

Word Bank
censures
transient
constrains
expunge
candid
abdicated
confiscation
magnanimity
renounce
acquiesce

The **etymology** of a word tells where it comes from, tracing its origins to other words in the language and often in earlier languages. By becoming familiar with a word's etymology, you can increase your vocabulary power.

Each of the Words to Own in boldface type in the following sentences has its origin in Latin. Using a dictionary and context clues, determine which word or phrase in the box titled **Latin Meanings** goes with each Word to Own, and write the letter of the correct meaning in the space provided.

Latin Meanings

a. back
b. to proclaim
c. to tax, value, judge
d. to go over or across
e. to become quiet
f. sincere, white, pure
g. great
h. money basket
i. to pluck out
j. to draw or bind together
k. to loosen

EXAMPLE: When something **dissolves**, its particles disperse, so it is not surprising that the word derives from the Latin *dissolvere,* meaning ___k___.

1. A boa constrictor **constrains** its victims, gathering them tightly to itself; this word is derived from the Latin *constringere,* meaning ______________.

2. The word **acquiesce,** meaning "to agree without complaint," comes from the Latin word meaning ______________.

3. When you **expunge** something, you remove it. It's easy to see how this word is related to the Latin *expungere,* meaning ______________.

4. The prefix *re–* often means "again." However, it can also mean ______________, as it does in the origin of the word **renounce.**

5. A business magnate may not always act with **magnanimity,** yet both words derive from the Latin *magnus,* meaning ______________.

6. **Censorship** and **censures,** often acts of official reprimand or decision making, both derive from the Latin verb *censere,* meaning ________________.

7. The word **transient** comes from the Latin *transire,* meaning ________________.

8. *Candidus* means ________________. From this Latin word comes the English word **candid,** meaning "open and honest."

9. In the word **abdicated,** meaning "renounced" or "formally gave up," you can find forms of the Latin words *ab,* or "off," and *dicare,* meaning ________________.

10. **Confiscation,** related to the word *fiscal* (that is, financial), has its root in the Latin *fiscus,* meaning ________________.

American Romanticism 1800–1860

CONNECT

Name three other classic stories (in literature, film, or folklore) that depict journeys.

The Pattern of the Journey

The journey—there is probably no pattern so common in all of narrative literature, from the Bible, to the Greek epic the *Odyssey,* to modern films like *The Wizard of Oz.* Very early in his *Autobiography,* Benjamin Franklin describes in great detail an important American journey: a personal quest in which the young Ben leaves his home in Boston and travels to Philadelphia. Franklin's journey is a declaration of independence, a move away from the constraints of his family and toward a city where he might prosper. We can see in this an expression of both his personal goals and the goals of eighteenth-century America: a reaching out for independence, prosperity, commerce, and urbane civilization—in other words, a quest for opportunity.

Franklin wrote about his journey to Philadelphia in 1771. In 1799, the American writer Charles Brockden Brown described a very different journey to Philadelphia in his Romantic novel *Arthur Mervyn.* In this tale a young farmboy hero leaves his home in the country for Philadelphia. Instead of finding a place of promise where he can make his dreams come true, however, the boy is plunged into a plague-ridden urban world of decay, corruption, and evil. The Philadelphia of this novel is no city of promise; it is an industrial hell that devours all hope and ambition.

COMPARE AND CONTRAST

Circle the words in this paragraph that characterize the rationalists' view of cities; underline the words that Romantics might have used.

The journeys described in Franklin's *Autobiography* and Brown's *Arthur Mervyn* make clear the differences between the views of the rationalists and those of the Romantics. To Franklin and other rationalists, the city was a place to find success and self-realization. To the Romantic writers who came after Franklin, though, the city, far from being the seat of civilization, was often a place of moral ambiguity and, worse, of corruption and death.

The characteristic Romantic journey is to the countryside, which Romantics associated with independence, moral clarity, and healthful living. Sometimes, though, as in the works of Gothic-influenced writers like Edgar Allan Poe (1809–1849), the Romantic journey was a voyage to the country of the imagination. But whatever the destination of the Romantic journey, it was a flight both *from* something and *to* something. In fact, America's first truly popular professional writer, Washington Irving (1783–1859), is today known principally for an immortal story about an escape from civilization and responsibility—"Rip Van Winkle."

American Romanticism can best be described as a journey away from the corruption of civilization and the limits of rational thought and toward the integrity of nature and the freedom of the imagination.

The Romantic Sensibility: Celebrating the Imagination

In general, **Romanticism** is the name given to those schools of thought that value feeling and intuition over reason. The first rumblings of Romanticism were felt in Germany in the second half of the eighteenth century. Romanticism had a strong influence on literature, music, and painting in Europe and England well into the nineteenth century. But Romanticism came relatively late to America, and it took different forms.

Romanticism, especially in Europe, developed in part as a reaction against **rationalism.** In the sooty wake of the Industrial Revolution, with its squalid cities and wretched working conditions, people had come to realize the limits of reason. The Romantics came to believe that the imagination was able to apprehend truths that the rational mind could not reach. These truths were usually accompanied by powerful emotion and associated with natural, unspoiled beauty. To the Romantic sensibility, the imagination, spontaneity, individual feelings, and wild nature were of greater value than reason, logic, planning, and civilization.

IDENTIFY

Underline the sentence that tells what the Romantics valued most.

To the Romantic mind, poetry was the highest and most sublime embodiment of the imagination. Romantic artists often contrasted poetry with science, which they saw as destroying the very truth it claimed to seek. Edgar Allan Poe, for example, called science a "vulture" with wings of "dull realities," preying on the hearts of poets.

Romanticism, originally a European movement, emphasized feeling and intuition over reason, sought wisdom in natural beauty, and valued poetry above all other works of the imagination.

Romantic Escapism: From Dull Realities to Higher Realms

The Romantics wanted to rise above "dull realities" to a realm of higher truth. They did this in two principal ways. First, the Romantics searched for exotic settings in the more "natural" past or in a world far removed from the grimy and noisy industrial age. Sometimes they found this world in the supernatural realm, or in old legends and folklore. Second, the Romantics tried to contemplate the natural world until dull reality fell away to reveal underlying beauty and truth.

We can most easily see the first Romantic approach in the development, in Britain, of Gothic novels like Mary Shelley's *Frankenstein* and

CONNECT

Can you name one or two other Gothic stories from literature or the movies?

Bram Stoker's *Dracula,* with their wild, haunted landscapes, supernatural events, and mysterious medieval castles. The Gothic, with its roots in French, German, and English literature, seemed an unlikely transplant to the new nation of America, where there were seemingly no places old enough to have accumulated ghosts or to reek of decay. But even writers in America, notably Edgar Allan Poe, were attracted to the exotic, otherworldly trappings of the Gothic. In America, particularly in the works of Poe, the Gothic took a turn toward the psychological exploration of the human mind.

The second Romantic approach, the contemplation of the natural world, is evident in many lyric poems, such as "Thanatopsis" by William Cullen Bryant (1794–1878). In a typical Romantic poem, a flower found by a stream or a waterfowl flying overhead brings the speaker to some important, deeply felt insight, which is then recorded in the poem. This contemplative process is similar to the way the Puritans drew moral lessons from nature. The difference is one of emphasis and goal. The Puritans' lessons were defined by their religion. In nature they found the God they knew from the Bible. The Romantics, on the other hand, found in nature a more generalized spiritual awakening.

American Romanticism took two roads on the journey to understanding higher truths. One road led to the exploration of the past and of exotic, even supernatural, realms; the other road led to the contemplation of the natural world.

COMPARE AND CONTRAST

Circle the items in this list that you think continue to characterize American culture today; underline those items that no longer seem true of modern life.

Characteristics of American Romanticism

- Values feeling and intuition over reason
- Places faith in inner experience and the power of the imagination
- Shuns the artificiality of civilization and seeks unspoiled nature
- Prefers youthful innocence to educated sophistication
- Champions individual freedom and the worth of the individual
- Contemplates nature's beauty as a path to spiritual and moral development
- Looks backward to the wisdom of the past and distrusts progress
- Finds beauty and truth in exotic locales, the supernatural realm, and the inner world of the imagination
- Sees poetry as the highest expression of the imagination
- Finds inspiration in myth, legend, and folk culture

The American Novel and the Wilderness Experience

During the Romantic period, the big question about American literature was: Would American writers continue to imitate the English and European models, or would they finally develop a distinctive literature of their own? America provided a sense of limitless frontiers that Europe, so long settled, simply did not possess. Thus, the development of the American novel coincided with westward expansion, with the growth of a nationalist spirit, and with the rapid spread of cities. All these factors tended to reinforce the idealization of frontier life—as they still do today.

Most Europeans had an image of the American as unsophisticated and uncivilized. But James Fenimore Cooper (1789–1851) and other Romantic novelists who followed him turned the insult on its head. Virtue, they implied, was in American innocence, not in European sophistication. Eternal truths were waiting to be discovered not in dusty libraries or crowded cities or glittering court life, but in the American wilderness that was unknown and unavailable to Europeans.

We can see how the novel developed in America by looking at Cooper's career. After writing two early novels based on British models, in his third novel Cooper finally broke free of European constraints. In this novel, *The Pioneers* (1823), Cooper explored uniquely American settings and characters: frontier communities, American Indians, backwoodsmen, and the wilderness of western New York and Pennsylvania. Most of all, he created the first American heroic figure: Natty Bumppo (also known variously as Hawkeye, Deerslayer, and Leatherstocking), virtuous, skillful frontiersman whose simple morality and almost superhuman resourcefulness mark him as a true Romantic hero.

A New Kind of Hero

Natty Bumppo was quite different from the hero of the Age of Reason. The rationalist hero—exemplified by a real-life figure such as Ben Franklin—was worldly, educated, sophisticated, and bent on making a place for himself in civilization. The typical hero of American Romantic fiction, on the other hand, was youthful, innocent, intuitive, and close to nature.

Today, Americans still create Romantic heroes; the twentieth-century descendants of Natty Bumppo are all around us. They can be found in the guise of dozens of pop-culture heroes: the Lone Ranger, Superman, Luke Skywalker, Indiana Jones, and any number of Western, detective, and fantasy heroes.

American novelists looked to westward expansion and the development of the frontier for inspiration, creating subject matter that broke with European tradition. They created the American Romantic hero, whose qualities of youthfulness, innocence, intuitiveness, and closeness to the natural world set him solidly apart from the hero of the Age of Reason.

INFER

What are three subjects or settings that a Romantic author like Cooper might write about today?

CONNECT

Name three other heroes of contemporary pop culture.

Characteristics of the American Romantic Hero

- Is young, or possesses youthful qualities
- Is innocent and pure of purpose
- Has a sense of honor based not on society's rules but on some higher principle
- Has a knowledge of people and of life based on deep, intuitive understanding, not on formal learning
- Loves nature and avoids town life
- Quests for some higher truth in the natural world

American Romantic Poetry: Read at Every Fireside

The American Romantic novelists looked for new subject matter and innovative themes, but the opposite tendency appears in the works of the Romantic poets. Like Franklin, they wanted to prove that Americans were not unsophisticated hicks, and they attempted to prove this by working solidly within literary traditions rather than by crafting a different and unique American voice. Even when they constructed poems with American settings and subject matter, the American Romantic poets used typically English themes, meter, and imagery. In a sense, they wrote in a style that a cultivated person from England who had recently immigrated to America might be expected to use.

The Fireside Poets were, in their own time and for many decades afterward, the most popular poets America had ever produced. In the era before mass media changed American family life, the Boston writers Henry Wadsworth Longfellow (1807–1882), John Greenleaf Whittier (1807–1892), Oliver Wendell Holmes (1809–1894), and James Russell Lowell (1819–1891) were known as the Fireside Poets because their poems were so often read aloud at the fireside as family entertainment.

The Fireside Poets' attempts to create a new American literature relied heavily on the literature of the past. Certainly, they were not great innovators, and their choice of subject matter—love, patriotism, nature, family, God, and religion—was, for the most part, comforting rather than challenging to their audience (though Whittier, for one, also wrote powerful antislavery poems). Still, the Fireside Poets furthered the evolution of American poetry by introducing uniquely American subject matter in their choices of topics: American folk themes, descriptions of the American landscape, American Indian culture, and celebrations of American people, places, and events.

Limited by their essential literary conservatism, the Fireside Poets were unable to recognize the poetry of the future, which was being written right under their noses. Whittier's response in 1855 to reading

IDENTIFY

What were the principal achievements of the Fireside Poets? Underline the answer in the text.

the first volume of a certain poet's work was to throw the book into the fire. Ralph Waldo Emerson's response was much more farsighted. "I greet you," Emerson wrote to this maverick new poet, Walt Whitman, "at the beginning of a great career."

The Fireside Poets, immensely popular in their time, created some poems of lasting merit, but their essential literary conservatism prevented them from being truly innovative. The first uniquely American poetry was yet to be created.

From Rip Van Winkle

Make the Connection

Suspended Animation

The very essence of life is constant change—growth, transformation, and death. But what if, instead of moving along with the rest of the world, you were placed in suspended animation for twenty years? That is, what if you remained unconscious but alive over a long period? When you woke from your "nap," your expectations and views would be the same as they were when you fell "asleep." The world, however, would be very different—and think how dramatic the changes of twenty years would seem if you experienced them all at once.

In "Rip Van Winkle," Washington Irving imagines a man who sleeps through the entire period of the American Revolution and the establishment of the United States under the Constitution. What if a modern-day Rip Van Winkle were to awaken after a twenty-year-long nap—what changes would seem most important, or most dramatic? And what if you were to awaken twenty years from *now*—what changes seem likely? Complete the following chart to explore the possibilities of suspended animation.

	Biggest Change in the Past Twenty Years	Biggest Change in the Next Twenty Years?
Technology	"Digital Revolution" in Computers	Intelligent Robots
Politics		
Music		
Movies		
Clothing		
Sports		
Environment		

FROM

Rip Van Winkle

Washington Irving

IDENTIFY

ircle a word in lines 5–7 that ıeans "hill"; underline a word ıat means "greenery."

VISUALIZE

'icture Rip, with his dog, Wolf, nd his hunting rifle, on a hill igh above the Hudson River nd the forests that line its hores.

INFER

Vhat does Rip's "heavy sigh" mply?

IDENTIFY

Circle a word in this passage that means "imagination"; underline a word that means "moved fearfully."

"Rip Van Winkle" takes place in a small village on the Hudson River. The story begins just before the Revolutionary War. Rip is a farmer who has no talent for his work. His is the "worst-conditioned farm in the neighborhood." Rip's wife complains constantly about his idleness and carelessness. To escape from the drudgery of farm labor and his wife's clamor, Rip frequently goes hunting in the Catskill Mountains, accompanied by his dog, Wolf.

In a long ramble of the kind on a fine autumnal day, Rip had unconsciously scrambled to one of the highest parts of the Kaatskill Mountains. He was after his favorite sport of squirrel shooting and the still solitudes had echoed and reechoed with the reports of his gun. Panting and fatigued he threw himself, late in the afternoon, on a green knoll, covered with mountain herbage, that crowned the brow of a precipice. From an opening between the trees he could overlook all the lower country for many a mile of rich woodland. He saw at a distance the lordly Hudson, far, far below him, moving on its silent but majestic course, with the reflection of a purple cloud, or the sail of a lagging bark[1] here and there sleeping on its glassy bosom, and at last losing itself in the blue highlands.

On the other side he looked down into a deep mountain glen, wild, lonely, and shagged, the bottom filled with fragments from the impending cliffs and scarcely lighted by the reflected rays of the setting sun. For some time Rip lay musing on this scene, evening was gradually advancing, the mountains began to throw their long blue shadows over the valleys, he saw that it would be dark, long before he could reach the village, and he heaved a heavy sigh when he thought of encountering the terrors of Dame Van Winkle.

As he was about to descend he heard a voice from a distance hallooing "Rip Van Winkle! Rip Van Winkle!" He looked around, but could see nothing but a crow winging its solitary flight across the mountain. He thought his fancy must have deceived him and turned again to descend, when he heard the same cry ring through the still evening air: "Rip Van Winkle! Rip Van Winkle!"—at the same time Wolf bristled up his back and giving a low growl, skulked to his master's side, looking fearfully down into the glen. Rip now felt a vague apprehension stealing over him; he looked anxiously in the same direction and perceived a strange figure slowly toiling up the rocks and bending under the weight of something he carried on his back. He was surprised to see any human being in this lonely and unfrequented place, but supposing it to be someone of the neighborhood in need of his assistance he hastened down to yield it.

---

1. **lagging bark:** slow-moving boat.

On nearer approach he was still more surprised at the singularity of the stranger's appearance. He was a short, square-built old fellow, with thick bushy hair and a grizzled beard. His dress was of the antique Dutch fashion, a cloth jerkin[2] strapped round the waist, several pair of breeches, the outer one of ample volume decorated with rows of buttons down the sides and bunches at the knees. He bore on his shoulder a stout keg that seemed full of liquor, and made signs for Rip to approach and assist him with the load. Though rather shy and distrustful of this new acquaintance Rip complied with his usual alacrity, and mutually relieving each other they clambered up a narrow gully apparently the dry bed of a mountain torrent. As they ascended, Rip every now and then heard long rolling peals like distant thunder, that seemed to issue out of a deep ravine or rather cleft between lofty rocks, toward which their rugged path conducted. He paused for an instant, but supposing it to be the muttering of one of those transient thundershowers which often take place in mountain heights, he proceeded. Passing through the ravine they came to a hollow like a small amphitheater, surrounded by perpendicular precipices, over the brinks of which impending trees shot their branches, so that you only caught glimpses of the azure sky and the bright evening cloud. During the whole time Rip and his companion had labored on in silence, for though the former marveled greatly what could be the object of carrying a keg of liquor up this wild mountain, yet there was something strange and incomprehensible about the unknown, that inspired awe and checked familiarity.

On entering the amphitheater new objects of wonder presented themselves. On a level spot in the center was a company of odd-looking personages playing at ninepins.[3] They were dressed in a quaint, outlandish fashion—some wore short doublets,[4] others jerkins with long knives in their belts and most of them had enormous breeches of similar style with that of the guide's. Their visages too were peculiar. One had a large head, broad face, and small piggish eyes. The face of another seemed to consist entirely of nose, and was surmounted by a white sugarloaf hat, set off with a little red cock's tail. They all had beards of various shapes and colors. There was one who seemed to be the commander. He was a stout old gentleman, with a weather-beaten countenance. He wore a laced doublet, broad belt and hanger,[5] high-crowned hat and feather, red stockings, and high-heeled shoes with roses[6] in them. The whole group reminded Rip of the figures in an old Flemish painting, in the parlor of Dominie Van Schaick the village parson, and which had been brought over from Holland at the time of the settlement.

---

2. jerkin (jur′kin): sleeveless jacket.
3. ninepins: a bowling game.
4. doublets: closefitting jackets.
5. hanger: short, curved sword hung from the belt.
6. roses: ornaments shaped like roses; often called rosettes.

IDENTIFY

Circle a word in this passage that means "oddness" or "peculiarity."

PREDICT

What might be the outcome of Rip's encounter with this stranger and the keg he's carrying?

IDENTIFY

Circle two words in this passage that mean "face."

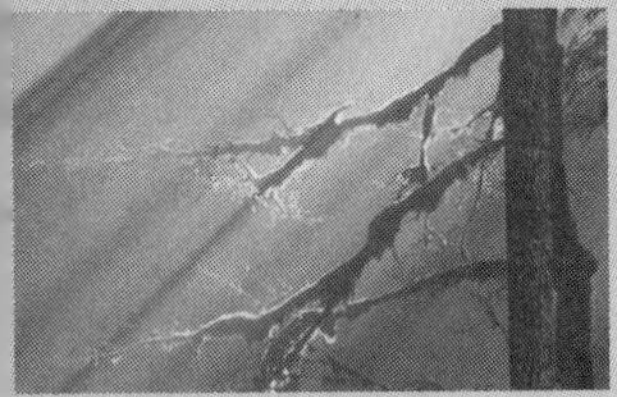

IDENTIFY

ircle a word in lines 82–85 hat means "stopped"; nderline a word that means 'outlandish" or "awkward."

WORDS TO OWN

eiterated (rē·it′ə·rāt′id) *v.:* epeated.

INFER

What kind of reception does Rip expect from his wife?

IDENTIFY

Circle a word in lines 106–114 that means "partygoers"; underline a word that refers to a kind of game bird.

What seemed particularly odd to Rip was, that though these folks were evidently amusing themselves, yet they maintained the gravest faces, the most mysterious silence, and were, withal, the most melancholy party of pleasure he had ever witnessed. Nothing interrupted the stillness of the scene, but the noise of the balls, which, whenever they were rolled, echoed along the mountains like rumbling peals of thunder.

As Rip and his companion approached them they suddenly desisted from their play and stared at him with such fixed statuelike gaze, and such strange uncouth, lackluster countenances, that his heart turned within him, and his knees smote together. His companion now emptied the contents of the keg into large flagons[7] and made signs to him to wait upon the company. He obeyed with fear and trembling; they quaffed the liquor in profound silence and then returned to their game.

By degrees Rip's awe and apprehension subsided. He even ventured, when no eye was fixed upon him, to taste the beverage, which he found had much of the flavor of excellent Hollands.[8] He was naturally a thirsty soul and was soon tempted to repeat the draft. One taste provoked another, and he reiterated his visits to the flagon so often that at length his senses were overpowered, his eyes swam in his head—his head gradually declined and he fell into a deep sleep.

On awaking he found himself on the green knoll from whence he had first seen the old man of the glen. He rubbed his eyes—it was a bright, sunny morning. The birds were hopping and twittering among the bushes, and the eagle was wheeling aloft and breasting the pure mountain breeze. "Surely," thought Rip, "I have not slept here all night." He recalled the occurrences before he fell asleep. The strange man with a keg of liquor—the mountain ravine—the wild retreat among the rocks—the woebegone party at ninepins—the flagon—"ah! that flagon! that wicked flagon!" thought Rip—"what excuse shall I make to Dame Van Winkle?"

He looked round for his gun, but in place of the clean well-oiled fowling piece he found an old firelock[9] lying by him, the barrel encrusted with rust; the lock falling off and the stock[10] worm-eaten. He now suspected that the grave roysters of the mountain had put a trick upon him, and having dosed him with liquor, had robbed him of his gun. Wolf too had disappeared, but he might have strayed away after a squirrel or partridge. He whistled after him and shouted his name—but all in vain; the echoes repeated his whistle and shout, but no dog was to be seen.

---

7. **flagons:** bottlelike containers for liquids.
8. **Hollands:** Dutch gin.
9. **firelock:** early type of gun.
10. **stock:** wooden handle attached to metal gun barrel.

He determined to revisit the scene of the last evening's gambol, and if he met with any of the party, to demand his dog and gun. As he arose to walk he found himself stiff in the joints and wanting in his usual activity. "These mountain beds do not agree with me," thought Rip, "and if this frolic should lay me up with a fit of the rheumatism, I shall have a blessed time with Dame Van Winkle." With some difficulty he got down into the glen; he found the gully up which he and his companion had ascended the preceding evening, but to his astonishment a mountain stream was now foaming down it; leaping from rock to rock, and filling the glen with babbling murmurs. He, however, made shift to scramble up its sides working his toilsome way through thickets of birch, sassafras, and witch hazel, and sometimes tripped up or entangled by the wild grapevines that twisted their coils and tendrils from tree to tree, and spread a kind of network in his path.

At length he reached to where the ravine had opened through the cliffs, to the amphitheater—but no traces of such opening remained. The rocks presented a high impenetrable wall over which the torrent came tumbling in a sheet of feathery foam, and fell into a broad deep basin black from the shadows of the surrounding forest. Here then poor Rip was brought to a stand. He again called and whistled after his dog—he was only answered by the cawing of a flock of idle crows, sporting high in air about a dry tree that overhung a sunny precipice; and who, secure in their elevation seemed to look down and scoff at the poor man's perplexities.

What was to be done? The morning was passing away and Rip felt famished for want of his breakfast. He grieved to give up his dog and gun; he dreaded to meet his wife; but it would not do to starve among the mountains. He shook his head, shouldered the rusty firelock, and with a heart full of trouble and anxiety, turned his steps homeward.

As he approached the village he met a number of people, but none whom he knew, which somewhat surprised him, for he had thought himself acquainted with everyone in the country round. Their dress too was of a different fashion from that to which he was accustomed. They all stared at him with equal marks of surprise, and whenever they cast their eyes upon him, invariably stroked their chins. The constant recurrence of this gesture induced Rip involuntarily to do the same, when to his astonishment he found his beard had grown a foot long!

He had now entered the skirts of the village. A troop of strange children ran at his heels, hooting after him and pointing at his gray beard. The dogs too, not one of which he recognized for an old acquaintance, barked at him as he passed. The very village was altered—it was larger and more populous. There were rows of houses which he had never seen before, and those which had been his familiar haunts had disappeared. Strange names were over the doors—strange faces at

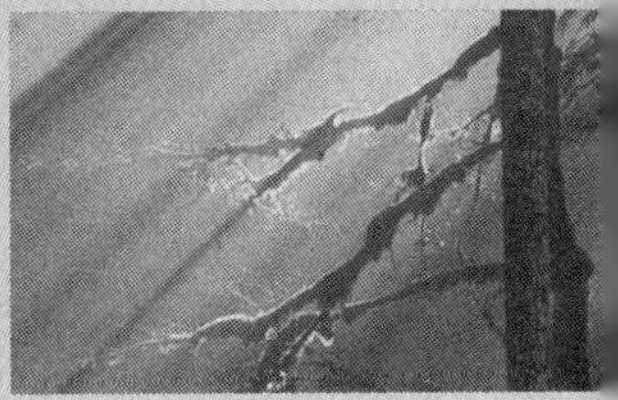

BUILD FLUENCY

Re-read this paragraph aloud, taking care to pronounce each word correctly and expressively.

COMPARE AND CONTRAST

Compare this description of the scene with the description of the same place during Rip's ascent of the mountain (lines 42–54). What is different now

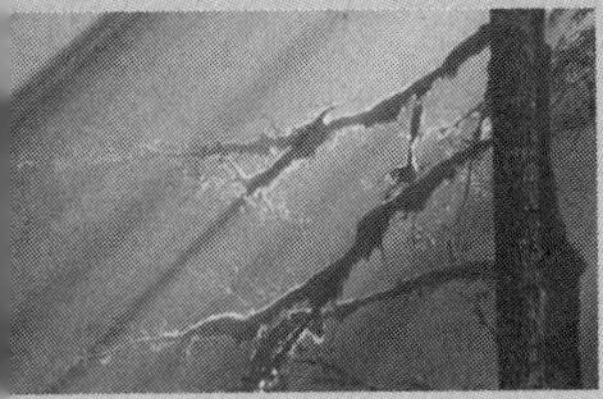

EVALUATE

ow successful is Irving in reating an impression of Rip's ewilderment at the strange et familiar appearance of his ative village?

the windows—everything was strange. His mind now misgave him; he began to doubt whether both he and the world around him were not bewitched. Surely this was his native village which he had left but the day before. There stood the Kaatskill Mountains—there ran the silver Hudson at a distance—there was every hill and dale precisely as it had always been—Rip was sorely perplexed—"That flagon last night," thought he, "has addled my poor head sadly!"

Setting

Misty mountaintops, a mysterious forest, an old-fashioned village, a distant era—these are some details of **setting** that Irving uses in "Rip Van Winkle." Like many Romantic writers, Irving was fascinated by times past and by wild, natural landscapes. In this story it is setting—that is, the story's physical, geographical, and historical environment—that brings about a magical change in the hero and sets the **plot** in motion. A master storyteller like Washington Irving makes the setting an integral part of the story; not only does the environment seem like the perfect place for the plot to unfold, but also the language that describes the setting contributes to the story's **tone,** or **mood.**

Examine the setting of Rip Van Winkle's strange ramble in the mountains by completing the chart below.

Description of Setting in the Story	Relation Between Setting and Plot	Mood Evoked by This Description
"He saw at a distance the lordly Hudson, far, far below him, moving on its silent but majestic course. . . ." (lines 8–10)	Rip has traveled far from his home into high mountains.	Reverent awe toward the power of the natural world
". . . he looked down into a deep mountain glen, wild, lonely, and shagged. . . ." (lines 13–14)		
". . . they came to a hollow like a small amphitheater, surrounded by perpendicular precipices, over the brinks of which impending trees shot their branches. . . ." (lines 51–52)		
"There were rows of houses which he had never seen before, and those which had been his familiar haunts had disappeared." (lines 156–158)		

Vocabulary: How to Own a Word

Using Context Clues

Using **context clues**—clues to meaning that are in the text—is the best way to figure out the meaning of a word without interrupting yourself to check a dictionary. "Rip Van Winkle" provides examples of six kinds of context clues that you will commonly encounter in your reading.

Example
". . . they ***quaffed*** the liquor in profound silence. . . ." (lines 87–88)

Liquor is something you can *quaff.* You can infer that *quaff* means "to drink."

Restatement
"He even ventured . . . to taste the beverage. . . . and was soon tempted to repeat the ***draft.***" (lines 89–92)

"Repeat the *draft*" seems to restate "taste the beverage," so you can infer that *draft* means "drinking."

Summary
"His mind now ***misgave*** him; he began to doubt whether both he and the world around him were not bewitched." (lines 159–161)

The clause after the semicolon tells you the meaning of *misgave*—"became filled with doubt."

Contrast
"Though rather shy and distrustful of this new acquaintance Rip complied with his usual ***alacrity.*** . . ." (lines 42–43)

The word *though* sets up an opposition—it helps you know that *alacrity* is not what you would expect from someone who is "rather shy and distrustful."

Items in a Series
"They were dressed in a ***quaint,*** outlandish fashion. . . ." (lines 61–62)

The comma between *quaint* and *outlandish* lets you know they may be close in meaning.

Cause and Effect
". . . Rip felt ***famished*** for want of his breakfast." (lines 139–140)

"For want of" indicates that being *famished* is a result of not having eaten breakfast. *Famished* means "extremely hungry."

Using context clues, circle the letter for the term that best corresponds to the word in boldface type.

1. "... Wolf bristled up his back and giving a low growl, **skulked** to his master's side, looking fearfully down into the glen." (lines 26–28)

   a. rowed boldly b. moved furtively c. nodded happily

2. "Rip now felt a vague **apprehension** stealing over him; he looked anxiously in the same direction. . . ." (lines 28–29)

   a. arrest b. sleepiness c. unease

3. "On nearer approach he was still more surprised at the **singularity** of the stranger's appearance." (lines 35–36)

   a. solitude b. ordinariness c. oddness

4. "... several pair of **breeches,** the outer one of ample volume decorated with rows of buttons down the sides and bunches at the knees." (lines 38–40)

   a. spectacles b. trousers c. shirts

5. "... so that you only caught glimpses of the **azure** sky and the bright evening cloud." (lines 53–54)

   a. blue b. darkened c. lofty

6. "... though these folks were evidently amusing themselves, yet they maintained the **gravest** faces. . . ." (lines 75–77)

   a. saddest b. happiest c. funniest

7. "As Rip and his companion approached them they suddenly **desisted from** their play. . . ." (lines 82–83)

   a. continued with b. broke off c. assisted with

8. "... and such strange **uncouth,** lackluster countenances . . ." (lines 83–84)

   a. bizarre b. uncovered c. expressive

9. "By degrees Rip's awe and apprehension **subsided.**" (line 89)

   a. increased b. returned c. decreased

10. "He determined to revisit the scene of the last evening's **gambol,** and if he met with any of the party, to demand his dog and gun." (lines 115–116)

    a. animal show b. frolic c. slumber

Thanatopsis

Make the Connection

The Endless Cycle

Following the creative method of the great English Romantic poet William Wordsworth, William Cullen Bryant wrote while taking long solitary rambles through the woods. Romantic poets looked to nature for lessons, and the chief lesson Bryant found was the organic cycle of birth, growth, death, and rebirth—nature endlessly renewing itself. *Thanatopsis* is a word Bryant coined by joining two Greek words, *thanatos* (death) and *opsis* (seeing). The word is defined by the poem: a way of looking at death and a way of thinking about it.

The idea that the way of the universe is cyclical, not linear, came to the Romantic poets instinctively, as a matter of sensibility. It's interesting that modern science has come to a similar understanding. Cosmologists, for example, now believe that the entire universe expands and contracts in an eternal cycle of "Big Bang" and "Big Crunch." Where else do we find cyclical patterns of renewal and rebirth? Complete the diagrams below.

The Water Cycle

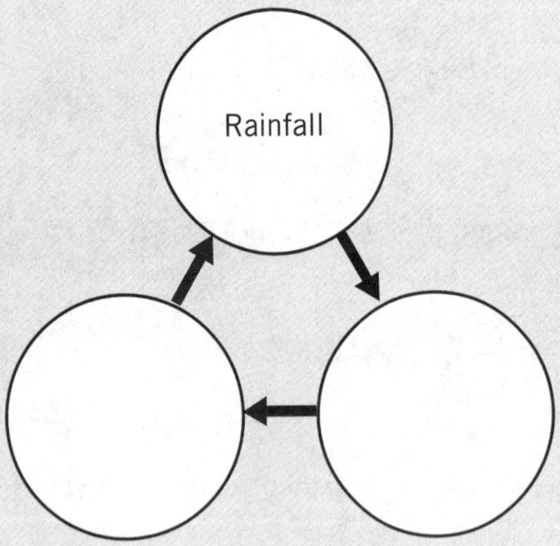

Forest Growth

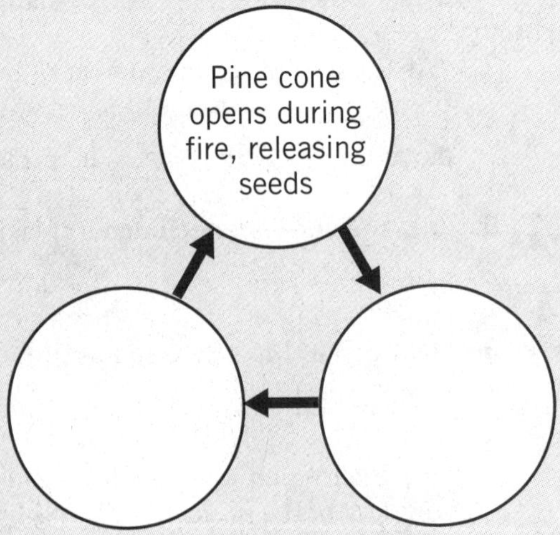

Thanatopsis

William Cullen Bryant

OMPARE AND CONTRAST

rcle the words and phrases lines 1–13 that suggest life d happiness; underline e words and phrases that ggest death and sadness.

REDICT

hat do you think Bryant ill present as nature's ndamental answer to the ar of death?

IDENTIFY

nderline the archaic terms hat Bryant uses in lines 7–30 instead of "you" and your."

RETELL

estate in simple terms ryant's message in lines 3–37. ("Thou shalt lie down . . one mighty sepulcher.")

To him who in the love of Nature holds
Communion with her visible forms, she speaks
A various language; for his gayer hours
She has a voice of gladness, and a smile
And eloquence of beauty, and she glides
Into his darker musings, with a mild
And healing sympathy, that steals away
Their sharpness, ere[1] he is aware. When thoughts
Of the last bitter hour come like a blight
Over thy spirit, and sad images
Of the stern agony, and shroud, and pall,[2]
And breathless darkness, and the narrow house,[3]
Make thee to shudder, and grow sick at heart;—
Go forth, under the open sky, and list[4]
To Nature's teachings, while from all around—
Earth and her waters, and the depths of air—
Comes a still voice.—
Yet[5] a few days, and thee
The all-beholding sun shall see no more
In all his course; nor yet in the cold ground,
Where thy pale form was laid, with many tears,
Nor in the embrace of ocean, shall exist
Thy image. Earth, that nourished thee, shall claim
Thy growth, to be resolved to earth again,
And, lost each human trace, surrendering up
Thine individual being, shalt thou go
To mix forever with the elements,
To be a brother to the insensible rock
And to the sluggish clod, which the rude swain[6]
Turns with his share,[7] and treads upon. The oak
Shall send his roots abroad, and pierce thy mold.

Yet not to thine eternal resting place
Shalt thou retire alone, nor couldst thou wish
Couch more magnificent. Thou shalt lie down
With patriarchs of the infant world—with kings,
The powerful of the earth—the wise, the good,
Fair forms, and hoary seers[8] of ages past,

---

1. **ere** (er): before.
2. **pall** (pôl): coffin cover.
3. **narrow house:** grave.
4. **list:** listen.
5. **Yet . . . :** Here, the voice of Nature begins to speak.
6. **rude swain:** uneducated country youth.
7. **share:** short for "plowshare."
8. **hoary seers:** white-haired prophets.

All in one mighty sepulcher.[9] The hills
Rock-ribbed and ancient as the sun,—the vales
Stretching in pensive quietness between;
The venerable woods—rivers that move
In majesty, and the complaining brooks
That make the meadows green; and, poured round all,
Old Ocean's gray and melancholy waste,—
Are but the solemn decorations all
Of the great tomb of man. The golden sun,
The planets, all the infinite host of heaven,
Are shining on the sad abodes of death,
Through the still lapse of ages. All that tread
The globe are but a handful to the tribes
That slumber in its bosom.—Take the wings
Of morning,[10] pierce the Barcan wilderness,[11]
Or lose thyself in the continuous woods
Where rolls the Oregon,[12] and hears no sound,
Save his own dashings—yet the dead are there:
And millions in those solitudes, since first
The flight of years began, have laid them down
In their last sleep—the dead reign there alone.
So shalt thou rest, and what if thou withdraw
In silence from the living, and no friend
Take note of thy departure? All that breathe
Will share thy destiny. The gay will laugh
When thou art gone, the solemn brood of care
Plod on, and each one as before will chase
His favorite phantom; yet all these shall leave
Their mirth and their employments, and shall come
And make their bed with thee. As the long train
Of ages glides away, the sons of men,
The youth in life's fresh spring, and he who goes
In the full strength of years, matron and maid,
The speechless babe, and the gray-headed man—
Shall one by one be gathered to thy side,
By those, who in their turn shall follow them.

So[13] live, that when thy summons comes to join
The innumerable caravan, which moves

IDENTIFY

Circle the words in lines 37–45 that suggest the great age of the earth.

EVALUATE

How much comfort is there in Bryant's assurance that we shouldn't fear death, since it comes to everyone?

INTERPRET

Why do you think Bryant uses the word *phantom* (line 64) to express the idea of goals, desires, and ambitions?

9. **sepulcher** (sep′əl·kər): burial place.
10. **Take . . . morning:** allusion to Psalm 139:9: "If I take the wings of the morning . . ."
11. **Barcan wilderness:** desert near Barca (now al-Marj), Libya, in North Africa.
12. **Oregon:** early name for the Columbia River, which flows between Washington and Oregon.
13. **So . . . :** The speaker's voice resumes here.

NFER

what, exactly, do you think yant wants the reader to ace "an unfaltering trust"?

BUILD FLUENCY

ead lines 73–81 aloud, king care to read expressively nd create a tone that suits e message of the poem.

To that mysterious realm, where each shall take
His chamber in the silent halls of death,
Thou go not, like the quarry slave at night,
Scourged to his dungeon, but, sustained and soothed
By an unfaltering trust, approach thy grave,
Like one who wraps the drapery of his couch
About him, and lies down to pleasant dreams.

Blank Verse

"Thanatopsis" is not written in rhyme, but it does have a regular rhythm, a pattern of stressed and unstressed syllables. If the opening line is broken down into syllables,

<table>
<tr><td>˘</td><td>´</td><td>˘</td><td>´</td><td>˘</td><td>´</td><td>˘</td><td>´</td><td>˘</td><td>´</td></tr>
<tr><td>To</td><td>him</td><td>who</td><td>in</td><td>the</td><td>love</td><td>of</td><td>Na-</td><td>ture</td><td>holds</td></tr>
<tr><td>1</td><td>2</td><td>3</td><td>4</td><td>5</td><td>6</td><td>7</td><td>8</td><td>9</td><td>10</td></tr>
</table>

we find a pattern of one unstressed syllable followed by one stressed syllable. English verse is based on stress, and the unit used to measure rhythm in a line of poetry is called a **foot.** A foot usually consists of two or three syllables, one of which is stressed. In the line above, each foot consists of one unstressed syllable followed by one stressed syllable. This kind of foot is called an **iamb.** Since the line has five such feet, its **meter,** or rhythmic pattern, is called **iambic pentameter.** (The prefix *penta–* means "five.") Poetry consisting of lines of unrhymed iambic pentameter is called **blank verse.**

Blank verse, which is close to normal speech in its rhythm, allows an extended development of thought, sometimes through many lines; it is common in poetry that deals with complex and profound subjects. And because of its speechlike rhythms, it is also suitable for dramatic poetry; Shakespeare used it in his plays. Bryant's choice of blank verse is appropriate for "Thanatopsis" for both reasons: the seriousness of the topic, death, and the poet's wish to address the reader directly, in the normal rhythms of speech. The poet who uses blank verse must keep the regular rhythm from becoming monotonous and singsong. Bryant accomplishes this by introducing slight variations in rhythm. Line 6, for instance, begins with a stressed syllable: "Into his darker musings . . ."

Complete the following chart, marking the stressed syllables and unstressed syllables. Then, analyze each line; if the iambic pattern (ta-DAH, ta-DAH, ta-DAH, etc.) is unbroken, write "regular" in the blank; otherwise, write "variation."

<table>
<tr><th>Lines from "Thanatopsis" Divided into Iambic Feet</th><th>Regular Line or Variation?</th></tr>
<tr><td>So live, | that when | thy sum- | mons comes | to join</td><td>regular</td></tr>
<tr><td>His cham- | ber in | the si- | lent halls | of death,</td><td></td></tr>
<tr><td>Thou go | not, like | the quar- | ry slave | at night</td><td></td></tr>
<tr><td>Scourged to | his dun- | geon, but, | sus·tained | and soothed</td><td></td></tr>
</table>

The Tide Rises, the Tide Falls

Make the Connection

Finite and Infinite

No other American poet has matched Henry Wadsworth Longfellow's popularity at the height of his career. Longfellow is now remembered as the foremost of the Fireside Poets. Longfellow believed his task as a poet was to create a common American heritage. This naturally led him to patriotic subjects like "Paul Revere's Ride," which quickly became a staple in schoolhouses across the nation. A greater challenge was to create poems of spiritual significance for a diverse people without a common religion.

Longfellow's solution was the same as William Cullen Bryant's—to seek and to find spiritual meaning in the natural world. Nature repeats its cycles without foreseeable end. Summer turns to winter, day follows night, and the tide rises and falls. In comparison, a person's lifetime is limited. There are no repeated cycles, just one journey from life's beginning to its end.

Complete the following chart to explore the ways we experience the finite and the infinite.

Natural Phenomenon	Represents the Finite or the Infinite?	Why?
Life Span of an Individual Human Being	Finite	A person's life span is short. Death is inevitable.
Succession of Generations in a Family		
Number of Stars in the Sky		
Cycle of Seasons		
Ocean Currents		

Henry Wadsworth Longfellow

The Tide Rises, the Tide Falls

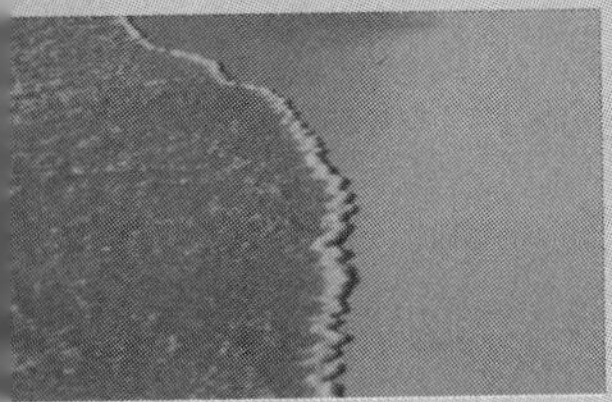

INTERPRET
low do the pauses in the niddle of each of the first two nes affect the rhythm of the oem and the way the lines re read?

VISUALIZE
icture the way the waves reak on the beach, smoothing he sand; what are the "soft, vhite hands" of the waves line 8)?

EVALUATE
What is the effect of concluding each stanza of the poem with the **refrain,** "And the tide rises, the tide falls"?

BUILD FLUENCY
Re-read the entire poem aloud, giving each line a natural rhythm without sounding too singsong.

The tide rises, the tide falls,
The twilight darkens, the curlew[1] calls;
Along the sea-sands damp and brown
The traveller hastens toward the town,
And the tide rises, the tide falls.

Darkness settles on roofs and walls,
But the sea, the sea in the darkness calls;
The little waves, with their soft, white hands,
Efface[2] the footprints in the sands,
And the tide rises, the tide falls.

The morning breaks; the steeds in their stalls
Stamp and neigh, as the hostler[3] calls;
The day returns, but nevermore
Returns the traveller to the shore,
And the tide rises, the tide falls.

1. **curlew** (kur'lo͞o'): large, brownish shorebird with long legs.
2. **Efface** (ə·fās'): wipe out; erase.
3. **hostler** (häs'lər): person who takes care of horses.

Meter: A Pattern of Sounds

Meter is a pattern of stressed and unstressed syllables in poetry. **Scanning** a poem means marking the stressed syllables with the symbol (´) and the unstressed syllables with the symbol (˘).

A metrical unit of poetry is called a **foot,** which always contains at least one stressed syllable and usually one or more unstressed syllables. A common type of foot is the **iamb**—an unstressed syllable followed by a stressed syllable. The meter of "The Tide Rises, the Tide Falls" is essentially iambic. Read this line aloud, giving special stress to syllables marked (´).

Alóng | the séa- | sands dámp | and brówn

Poets usually include variations within a metrical pattern in order to avoid a mechanical, singsong effect. In the poem's first line, notice how Longfellow avoids a purely iambic meter by pairing two stressed syllables, which is a metrical foot called a **spondee.**

Mark each line in "The Tide Rises, the Tide Falls" for stressed and unstressed syllables. Then, read the poem aloud once again, noting which lines are regular in their meter and which are variations from a strict pattern.

The Chambered Nautilus

Make the Connection

Things Change

A nautilus is a squidlike sea creature that lives in a shell that grows year by year from the size of a tiny bead to the size of a pumpkin. The word *nautilus* comes from the Greek word for "sailor," reminding us that the Greeks thought this shell could actually move on the surface of the water, using a membrane as its sail.

The first three stanzas of "The Chambered Nautilus" are a meditation upon the life and death of the nautilus. In the next-to-last stanza, the poet begins an **apostrophe** (a direct address to an object or to someone who is not present). And in the final stanza he imagines hearing an answering voice—perhaps the voice of nature, or of life itself—urging him, like the nautilus, to grow ever-larger chambers to house his ever-growing spirit.

Throughout our lives we outgrow old things and move on to new ones: clothes, attitudes, interests, jobs, types of entertainment—even friendships. Complete the following chart to consider various ways we grow and change.

Experience of Change	What We Fear from the Change	How We Might Benefit from the Change
Graduating from high school	Losing friends and familiar routines	Developing new friendships and interests
Moving out of family home		
Getting engaged to be married		
Joining the military		
Traveling to a distant country		

Oliver Wendell Holmes

The Chambered Nautilus

INTERPRET

'hy is the "main" (that is, ıe sea) "unshadowed"?

IDENTIFY

:ircle words in the second tanza that suggest the fragile ıature of the nautilus.

VISUALIZE

'icture the shell as a series of ever-larger chambers growing n a spiral, like a snail shell.

INTERPRET

Vhat does the poet mean by "deep caves of thought" (line 28), and what voice might come from those caves?

INTERPRET

When will the soul be "free" from the series of "stately mansions" it builds for itself?

This is the ship of pearl, which, poets feign,[1]
Sails the unshadowed main,—
The venturous bark that flings
On the sweet summer wind its purpled wings
In gulfs enchanted, where the siren[2] sings,
And coral reefs lie bare,
Where the cold sea maids[3] rise to sun their streaming hair.

Its webs of living gauze no more unfurl;
Wrecked is the ship of pearl!
And every chambered cell,
Where its dim dreaming life was wont to dwell,
As the frail tenant shaped his growing shell,
Before thee lies revealed,—
Its irised[4] ceiling rent,[5] its sunless crypt unsealed!

Year after year beheld the silent toil
That spread his lustrous coil;
Still, as the spiral grew,
He left the past year's dwelling for the new,
Stole with soft step its shining archway through,
Built up its idle door,
Stretched in his last-found home, and knew the old no more.

Thanks for the heavenly message brought by thee,
Child of the wandering sea,
Cast from her lap, forlorn!
From thy dead lips a clearer note is born
Than ever Triton blew from wreathèd horn![6]
While on mine ear it rings,
Through the deep caves of thought I hear a voice that sings:—

Build thee more stately mansions, O my soul,
As the swift seasons roll!
Leave thy low-vaulted past!
Let each new temple, nobler than the last,

1. **feign** (fān): archaic for "imagine."
2. **siren** (sī′rən): in Greek mythology, one of a group of sea maidens whose seductive singing lures sailors to wreck their ships on coastal rocks.
3. **sea maids:** mermaids or sea nymphs.
4. **irised** (ī′risd): iridescent; rainbowlike. Iris is the Greek goddess of the rainbow.
5. **rent:** torn.
6. **than . . . wreathèd** (rē*th*′id) **horn:** echoes a line from "The World Is Too Much with Us," a sonnet by English poet William Wordsworth (1770–1850): "Or hear old Triton blow his wreathèd horn." In Greek mythology, Triton is a sea god, often represented as blowing a trumpet made from a conch shell. *Wreathèd* means "coiled" or "spiral-shaped."

Shut thee from heaven with a dome more vast,
    Till thou at length art free,
Leaving thine outgrown shell by life's unresting sea!

BUILD FLUENCY

Read the last two stanzas of this poem aloud, pronouncing each word clearly and expressively.

Extended Metaphor

A **metaphor** is a figure of speech that makes a comparison between two very unlike things. Sometimes writers extend a metaphor—that is, they take it as far as it can logically be developed. An **extended metaphor** may continue for several lines, or it may be developed throughout an entire work.

Step by step, describe the extended metaphor in the last stanza of the poem.

1. What are the "stately mansions" (line 29)?

2. What is the "low-vaulted past" (line 31)?

3. What is "each new temple" (line 32)?

4. What is the "outgrown shell" (line 35)?

5. What is the "unresting sea" (line 35)?

Sound Effects

Writers use devices such as **rhythm, meter, rhyme, alliteration, assonance, onomatopoeia, consonance,** and **refrain** to make the sounds of a work convey and enhance its meaning.

Rhythm refers to the alternation of stressed and unstressed syllables in language (see page 77). The most obvious kind of rhythm is produced by **meter,** the regular pattern of stressed and unstressed syllables (see page 81).

Rhyme refers to the repetition of vowel sounds in accented syllables and all succeeding syllables. **End rhyme** refers to rhyming words at the ends of lines. When words within the same line of poetry have repeated sounds, we have an example of **internal rhyme.** The pattern of rhyme in a poem is called a **rhyme scheme.**

Alliteration refers to the repetition of the same or similar consonant sounds at the beginning of words or stressed syllables.

> The morning breaks; the **st**eeds in their **st**alls
> **St**amp and neigh,

Assonance refers to the repetition of similar vowel sounds followed by different consonant sounds, especially in words close together:

> The t**i**de r**i**ses, the t**i**de falls,

Onomatopoeia refers to the use of a word whose sound imitates or suggests its meaning. The word *buzz* is onomatopoeic; it imitates the sound it names.

Consonance refers to the repetition of the same or similar final consonant sounds in accented syllables or in important words. The word *singsong* is an example of consonance.

A **refrain** is a word, phrase, line, or group of lines that is repeated, for effect, several times in a poem. In Longfellow's poem (page 80), the refrain occurs at the end of each stanza:

> And the tide rises, the tide falls.

The American Renaissance:
A Literary Coming of Age
1840–1860

A remarkable party took place on August 5, 1850, in Stockbridge, Massachusetts. Among those attending were two writers living nearby: Nathaniel Hawthorne (1804–1864) and Herman Melville (1819–1891). After a fine day of vigorous hiking in the Berkshire Mountains, the group settled down for a long dinner. Soon the table conversation turned to American literature.

Would there ever be an American writer as great as England's William Shakespeare? This question started a heated discussion, with Melville firmly supporting the American side. Hawthorne found himself agreeing with Melville, whom he had never met before.

It seemed highly unlikely that these two writers would become friends. Herman Melville was an ex-sailor with little formal education. He had lived in the South Seas and had written a remarkable first novel, *Typee* (1846), about his adventures. At the time of the party, Melville was hard at work on his fifth novel, *Moby-Dick,* which, it appeared, would be very long.

Nathaniel Hawthorne, who was fifteen years older than Melville, was well educated, reserved, and a bit of a loner. He had written many short stories and had recently published *The Scarlet Letter* (1850), a novel about sin and hypocrisy in Puritan New England.

Despite their different backgrounds, a friendship sprang up between the two writers. Melville read Hawthorne's works and soon wrote a magazine essay in which he urged American readers to "prize and cherish" their own writers. In a burst of literary patriotism, Melville claimed that, in Hawthorne, America was very close to producing its own Shakespeare.

Nathaniel Hawthorne and Herman Melville firmly agreed that America was finally capable as a nation of producing great writing. They both saw a dark side to human existence, and they sought to record this aspect of human nature in their works.

EVALUATE

Do you agree that "great writing" can or should include the "dark side to human existence"? Explain your answer.

First Flowering: A Declaration of Literary Independence

Melville's horn blowing for American writing came at a time when the American landscape and American culture would finally find their place in a literature distinct from European models. Writers were aware of this, and they sometimes used the word *renaissance* (ren′ə·säns′), meaning "rebirth," to describe this extraordinary explosion of American literary genius.

When Americans referred to themselves as living in a renaissance, they were comparing their times to the European Renaissance, a period of extraordinary cultural vitality that lasted from about the fourteenth to the sixteenth century. A better term, however, for what happened in the still-raw America of the mid-1800s might be "coming of age." From 1849 to 1855, American writers produced a remarkable body of work, enough masterpieces for a national literature.

In the mid-nineteenth century, writers such as Nathaniel Hawthorne, Ralph Waldo Emerson, Henry David Thoreau, and Herman Melville produced some of the early masterpieces of American literature.

Intellectual and Social Life in New England

This burst of American literature can be traced in large measure to the intellectual and social ferment in New England, long known for its interest in self-improvement and intellectual inquiry. This interest found expression in the Lyceum (lī·sē′əm) movement, begun in 1826 in Millbury, Massachusetts. Lyceum organizations, soon established in many communities, had a number of goals, including educating adults, training teachers, establishing museums, and instituting social reforms. A typical part of a Lyceum program was a course of lectures in winter. These became immensely popular in New England and the Midwest. One of the most popular speakers was Ralph Waldo Emerson (1803–1882).

By the middle of the nineteenth century, New England was a hotbed of social causes: abolition of slavery, women's rights, improved public education, and better treatment for the mentally ill. Numerous utopian (yo͞o·tō′pē·ən) projects—plans for creating a more perfect society—were developed. In 1840, Emerson wryly remarked that every man who could read had plans in his pocket for a new community.

Ralph Waldo Emerson was a primary force behind the flowering of American culture. He helped inspire numerous reform movements that aimed to improve public education, end slavery, elevate the status of women, and generally ease the rough social conditions of the time. Various utopian groups drew up comprehensive plans for a better society.

CONNECT

What are some of the organizations and institutions devoted to "self-improvement" in the area where you live?

CONNECT

What, in your opinion, are some of the best and the worst ideas that people are presently considering for improving society?

Utopian Ventures

Utopian communities flourished in the United States during the mid-nineteenth century. Rebelling against the status quo, utopian communities tried to create prosperous and harmonious environments. Many were religious communities founded on ideals of nonviolence and communal ownership. In many utopian communities, African Americans and women could find more equality than in society at large.

Community members often had to abide by rules that were quite restrictive. At Fruitlands, the short-lived vegetarian community established by Bronson Alcott (father of Louisa May Alcott), residents were permitted to eat only vegetables that grew up toward heaven—no root vegetables such as carrots and potatoes were allowed! They also did not take milk from cows or wool from sheep. Nor would they use animals to pull plows.

Most utopian ventures failed within a few years. As the members of Brook Farm in Massachusetts discovered, innovative thinkers aren't necessarily willing or successful farmers. But several utopian communities did endure for decades. In all, more than 100,000 Americans participated in utopian communities in the nineteenth century.

The Transcendentalists: True Reality Is Spiritual

Emerson could speak of utopian projects from personal experience, for he was a member of one of the most influential utopian groups, "The Transcendental Club." The term *transcendental* comes from the eighteenth-century German philosopher Immanuel Kant. The word refers to the idea that in determining the ultimate reality of God, the universe, the self, and other important matters, one must transcend, or go beyond, everyday human experience in the physical world. Intuition is an important tool for discovering truth.

For Emerson, **Transcendentalism** was not a new philosophy but "the very oldest of thoughts cast into the mold of these new times." That "oldest of thoughts" was Idealism, which had already been articulated by the Greek philosopher Plato in the fourth century B.C. Idealists said that true reality involved ideas rather than the world as perceived by the senses. Idealists sought the permanent reality that underlay physical appearances. The Americans who called themselves Transcendentalists were idealists, but in a broader, more practical sense. Like many Americans today, they believed in human perfectibility, and they worked to achieve this goal.

INFER
In what sense were the Transcendentalists idealists?

A Transcendentalist's View of the World

- Everything in the world, including human beings, is a reflection of the Divine Soul.

- The physical facts of the natural world are a doorway to the spiritual or ideal world.
- People can use their intuition to behold God's spirit revealed in nature or in their own souls.
- Self-reliance and individualism must outweigh external authority and blind conformity to custom and tradition.
- Spontaneous feelings and intuition are superior to deliberate intellectualism and rationality.

CONNECT

In your opinion, are most modern-day Americans "mystical" in this sense of believing in a higher reality beyond the world of observable facts? Why or why not?

Emerson and Transcendentalism: The American Roots

Though Emerson was skeptical of many of the Transcendentalists' ideas and projects, he was the most influential and best-known member of the group, largely because of his lectures and books. His writing and that of his friend Henry David Thoreau (1817–1862) clearly and forcefully expressed Transcendental ideas. As developed by Emerson, Transcendentalism grafted ideas from Europe and Asia onto a homegrown American philosophical stem. Its American roots included Puritan thought and the Romantic tradition.

The Puritans believed that God revealed himself to people through the Bible and through the physical world. William Bradford, for example, saw the death of an abusive sailor on the *Mayflower* as the direct action of God in the human world. Anne Bradstreet saw evidence of God in the grandeur of nature. Jonathan Edwards found God's wisdom, purity, and love in the sun, moon, and stars—in fact, in all of nature. This native mysticism—also typical of Romanticism—reappears in Emerson's thought. "Every natural fact," Emerson wrote, "is a symbol of some spiritual fact."

Transcendentalism was based partly on the philosophy of Idealism, which dated back to ancient Greece. It was based also on the ideas of American thinkers ranging from the Puritans to the nineteenth-century Romantics. Transcendentalists viewed nature as a doorway to a mystical world holding important truths.

Emerson's Optimistic Outlook

Emerson's mystical view of the world sprang not from logic but from intuition. Intuition is our capacity to know things spontaneously and immediately through our emotions rather than through our reasoning abilities. Intuitive thought—the kind Emerson believed in—contrasts with the rational thinking of someone like Benjamin Franklin. Franklin did not gaze on nature and feel the presence of a Divine Soul; Franklin looked at nature and saw something to be examined scientifically and used to help

CONNECT

What are some of the ways people use intuition in their everyday lives?

IDENTIFY

Underline three sentences in lines 144–166 that help to define Emerson's philosophy of Transcendentalism.

INTERPRET

What did Melville mean by his remark about Transcendentalism, "what stuff all this is"?

humanity. Emerson's mode of examination, though, was completely different. "I unsettle all things," he wrote. "No facts are to me sacred; none are profane; I simply experiment, an endless seeker, with no Past at my back."

An intense feeling of optimism was one product of Emerson's belief that we can find God directly in nature. God is good, and God works through nature, Emerson believed. If we simply trust ourselves—that is, trust in the power each of us has to know God directly—then we will realize that each of us is also part of the Divine Soul, the source of all good.

Emerson's sense of optimism and hope appealed to audiences who lived in a period of economic downturns, regional strife, and conflict over slavery. Your condition today, Emerson seemed to tell his readers and listeners, may seem dull and disheartening, but it need not be. If you discover the God within you, he suggested, your lives will partake of the grandeur of the universe.

> ***Emerson believed in the power of intuition, our ability to learn directly without conscious use of reasoning. He emphasized the importance of each individual, and his outlook was optimistic.***

Melville, Hawthorne, and Poe: A Challenge to the Transcendentalists

Emerson's idealism was exciting for his audiences, but not all the writers and thinkers of the time agreed with Transcendentalist thought. "To one who has weathered Cape Horn as a common sailor," Herman Melville wrote of Emerson's ideas, "what stuff all this is."

Some people think of Nathaniel Hawthorne, Herman Melville, and Edgar Allan Poe (1809–1849) as anti-Transcendentalists, because their view of the world seems so profoundly opposed to the optimistic view of Emerson and his followers. But these Dark Romantics, as they are known, had much in common with the Transcendentalists. Both groups valued intuition over logic and reason. Both groups, like the Puritans before them, saw signs and symbols in human events—as Anne Bradstreet found spiritual significance in the fire that destroyed her house. (Not surprisingly, the Dark Romantics used the literary technique of **symbolism** to great effect in their works.)

The Dark Romantics didn't disagree with Emerson's belief that spiritual facts lie behind the appearances of nature; they disagreed with the premise that those facts are necessarily good, or harmless. Emerson, they felt, had taken the ecstatic, mystical elements of Puritan thought and ignored its dark side. The Dark Romantics came along to redress the balance. Their view of existence developed from both the mystical and the melancholy aspects of Puritan thought. In their works, they explored the conflict between good and evil, the psychological effects of guilt and sin, and even madness and derangement in the human psyche. Behind the pasteboard masks of social respectability, the Dark Romantics saw the blankness and the horror of evil. From this imaginative, unflinching vision they shaped a uniquely American literature.

The works of writers such as Hawthorne, Melville, and Poe acknowledged the existence of sin, pain, and evil in human life and formed a counterpoint to the optimism of the Transcendentalists.

COMPARE AND CONTRAST

List five words that an idealis might apply to the human race; then, list five words tha a pessimist might use.

From Self-Reliance

Make the Connection

Rugged Individualism

In the decades before the Civil War, Ralph Waldo Emerson became an immensely popular writer and lecturer. At the center of Transcendentalism lay the supreme right of the individual to chart his or her own path.

This was exactly the message that the young republic wanted to hear. In 1841, Emerson nourished this creed of individualism with his essay "Self-Reliance," perhaps the single most influential work of this essayist, philosopher, and poet. "Trust thyself," he counsels. "Every heart vibrates to that iron string."

If Transcendentalism seems to have disappeared, it is only because its main ideas have been so thoroughly absorbed into the fabric of American life. Explore the continuing influence of Emerson by completing the following chart.

	Typical "American Hero"	This Person's "Rugged Individual" Traits	This Person's "Team Player" Traits
History	Abraham Lincoln	Courage to make unpopular decisions Frontier upbringing	Devotion to the Union Political skill
Movies			
Sports			
Art & Music			

FROM **Self-Reliance**

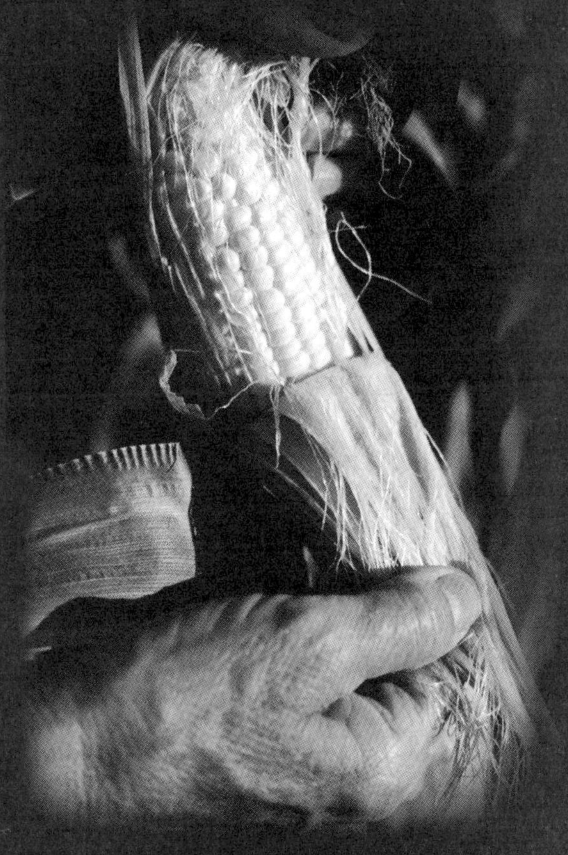

. . . no kernel of nourishing corn can come to him but through his toil . . .

Ralph Waldo Emerson

. . . There is a time in every man's education when he arrives at the conviction that envy is ignorance; that imitation is suicide; that he must take himself for better, for worse, as his portion; that though the wide universe is full of good, no kernel of nourishing corn can come to him but through his toil bestowed on that plot of ground which is given to him to till. The power which resides in him is new in nature, and none but he knows what that is which he can do, nor does he know until he has tried. Not for nothing one face, one character, one fact makes much impression on him, and another none. This sculpture in the memory is not without preestablished harmony. The eye was placed where one ray should fall, that it might testify of that particular ray. We but half express ourselves, and are ashamed of that divine idea which each of us represents. It may be safely trusted as proportionate and of good issues, so it be faithfully imparted, but God will not have his work made manifest by cowards. A man is relieved and gay when he has put his heart into his work and done his best; but what he has said or done otherwise, shall give him no peace. It is a deliverance which does not deliver. In the attempt his genius deserts him; no muse befriends; no invention, no hope.

Trust thyself: Every heart vibrates to that iron string. Accept the place the divine Providence has found for you; the society of your contemporaries, the connection of events. Great men have always done so and confided themselves childlike to the genius of their age, betraying their perception that the absolutely trustworthy was seated at their heart, working through their hands, predominating in all their being. And we are now men, and must accept in the highest mind the same transcendent destiny; and not minors and invalids in a protected corner, not cowards fleeing before a revolution, but guides, redeemers, and benefactors, obeying the Almighty effort, and advancing on Chaos and the Dark. . . .

These are the voices which we hear in solitude, but they grow faint and inaudible as we enter into the world. Society everywhere is in conspiracy against the manhood of every one of its members. Society is a joint-stock company in which the members agree for the better securing of his bread to each shareholder, to surrender the liberty and culture of the eater. The virtue in most request is conformity. Self-reliance is its aversion. It loves not realities and creators, but names and customs.

Whoso would be a man must be a nonconformist. He who would gather immortal palms[1] must not be hindered by the name of goodness, but must explore if it be goodness. Nothing is at last sacred but the integrity of your own mind. Absolve you to yourself, and you shall have the suffrage of the world. . . .

VORDS TO OWN

onviction (kən·vik′shən) *n.:* elief.

VORDS TO OWN

roportionate (prə·pôr′shə·nit) *dj.:* having a correct elationship between parts; alanced.
mparted (im·pärt′id) *v.:* evealed.
nanifest (man′ə·fest′) *adj.:* lain; clear.

WORDS TO OWN

predominating (prē·däm′ə·nāt′iŋ) *v.* used as *adj.:* having influence.
transcendent (tran·sen′dənt) *adj.:* excelling; surpassing.
benefactors (ben′ə·fak′tərz) *n. pl.:* people who help others.

WORDS TO OWN

conspiracy (kən·spir′ə·sē) *n.:* secret plot with a harmful or illegal purpose.
aversion (ə·vur′zhən) *n.:* intense dislike.
integrity (in·teg′rə·tē) *n.:* sound moral principles; honesty.

1. **he who . . . immortal palms:** he who would win fame. In ancient times, palm leaves were carried as a symbol of victory or triumph.

A foolish consistency is the hobgoblin of little minds, adored by little statesmen and philosophers and divines. With consistency a great soul has simply nothing to do. He may as well concern himself with his shadow on the wall. Speak what you think now in hard words, and tomorrow speak what tomorrow thinks in hard words again, though it contradict everything you said today—"Ah, so you shall be sure to be misunderstood"—Is it so bad then to be misunderstood? Pythagoras was misunderstood, and Socrates, and Jesus, and Luther, and Copernicus, and Galileo, and Newton,[2] and every pure and wise spirit that ever took flesh. To be great is to be misunderstood. . . .

INTERPRET

What does Emerson mean by "foolish consistency"?

IDENTIFY

Name some great figures from history who seem to have been misunderstood in their own times.

BUILD FLUENCY

Re-read the final paragraph aloud, taking care to pronounce each word clearly and expressively.

---

2. **Pythagoras . . . Newton:** people whose contributions to scientific, philosophical, and religious thought were ignored or suppressed during their lifetimes.

Figures of Speech

Emerson makes many of his points through a series of **figures of speech** that compare abstract ideas with ordinary things or events, such as "Society is a joint-stock company." Some of Emerson's figures of speech are difficult; in fact, he seems to have cultivated their difficulty quite deliberately. After hearing Emerson lecture, Herman Melville wrote, "I had heard of him as full of transcendentalisms, myths, and oracular gibberish. To my surprise, I found him quite intelligible. To say truth, they told me that that night he was unusually plain."

For generations, readers have found that the extra effort it takes to read and understand the writing of Ralph Waldo Emerson is well rewarded. To sharpen your skill as a reader, complete the following chart.

Emerson's Figure of Speech	Paraphrase in Contemporary English
"Society is a joint-stock company. . . ." (lines 33–34)	Every member of a society has a share of the responsibilities and will receive a share of benefits.
". . . imitation is suicide. . . ." (line 2)	
"Trust thyself: Every heart vibrates to that iron string." (line 20)	
"A foolish consistency is the hobgoblin of little minds. . . ." (line 43)	

Vocabulary: How to Own a Word

Vocabulary and Context Clues

Word Bank
conviction
proportionate
imparted
manifest
predominating
transcendent
benefactors
conspiracy
aversion
integrity

In each sentence below, use the list of Words to Own and context clues to find the word that has the same meaning as the italicized word or words. Write the word on the line in front of the sentence. Underline any context clues that help you find the answer.

EXAMPLE: divinity Believing in the essential *godliness* of all people, Emerson always looked for their superhuman qualities.

_______________ **1.** In Emerson's view, a person of *good moral character* is first of all honest with himself or herself.

_______________ **2.** A *strong opinion* of your own worth—belief in yourself—is a good start toward self-reliance.

_______________ **3.** With one's own inner voices *prevailing*, Emerson believes, a person will take the correct path through life. It may be difficult to let inner voices be one's major influence.

_______________ **4.** A person's special inborn talent may not be *apparent*. The talent cannot show itself without the opportunity to develop it.

_______________ **5.** Emerson *disclosed* his philosophy of self-reliance to students, rather than let them discover it on their own.

_______________ **6.** *Philanthropists* have good intentions, but they should ensure that their gifts do not stifle a recipient's self-reliance.

_______________ **7.** People with an *intense dislike* of hard thinking may find it easier to rely on the ideas of others.

_______________ **8.** Emerson believes that an individual's trust of self is of *exceeding* importance. It surpasses trust in any authority.

_______________ **9.** When Emerson talks about a *secret plan* to rob people of their individuality, he is exaggerating the truth. It is unlikely that a group of people would actually conceive of such a plot.

_______________ **10.** A child's level of self-reliance must be *related* to his or her chronological age, just as the ability to make judgments is equal to his or her maturity.

From Resistance to Civil Government

Make the Connection

Civil Disobedience

In July 1846, Thoreau was arrested because he refused to pay a tax to the state—primarily because he was opposed to the government's support of slavery and the war against Mexico. The Concord, Massachusetts, police offered to pay the tax for Thoreau, but he refused that also. He was forced, therefore, to spend the night in jail, and he might have spent more time there, except that someone, probably his aunt, paid the tax for him. This night in jail inspired the essay known as "Resistance to Civil Government" or "Civil Disobedience."

The idea of civil disobedience is probably familiar to you if you know anything about the U.S. civil rights struggles of the 1960s or the efforts of Mohandas K. ("Mahatma") Gandhi and his followers to achieve independence for India in the first half of the twentieth century. (Both movements, incidentally, were inspired by Thoreau's essay.) The essence of civil disobedience is principled, nonviolent resistance to policies deemed immoral, and a willingness to accept the ensuing consequences.

Where can we draw the lines between mere criminality and real civil disobedience? Complete the following chart to explore this very American form of political expression.

Act of Resistance	Can this be a form of civil disobedience?	What would make this legitimate as civil disobedience?
Refusal to pay taxes	yes	very specific grievance, not just greed willingness to take a public stand, and to accept legal consequences
Peaceful demonstration		
Blocking traffic		
Exposing secret government documents		

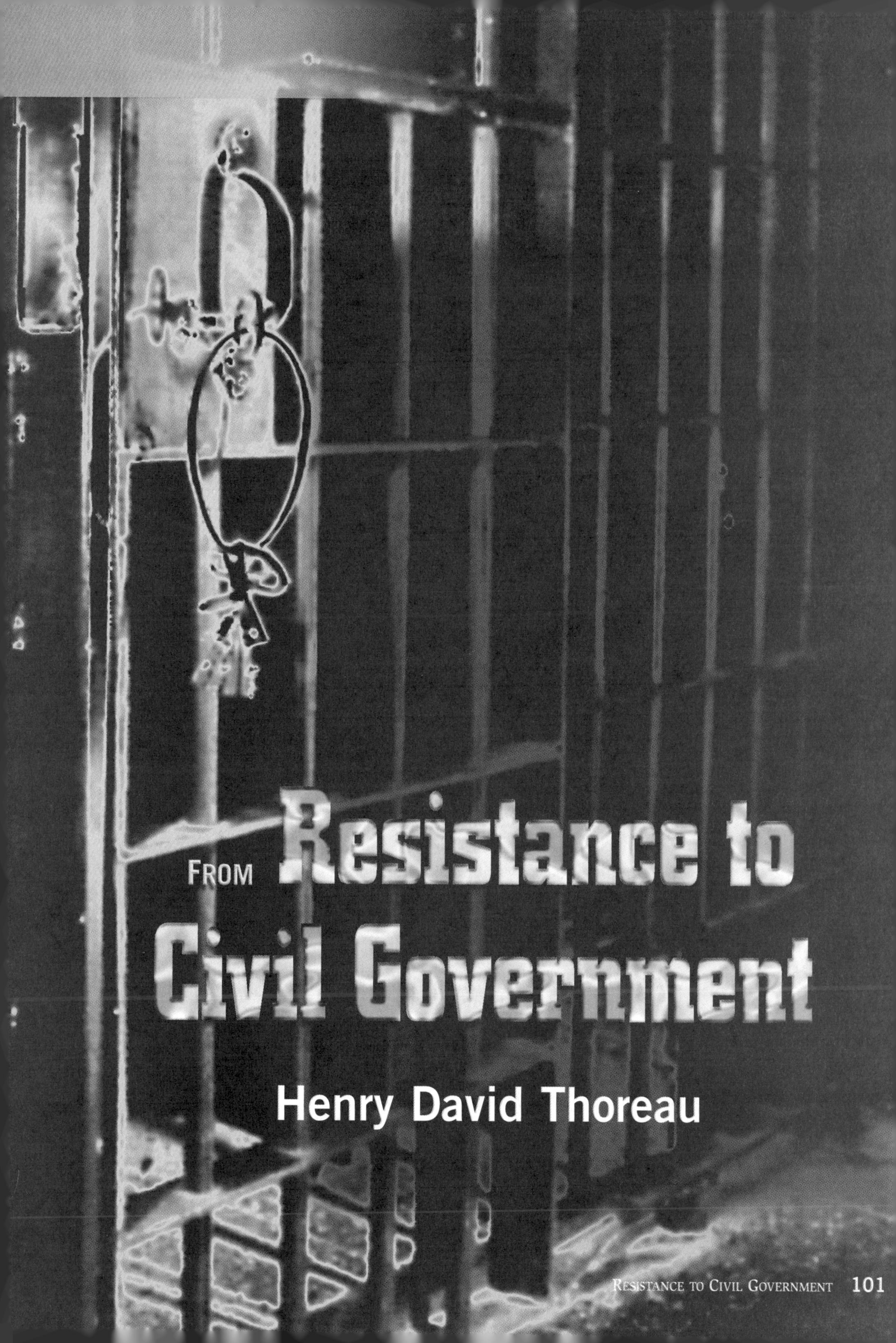

FROM Resistance to Civil Government

Henry David Thoreau

NTERPRET

ɔw does Thoreau's statement of the motto ange its meaning?

ORDS TO OWN

xpedient (ek·spē′dē·ənt) *n.:* onvenience; means to an end.

erverted (pər·vʉrt′id) *v.:* isdirected; corrupted.

osterity (päs·ter′ə·tē) *n.:* enerations to come.

INTERPRET

hat does Thoreau mean in aying that "the people must ave" something to satisfy heir "idea of government" ines 23–25)?

ORDS TO OWN

lacrity (ə·lak′rə·tē) *n.:* romptness in responding; agerness.

nherent (in·hir′ənt) *adj.:* nborn.

I heartily accept the motto—"That government is best which governs least";[1] and I should like to see it acted up to more rapidly and systematically. Carried out, it finally amounts to this, which also I believe—"That government is best which governs not at all"; and when men are prepared for it, that will be the kind of government which they will have. Government is at best but an expedient; but most governments are usually, and all governments are sometimes, inexpedient. The objections which have been brought against a standing army, and they are many and weighty, and deserve to prevail, may also at last be brought against a standing government. The standing army is only an arm of the standing government. The government itself, which is only the mode which the people have chosen to execute their will, is equally liable to be abused and perverted before the people can act through it. Witness the present Mexican war, the work of comparatively a few individuals using the standing government as their tool; for, in the outset, the people would not have consented to this measure.[2]

This American government—what is it but a tradition, though a recent one, endeavoring to transmit itself unimpaired to posterity, but each instant losing some of its integrity? It has not the vitality and force of a single living man; for a single man can bend it to his will. It is a sort of wooden gun to the people themselves; and, if ever they should use it in earnest as a real one against each other, it will surely split. But it is not the less necessary for this; for the people must have some complicated machinery or other, and hear its din, to satisfy that idea of government which they have. Governments show thus how successfully men can be imposed on, even impose on themselves, for their own advantage. It is excellent, we must all allow; yet this government never of itself furthered any enterprise, but by the alacrity with which it got out of its way. *It* does not keep the country free. *It* does not settle the West. *It* does not educate. The character inherent in the American people has done all that has been accomplished; and it would have done somewhat more, if the government had not sometimes got in its way. For government is an expedient by which men would fain[3] succeed in letting one another alone; and, as has been said, when it is most expedient, the governed are most let alone by it. Trade and commerce, if they were not made of India rubber, would never manage to bounce over the obstacles which legislators are continually putting in their way; and, if one were to judge these men wholly by the effects of their actions, and not partly by

1. **"That . . . least":** This statement, attributed to Thomas Jefferson, was the motto of the New York *Democratic Review*, which had published two of Thoreau's essays.
2. **this measure:** On May 9, 1846, President James K. Polk (1795–1849) received word that Mexico had attacked United States troops. He then asked Congress to declare war, which they did on May 13. Some Americans, including Thoreau, thought the war was unjustified. Because Thoreau would not support the war with his taxes, he went to jail.
3. **fain:** archaic for "gladly" or "willingly."

their intentions, they would deserve to be classed and punished with those mischievous persons who put obstructions on the railroads.

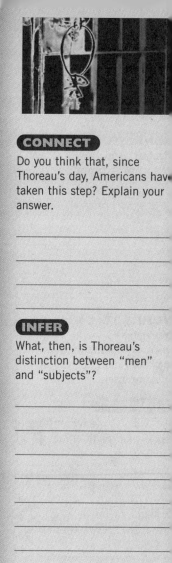

But, to speak practically and as a citizen, unlike those who call themselves no-government men, I ask for, not at once no government, but *at once* a better government. Let every man make known what kind of government would command his respect, and that will be one step toward obtaining it.

After all, the practical reason why, when the power is once in the hands of the people, a majority are permitted, and for a long period continue, to rule, is not because they are most likely to be in the right, nor because this seems fairest to the minority, but because they are physically the strongest. But a government in which the majority rule in all cases cannot be based on justice, even as far as men understand it. Can there not be a government in which majorities do not virtually decide right and wrong, but conscience?—in which majorities decide only those questions to which the rule of expediency is applicable? Must the citizen ever for a moment, or in the least degree, resign his conscience to the legislator? Why has every man a conscience, then? I think that we should be men first, and subjects afterward. It is not desirable to cultivate a respect for the law, so much as for the right. The only obligation which I have a right to assume, is to do at any time what I think right. . . .

It is not a man's duty, as a matter of course, to devote himself to the eradication of any, even the most enormous wrong; he may still properly have other concerns to engage him; but it is his duty, at least, to wash his hands of it, and, if he gives it no thought longer, not to give it practically his support. If I devote myself to other pursuits and contemplations, I must first see, at least, that I do not pursue them sitting upon another man's shoulders. I must get off him first, that he may pursue his contemplations too. See what gross inconsistency is tolerated. I have heard some of my townsmen say, "I should like to have them order me out to help put down an insurrection of the slaves, or to march to Mexico—see if I would go"; and yet these very men have each, directly by their allegiance, and so indirectly, at least, by their money, furnished a substitute. The soldier is applauded who refuses to serve in an unjust war by those who do not refuse to sustain the unjust government which makes the war; is applauded by those whose own act and authority he disregards and sets at nought; as if the State were penitent to that degree that it hired one to scourge it while it sinned, but not to that degree that it left off sinning for a moment. Thus, under the name of order and civil government, we are all made at last to pay homage to and support our own meanness. After the first blush of sin, comes its indifference and from immoral it becomes, as it were, *un*moral, and not quite unnecessary to that life which we have made. . . .

CONNECT

Do you think that, since Thoreau's day, Americans hav[e] taken this step? Explain your answer.

INFER

What, then, is Thoreau's distinction between "men" and "subjects"?

RETELL

The sentence in lines 61–65 contains the essence of Thoreau's definition of a citizen's moral responsibility. Restate it in your own words.

WORDS TO OWN

insurrection (in′sə·rek′shən) *n.*: rebellion; revolt.

penitent (pen′i·tənt) *adj.*: sorry for doing wrong.

VORDS TO OWN
ffectual (e·fek'cho͞o·əl) *adj.:* roductive; efficient.

VORDS TO OWN
bstruction (əb·struk'shən) *n.:* lockage; hindrance.
npetuous (im·pech'o͞o·əs) *dj.:* impulsive.

CONNECT
.ist two or three present-day ssues that might attract a imilarly passionate stand.

INTERPRET
Thoreau speaks of a "still nore difficult" wall than the wall of stone (lines 114–115). What was this other "wall"?

IDENTIFY
Underline at least two **figures of speech** in this paragraph in which Thoreau illustrates his idea with a comparison.

I meet this American government, or its representative the State government, directly, and face to face, once a year, no more, in the person of its tax-gatherer; this is the only mode in which a man situated as I am necessarily meets it; and it then says distinctly, Recognize me; and the simplest, the most effectual, and, in the present posture of affairs, the indispensablest mode of treating with it on this head, of expressing your little satisfaction with and love for it, is to deny it then. My civil neighbor, the tax-gatherer, is the very man I have to deal with—for it is, after all, with men and not with parchment that I quarrel—and he has voluntarily chosen to be an agent of the government. How shall he ever know well what he is and does as an officer of the government, or as a man, until he is obliged to consider whether he shall treat me, his neighbor, for whom he has respect, as a neighbor and well-disposed man, or as a maniac and disturber of the peace, and see if he can get over this obstruction to his neighborliness without a ruder and more impetuous thought or speech corresponding with his action? I know this well, that if one thousand, if one hundred, if ten men whom I could name—if ten *honest* men only—aye, if *one* HONEST man, in this State of Massachusetts, *ceasing to hold slaves,* were actually to withdraw from this copartnership, and be locked up in the county jail therefor, it would be the abolition of slavery in America. For it matters not how small the beginning may seem to be: What is once well done is done forever. . . .

I have paid no poll tax[4] for six years. I was put into a jail once on this account, for one night; and, as I stood considering the walls of solid stone, two or three feet thick, the door of wood and iron, a foot thick, and the iron grating which strained the light, I could not help being struck with the foolishness of that institution which treated me as if I were mere flesh and blood and bones, to be locked up. I wondered that it should have concluded at length that this was the best use it could put me to, and had never thought to avail itself of my services in some way. I saw that, if there was a wall of stone between me and my townsmen, there was a still more difficult one to climb or break through, before they could get to be as free as I was. I did not for a moment feel confined, and the walls seemed a great waste of stone and mortar. I felt as if I alone of all my townsmen had paid my tax. They plainly did not know how to treat me, but behaved like persons who are underbred. In every threat and in every compliment there was a blunder; for they thought that my chief desire was to stand the other side of that stone wall. I could not but smile to see how industriously they locked the door on my meditations, which followed them out again without let or hindrance, and *they* were really all that was dangerous. As they could not reach me, they had resolved to punish my body; just as boys, if they cannot

4. **poll tax:** fee some states and localities required from each citizen as a qualification for voting. It is now considered unconstitutional in the United States to charge such a tax.

come at some person against whom they have a spite, will abuse his dog. I saw that the State was half-witted, that it was timid as a lone woman with her silver spoons, and that it did not know its friends from its foes, and I lost all my remaining respect for it, and pitied it. . . .

The night in prison was novel and interesting enough. The prisoners in their shirt sleeves were enjoying a chat and the evening air in the doorway, when I entered. But the jailer said, "Come, boys, it is time to lock up"; and so they dispersed, and I heard the sound of their steps returning into the hollow apartments. My roommate was introduced to me by the jailer, as "a first-rate fellow and a clever man." When the door was locked, he showed me where to hang my hat, and how he managed matters there. The rooms were whitewashed once a month; and this one, at least, was the whitest, most simply furnished, and probably the neatest apartment in the town. He naturally wanted to know where I came from, and what brought me there; and, when I had told him, I asked him in my turn how he came there, presuming him to be an honest man, of course; and, as the world goes, I believe he was. "Why," said he, "they accuse me of burning a barn; but I never did it." As near as I could discover, he had probably gone to bed in a barn when drunk, and smoked his pipe there; and so a barn was burnt. He had the reputation of being a clever man, had been there some three months waiting for his trial to come on, and would have to wait as much longer; but he was quite domesticated and contented, since he got his board for nothing, and thought that he was well treated.

He occupied one window, and I the other; and I saw, that, if one stayed there long, his principal business would be to look out the window. I had soon read all the tracts that were left there, and examined where former prisoners had broken out, and where a grate had been sawed off, and heard the history of the various occupants of that room; for I found that even here there was a history and a gossip which never circulated beyond the walls of the jail. Probably this is the only house in the town where verses are composed, which are afterward printed in a circular form, but not published. I was shown quite a long list of verses which were composed by some young men who had been detected in an attempt to escape, who avenged themselves by singing them.

I pumped my fellow prisoner as dry as I could, for fear I should never see him again; but at length he showed me which was my bed, and left me to blow out the lamp.

It was like traveling into a far country, such as I had never expected to behold, to lie there for one night. It seemed to me that I never had heard the town-clock strike before, nor the evening sounds of the village; for we slept with the windows open, which were inside the grating. It was to see my native village in the light of the middle ages, and our Concord was turned into a Rhine stream, and visions of knights and

EVALUATE

Do you think that this account of Thoreau's experience in the jail distracts from his main point, or adds something valuable to the essay? Explain your answer.

INTERPRET

What does Thoreau mean by the **figure of speech** in line 161?

INTERPRET

'hy did everything suddenly ɜem so strange to Thoreau om the new perspective of ıe jail?

INFER

/hat does his use of the word *ıterfered* (line 185) tell us bout Thoreau's attitude?

EVALUATE

n his characterization of his ellow citizens, is Thoreau ndeed being "harsh"? Explain 'our answer.

castles passed before me. They were the voices of old burghers that I heard in the streets. I was an involuntary spectator and auditor of whatever was done and said in the kitchen of the adjacent village inn—a wholly new and rare experience to me. It was a closer view of my native town. I was fairly inside of it. I never had seen its institutions before. This is one of its peculiar institutions; for it is a shire town.[5] I began to comprehend what its inhabitants were about.

In the morning, our breakfasts were put through the hole in the door, in small oblong-square tin pans, made to fit, and holding a pint of chocolate, with brown bread, and an iron spoon. When they called for the vessels again, I was green enough to return what bread I had left; but my comrade seized it, and said that I should lay that up for lunch or dinner. Soon after, he was let out to work at haying in a neighboring field, whither he went every day, and would not be back till noon; so he bade me good day, saying that he doubted if he should see me again.

When I came out of prison—for someone interfered, and paid the tax—I did not perceive that great changes had taken place on the common, such as he observed who went in a youth, and emerged a tottering and gray-headed man; and yet a change had to my eyes come over the scene—the town, and State, and country—greater than any that mere time could effect. I saw yet more distinctly the State in which I lived. I saw to what extent the people among whom I lived could be trusted as good neighbors and friends; that their friendship was for summer weather only; that they did not greatly purpose to do right; that they were a distinct race from me by their prejudices and superstitions, as the Chinamen and Malays are; that, in their sacrifices to humanity, they ran no risks, not even to their property; that, after all, they were not so noble but they treated the thief as he had treated them, and hoped, by a certain outward observance and a few prayers, and by walking in a particular straight though useless path from time to time, to save their souls. This may be to judge my neighbors harshly; for I believe that most of them are not aware that they have such an institution as the jail in their village.

It was formerly the custom in our village, when a poor debtor came out of jail, for his acquaintances to salute him, looking through their fingers, which were crossed to represent the grating of a jail window, "How do ye do?" My neighbors did not thus salute me, but first looked at me, and then at one another, as if I had returned from a long journey. I was put into jail as I was going to the shoemaker's to get a shoe which was mended. When I was let out the next morning, I proceeded to finish my errand, and, having put on my mended shoe, joined a huckleberry party, who were impatient to put themselves under my conduct; and in

---

5. **shire town:** town where a court sits, like a county seat.

half an hour—for the horse was soon tackled[6]—was in the midst of a huckleberry field, on one of our highest hills, two miles off; and then the State was nowhere to be seen.

This is the whole history of "My Prisons." . . .

The authority of government, even such as I am willing to submit to—for I will cheerfully obey those who know and can do better than I, and in many things even those who neither know nor can do so well-- is still an impure one: To be strictly just, it must have the sanction and consent of the governed. It can have no pure right over my person and property but what I concede to it. The progress from an absolute to a limited monarchy, from a limited monarchy to a democracy, is a progress toward a true respect for the individual. Is a democracy, such as we know it, the last improvement possible in government? Is it not possible to take a step further toward recognizing and organizing the rights of man? There will never be a really free and enlightened State, until the State comes to recognize the individual as a higher and independent power, from which all its own power and authority are derived, and treats him accordingly. I please myself with imagining a State at last which can afford to be just to all men, and to treat the individual with respect as a neighbor; which even would not think it inconsistent with its own repose, if a few were to live aloof from it, not meddling with it, nor embraced by it, who fulfilled all the duties of neighbors and fellow men. A State which bore this kind of fruit, and suffered it to drop off as fast as it ripened, would prepare the way for a still more perfect and glorious State, which also I have imagined, but not yet anywhere seen.

EVALUATE

Although Thoreau presents a **rhetorical question** in lines 224–226 to which his answe is clearly "yes, it *is* possible,' we can still wonder whether such progress is indeed possible. What do you think?

BUILD FLUENCY

Re-read the final paragraph of this essay aloud, clearly, expressively, and persuasively, in the manner that Thoreau himself might have read it.

6. **tackled:** harnessed.

Paradox

A **paradox** is a statement that expresses the complexity of life by showing how opposing ideas can be both contradictory and true. Paradox was one of Thoreau's favorite literary devices. The idea that a contradiction can contain a truth is in itself paradoxical—and truthful.

Complete the following chart.

Paradoxical Statement by Thoreau	One "Leg" of the Paradox	Other "Leg" of the Paradox	Deeper Truth Revealed by the Paradox
"I saw that, if there was a wall of stone between me and my townsmen, there was a still more difficult one to climb or break through, before they could get to be as free as I was." (lines 114–116)	Thoreau was in jail; the other townsmen were free.	Thoreau felt more free than the townsmen.	The freedom of the conscience has nothing to do with the freedom of the body.
". . . That government is best which governs least. . . ." (lines 1–2)			
"I felt as if I alone of all my townsmen had paid my tax." (lines 117–118)			

Vocabulary: How to Own a Word

Vocabulary and Context Clues

Word Bank
expedient
perverted
posterity
alacrity
inherent
insurrection
penitent
effectual
obstruction
impetuous

In each sentence below, use the list of Words to Own and context clues to find the word that has the same meaning as the italicized word or words. Write the word on the line in front of the sentence. Underline any context clues that help you find the answer.

EXAMPLE: indubitably Thoreau was *undoubtedly* an influence on Martin Luther King, Jr. That much is certain.

______________ 1. Thoreau wasn't *remorseful* about not paying his poll taxes. He did not think he had done anything wrong.

______________ 2. He believed his imprisonment was further evidence of the government's *warped* sense of right and wrong—morality turned upside down.

______________ 3. Is a washing machine a necessity? Thoreau would consider it a mere *convenience.*

______________ 4. Though Thoreau supported resistance to the government when it was "*un*moral," he did not actively encourage *rebellion.*

______________ 5. Did Thoreau foresee the effect his writings would have on *his descendants*? Do you think he wondered how future generations would respond?

______________ 6. Sit-ins and marches have sometimes proven to be *effective* methods of protest. They have gotten results.

______________ 7. Protesters have often been arrested with *great speed*. They have been quickly swept off the streets.

______________ 8. Sitting in the street to cause an *impediment* to traffic might be considered an extreme measure. Blocking the flow of traffic could be dangerous.

______________ 9. Do you think the existence of authority is *inborn* in any concept of government? That is, is it inseparable from government?

______________ 10. The decision to protest a government action should not be *impulsive,* but should be considered carefully.

The Raven

Make the Connection

Exploring the Dark Side

Although Poe's literary achievements are astonishing, he spent most of his career in humiliating poverty. Desperate for fame, he finally attained a measure of success with "The Raven," which may well be the single most famous American poem. First published in 1845, the poem was an immediate sensation. It seemed as though everyone read "The Raven," recited it, and talked about it. Poe became a household name with this poem—yet he received only about ten dollars for it.

"The Raven" was written to create an effect on readers that Poe called *"Mournful and never-ending Remembrance."* Though it has the sound of a lyric, "The Raven" is actually a narrative poem with a plot that leads the reader from curiosity to horror. In the jargon of psychology, the narrator "projects" onto the bird whatever his own wild imagination dredges up. The poem explores one aspect of the dark side of human nature: what Poe himself called "that species of despair which delights in self-torture"—a kind of despair that Poe seems to have understood better than almost anyone else.

What might have inspired Poe to choose a raven for his poem? What associations do you have with ravens, both in fact and in legend?

Jot down your ideas. Then, see if Poe's poem makes use of any of these ideas.

Edgar Allan Poe

The Raven

IDENTIFY

lliteration refers to the epetition of consonant *ounds.* Circle two words in ne 2 that alliterate.

IDENTIFY

The Raven" makes frequent se of **internal rhyme.** nderline all the rhyming ords in lines 3–5.

IDENTIFY

ssonance, like **alliteration,** neans a repetition of *sounds* n the case of assonance, owel sounds) rather than imply *letters.* Circle three xamples of assonance in ne 13.

IDENTIFY

Jnderline at least two physical etails in lines 13–18 that elp to create **suspense.**

INTERPRET

What are some of the ideas hat might be signified by arkness?

PREDICT

The narrator has investigated he "tapping" that he thought ne heard and has found nothing. What might be the eal cause of this "tapping"?

Once upon a midnight dreary, while I pondered, weak and weary,
Over many a quaint and curious volume of forgotten lore—
While I nodded, nearly napping, suddenly there came a tapping,
As of someone gently rapping, rapping at my chamber door—
" 'Tis some visitor," I muttered, "tapping at my chamber door—
Only this and nothing more."

Ah, distinctly I remember it was in the bleak December;
And each separate dying ember wrought its ghost upon the floor.
Eagerly I wished the morrow;—vainly I had sought to borrow
From my books surcease[1] of sorrow—sorrow for the lost Lenore—
For the rare and radiant maiden whom the angels name Lenore—
Nameless *here* for evermore.

And the silken, sad, uncertain rustling of each purple curtain
Thrilled me—filled me with fantastic terrors never felt before;
So that now, to still the beating of my heart, I stood repeating
" 'Tis some visitor entreating entrance at my chamber door—
Some late visitor entreating entrance at my chamber door;—
This it is and nothing more."

Presently my soul grew stronger; hesitating then no longer,
"Sir," said I, "or Madam, truly your forgiveness I implore;
But the fact is I was napping, and so gently you came rapping,
And so faintly you came tapping, tapping at my chamber door,
That I scarce was sure I heard you"—here I opened wide the door;——
Darkness there and nothing more.

Deep into that darkness peering, long I stood there wondering, fearing,
Doubting, dreaming dreams no mortal ever dared to dream before;
But the silence was unbroken, and the stillness gave no token,
And the only word there spoken was the whispered word, "Lenore?"
This I whispered, and an echo murmured back the word, "Lenore!"
Merely this and nothing more.

Back into the chamber turning, all my soul within me burning,
Soon again I heard a tapping somewhat louder than before.
"Surely," said I, "surely that is something at my window lattice;
Let me see, then, what thereat is, and this mystery explore—
Let my heart be still a moment and this mystery explore;—
'Tis the wind and nothing more!"

1. **surcease:** an end.

Open here I flung the shutter, when, with many a flirt and flutter,
In there stepped a stately Raven of the saintly days of yore;[2]
Not the least obeisance[3] made he; not a minute stopped or stayed he;
But, with mien of lord or lady, perched above my chamber door—
Perched upon a bust of Pallas[4] just above my chamber door—
Perched, and sat, and nothing more.

Then this ebony bird beguiling my sad fancy into smiling,
By the grave and stern decorum of the countenance it wore,
"Though thy crest be shorn and shaven, thou," I said, "art sure no
craven,
Ghastly grim and ancient Raven wandering from the Nightly shore—
Tell me what thy lordly name is on the Night's Plutonian shore!"[5]
Quoth the Raven "Nevermore."

Much I marveled this ungainly fowl to hear discourse so plainly,
Though its answer little meaning—little relevancy bore;
For we cannot help agreeing that no living human being
Ever yet was blessed with seeing bird above his chamber door—
Bird or beast upon the sculptured bust above his chamber door,
With such name as "Nevermore."

But the Raven, sitting lonely on the placid bust, spoke only
That one word, as if his soul in that one word he did outpour.
Nothing farther then he uttered—not a feather then he fluttered—
Till I scarcely more than muttered "Other friends have flown before—
On the morrow *he* will leave me, as my Hopes have flown before."
Then the bird said "Nevermore."

Startled at the stillness broken by reply so aptly spoken,
"Doubtless," said I, "what it utters is its only stock and store
Caught from some unhappy master whom unmerciful Disaster
Followed fast and followed faster till his songs one burden bore—
Till the dirges of his Hope that melancholy burden bore
Of 'Never—nevermore.' "

2. **Raven . . . of yore:** "Of yore" is an obsolete way of saying "of time long past." Poe's allusion is to 1 Kings 17:1–6, which tells of the prophet Elijah being fed by ravens in the wilderness.
3. **obeisance** (ō·bā′səns): gesture of respect or subservience.
4. **Pallas:** Pallas Athena, the Greek goddess of wisdom.
5. **Plutonian shore:** Pluto is the Greek god of the underworld—the land of darkness—called Hades (hā′dēz′). Hades is separated from the world of the living by several rivers, hence the mention of a shore.

INTERPRET

Why do you think Poe has chosen a raven and not some other kind of bird?

INTERPRET

What clues do we get in lines 43–48 that the narrator is "projecting" his own inner thoughts onto the raven?

INTERPRET

What evidence does the narrator have that the raven has learned his one word from "some unhappy master" whose hopes were all frustrated?

But the Raven still beguiling my sad fancy into smiling,
Straight I wheeled a cushioned seat in front of bird, and bust and door;
Then, upon the velvet sinking, I betook myself to linking
Fancy unto fancy, thinking what this ominous bird of yore—
What this grim, ungainly, ghastly, gaunt, and ominous bird of yore
Meant in croaking "Nevermore."

This I sat engaged in guessing, but no syllable expressing
To the fowl whose fiery eyes now burned into my bosom's core;
This and more I sat divining, with my head at ease reclining
On the cushion's velvet lining that the lamplight gloated o'er,
But whose velvet-violet lining with the lamplight gloating o'er,
She shall press, ah, nevermore!

Then, methought, the air grew denser, perfumed from an unseen censer
Swung by seraphim[6] whose footfalls tinkled on the tufted floor.
"Wretch," I cried, "thy God hath lent thee—by these angels he hath sent thee
Respite—respite and nepenthe[7] from thy memories of Lenore;
Quaff, oh quaff this kind nepenthe and forget this lost Lenore!"
Quoth the Raven "Nevermore."

"Prophet!" said I, "thing of evil!—prophet still, if bird or devil!—
Whether Tempter sent, or whether tempest tossed thee here ashore,
Desolate yet all undaunted, on this desert land enchanted—
On this home by Horror haunted—tell me truly, I implore—
Is there—*is* there balm in Gilead?[8]—tell me—tell me, I implore!"
Quoth the Raven "Nevermore."

"Prophet!" said I, "thing of evil!—prophet still, if bird or devil!
By that Heaven that bends above us—by that God we both adore—
Tell this soul with sorrow laden if, within the distant Aidenn,[9]
It shall clasp a sainted maiden whom the angels name Lenore—
Clasp a rare and radiant maiden whom the angels name Lenore."
Quoth the Raven "Nevermore."

INFER

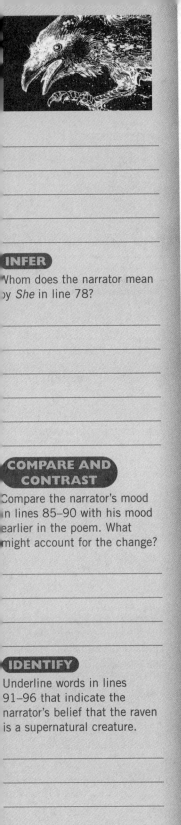

Whom does the narrator mean by *She* in line 78?

COMPARE AND CONTRAST

Compare the narrator's mood in lines 85–90 with his mood earlier in the poem. What might account for the change?

IDENTIFY

Underline words in lines 91–96 that indicate the narrator's belief that the raven is a supernatural creature.

---

6. **seraphim:** the highest of the nine ranks of angels; often pictured as having three sets of wings.
7. **nepenthe** (nē·pen′thē): a sleeping potion that people once believed would relieve pain and sorrow. Eventually it came to stand for anything that brought such relief.
8. **Is . . . Gilead:** "Is there any relief from my sorrow?" Poe paraphrases a line from Jeremiah 8:22: "Is there no balm in Gilead?" Gilead was a region in ancient Palestine known for its healing herbs, such as balm. Balm has come to mean any healing ointment.
9. **Aidenn:** Arabic for "Eden" or "Heaven."

"Be that word our sign of parting, bird or fiend!" I shrieked, upstarting—
"Get thee back into the tempest and the Night's Plutonian shore!
Leave no black plume as a token of that lie thy soul hath spoken!
Leave my loneliness unbroken!—quit the bust above my door!
Take thy beak from out my heart, and take thy form from off my door!"
Quoth the Raven "Nevermore."

And the Raven, never flitting, still is sitting, *still* is sitting
On the pallid bust of Pallas just above my chamber door;
And his eyes have all the seeming of a demon's that is dreaming,
And the lamplight o'er him streaming throws his shadow on the floor;
And my soul from out that shadow that lies floating on the floor
Shall be lifted—nevermore!

INTERPRET

What is the effect of shifting to the present tense here in the final stanza?

BUILD FLUENCY

To get the full flavor of "The Raven," you should read the entire poem aloud, letting yourself be swept up in its rhythm and music. Practice first on the final two stanzas, taking care to express the **tone** of real horror and despair.

Sound Effects

One of the reasons "The Raven" became so popular was that it was catchy in the way a song can be. Like many songs, the poem uses evocative rhythms, clever rhymes, alliteration, and other sound effects. These elements make the poem cry out for oral interpretation.

For example, skillful use of repetition occurs with the **refrain** "Nevermore"; it is also an important element in the **rhyme scheme** of the poem. Poe keeps the sound of the word echoing in our ears through repetition combined with changes in tone.

"The Raven" is a virtuoso performance in the use of **internal rhyme** (rhyme that occurs within the lines, as well as **alliteration** (the repetition of a consonant sound), **assonance** (the repetition of a vowel sound), and **onomatopoeia** (the use of words with sounds that actually echo their sense).

Complete the following chart by locating examples of Poe's use of sound effects in "The Raven."

Sound Effect	Examples in "The Raven"	Line(s)
End Rhyme	floor/nevermore	107, 108
Internal Rhyme	turning/burning	31
Alliteration	silken, sad, uncertain	13

Assonance	fl<u>u</u>ng, fl<u>u</u>tter	37
Onomatopoeia	tapping, rapping	3, 4

The Minister's Black Veil

Make the Connection

Secret Sin

The following story, "The Minister's Black Veil," concerns what Hawthorne calls "that saddest of all prisons"—the human heart. It was inspired by a New England clergyman who, Hawthorne learned, "in early life had accidentally killed a beloved friend; and from that day till the hour of his own death, he hid his face from men." The Reverend Hooper, Hawthorne's main character, experiences powerful feelings of shame and remorse for the "secret sins" that isolate people from the world and from their relationships with others.

Hawthorne added the subtitle "A Parable" to his story. A **parable** is a short, simple story from which a moral or religious lesson can be drawn. Many of the world's parables come from religious scripture, such as the Bible. Hawthorne's story is a literary parable with meanings that may be ambiguous rather than clear-cut.

Explore Hawthorne's concept of secret sin. Almost all people, at some point in life, have done things that make them feel guilty and that they have concealed from others. What do you think is useful and beneficial about having a sense of guilt? What is harmful about it? In what ways can guilt isolate people, and in what ways can it bring people together?

Using examples from literature, film, or real-life experience, respond to these questions.

Nathaniel Hawthorne

The Minister's Black Veil

A Parable

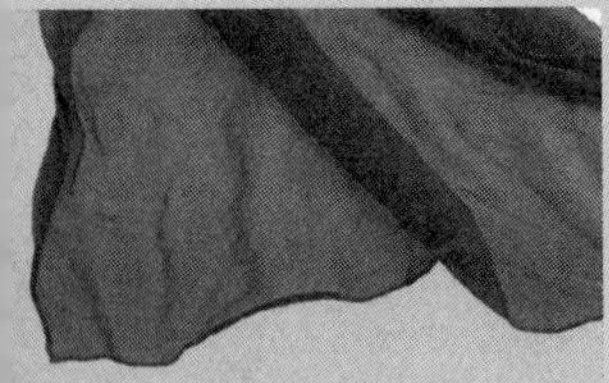

IDENTIFY

ircle words in this opening aragraph that create a lively, ghthearted **tone.**

VORDS TO OWN

emblance (sem′bləns) *n.:* utward appearance.

IDENTIFY

Jnderline words and phrases n this paragraph that alter he **tone** from liveliness to omething moodier and darker.

INFER

Vhat might be the "something wful" that the old woman ees in Mr. Hooper?

The sexton[1] stood in the porch of Milford meetinghouse, pulling lustily at the bell rope. The old people of the village came stooping along the street. Children, with bright faces, tripped merrily beside their parents, or mimicked a graver gait, in the conscious dignity of their Sunday clothes. Spruce bachelors looked sidelong at the pretty maidens, and fancied that the Sabbath sunshine made them prettier than on weekdays. When the throng had mostly streamed into the porch, the sexton began to toll the bell, keeping his eye on the Reverend Mr. Hooper's door. The first glimpse of the clergyman's figure was the signal for the bell to cease its summons.

"But what has good Parson Hooper got upon his face?" cried the sexton in astonishment.

All within hearing immediately turned about, and beheld the semblance of Mr. Hooper, pacing slowly his meditative way toward the meetinghouse. With one accord they started, expressing more wonder than if some strange minister were coming to dust the cushions of Mr. Hooper's pulpit.

"Are you sure it is our parson?" inquired Goodman[2] Gray of the sexton.

"Of a certainty it is good Mr. Hooper," replied the sexton. "He was to have exchanged pulpits with Parson Shute of Westbury; but Parson Shute sent to excuse himself yesterday, being to preach a funeral sermon."

The cause of so much amazement may appear sufficiently slight. Mr. Hooper, a gentlemanly person of about thirty, though still a bachelor, was dressed with due clerical neatness, as if a careful wife had starched his band, and brushed the weekly dust from his Sunday's garb. There was but one thing remarkable in his appearance. Swathed about his forehead, and hanging down over his face, so low as to be shaken by his breath, Mr. Hooper had on a black veil. On a nearer view, it seemed to consist of two folds of crape,[3] which entirely concealed his features, except the mouth and chin, but probably did not intercept his sight, farther than to give a darkened aspect to all living and inanimate things. With this gloomy shade before him, good Mr. Hooper walked onward, at a slow and quiet pace, stooping somewhat and looking on the ground, as is customary with abstracted men, yet nodding kindly to those of his parishioners who still waited on the meetinghouse steps. But so wonder-struck were they, that his greeting hardly met with a return.

"I can't really feel as if good Mr. Hooper's face was behind that piece of crape," said the sexton.

"I don't like it," muttered an old woman, as she hobbled into the meetinghouse. "He has changed himself into something awful, only by hiding his face."

1. **sexton:** church officer or employee whose duties may include maintenance, ringing the bells, and digging graves.
2. **Goodman:** form of polite address similar to *mister*.
3. **crape:** kind of black cloth worn as a sign of mourning; from the French word *crêpe*.

"Our parson has gone mad!" cried Goodman Gray, following him across the threshold.

A rumor of some unaccountable phenomenon had preceded Mr. Hooper into the meetinghouse, and set all the congregation astir. Few could refrain from twisting their heads toward the door; many stood upright, and turned directly about; while several little boys clambered upon the seats, and came down again with a terrible racket. There was a general bustle, a rustling of the women's gowns and shuffling of the men's feet, greatly at variance with that hushed repose which should attend the entrance of the minister. But Mr. Hooper appeared not to notice the perturbation of his people. He entered with an almost noiseless step, bent his head mildly to the pews on each side, and bowed as he passed his oldest parishioner, a white-haired great-grandsire, who occupied an armchair in the center of the aisle. It was strange to observe, how slowly this venerable man became conscious of something singular in the appearance of his pastor. He seemed not fully to partake of the prevailing wonder, till Mr. Hooper had ascended the stairs, and showed himself in the pulpit, face to face with his congregation, except for the black veil. That mysterious emblem was never once withdrawn. It shook with his measured breath as he gave out the psalm; it threw its obscurity between him and the holy page, as he read the Scriptures; and while he prayed, the veil lay heavily on his uplifted countenance. Did he seek to hide it from the dread Being whom he was addressing?

Such was the effect of this simple piece of crape, that more than one woman of delicate nerves was forced to leave the meetinghouse. Yet perhaps the pale-faced congregation was almost as fearful a sight to the minister, as his black veil to them.

Mr. Hooper had the reputation of a good preacher, but not an energetic one: He strove to win his people heavenward, by mild persuasive influences, rather than to drive them thither, by the thunders of the Word. The sermon which he now delivered, was marked by the same characteristics of style and manner, as the general series of his pulpit oratory. But there was something, either in the sentiment of the discourse itself, or in the imagination of the auditors, which made it greatly the most powerful effort that they had ever heard from their pastor's lips. It was tinged, rather more darkly than usual, with the gentle gloom of Mr. Hooper's temperament. The subject had reference to secret sin, and those sad mysteries which we hide from our nearest and dearest, and would fain conceal from our own consciousness, even forgetting that the Omniscient[4] can detect them. A subtle power was breathed into his words. Each member of the congregation, the most innocent girl, and the man of hardened breast, felt as if the preacher had crept upon them, behind his awful veil, and discovered their hoarded

4. the Omniscient: the all-knowing God.

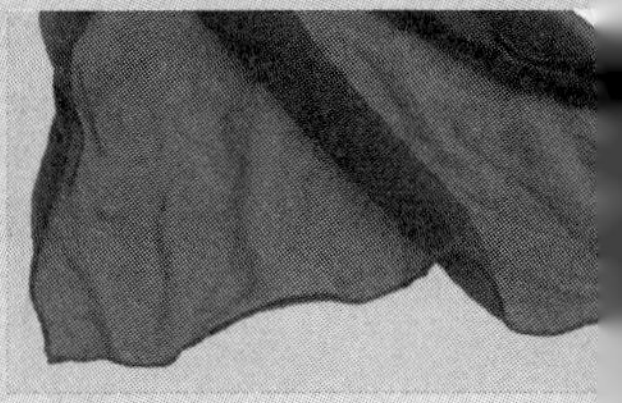

VISUALIZE

Picture how the appearance of the veiled minister among the congregation has abruptly changed their mood to confusion and consternation.

INTERPRET

If the veil is an "emblem" (line 60), then what does it **symbolize,** both to Mr. Hooper and to the congregation?

INFER

In lines 70–72, Hawthorne presents two very different ways of preaching. What is meant by "the thunders of the Word"?

INFER

What might Hawthorne mean by "secret sin"—do you think he refers to sins of action or sins of thought?

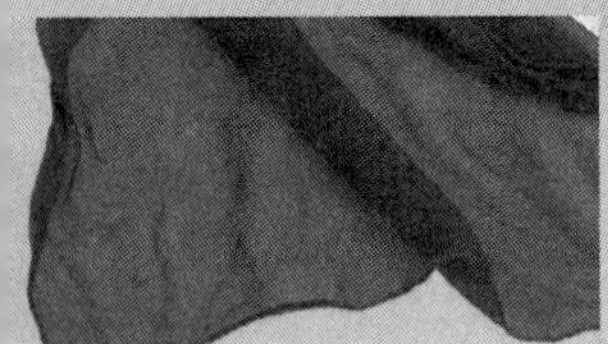

VORDS TO OWN
iiquity (i·nik'wi·tē) *n.:* ickedness.

IDENTIFY
ow do the parishioners react) the sermon? Underline the assage that tells you.

VORDS TO OWN
stentatious (äs'tən·tā'shəs) *dj.:* conspicuous.
agacious (sə·gā'shəs) *adj.:* vise; keenly perceptive.

INFER
s it an "accidental lapse of nemory" that Squire Saunders loesn't invite Mr. Hooper to line with him, or is Hawthorne eing **ironic** here?

INTERPRET
)oes the veil primarily affect Mr. Hooper or those who observe Mr. Hooper? Explain.

iniquity of deed or thought. Many spread their clasped hands on their bosoms. There was nothing terrible in what Mr. Hooper said; at least, no violence; and yet, with every tremor of his melancholy voice, the hearers quaked. An unsought pathos came hand in hand with awe. So sensible were the audience of some unwonted attribute in their minister, that they longed for a breath of wind to blow aside the veil, almost believing that a stranger's visage would be discovered, though the form, gesture, and voice were those of Mr. Hooper.

At the close of the services, the people hurried out with indecorous confusion, eager to communicate their pent-up amazement, and conscious of lighter spirits, the moment they lost sight of the black veil. Some gathered in little circles, huddled closely together, with their mouths all whispering in the center; some went homeward alone, wrapped in silent meditation; some talked loudly, and profaned the Sabbath day with ostentatious laughter. A few shook their sagacious heads, intimating that they could penetrate the mystery; while one or two affirmed that there was no mystery at all, but only that Mr. Hooper's eyes were so weakened by the midnight lamp, as to require a shade. After a brief interval, forth came good Mr. Hooper also, in the rear of his flock. Turning his veiled face from one group to another, he paid due reverence to the hoary heads, saluted the middle-aged with kind dignity, as their friend and spiritual guide, greeted the young with mingled authority and love, and laid his hands on the little children's heads to bless them. Such was always his custom on the Sabbath day. Strange and bewildered looks repaid him for his courtesy. None, as on former occasions, aspired to the honor of walking by their pastor's side. Old Squire Saunders, doubtless by an accidental lapse of memory, neglected to invite Mr. Hooper to his table, where the good clergyman had been wont to bless the food, almost every Sunday since his settlement. He returned, therefore, to the parsonage, and, at the moment of closing the door, was observed to look back upon the people, all of whom had their eyes fixed upon the minister. A sad smile gleamed faintly from beneath the black veil, and flickered about his mouth, glimmering as he disappeared.

"How strange," said a lady, "that a simple black veil, such as any woman might wear on her bonnet, should become such a terrible thing on Mr. Hooper's face!"

"Something must surely be amiss with Mr. Hooper's intellects," observed her husband, the physician of the village. "But the strangest part of the affair is the effect of this vagary, even on a sober-minded man like myself. The black veil, though it covers only our pastor's face, throws its influence over his whole person, and makes him ghostlike from head to foot. Do you not feel it so?"

"Truly do I," replied the lady; "and I would not be alone with him for the world. I wonder he is not afraid to be alone with himself!"

"Men sometimes are so," said her husband.

The afternoon service was attended with similar circumstances. At its conclusion, the bell tolled for the funeral of a young lady. The relatives and friends were assembled in the house, and the more distant acquaintances stood about the door, speaking of the good qualities of the deceased, when their talk was interrupted by the appearance of Mr. Hooper, still covered with his black veil. It was now an appropriate emblem. The clergyman stepped into the room where the corpse was laid, and bent over the coffin, to take a last farewell of his deceased parishioner. As he stooped, the veil hung straight down from his forehead, so that, if her eyelids had not been closed forever, the dead maiden might have seen his face. Could Mr. Hooper be fearful of her glance, that he so hastily caught back the black veil? A person, who watched the interview between the dead and living, scrupled[5] not to affirm, that, at the instant when the clergyman's features were disclosed, the corpse had slightly shuddered, rustling the shroud and muslin cap, though the countenance retained the composure of death. A superstitious old woman was the only witness of this prodigy.[6] From the coffin, Mr. Hooper passed into the chamber of the mourners, and thence to the head of the staircase, to make the funeral prayer. It was a tender and heart-dissolving prayer, full of sorrow, yet so imbued with celestial hopes, that the music of a heavenly harp, swept by the fingers of the dead, seemed faintly to be heard among the saddest accents of the minister. The people trembled, though they but darkly understood him, when he prayed that they, and himself, and all of mortal race, might be ready, as he trusted this young maiden had been, for the dreadful hour that should snatch the veil from their faces. The bearers went heavily forth, and the mourners followed, saddening all the street, with the dead before them, and Mr. Hooper in his black veil behind.

"Why do you look back?" said one in the procession to his partner.

"I had a fancy," replied she, "that the minister and the maiden's spirit were walking hand in hand."

"And so had I, at the same moment," said the other.

That night, the handsomest couple in Milford village were to be joined in wedlock. Though reckoned a melancholy man, Mr. Hooper had a placid cheerfulness for such occasions, which often excited a sympathetic smile, where livelier merriment would have been thrown away. There was no quality of his disposition which made him more beloved than this. The company at the wedding awaited his arrival with impatience, trusting that the strange awe, which had gathered over him throughout the day, would now be dispelled. But such was not the result. When Mr. Hooper came, the first thing that their eyes rested on

5. **scrupled:** hesitated.
6. **prodigy:** extraordinary act that foretells the future.

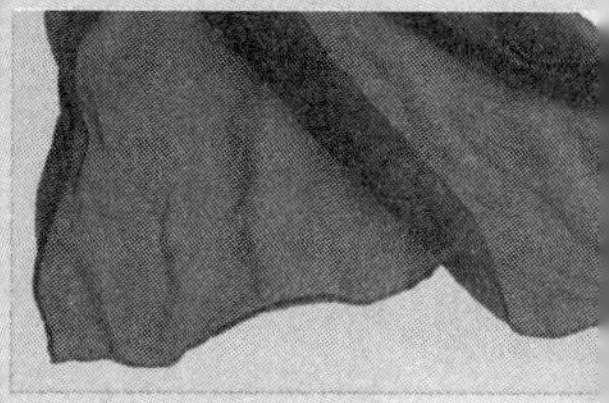

INTERPRET

This is the second appearance of the word *emblem* (line 137). How does the appearance of the veil at a funeral change its **symbolic** character?

INFER

What is the "veil" that "the dreadful hour" of death might snatch from the faces of the living? Is it the same as the literal veil that Mr. Hooper wears?

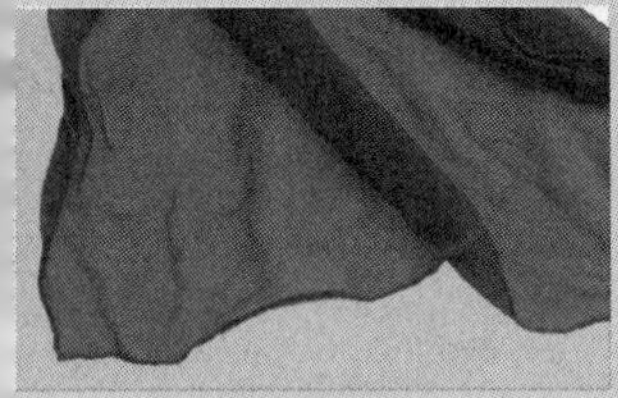

VORDS TO OWN

ortend (pôr·tend′) *v.:* signify.

INTERPRET

Vhy do you think no one in he parish asks Mr. Hooper vhy he is wearing a black veil?

was the same horrible black veil, which had added deeper gloom to the funeral, and could portend nothing but evil to the wedding. Such was its immediate effect on the guests, that a cloud seemed to have rolled duskily from beneath the black crape, and dimmed the light of the candles. The bridal pair stood up before the minister. But the bride's cold fingers quivered in the tremulous hand of the bridegroom, and her deathlike paleness caused a whisper, that the maiden who had been buried a few hours before, was come from her grave to be married. If ever another wedding were so dismal, it was that famous one, where they tolled the wedding knell.[7] After performing the ceremony, Mr. Hooper raised a glass of wine to his lips, wishing happiness to the new-married couple, in a strain of mild pleasantry that ought to have brightened the features of the guests, like a cheerful gleam from the hearth. At that instant, catching a glimpse of his figure in the looking glass, the black veil involved his own spirit in the horror with which it overwhelmed all others. His frame shuddered—his lips grew white—he spilt the untasted wine upon the carpet—and rushed forth into the darkness. For the Earth, too, had on her Black Veil.

The next day, the whole village of Milford talked of little else than Parson Hooper's black veil. That, and the mystery concealed behind it, supplied a topic for discussion between acquaintances meeting in the street, and good women gossiping at their open windows. It was the first item of news that the tavern keeper told to his guests. The children babbled of it on their way to school. One imitative little imp covered his face with an old black handkerchief, thereby so affrighting his playmates, that the panic seized himself, and he well nigh lost his wits by his own waggery.[8]

It was remarkable, that, of all the busybodies and impertinent people in the parish, not one ventured to put the plain question to Mr. Hooper, wherefore he did this thing. Hitherto, whenever there appeared the slightest call for such interference, he had never lacked advisers, nor shown himself averse to be guided by their judgment. If he erred at all, it was by so painful a degree of self-distrust, that even the mildest censure would lead him to consider an indifferent action as a crime. Yet, though so well acquainted with this amiable weakness, no individual among his parishioners chose to make the black veil a subject of friendly remonstrance. There was a feeling of dread, neither plainly confessed nor carefully concealed, which caused each to shift the responsibility upon another, till at length it was found expedient to send a deputation of the church, in order to deal with Mr. Hooper about the mystery, before it should grow into a scandal. Never did an embassy so ill discharge its

---

7. **If . . . wedding knell:** reference to Hawthorne's story "The Wedding Knell." A knell is the ringing of a bell.
8. **waggery:** joke.

duties. The minister received them with friendly courtesy, but became silent, after they were seated, leaving to his visitors the whole burden of introducing their important business. The topic, it might be supposed, was obvious enough. There was the black veil, swathed round Mr. Hooper's forehead, and concealing every feature above his placid mouth, on which, at times, they could perceive the glimmering of a melancholy smile. But that piece of crape, to their imagination, seemed to hang down before his heart, the symbol of a fearful secret between him and them. Were the veil but cast aside, they might speak freely of it, but not till then. Thus they sat a considerable time, speechless, confused, and shrinking uneasily from Mr. Hooper's eye, which they felt to be fixed upon them with an invisible glance. Finally, the deputies returned abashed to their constituents, pronouncing the matter too weighty to be handled, except by a council of the churches, if, indeed, it might not require a general synod.[9]

But there was one person in the village, unappalled by the awe with which the black veil had impressed all beside herself. When the deputies returned without an explanation, or even venturing to demand one, she, with the calm energy of her character, determined to chase away the strange cloud that appeared to be settling round Mr. Hooper, every moment more darkly than before. As his plighted[10] wife, it should be her privilege to know what the black veil concealed. At the minister's first visit, therefore, she entered upon the subject, with a direct simplicity, which made the task easier both for him and her. After he had seated himself, she fixed her eyes steadfastly upon the veil, but could discern nothing of the dreadful gloom that had so overawed the multitude: It was but a double fold of crape, hanging down from his forehead to his mouth, and slightly stirring with his breath.

"No," said she aloud, and smiling, "there is nothing terrible in this piece of crape, except that it hides a face which I am always glad to look upon. Come, good sir, let the sun shine from behind the cloud. First lay aside your black veil: Then tell me why you put it on."

Mr. Hooper's smile glimmered faintly.

"There is an hour to come," said he, "when all of us shall cast aside our veils. Take it not amiss, beloved friend, if I wear this piece of crape till then."

"Your words are a mystery too," returned the young lady. "Take away the veil from them, at least."

"Elizabeth, I will," said he, "so far as my vow may suffer me. Know, then, this veil is a type and a symbol, and I am bound to wear it ever, both in light and darkness, in solitude and before the gaze of multitudes, and as with strangers, so with my familiar friends. No mortal eye will see

9. **synod** (sin′əd): governing body of a group of churches.
10. **plighted:** promised.

INFER

Is this "fearful secret" (line 220) the same as the "secret sin" that was the subject of Mr. Hooper's sermon? Explain your answer.

RETELL

In your own words, restate Mr. Hooper's explanation for wearing the veil.

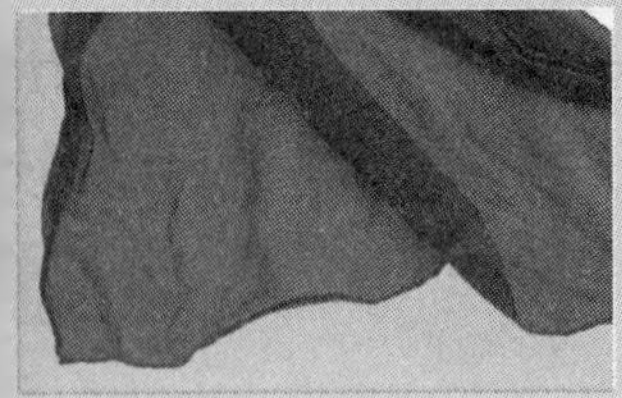

it withdrawn. This dismal shade must separate me from the world: Even you, Elizabeth, can never come behind it!"

"What grievous affliction hath befallen you," she earnestly inquired, "that you should thus darken your eyes forever?"

"If it be a sign of mourning," replied Mr. Hooper, "I, perhaps, like most other mortals, have sorrows dark enough to be typified by a black veil."

"But what if the world will not believe that it is the type of an innocent sorrow?" urged Elizabeth. "Beloved and respected as you are, there may be whispers, that you hide your face under the consciousness of secret sin. For the sake of your holy office, do away this scandal!"

The color rose into her cheeks, as she intimated the nature of the rumors that were already abroad in the village. But Mr. Hooper's mildness did not forsake him. He even smiled again—that same sad smile, which always appeared like a faint glimmering of light, proceeding from the <u>obscurity</u> beneath the veil.

"If I hide my face for sorrow, there is cause enough," he merely replied; "and if I cover it for secret sin, what mortal might not do the same?"

And with this gentle, but unconquerable obstinacy, did he resist all her entreaties. At length Elizabeth sat silent. For a few moments she appeared lost in thought, considering, probably, what new methods might be tried, to withdraw her lover from so dark a fantasy, which, if it had no other meaning, was perhaps a symptom of mental disease. Though of a firmer character than his own, the tears rolled down her cheeks. But, in an instant, as it were, a new feeling took the place of sorrow: Her eyes were fixed insensibly on the black veil, when, like a sudden twilight in the air, its terrors fell around her. She arose, and stood trembling before him.

"And do you feel it then at last?" said he mournfully.

She made no reply, but covered her eyes with her hand, and turned to leave the room. He rushed forward and caught her arm.

"Have patience with me, Elizabeth!" cried he passionately. "Do not desert me, though this veil must be between us here on earth. Be mine, and hereafter there shall be no veil over my face, no darkness between our souls! It is but a mortal veil—it is not for eternity! Oh! you know not how lonely I am, and how frightened to be alone behind my black veil. Do not leave me in this miserable obscurity forever!"

"Lift the veil but once, and look me in the face," said she.

"Never! It cannot be!" replied Mr. Hooper.

"Then, farewell!" said Elizabeth.

She withdrew her arm from his grasp, and slowly departed, pausing at the door, to give one long, shuddering gaze, that seemed almost to penetrate the mystery of the black veil. But, even amid his grief, Mr. Hooper smiled to think that only a material emblem had separated him

COMPARE AND CONTRAST

What distinction does Elizabeth seem to be making between, on the one hand, "innocent sorrow," and on the other, guilt?

WORDS TO OWN

obscurity (əb·skyoor′ə·tē) *n.:* something hidden or concealed.

INTERPRET

With the third use of the word *emblem* (line 299), what additional layers of meaning has the veil acquired?

from happiness, though the horrors which it shadowed forth, must be drawn darkly between the fondest of lovers.

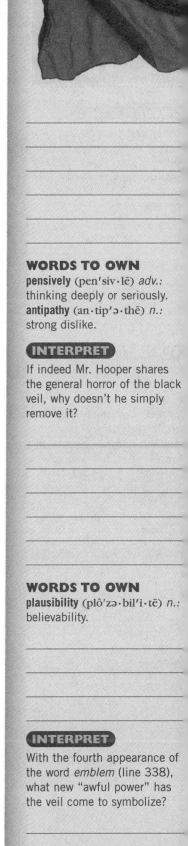

From that time no attempts were made to remove Mr. Hooper's black veil, or, by a direct appeal, to discover the secret which it was supposed to hide. By persons who claimed a superiority to popular prejudice, it was reckoned merely an eccentric whim, such as often mingles with the sober actions of men otherwise rational, and tinges them all with its own semblance of insanity. But with the multitude, good Mr. Hooper was irreparably a bugbear.[11] He could not walk the streets with any peace of mind, so conscious was he that the gentle and timid would turn aside to avoid him, and that others would make it a point of hardihood to throw themselves in his way. The impertinence of the latter class compelled him to give up his customary walk, at sunset, to the burial ground; for when he leaned pensively over the gate, there would always be faces behind the gravestones, peeping at his black veil. A fable went the rounds, that the stare of the dead people drove him thence. It grieved him, to the very depth of his kind heart, to observe how the children fled from his approach, breaking up their merriest sports, while his melancholy figure was yet afar off. Their instinctive dread caused him to feel, more strongly than aught else, that a preternatural[12] horror was interwoven with the threads of the black crape. In truth, his own antipathy to the veil was known to be so great, that he never willingly passed before a mirror, nor stooped to drink at a still fountain, lest, in its peaceful bosom, he should be affrighted by himself. This was what gave plausibility to the whispers, that Mr. Hooper's conscience tortured him for some great crime, too horrible to be entirely concealed, or otherwise than so obscurely intimated. Thus, from beneath the black veil, there rolled a cloud into the sunshine, an ambiguity of sin or sorrow, which enveloped the poor minister, so that love or sympathy could never reach him. It was said, that ghost and fiend consorted with him there. With self-shudderings and outward terrors, he walked continually in its shadow, groping darkly within his own soul, or gazing through a medium that saddened the whole world. Even the lawless wind, it was believed, respected his dreadful secret, and never blew aside the veil. But still good Mr. Hooper sadly smiled, at the pale visages of the worldly throng as he passed by.

Among all its bad influences, the black veil had the one desirable effect, of making its wearer a very efficient clergyman. By the aid of his mysterious emblem—for there was no other apparent cause—he became a man of awful power, over souls that were in agony for sin. His converts always regarded him with a dread peculiar to themselves, affirming, though but figuratively, that, before he brought them to

11. **bugbear:** source of irrational fears.
12. **preternatural:** abnormal; supernatural.

WORDS TO OWN
pensively (pen′siv·lē) *adv.:* thinking deeply or seriously.
antipathy (an·tip′ə·thē) *n.:* strong dislike.

INTERPRET
If indeed Mr. Hooper shares the general horror of the black veil, why doesn't he simply remove it?

WORDS TO OWN
plausibility (plô′zə·bil′i·tē) *n.:* believability.

INTERPRET
With the fourth appearance of the word *emblem* (line 338), what new "awful power" has the veil come to symbolize?

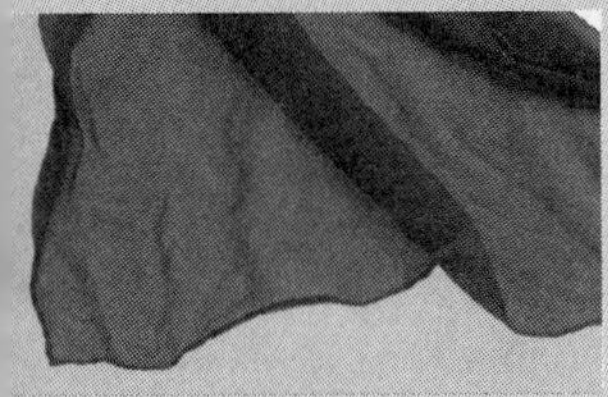

BUILD FLUENCY

his crucial paragraph details ome of the powerful positive ffects of the black veil. Re- ead it aloud, taking care to ronounce each word clearly nd expressively.

EVALUATE

Hawthorne devotes several ages to the day on which Mr. Hooper makes his first ppearance in the black veil, et here he compresses many ears into a single paragraph. How effective is this technique f storytelling, and why?

INTERPRET

Mr. Hooper has spent most of his life in "that saddest of all prisons, his own heart." Is his decision to wear the veil the *cause* of that imprisonment, or merely an emblem of it? Explain your answer.

celestial light, they had been with him behind the black veil. Its gloom, indeed, enabled him to sympathize with all dark affections. Dying sinners cried aloud for Mr. Hooper, and would not yield their breath till he appeared; though ever, as he stooped to whisper consolation, they shuddered at the veiled face so near their own. Such were the terrors of the black veil, even when Death had bared his visage! Strangers came long distances to attend service at his church, with the mere idle purpose of gazing at his figure, because it was forbidden them to behold his face. But many were made to quake ere they departed! Once, during Governor Belcher's[13] administration, Mr. Hooper was appointed to preach the election sermon. Covered with his black veil, he stood before the chief magistrate, the council, and the representatives, and wrought so deep an impression, that the legislative measures of that year were characterized by all the gloom and piety of our earliest ancestral sway.

In this manner Mr. Hooper spent a long life, irreproachable in outward act, yet shrouded in dismal suspicions; kind and loving, though unloved, and dimly feared; a man apart from men, shunned in their health and joy, but ever summoned to their aid in mortal anguish. As years wore on, shedding their snows above his sable veil, he acquired a name throughout the New England churches, and they called him Father Hooper. Nearly all his parishioners, who were of mature age when he was settled, had been borne away by many a funeral: He had one congregation in the church, and a more crowded one in the churchyard; and having wrought so late into the evening, and done his work so well, it was now good Father Hooper's turn to rest.

Several persons were visible by the shaded candlelight, in the death chamber of the old clergyman. Natural connections he had none. But there was the decorously grave, though unmoved physician, seeking only to mitigate the last pangs of the patient whom he could not save. There were the deacons, and other eminently pious members of his church. There, also, was the Reverend Mr. Clark, of Westbury, a young and zealous divine, who had ridden in haste to pray by the bedside of the expiring minister. There was the nurse, no hired handmaiden of death, but one whose calm affection had endured thus long, in secrecy, in solitude, amid the chill of age, and would not perish, even at the dying hour. Who, but Elizabeth! And there lay the hoary head of good Father Hooper upon the death-pillow, with the black veil still swathed about his brow and reaching down over his face, so that each more difficult gasp of his faint breath caused it to stir. All through life that piece of crape had hung between him and the world: It had separated him from cheerful brotherhood and woman's love, and kept him in that saddest of all prisons, his own heart; and still it lay upon his face, as if to deepen

13. **Governor Belcher's:** Jonathan Belcher (1682–1757) was governor of the Massachusetts Bay Colony from 1730 to 1741.

the gloom of his darksome chamber, and shade him from the sunshine of eternity.

For some time previous, his mind had been confused, wavering doubtfully between the past and the present, and hovering forward, as it were, at intervals, into the indistinctness of the world to come. There had been feverish turns, which tossed him from side to side, and wore away what little strength he had. But in his most convulsive struggles, and in the wildest vagaries of his intellect, when no other thought retained its sober influence, he still showed an awful solicitude lest the black veil should slip aside. Even if his bewildered soul could have forgotten, there was a faithful woman at his pillow, who, with averted eyes, would have covered that aged face, which she had last beheld in the comeliness of manhood. At length the death-stricken old man lay quietly in the torpor of mental and bodily exhaustion, with an imperceptible pulse, and breath that grew fainter and fainter, except when a long, deep, and irregular inspiration seemed to prelude the flight of his spirit.

The minister of Westbury approached the bedside.

"Venerable Father Hooper," said he, "the moment of your release is at hand. Are you ready for the lifting of the veil, that shuts in time from eternity?"

Father Hooper at first replied merely by a feeble motion of his head; then, apprehensive, perhaps, that his meaning might be doubtful, he exerted himself to speak.

"Yea," said he, in faint accents, "my soul hath a patient weariness until that veil be lifted."

"And is it fitting," resumed the Reverend Mr. Clark, "that a man so given to prayer, of such a blameless example, holy in deed and thought, so far as mortal judgment may pronounce; is it fitting that a father in the church should leave a shadow on his memory, that may seem to blacken a life so pure? I pray you, my venerable brother, let not this thing be! Suffer us to be gladdened by your triumphant aspect, as you go to your reward. Before the veil of eternity be lifted, let me cast aside this black veil from your face!"

And thus speaking, the Reverend Mr. Clark bent forward to reveal the mystery of so many years. But, exerting a sudden energy, that made all the beholders stand aghast, Father Hooper snatched both his hands from beneath the bedclothes, and pressed them strongly on the black veil, resolute to struggle, if the minister of Westbury would contend with a dying man.

"Never!" cried the veiled clergyman. "On earth, never!"

"Dark old man!" exclaimed the affrighted minister, "with what horrible crime upon your soul are you now passing to the judgment?"

Father Hooper's breath heaved; it rattled in his throat; but, with a mighty effort, grasping forward with his hands, he caught hold of life, and held it back till he should speak. He even raised himself in bed; and

RETELL

Put into your own words the sentence in lines 390–393.

WORDS TO OWN

resolute (rez′ə·lo͞ot′) *adj.:* determined.

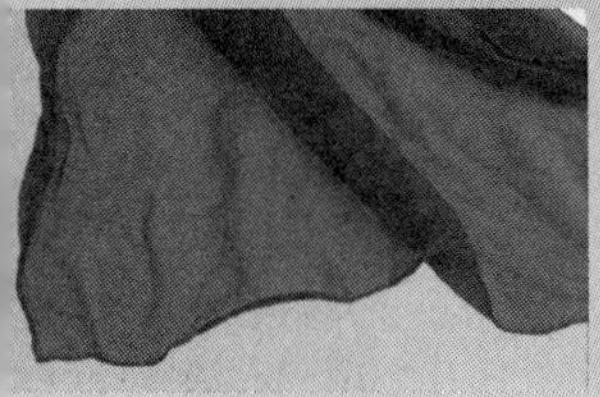

there he sat, shivering with the arms of death around him, while the black veil hung down, awful, at that last moment, in the gathered terrors of a lifetime. And yet the faint, sad smile, so often there, now seemed to glimmer from its obscurity, and linger on Father Hooper's lips.

"Why do you tremble at me alone?" cried he, turning his veiled face round the circle of pale spectators. "Tremble also at each other! Have men avoided me, and women shown no pity, and children screamed and fled, only for my black veil? What, but the mystery which it obscurely typifies, has made this piece of crape so awful? When the friend shows his inmost heart to his friend; the lover to his best-beloved; when man does not vainly shrink from the eye of his Creator, loathsomely treasuring up the secret of his sin; then deem me a monster, for the symbol beneath which I have lived, and die! I look around me, and, lo! on every visage a Black Veil!"

While his auditors shrank from one another, in mutual affright, Father Hooper fell back upon his pillow, a veiled corpse, with a faint smile lingering on the lips. Still veiled, they laid him in his coffin, and a veiled corpse they bore him to the grave. The grass of many years has sprung up and withered on that grave, the burial-stone is moss-grown, and good Mr. Hooper's face is dust; but awful is still the thought, that it moldered beneath the Black Veil!

UILD FLUENCY

is dramatic speech is the **imax** of the story. Re-read it oud so that its meaning and nportance are clear.

VALUATE

r. Hooper's decision to wear e black veil caused him great rrow over the course of his e, but he never wavered in s resolution. Was it a good e?

Symbol

A **symbol** is something that has meaning in itself but also stands for something more than itself. In Hawthorne's story the central symbol is a "horrible black veil," a "dismal shade" that separates its wearer from the world. The veil accumulates layers of meaning as the events of the story unfold, and by the end of the story the veil has become richly ambiguous in its associations.

Simple or complex, symbols are everywhere, and every culture defines itself both by the creation of symbols and by the interpretation of those symbols—and by the way it interprets the symbols of others. Complete the following chart to investigate the workings of symbolism in the world around us.

Symbol	Literal Meaning	Figurative Meaning
Flag Made of Stars and Stripes	Citizens, territory, and government of the United States	American ideals of democracy and liberty
Flag Showing Hammer and Sickle		
Five Interlocking Rings		
Scales Held Up by Blindfolded Woman		
White Dove		
Heart Pierced by Arrow		

Vocabulary: How to Own a Word

Vocabulary Comprehension

Word Bank
semblance
iniquity
ostentatious
sagacious
portend
obscurity
pensively
antipathy
plausibility
resolute

Each sentence below uses one Word to Own (in boldface type). If the Word to Own is used correctly, write *Correct* on the line provided. If it is used incorrectly, write *Incorrect* on the line and explain your answer.

EXAMPLE: The church **sexton** preached a powerful sermon.

Incorrect *A sexton is a church maintenance worker, not a preacher.*

1. The veil was so **ostentatious** that it was hardly noticed by the congregation.

______ ____
____

2. In his former days, Hooper's **semblance** had been so kindly and bland that he never startled anyone.

______ ____
____

3. The congregation wondered what deep significance Hooper's veil might **portend.**

______ ____
____

4. If you were distracted or cheerful, you would listen **pensively** to Hooper's explanation of why he wears the veil.

______ ____
____

5. People on the verge of death found **plausibility** in Hooper's veil, for they didn't understand the veil or believe it had any meaning.

______ ____
____

6. Although they had always liked and admired Hooper, many in his congregation felt a strong **antipathy** toward his veil.

______ ____
____

7. Elizabeth argued with **iniquity,** giving several reasons why Hooper should remove the veil.

8. Even the most **sagacious** parishioners did not foolishly ask Hooper to explain.

9. Perhaps Hooper would have preferred to live a life of **obscurity,** but his decision to wear the veil made it impossible for him to hide away.

10. However **resolute** the reverend was, his determination to have Hooper remove the veil was no match for Hooper's resistance.

A New American Poetry:
Whitman and Dickinson

The two greatest American poets of the nineteenth century were so different from one another, both as artists and as personalities, that only a nation as varied in character as the United States could possibly contain them.

Walt Whitman (1819–1892) worked with bold strokes on a broad canvas; Emily Dickinson (1830–1886) worked with the delicacy of a miniaturist. Whitman was sociable and gregarious, a traveler; Dickinson was private and shy, content to remain in one secluded spot through all of her lifetime.

While both poets were close observers of people and of life's daily activities, the emphasis they gave to what impressed them was so distinct as to make them opposites. Whitman was the public spokesman of the masses and the prophet of progress. "I hear America singing," he said, and he joined his eloquent voice to that chorus. Dickinson was the obscure homebody, peering through the curtains of her house in a country village, who found in nature metaphors for the spirit and recorded them with no thought of an audience. Whitman expected that his celebration of universal brotherhood and the bright destiny of democracy would be carried like a message into the future. Dickinson expected nothing but oblivion for the poetry that was her "letter to the World."

Whitman and Dickinson were true innovators who expressed themselves in poetic voices that broke with the established literary traditions of their time.

Two Seams in the Fabric

Whitman's career might be regarded as another American success story—the story of an amiable young man who drifted into his thirties, working at one job after another, never "finding himself" until, at his own expense, he boldly published *Leaves of Grass* (1855). The book made him famous around the world. Dickinson's career as a poet began after her death. It is one of those ironies of history in which a writer dies unknown, only to have fame thrust upon her by succeeding generations.

Whitman and Dickinson represent two distinct seams in the fabric of American poetry, one slightly uneven and the other carefully measured and stitched tight. Whitman was as extravagant with words as he was careless with repetition and self-contradiction. Aiming for the large,

CONNECT
/hat contemporary figures in ny field (e.g., literature, olitics, art, sports, music, etc.) lay this "Whitmanesque" role f speaking for all Americans?

CONNECT
:an you think of any recent gures who, like Emily)ickinson, seem to have risen o prominence despite no vident desire to do so?

IDENTIFY
:ircle five words or phrases in his paragraph that characterize he work of Walt Whitman.

overall impression, he filled his pages with long lists as he strained to catalog everything in sight. His technique is based on **cadence**—the long, easy sweep of sound that echoes the Bible and the speeches of orators and preachers. This cadence is the basis for his **free verse:** poetry without rhyme or meter.

Dickinson, on the other hand, wrote with the precision of a diamond cutter. Meticulous in her choice of words, she aimed to evoke the feelings of things rather than simply to name them. She was always searching for the one right phrase that would fix a thought in the mind. Her technique is economical, and her neat stanzas are controlled by the demands of rhyme and the meters she found in her hymnbook.

Dickinson used precise language and unique poetic forms to simultaneously reveal and conceal her private thoughts and feelings. Whitman, on the other hand, let loose his passion, philosophy, and observations in a torrent of language shaped by cadence rather than traditional meter.

Models for Future Poets

As the history of our poetry shows, both modes of expression have continued to be used by American writers. Both poets have served as models for modern poets who have been drawn to the visions they fulfilled and the techniques they mastered. Poetry as public speech written in the cadences of free verse remains a part of our literature; poetry as private observation, carefully crafted in rhyme and meter, still attracts writers who prize the musical effects of patterned sound.

Together, the gemlike artistry of Dickinson and the all-embracing power of Whitman represent the astonishing range of the American poetic tradition—a tradition that remains a vibrant source of instruction and inspiration to countless poets today.

IDENTIFY

Underline five words or phrases in this paragraph that characterize the work of Emily Dickinson.

CONNECT

What are a few important forms of public speech today?

CONNECT

Name any contemporary poets or musicians who use words with particular emphasis on the sound or musical quality.

From Song of Myself

Make the Connection

Singing His Own Song

Before Walt Whitman, virtually all American poets strove to imitate the forms, the language, and the subject matter of English verse. To be sure, there were great American poems before Whitman—Bryant's "Thanatopsis," for example, or Poe's "The Raven"—but it was Whitman's great achievement to create a uniquely *American* style of poetry, a style that celebrated American life and did so in an American voice.

What makes Whitman's poetic voice so very American? Partly it's the **diction.** Whitman used a great range of language, from elegant "poetic" terms to the ordinary words of the American worker. And partly it's the **rhythm**—Whitman's long, free-flowing lines closely imitate American speech patterns, or **cadence.** Mainly, though, the Americanness of Whitman's poetry stems from its **tone,** a brashly assertive, exuberant, unapologetic, life-loving tone that seems the very voice of a young, confident, democratic nation.

So largely does Whitman define himself that, paradoxically, his "Song of Myself" seems not to be about an individual but about all the selves that make up America. His voice encompasses the frontiersman, the sailor, the mother condemned as a witch, the escaped slave. Is this egotism? Yes, and something much more—Whitman's voice is an egotism that transcends ego and becomes a purely *human* voice, every American's voice.

Suppose you wanted to "sing your own song." What aspects of yourself would you include? Make a list of the characteristics that would give a reader a vivid idea of the kind of person you are.

A "Song of Myself"—the Key Ingredients

Walt Whitman

FROM *Song of Myself*

BUILD FLUENCY

he poetry of Walt Whitman is eant not so much to be seen s *heard*. After you have read e first section of "Song of yself," re-read these lines oud as expressively as you an.

IDENTIFY

hese stanzas are knit together y several key words that are epeated. What are they? Circle em.

RETELL

/hat does Whitman mean by Nature without check with riginal energy"? Put this in our own words.

INFER

Why might the speaker be shouting joyously from the deck of the ship?

1.

I celebrate myself, and sing myself,
And what I assume you shall assume,
For every atom belonging to me as good belongs to you.

I loaf and invite my soul,
I lean and loaf at my ease observing a spear of summer grass.

My tongue, every atom of my blood, form'd from this soil, this air,
Born here of parents born here from parents the same, and their parents the same,
I, now thirty-seven years old in perfect health begin,
Hoping to cease not till death.

Creeds and schools in abeyance,
Retiring back a while sufficed at what they are, but never forgotten,
I harbor for good or bad, I permit to speak at every hazard,
Nature without check with original energy.

Here the speaker both observes and participates in the diversity of American experience. Whitman carefully juxtaposes different scenes and emotions in these movielike glimpses into the broad American scene. The speaker presents himself as though he were not only the cinematographer who shoots the pictures but also the director behind each scene who arranges just what each frame will look like.

10.

Alone far in the wilds and mountains I hunt,
Wandering amazed at my own lightness and glee,
In the late afternoon choosing a safe spot to pass the night,
Kindling a fire and broiling the fresh-kill'd game,
Falling asleep on the gather'd leaves with my dog and gun by my side.

The Yankee clipper is under her sky-sails,[1] she cuts the sparkle and scud,[2]
My eyes settle the land, I bend at her prow or shout joyously from the deck.

---

1. **sky-sails:** small sails atop a square-rigged mast.
2. **scud:** windblown sea spray or foam.

The boatmen and clam-diggers arose early and stopt for me,
I tuck'd my trowser-ends in my boots and went and had a good time;
You should have been with us that day round the chowder-kettle.

I saw the marriage of the trapper in the open air in the far west, the bride was a red girl,
Her father and his friends sat near cross-legged and dumbly smoking, they had moccasins to their feet and large thick blankets hanging from their shoulders,
On a bank lounged the trapper, he was drest mostly in skins, his luxuriant beard and curls protected his neck, he held his bride by the hand,
She had long eyelashes, her head was bare, her coarse straight locks descended upon her voluptuous limbs and reach'd to her feet.

The runaway slave came to my house and stopt outside,
I heard his motions crackling the twigs of the woodpile,
Through the swung half-door of the kitchen I saw him limpsy[3] and weak,
And went where he sat on a log and led him in and assured him,
And brought water and fill'd a tub for his sweated body and bruis'd feet,
And gave him a room that enter'd from my own, and gave him some coarse clean clothes,
And remember perfectly well his revolving eyes and his awkwardness,
And remember putting plasters on the galls[4] of his neck and ankles;
He stayed with me a week before he was recuperated and pass'd north,
I had him sit next me at table, my fire-lock lean'd in the corner.

*Much of Whitman's work is distinguished by his attempt to erase the line between observer and object. The poet does this in order to—imaginatively speaking—*become *the thing or person he is talking about. Whitman is capable not only of sympathy, but also of* empathy—*the ability to share in another's thoughts or feelings. This excerpt from the thirty-third section of "Song of Myself" includes one of Whitman's most famous lines: "I am the man, I suffer'd, I was there." Through empathy, Whitman explores the greatness of heart that characterizes some unlikely heroes.*

from 33.

I understand the large hearts of heroes,
The courage of present times and all times,
How the skipper saw the crowded and rudderless wreck of the steam-ship, and Death chasing it up and down the storm,

---

3. **limpsy:** limp; exhausted.
4. **galls:** sores.

VISUALIZE
Picture the scene of this marriage between two worlds: the trapper representing the newcomers to America, and the Indians native to the land.

IDENTIFY
Underline some of the visual details that indicate the physical and emotional condition of the escaped slave.

BUILD FLUENCY
Re-read this passage aloud, using your voice to indicate the change of tone from the joyousness of the previous stanzas to the attentive concern in this one.

PREDICT
From what you have seen of Whitman's poetic methods in the previous sections, what do you think will follow this section's thematic opening lines?

BUILD FLUENCY

e-read aloud the opening 1 lines of this section, which ontains some of Whitman's ost famous lines. Try to read the way Whitman would ad it.

COMPARE AND CONTRAST

o you think that this hounded slave" is the same an we met in section 10 age 139)? What evidence oes the poem itself provide?

INFER

Vhy doesn't the speaker "ask he wounded person how he eels"?

How he knuckled tight and gave not back an inch, and was faithful of
days and faithful of nights,
And chalk'd in large letters on a board, *Be of good cheer, we will not*
desert you;
How he follow'd with them and tack'd with them three days and would
not give it up,
How he saved the drifting company at last,
How the lank loose-gown'd women look'd when boated from the side
of their prepared graves,
How the silent old-faced infants and the lifted sick, and the sharp-lipp'd
unshaved men;
All this I swallow, it tastes good, I like it well, it becomes mine,
I am the man, I suffer'd, I was there.[1]

The disdain and calmness of martyrs,
The mother of old, condemn'd for a witch, burnt with dry wood, her
children gazing on,
The hounded slave that flags in the race, leans by the fence, blowing,
cover'd with sweat,
The twinges that sting like needles his legs and neck, the murderous
buckshot and the bullets,
All these I feel or am.

I am the hounded slave, I wince at the bite of the dogs,
Hell and despair are upon me, crack and again crack the marksmen,
I clutch the rails of the fence, my gore dribs,[2] thinn'd with the ooze of
my skin,
I fall on the weeds and stones,
The riders spur their unwilling horses, haul close,
Taunt my dizzy ears and beat me violently over the head with
whip-stocks.

Agonies are one of my changes of garments,
I do not ask the wounded person how he feels, I myself become the
wounded person,
My hurts turn livid upon me as I lean on a cane and observe.

1. **I understand . . . I was there:** This stanza was inspired by an actual incident that occurred in 1853. According to reports in the New York *Weekly Tribune* of January 21, 1854, the ship *San Francisco* sailed from New York City on December 22, 1853, destined for South America. A violent storm hit the ship several hundred miles out of port, washing many passengers overboard. The captain of another ship helped rescue the survivors. A copy of the newspaper story was found among Whitman's papers after his death.
2. **dribs:** dribbles.

I am the mash'd fireman with breast-bone broken,
Tumbling walls buried me in their debris,
Heat and smoke I inspired,[3] I heard the yelling shouts of my comrades,
I heard the distant click of their picks and shovels,
They have clear'd the beams away, they tenderly lift me forth.

I lie in the night air in my red shirt, the pervading hush is for my sake,
Painless after all I lie exhausted but not so unhappy,
White and beautiful are the faces around me, the heads are bared of
    their fire-caps,
The kneeling crowd fades with the light of the torches.

Distant and dead resuscitate,
They show as the dial or move as the hands of me, I am the clock
    myself.

I am an old artillerist, I tell of my fort's bombardment,
I am there again.

Again the long roll of the drummers,
Again the attacking cannon, mortars,
Again to my listening ears the cannon responsive.

I take part, I see and hear the whole,
The cries, curses, roar, the plaudits for well-aim'd shots,
The ambulanza[4] slowly passing trailing its red drip,
Workmen searching after damages, making indispensable repairs,
The fall of grenades through the rent roof, the fan-shaped explosion,
The whizz of limbs, heads, stone, wood, iron, high in the air.

Again gurgles the mouth of my dying general, he furiously waves with
    his hand,
He gasps through the clot *Mind not me—mind—the entrenchments.*

INTERPRET

What do you think has happened to the fireman, especially at the end of this passage when the "kneeling crowd fades"?

IDENTIFY

Using circles, boxes, or underlining, note some of the words that Whitman uses to create a pattern of similar phrases throughout lines 37–49.

---

3. **inspired:** breathed in.
4. **ambulanza** (äm·bo͞o·länt'sə): Italian for "ambulance."

NTERPRET

hat does Whitman mean
"barbaric yawp"? Why has
chosen the phrase to
aracterize the sound of his
vn voice?

DENTIFY

rcle words in section 52
at evoke the four elements—
arth, air, fire, and water.

BUILD FLUENCY

e-read aloud the conclusion
"Song of Myself," lines
–16. Read expressively and
early.

In this final song, Whitman restates some of the **themes** *that have run throughout "Song of Myself." The poet weaves these themes in and out of this final verse like a composer filling a song with familiar refrains. Since the most insistently present element throughout "Song of Myself" is the mind and spirit of the speaker himself, this passage is highly personal. True to his nature, Whitman mocks his own egotism. But, true to his confidence in himself, he also proclaims his importance—and his inescapability.*

52.

The spotted hawk swoops by and accuses me, he complains of my gab
    and my loitering.

I too am not a bit tamed, I too am untranslatable,
I sound my barbaric yawp over the roofs of the world.

The last scud of day holds back for me,
It flings my likeness after the rest and true as any on the shadow'd wilds,
It coaxes me to the vapor and the dusk.

I depart as air, I shake my white locks at the runaway sun,
I effuse[1] my flesh in eddies, and drift it in lacy jags.

I bequeath myself to the dirt to grow from the grass I love,
If you want me again look for me under your boot-soles.

You will hardly know who I am or what I mean,
But I shall be good health to you nevertheless,
And filter and fiber your blood.

Failing to fetch me at first keep encouraged,
Missing me one place search another,
I stop somewhere waiting for you.

1. **effuse:** spread out.

Free Verse

Today we are so used to poetry written in free verse that we take it for granted. But in Whitman's time, Americans expected a poem to show the very strictest concern for **meter** and **rhyme.** Thus, Whitman's sprawling lines were revolutionary, as was his daring use of American slang, foreign words, and words he occasionally made up to suit his purpose.

Free verse is poetry that is written without concern for regular rhyme schemes and meter. But *free* verse does not mean "random" verse. Though Whitman abandoned meter and regular rhyme schemes, he made full use of **cadence**—the run of words that rise and fall in emphasis. As you can see from Whitman's poems, cadence does not depend on any strict count of stressed syllables.

Further, Whitman made extensive use of these other literary elements:

- **Alliteration:** the repetition of similar consonant sounds
- **Assonance:** the repetition of similar vowel sounds
- **Imagery:** the use of language to evoke visual pictures, as well as sensations of smell, hearing, taste, and touch
- **Onomatopoeia:** the use of words whose sounds echo their meaning (such as *buzz*)
- **Parallel structure:** the repetition of the same or similar words, phrases, clauses, or sentences

Find two examples of each of these techniques in "Song of Myself," and complete the following chart.

Poetic Technique	Example(s) from "Song of Myself"	Section and Line(s) "Song of Myself"
Alliteration	"I celebrate myself, and sing myself"	s. 1, l. 1
Assonance		
Imagery		
Onomatopoeia		
Parallel Structure		

Vocabulary: How to Own a Word

Developing Vocabulary

Read carefully the explanation of each word. Then, write an original sentence of your own using that word. Include in your sentence clues to the meaning of the word.

1. **abeyance** (ə·bā′əns) *n.:* temporary suspension of an activity. ("Song of Myself," 1, line 10)
   - This word is derived from the Old French *bayer,* which means "to wait expectantly."
     The soccer game on the field next to us was in full swing, but ours was in abeyance.

   Original Sentence: ______________________________

   ____

2. **prow** (prou) *n.:* forward part of a ship or boat. ("Song of Myself," 10, line 7)
   - The rear end of a ship is called the *stern.*
     The prow of the ship was seriously damaged when it sailed straight into a barrier reef.

   Original Sentence: ______________________________

   ____

3. **tacked** (takt) *v.:* past tense of *to tack,* which means "to sail against the wind in a zigzag course." ("Song of Myself," 33, line 6)
   - The noun *tack* can refer to a rope used for securing sails.
     Despite a strong headwind, the ship tacked for several days in pursuit of the white whale.

   Original Sentence: ______________________________

   ____

4. **martyrs** (märt′ərz) *n. pl.:* persons tortured or killed for their beliefs. ("Song of Myself," 33, line 12)
   - Originally a religious term meaning "witness," *martyr* comes from an Indo-European root meaning "to remember or care."
     Saint Stephen, stoned to death for his beliefs, is considered the first Christian martyr.

   Original Sentence: ______________________________

   ____

5. **flags** (flagz) *vi.:* present tense of the verb *to flag,* which means "to lose strength or grow tired." ("Song of Myself," 33, line 14)
   - This verb stems from an Old Norse word meaning "to flutter."
     A poor runner flags toward the end of a long race; a well-trained runner gains strength.

Original Sentence: ______________________________

____

6. **livid** (liv′id) *adj.:* colored grayish blue or black and blue; also can mean ashen or pale. ("Song of Myself," 33, line 25)

- *Livid* comes from an Indo-European root meaning "bluish."
  John, who was normally of a ruddy complexion, turned livid upon hearing the news.

Original Sentence: ______________________________

____

7. **resuscitate** (ri·sus′ə·tāt′) *v.:* to revive. ("Song of Myself," 33, line 35)

- *Resuscitate* stems from a Latin word meaning "to raise up."
  The medics tried to resuscitate the unconscious man by using CPR.

Original Sentence: ______________________________

____

8. **plaudits** (plô′dits) *n. pl.:* applause; praise. ("Song of Myself," 33, line 43)

- The adjective *plausible,* which means "seemingly true," and the noun *plaudits* both derive from the same Latin root meaning "to applaud."
  The violinist received plaudits from the critics for her extraordinary performance.

Original Sentence: ______________________________

____

9. **eddies** (ed′ēz) *n. pl.:* circular currents of air or water. ("Song of Myself," 52, line 8)

- This word derives from the Old Norse *itha,* which means "whirlpool."
  The half-sunken tree created currents and eddies in the fast-moving stream.

Original Sentence: ______________________________

____

10. **bequeath** (bē·kwēth′) *v.:* to hand down; leave property in a will. ("Song of Myself," 52, line 9)

- This verb is descended from the Old English *becwethan,* which means "to declare."
  The millionaire decided to bequeath her vast fortune to charitable organizations.

Original Sentence: ______________________________

____

The Soul selects her own Society; Some keep the Sabbath going to Church; Because I could not stop for Death

Make the Connection

Choices of the Soul

No one knows why Emily Dickinson quietly and abruptly withdrew from all social life except that involving her immediate family. In the seclusion of her bedroom, she spent the decades of her adulthood writing letters and an astonishing number of poems, most of which were never seen by anyone else until, after she died at the age of fifty-five, her sister Lavinia discovered them in dozens of neatly tied packets.

What was the nature of the choice that Dickinson seems to have made for the course of her life? Why did she suddenly choose seclusion and solitude? Did she make a conscious choice, or was she blindly following the instincts and yearnings of the soul?

Few of us fully understand our reasoning as we "select our own society"—that is, as we pick our friends, form our tastes, make our plans. In the chart below, consider the ways we make the decisions that determine the course of our lives.

Choice of . . .	Rational Considerations (Thoughts)	Nonrational Considerations (Feelings)
Friends	similarity of interests, shared sense of humor, mutual acquaintances	fun to be around, easy to get to know, cares about me
Career		
Hobbies		
Places to Visit		
Location of Home		
Religious Beliefs		

The Soul selects her own Society

Some keep the Sabbath going to Church

Because I could not stop for Death

Emily Dickinson

The Soul selects her own Society

The Soul selects her own Society—
Then—shuts the Door—
To her divine Majority—
Present no more—

Unmoved—she notes the Chariots—pausing—
At her low Gate—
Unmoved—an Emperor be kneeling
Upon her Mat—

I've known her—from an ample nation—
Choose One—
Then—close the Valves of her attention—
Like Stone—

The fifth of only seven poems published in Dickinson's lifetime, "Some keep the Sabbath going to Church" first appeared as "My Sabbath." Like so many of her poems, it seems to reflect upon the singular path she followed. She rejected the teachings of her family's Congregational church, but Dickinson was a deeply spiritual poet who constantly meditated on the divine—who indeed seemed to be "going, all along," to her own private church and her own private heaven.

Some keep the Sabbath going to Church

Some keep the Sabbath going to Church—
I keep it, staying at Home—
With a Bobolink[1] for a Chorister[2]—
And an Orchard, for a Dome—

Some keep the Sabbath in Surplice[3]—
I just wear my Wings—

1. **bobolink:** small bird.
2. **chorister:** choir member.
3. **surplice** (sur′plis): loose white vestment worn by clergy or choir members on top of longer robes.

INTERPRET

o what is the soul compared?

COMPARE AND CONTRAST

\n editor once altered "Valves" n line 11 to "lids." How does his change the poem's final mage?

BUILD FLUENCY

Re-read the entire poem aloud, keeping in mind that Dickinson used capital letters as a means of emphasizing key words.

IDENTIFY

Circle two different examples of **alliteration** in the second stanza.

And instead of tolling the Bell, for Church,
Our little Sexton[4]—sings.

God preaches, a noted Clergyman—
And the sermon is never long,
So instead of getting to Heaven, at last—
I'm going, all along.

*Like many other **metaphors** in Dickinson's poetry, the one in "Because I could not stop for Death" imaginatively captures the most awesome and inevitable of human experiences—death—and does so with playfulness and wit. The literal elements of the metaphor are simple: Dying is compared to an unexpected ride in a horse-drawn carriage. But these are just about the only simple elements in a poem that depends for its effect on **irony,** on gradual comprehension, and on a blithe **tone** that is much at odds with the subject of the story being told.*

Because I could not stop for Death

Because I could not stop for Death—
He kindly stopped for me—
The Carriage held but just Ourselves—
And Immortality.

We slowly drove—He knew no haste
And I had put away
My labor and my leisure too,
For His Civility—

We passed the School, where Children strove
At Recess—in the Ring—
We passed the Fields of Gazing Grain—
We passed the Setting Sun—

Or rather—He passed Us—
The Dews drew quivering and chill—

4. **sexton:** church officer or employee whose various duties may include maintenance and ringing the bells.

INTERPRET
From clues in the poem, who is the speaker and where is he "Home"?

BUILD FLUENCY
Re-read the entire poem aloud pronouncing each word carefully and expressively.

VISUALIZE
Notice that Dickinson pictures Death as the patient driver of a carriage who inspires not terror but trust "For His Civility" (that is, because of his courtesy). Why do you think Dickinson imagines Death in this way?

INFER

hat is the "House" where the arriage stopped?

INTERPRET

/hy do you think that the assage of "Centuries" seems ke so little time to the poet?

BUILD FLUENCY

e-read the entire poem aloud, eading slowly and expressively o convey the poem's tone of lignified wonder.

For only Gossamer,[1] my Gown—
My Tippet—only Tulle[2]—

We paused before a House that seemed
A Swelling of the Ground—
The Roof was scarcely visible—
The Cornice[3]—in the Ground—

Since then—'tis Centuries—and yet
Feels shorter than the Day
I first surmised the Horses Heads
Were toward Eternity—

1. **gossamer:** thin, soft material.
2. **tippet . . . tulle:** shawl made of fine netting.
3. **cornice:** projecting horizontal molding at the top of a building.

Slant Rhyme

Not long ago, **exact rhyme**—two or more words whose syllables share identical sounds, as in the words *free* and *bee*—was part of every poet's craft. Today it is still the most familiar aspect of sound in poetry. But rhyme has, over the years, fallen out of favor with many poets. One reason is that English, unlike languages such as Spanish and Russian, is comparatively "rhyme poor." (Some English words, like *orange* and *purple,* have no rhymes at all.) Over the centuries, some rhymes, like *love/above,* have become overused—and therefore overfamiliar to readers. Another reason is that imposed rhymes can act as a constraint and can limit expression. Some poets, as a solution, have abandoned rhyme altogether. Other poets, like Dickinson, use slant rhyme.

Slant rhyme is a close, but not exact, rhyming sound. (It is also called **off rhyme, half rhyme,** or **approximate rhyme.**) Word pairs like *society/majority* or *nerve/love* are examples of slant rhymes—"not quite, but almost" rhyming sounds.

Part of the shock value of Dickinson's poems comes from her use of slant rhyme, which she often used to force our attention onto particular words. For example, the last word in "The Soul selects her own Society," *Stone,* stands out because it doesn't match exactly in sound with the word *One.* Why is it important that the word *Stone* be emphasized?

What are the other slant rhymes in two of the poems by Emily Dickinson? Complete the chart below with as many examples as you can find.

Poem	Examples of Slant Rhyme
"The Soul selects her own Society"	Society/Majority
"Because I could not stop for Death"	

The Rise of Realism: The Civil War and Postwar Period 1850–1900

On the evening of April 12, 1861, Walt Whitman attended the opera at the Academy of Music in Manhattan. After the opera, he was walking down Broadway toward Brooklyn when, as he later wrote, "I heard in the distance the loud cries of the newsboys, who came presently tearing and yelling up the street, rushing from side to side even more furiously than usual. I bought an extra and crossed to the Metropolitan Hotel . . . where the great lamps were still brightly blazing, and, with a crowd of others, who gathered impromptu, read the news, which was evidently authentic."

VISUALIZE
magine the way scenes like his took place all over the country when the Civil War proke out. Why do you think hat Whitman assumed that he news was "authentic"?

The news that Whitman and the others read so avidly was of the Confederate attack on Fort Sumter, the opening shots of the Civil War. Thus solemnly began, for one of the few American poets or novelists who would witness it firsthand, the greatest cataclysm in United States history.

Responses to the War: Idealism

In Concord, Massachusetts, home of Ralph Waldo Emerson, army volunteers met soon after the war's opening battle. Emerson had for decades warned that this day would come if slavery were not abolished. Now that the day had arrived, he was filled with patriotic fervor. Emerson had great respect for the Southern will to fight, however, and he suspected, quite rightly, that the war would not be over in a few months as people had predicted. When the Concord volunteers returned later that summer from the First Battle of Bull Run (July 1861), defeated and disillusioned, many of them unwilling to reenlist, Emerson maintained his conviction that the war must be pursued.

COMPARE AND CONTRAST
What similarities and differences do you see between the mixed reaction to the outset of the Civil War, on the one hand, and the reaction of present-day Americans to involvement in conflicts between other nations?

Late in 1862, Walt Whitman traveled to Virginia to find his brother George, who had been wounded in battle. After George was nursed back to health, Whitman remained in Washington off and on, working part time and serving as a volunteer hospital visitor, comforting the wounded and writing to their loved ones. The condition of the wounded was appalling. Many of the injured had to remain on the battlefield for two or three days until the camp hospitals had room for them. Antiseptics were primitive, as were operating-room techniques. Anesthesia was virtually unknown. A major wound meant amputation or even death.

Whitman estimated that in three years as a camp hospital volunteer, he visited tens of thousands of wounded men. In his poems, he had presented a panoramic vision of America; now America passed through the hospital tents in the form of wounded men from every state in the Union and the Confederacy. Nevertheless, out of the horror that he viewed, Whitman was able to derive a hopeful vision of the American character, of "the actual soldier of 1862–65 . . . with all his ways, his incredible dauntlessness, habits, practices, tastes, language, his fierce friendship, his appetite, rankness, his superb strength—and a hundred unnamed lights and shades."

RETELL
What seems to be the "common denominator" in this list of the traits of soldiers? Restate Whitman's point in your own words.

Disillusionment

The war that strengthened Whitman's optimism served at the same time to justify Herman Melville's pessimism. Melville's poems about the war, collected in *Battle-Pieces* and *Aspects of the War* (1866), were often dark and foreboding. Of the elation following the firing on Fort Sumter, Melville wrote:

O, the rising of the People
    Came with the springing of the grass,
They rebounded from dejection
    After Easter came to pass.
And the young were all elation
    Hearing Sumter's cannon roar. . . .
But the elders with foreboding
    Mourned the days forever o'er,
And recalled the forest proverb,
    The Iroquois' old saw:
Grief to every graybeard
    When young Indians lead the war

INTERPRET
Why do you think Melville has marked the time when people "rebounded from dejection" with a mention of Easter, rather than simply the month or the season?

RETELL
Restate the "old saw" (that is, old saying) of the Iroquois in your own words.

Melville was fascinated by the war, but he never wrote a novel about it. The poems in *Battle-Pieces,* based on newspaper accounts of the battles as well as visits to battlefields, record the heroism and futility of the fighting on both sides and demonstrate respect for Southern soldiers as well as Northern troops. But in some of the best poems, there is a sense of human nature being stripped bare, revealing not the heroism and strength that Whitman found, but rather humanity's basic evil.

The American Civil War (1861–1865) resulted in terrible bloodshed as the national government sought to preserve the Union. Despite his firsthand experience of the aftermath of battle, Walt Whitman retained an optimistic view of the American character. But the horrors of war merely reinforced the pessimism of Herman Melville.

BUILD FLUENCY
Re-read Melville's poem aloud, avoiding a singsong rhythm by paying careful attention to the meanings of the words.

CONNECT

Vill historians of the future e able to construct an ccurate record of our own mes from the many sources f information we're leaving ehind—newspapers, nagazines, and videotapes?

IDENTIFY

Vhat are two reasons for the neager literary record of he Civil War? Underline the nswers.

The War in Literature

There was enough atrocity and heroism in the war to feed the views of both Melville and Whitman. What is odd, though, is that Melville's *Battle-Pieces* (which was ignored until the twentieth century) and Whitman's *Drum-Taps* (1865) and *Specimen Days and Collect* (1882) make up the bulk of the war's immediate legacy of poetry and fiction. Although there were many works of historical interest—soldiers' letters and diaries, as well as journalistic writings—works of literary significance were rare. Whitman himself wrote, "Future years will never know the seething hell and the black infernal background of the countless minor scenes and interiors . . . and it is best they should not—the real war will never get in the books."

Why did an event of such magnitude result in such a scant literary output? One reason is simply that few major American writers saw the Civil War firsthand. Emerson was in Concord during most of the war, "knitting socks and mittens for soldiers," as he wrote to his son, and "writing patriotic lectures." Thoreau, who had been a fervent abolitionist, died in 1862, and Hawthorne died two years later. Emily Dickinson remained in Amherst, Massachusetts, though the country's grief over the war seems to have informed her poetry. Of the younger generation of writers, William Dean Howells, Henry James, and Henry Adams were abroad.

Perhaps most important, though, traditional literary forms of the time were inadequate to express the horrifying details of the Civil War. The literary form most appropriate for handling such strong material—the realistic novel—had not yet been fully developed in the United States. Thus, the great novel of the war, *The Red Badge of Courage,* had to wait to be written by a man who was not born until six years after the war had ended: Stephen Crane (1871–1900).

Very little important poetry and fiction issued directly from the Civil War, largely because few major American writers experienced the war firsthand. Direct accounts of the war found their way into other types of literature, however, including poignant letters and diaries. The "real war" would not find a place in American fiction until the development of the realistic novel.

The Rise of Realism

One of the most enduring subjects for prose has always been the exploits of larger-than-life heroes. Born of epic poetry and the chivalric romance, the **romantic novel** presents readers with lives lived idealistically—

beyond the level of everyday life. The heroes and heroines of the novels of James Fenimore Cooper, for example, engage in romantic adventures filled with courageous acts, daring chases, and exciting escapes. Such exciting exploits have always been a staple of prose fiction—and today, of action movies featuring James Bond, Indiana Jones, and Luke Skywalker.

In America, the great fiction writers of the mid-nineteenth century, Edgar Allan Poe, Nathaniel Hawthorne, and Herman Melville, shared an aversion to simple realism. These writers used romance not simply to entertain readers, but to reveal truths that would be hidden in a realistic story.

After the Civil War, however, a new generation of writers came of age. They were known as **realists,** writers who aimed at a "very minute fidelity" to the common course of ordinary life. Their subjects were drawn from the slums of the rapidly growing cities, from the factories that were rapidly covering farmlands, and from the lives of far-from-idealized characters: poor factory workers, corrupt politicians, even prostitutes.

Realism was well entrenched in Europe by the time it began to flower in the United States. It developed in the work of writers who tried to represent faithfully the environment and the manners of everyday life: the way ordinary people lived and dressed, and what they thought and felt and talked about. But realism was not simply concerned with recording wallpaper patterns, hairstyles, or the subjects of conversations. It sought also to explain *why* ordinary people behave the way they do. Realistic novelists often relied on the emerging sciences of human and animal behavior—biology, psychology, and sociology—as well as on their own insights and observations.

The literary movement known as realism dominated American fiction from the late nineteenth century to the middle of the twentieth. Realists sought to portray real life accurately, without the filters of romanticism or idealism.

American Regionalism: Brush Strokes of Local Color

In America, realism had its roots in **regionalism,** literature that emphasizes a specific geographic setting and that makes use of the speech and manners of the people who live in that region. Sarah Orne Jewett, Kate Chopin, Harriet Beecher Stowe, Bret Harte, and Charles W. Chesnutt are noted early regionalists who recorded the peculiarities of speech and temperament in their parts of a rapidly expanding nation.

CONNECT

Name three more romantic figures from books, movies, or television. (Notice that, in the study of literature, "romantic novels" are unrealistic, "larger-than-life stories," not "love stories.")

IDENTIFY

Underline three subjects of realistic fiction, and circle the names of three behavioral sciences that contributed to the rise of realistic fiction.

IDENTIFY
nderline a phrase that ndicates the technique used y regional writers.

While regional writers strove to be realistic in their depiction of speech patterns and manners, though, they were often unrealistic—even sentimental—in their depiction of character and social environment. Realism as a literary movement in the United States went far beyond regionalism in its concern for accuracy in portraying social conditions and human motivation.

Mark Twain (1835–1910) is the best-known example of a regional writer whose realism far surpassed local bounds. Although he first established his reputation as a regional humorist, Twain evolved into a writer whose comic view of society became increasingly satiric. His best novel, *Adventures of Huckleberry Finn* (1884), combines a biting picture of some of the injustices inherent in pre–Civil War life with a lyrical portrait of the American landscape.

American realism had its roots in regionalism, literature that focuses on a relatively small geographical area and attempts to accurately reproduce the speech and manners of that region.

Realism and Naturalism: A Lens on Everyday Life

The most active proponent of realism in American fiction was William Dean Howells (1837–1920), editor of the influential magazine *The Atlantic Monthly.* In both his fiction and his critical writings, Howells insisted that realism should deal with the lives of ordinary people, be faithful to the development of character even at the expense of action, and discuss the social questions perplexing Americans. Howells's "smiling realism" portrayed an America where people may act foolishly but where their good qualities eventually win out.

Other realistic novelists viewed life as a much rougher clash of contrary forces. The Californian Frank Norris (1870–1902), for example, agreed with Howells that the proper subject for fiction was the ordinary person, but he found Howells's fiction too strait-laced and narrow—"as respectable as a church and proper as a deacon." Norris was an earthier writer, interested in the impact of large social forces on individuals. His best-known novel, *The Octopus* (1901), is about the struggles between wheat farmers and the railroad monopoly in California. Norris was not the first to use the novel to examine social institutions with the aim of reforming them. Decades earlier, Harriet Beecher Stowe's antislavery novel *Uncle Tom's Cabin* (1852) was credited by President Lincoln (and many historians) with helping to cause the war. But *Uncle Tom's Cabin* was more melodrama than realistic fiction.

Norris is generally considered to be a **naturalist.** Following the lead of the French novelist Emile Zola, naturalists relied heavily on the growing scientific disciplines of psychology and sociology. In their fiction, they attempted to dissect human behavior with as much objectivity as a scientist would dissect a frog or a cadaver. For naturalists, human behavior was determined by forces beyond the individual's power, especially by biology and environment. The naturalists tended to look at human life as a grim losing battle. Their characters often had only limited choices and motivations. In the eyes of some naturalist writers, human beings were totally subject to the natural laws of the universe; like animals, they lived crudely, by instinct, unable to control or understand their own desires.

RETELL

Briefly summarize three characteristics of realistic fiction.

Psychological Fiction: Inside the Human Mind

On the other hand, the New York–born Henry James (1843–1916), considered America's greatest writer of the psychological novel, concentrated principally on fine distinctions in character motivation. James was a realist, but no realist could be further from the blunt, naturalistic view that people were driven by animal-like instincts. In his finely tuned studies of human motivation, James opened the inner mind to the techniques of fiction. He was mainly interested in complex social and psychological situations. Many of his novels, including *Daisy Miller* (1878) and *The Portrait of a Lady* (1881), take place in Europe, because James considered European society to be both more complex and more sinister than American society. He frequently contrasts innocent, eager Americans with sophisticated, more reserved Europeans.

Stephen Crane was as profound a psychologist as James, but his principal interest was the human character at moments of stress—on the battlefield, the streets of a slum, or a lifeboat lost at sea. Although Crane is sometimes referred to as a naturalist, he is probably best thought of as an **ironist;** he was the first of many modern American writers—later including Ernest Hemingway and Kurt Vonnegut, Jr.—to juxtapose human pretensions with the indifference of the universe. Of all the nineteenth-century realists, only Crane could describe a stabbing death (in his story "The Blue Hotel") in this coolly cynical manner: "[The blade] shot forward, and a human body, this citadel of virtue, wisdom, power, was pierced as easily as if it had been a melon." It would take this sensibility to get the "real war" in the books at last.

IDENTIFY

Circle the names of three important realist novelists.

Realism in American literature branched out in several directions, from the "smiling realism" of William Dean Howells to the gritty naturalism of Frank Norris, and from the psychological realism of Henry James to the ironic stance of Stephen Crane.

From The Narrative of the Life of Frederick Douglass

Make the Connection

The Turning Point

Frederick Douglass's account of his slavery and his freedom is one of the great American autobiographies. Early in *The Narrative of the Life of Frederick Douglass,* he explains "how a man was made a slave." In the following selection from later in the book, though, he promises to show the reader "how a slave was made a man." Douglass was a sixteen-year-old slave when his owner, a man named Thomas, rented him out for a year to Mr. Covey, a farmer with a brutal temper.

Douglass focuses our attention on a **turning point**—a moment in his life when the course of his fortunes changed. Such moments provide not only the dramatic highlights in a story, but also, for an insightful writer like Douglass, an opportunity to establish clear themes. That is, at turning points we often see a story's "big ideas" emerge clearly.

Every life has its turning points. Some are predictable and traditional, like graduations and weddings. Others occur unexpectedly, but their effects can be every bit as profound. Think of some turning point in your own life—a moment of major and permanent change—and explore its importance by completing the chart below.

Initial Circumstance(s)	Turning Point	Resulting Circumstance(s)	Importance of the Changed Circumstances

FROM The Narrative of the Life of Frederick Douglass

Frederick Douglass

ORDS TO OWN
timated (in′tə·māt′əd) *v.:* ated indirectly; hinted.

INFER
'hom might Douglass be ddressing as "you" here?

IDENTIFY
ircle the words in this passage iat indicate Douglass's hysical condition.

ORDS TO OWN
omply (kəm·plī′) *v.:* to obey; gree to a request.

The Battle with Mr. Covey

I have already intimated that my condition was much worse, during the first six months of my stay at Mr. Covey's, than in the last six. The circumstances leading to the change in Mr. Covey's course toward me form an epoch in my humble history. You have seen how a man was made a slave; you shall see how a slave was made a man. On one of the hottest days of the month of August, 1833, Bill Smith, William Hughes, a slave named Eli, and myself, were engaged in fanning wheat.[1] Hughes was clearing the fanned wheat from before the fan, Eli was turning, Smith was feeding, and I was carrying wheat to the fan. The work was simple, requiring strength rather than intellect; yet, to one entirely unused to such work, it came very hard.

About three o'clock of that day, I broke down; my strength failed me; I was seized with a violent aching of the head, attended with extreme dizziness; I trembled in every limb. Finding what was coming, I nerved myself up, feeling it would never do to stop work. I stood as long as I could stagger to the hopper with grain. When I could stand no longer, I fell, and felt as if held down by an immense weight. The fan of course stopped; everyone had his own work to do; and no one could do the work of the other, and have his own go on at the same time.

Mr. Covey was at the house, about one hundred yards from the treading yard where we were fanning. On hearing the fan stop, he left immediately, and came to the spot where we were. He hastily inquired what the matter was. Bill answered that I was sick, and there was no one to bring wheat to the fan. I had by this time crawled away under the side of the post-and-rail fence by which the yard was enclosed, hoping to find relief by getting out of the sun. He then asked where I was. He was told by one of the hands.

He came to the spot, and, after looking at me awhile, asked me what was the matter. I told him as well as I could, for I scarce had strength to speak. He then gave me a savage kick in the side, and told me to get up. I tried to do so, but fell back in the attempt. He gave me another kick, and again told me to rise. I again tried, and succeeded in gaining my feet; but, stooping to get the tub with which I was feeding the fan, I again staggered and fell. While down in this situation, Mr. Covey took up the hickory slat with which Hughes had been striking off the half-bushel measure, and with it gave me a heavy blow upon the head, making a large wound, and the blood ran freely; and with this again told me to get up. I made no effort to comply, having now made up my mind to let him do his worst. In a short time after receiving this blow, my head grew better. Mr. Covey had now left me to my fate.

At this moment I resolved, for the first time, to go to my master, enter a complaint, and ask his protection. In order to [do] this, I must

1. **fanning wheat:** separating usable grain.

that afternoon walk seven miles; and this, under the circumstances, was truly a severe undertaking. I was exceedingly feeble; made so as much by the kicks and blows which I received, as by the severe fit of sickness to which I had been subjected. I, however, watched my chance, while Covey was looking in an opposite direction, and started for St. Michael's. I succeeded in getting a considerable distance on my way to the woods, when Covey discovered me, and called after me to come back, threatening what he would do if I did not come. I disregarded both his calls and his threats, and made my way to the woods as fast as my feeble state would allow; and thinking I might be overhauled by him if I kept the road, I walked through the woods, keeping far enough from the road to avoid detection, and near enough to prevent losing my way.

I had not gone far before my little strength again failed me. I could go no farther. I fell down, and lay for a considerable time. The blood was yet oozing from the wound on my head. For a time I thought I should bleed to death; and think now that I should have done so, but that the blood so matted my hair as to stop the wound. After lying there about three quarters of an hour, I nerved myself up again, and started on my way, through bogs and briers, barefooted and bareheaded, tearing my feet sometimes at nearly every step; and after a journey of about seven miles, occupying some five hours to perform it, I arrived at master's store. I then presented an appearance enough to affect any but a heart of iron. From the crown of my head to my feet, I was covered with blood. My hair was all clotted with dust and blood; my shirt was stiff with blood. My legs and feet were torn in sundry places with briers and thorns, and were also covered with blood. I suppose I looked like a man who had escaped a den of wild beasts, and barely escaped them.

In this state I appeared before my master, humbly entreating him to interpose his authority for my protection. I told him all the circumstances as well as I could, and it seemed, as I spoke, at times to affect him. He would then walk the floor, and seek to justify Covey by saying he expected I deserved it. He asked me what I wanted. I told him, to let me get a new home; that as sure as I lived with Mr. Covey again, I should live with but to die with him; that Covey would surely kill me; he was in a fair way for it. Master Thomas ridiculed the idea that there was any danger of Mr. Covey's killing me, and said that he knew Mr. Covey; that he was a good man, and that he could not think of taking me from him; that, should he do so, he would lose the whole year's wages; that I belonged to Mr. Covey for one year, and that I must go back to him, come what might; and that I must not trouble him with any more stories, or that he would himself *get hold of me.* After threatening me thus, he gave me a very large dose of salts, telling me that I might remain in St. Michael's that night (it being quite late), but that I must be off back to Mr. Covey's early in the morning; and that if I did not, he would *get hold of me,* which meant that he would whip me.

INFER

Douglass reveals how few options were available to a slave. What seems to be his attitude toward his master?

IDENTIFY

Underline the words or phrase in this paragraph that help to create **suspense.**

WORDS TO OWN

interpose (in′tər·pōz′) *v.:* to put forth in order to intervene

IDENTIFY

Underline the phrase in this paragraph that explains what Douglass means by *"get hold of me."*

INFER

'hy might Mr. Covey have •und Douglass's behavior ıltogether unaccountable"?

INTERPRET

'hat does Douglass mean by 'free wife"?

VORDS TO OWN

olemnity (sə·lem'nə·tē) *n.:* ɜriousness.

ender (ren'dər) *v.:* make.

IDENTIFY

nderline words in this aragraph that indicate ouglass's opinions about andy's advice.

VORDS TO OWN

ngular (siŋ'gyə·lər) *adj.:* ɜmarkable.

ttributed (ə·trib'yoot·id) *v.:* elieved to result from.

PREDICT

/hat do you think will test the virtue of the *root*"?

I remained all night, and, according to his orders, I started off to Covey's in the morning (Saturday morning), wearied in body and broken in spirit. I got no supper that night, or breakfast that morning. I reached Covey's about nine o'clock; and just as I was getting over the fence that divided Mrs. Kemp's fields from ours, out ran Covey with his cowskin, to give me another whipping. Before he could reach me, I succeeded in getting to the cornfield; and as the corn was very high, it afforded me the means of hiding. He seemed very angry, and searched for me a long time. My behavior was altogether unaccountable. He finally gave up the chase, thinking, I suppose, that I must come home for something to eat; he would give himself no further trouble in looking for me. I spent that day mostly in the woods, having the alternative before me—to go home and be whipped to death, or stay in the woods and be starved to death.

That night, I fell in with Sandy Jenkins, a slave with whom I was somewhat acquainted. Sandy had a free wife who lived about four miles from Mr. Covey's; and it being Saturday, he was on his way to see her. I told him my circumstances, and he very kindly invited me to go home with him. I went home with him, and talked this whole matter over, and got his advice as to what course it was best for me to pursue. I found Sandy an old advisor.[2] He told me, with great solemnity, I must go back to Covey; but that before I went, I must go with him into another part of the woods, where there was a certain *root,* which, if I would take some of it with me, carrying it *always on my right side,* would render it impossible for Mr. Covey, or any other white man, to whip me. He said he had carried it for years; and since he had done so, he had never received a blow, and never expected to while he carried it. I at first rejected the idea, that the simple carrying of a root in my pocket would have any such effect as he had said, and was not disposed to take it; but Sandy impressed the necessity with much earnestness, telling me it could do no harm, if it did no good. To please him, I at length took the root, and, according to his direction, carried it upon my right side. This was Sunday morning.

I immediately started for home; and upon entering the yard gate, out came Mr. Covey on his way to meeting. He spoke to me very kindly, made me drive the pigs from a lot near by, and passed on toward the church. Now, this singular conduct of Mr. Covey really made me begin to think that there was something in the *root* which Sandy had given me; and had it been on any other day than Sunday, I could have attributed the conduct to no other cause than the influence of that root; and as it was, I was half inclined to think the *root* to be something more than I at first had taken it to be. All went well till Monday morning. On this morning, the virtue of the *root* was fully tested.

2. **an old advisor:** someone who can offer good advice.

Long before daylight, I was called to go and rub, curry, and feed the horses. I obeyed, and was glad to obey. But while thus engaged, while in the act of throwing down some blades from the loft, Mr. Covey entered the stable with a long rope; and just as I was half out of the loft, he caught hold of my legs, and was about tying me. As soon as I found what he was up to, I gave a sudden spring, and as I did so, he holding to my legs, I was brought sprawling on the stable floor. Mr. Covey seemed now to think he had me, and could do what he pleased; but at this moment—from whence came the spirit I don't know—I resolved to fight; and, suiting my action to the resolution, I seized Covey hard by the throat; and as I did so, I rose. He held on to me, and I to him. My resistance was so entirely unexpected, that Covey seemed taken all aback. He trembled like a leaf. This gave me assurance, and I held him uneasy, causing the blood to run where I touched him with the ends of my fingers. Mr. Covey soon called out to Hughes for help. Hughes came, and, while Covey held me, attempted to tie my right hand. While he was in the act of doing so, I watched my chance, and gave him a heavy kick close under the ribs. This kick fairly sickened Hughes, so that he left me in the hands of Mr. Covey.

This kick had the effect of not only weakening Hughes, but Covey also. When he saw Hughes bending over with pain, his courage quailed.[3] He asked me if I meant to persist in my resistance. I told him I did, come what might; that he had used me like a brute for six months, and that I was determined to be used so no longer. With that, he strove to drag me to a stick that was lying just out of the stable door. He meant to knock me down. But just as he was leaning over to get the stick, I seized him with both hands by his collar, and brought him by a sudden snatch to the ground. By this time, Bill came. Covey called upon him for assistance. Bill wanted to know what he could do. Covey said, "Take hold of him, take hold of him!" Bill said his master hired him out to work, and not to help to whip me; so he left Covey and myself to fight our own battle out. We were at it for nearly two hours. Covey at length let me go, puffing and blowing at a great rate, saying that if I had not resisted, he would not have whipped me half so much. The truth was, that he had not whipped me at all. I considered him as getting entirely the worst end of the bargain; for he had drawn no blood from me, but I had from him. The whole six months afterward, that I spent with Mr. Covey, he never laid the weight of his finger upon me in anger. He would occasionally say, he didn't want to get hold of me again. "No," thought I, "you need not; for you will come off worse than you did before."

This battle with Mr. Covey was the turning point in my career as a slave. It rekindled the few expiring embers of freedom, and revived

3. **quailed:** faltered.

WORDS TO OWN
curry (kur'ē) *v.:* to groom.

VISUALIZE
What is the "loft" in a stable Visualize the way the battle begins as Douglass is descending from the loft.

IDENTIFY
Underline the sentence in this paragraph that marks the **turning point** in this story.

INTERPRET
Why does Douglass, througho most of this paragraph, refer Mr. Covey simply as "Covey"?

INTERPRET
What does Douglass mean by the phrase "entirely the worst end of the bargain"?

WORDS TO OWN
expiring (ek·spīr'iŋ) *v.* used as *adj.:* dying.

'ORDS TO OWN

forded (ə·fôrd′əd) *v.* used *adj.:* given; provided.

NTERPRET

nderline the sentences in is paragraph that reveal the sults of Douglass's fight with r. Covey.

BUILD FLUENCY

ead the last paragraph aloud, aying careful attention to e words and phrases that ouglass uses to convey owerful feelings.

within me a sense of my own manhood. It recalled the departed self-confidence, and inspired me again with a determination to be free. The gratification afforded by the triumph was a full compensation for whatever else might follow, even death itself. He only can understand the deep satisfaction which I experienced, who has himself repelled by force the bloody arm of slavery. I felt as I never felt before. It was a glorious resurrection, from the tomb of slavery, to the heaven of freedom. My long-crushed spirit rose, cowardice departed, bold defiance took its place; and I now resolved that, however long I might remain a slave in form, the day had passed forever when I could be a slave in fact.

Conflict

Conflict, the struggle between opposing forces that lies at the heart of any dramatic situation, can be of two types. **External** conflict occurs between people and can range from gentle teasing to brutal physical combat. **Internal** conflict, as the term implies, occurs within a person's mind and might express itself as doubt, confusion, or indecision. In the best literature—just as in real life—both kinds of conflict, internal and external, occur simultaneously, and the resolution of one may or may not bring about the resolution of the other.

Frederick Douglass's account of his battle with Mr. Covey is rich in conflict. Complete the chart below, taking care to show clearly the opposing forces, the causes of the conflict, and the outcomes.

The Opposing Parties of Douglass's *External* Conflict	The *Cause* of Douglass's *External* Conflict	The *Outcome* of Douglass's *External* Conflict

The Opposing Emotions or Ideals of Douglass's *Internal* Conflict	The *Cause* of Douglass's *Internal* Conflict	The *Outcome* of Douglass's *Internal* Conflict

Vocabulary: How to Own a Word

Synonyms and Context Clues

Each item below contains italicized words that are synonyms for your Words to Own. By using context clues from the sentence, determine the meaning of the italicized word and write its synonym from the Word Bank in the blank provided. After you have determined the synonym, underline the words in the sentence that provide the clues to the italicized word's meaning.

Word Bank
intimated
comply
interpose
solemnity
render
singular
attributed
curry
expiring
afforded

Example: Douglass was not *freed* for four years after his battle with Covey, though he often dreamed of the day he'd no longer be enslaved.

emancipated

1. One of Douglass's regular chores is to *brush* the horses, eliminating any burrs or tangles. ______________________
2. Master Thomas chooses not to *put* himself *between* Douglass and Mr. Covey. ______________________
3. Sandy Jenkins tells Douglass of a talisman, a magic root that will *make* it impossible for anyone to harm him. ______________________
4. The standoff with Covey gave Douglass something special: It *furnished* him *with* a renewed sense of dignity. ______________________
5. Covey's behavior is *extraordinary,* unlike anything Douglass has ever seen. ______________________

6. Although Douglass was frequently forced to follow Covey's commands, the day finally came when he refused to *obey.* ____________________

7. Douglass *implied* his feelings instead of stating them directly.

____

8. Rather than make light of the situation, Sandy speaks with great *gravity.*

____

9. Douglass *ascribed* Covey's surprisingly pleasant greeting to the power of the root, which is supposed to have this effect. ____________________

10. Like wind blowing on the glowing embers of a campfire, the altercation rekindles the *dying* flames of pride within Douglass. ____________________

A Pair of Silk Stockings

Make the Connection

Escaping the Humdrum

Mrs. Sommers, the main character in "A Pair of Silk Stockings," is a nineteenth-century woman of limited means trying to satisfy the needs of her family. For her, even a brief reprieve from the demands of domesticity could be a life-changing bid for freedom and a temporary escape from day-to-day duties. Because everyone—even those who seem to lead exciting lives—sometimes feels trapped by the sameness of everyday existence, escaping the humdrum is a popular theme among writers. Using the chart below, choose a character from a favorite book, film, or television program, and explore how he or she escaped the drudgery of everyday life.

Title of Work
Characters
Problem (What makes his or her life humdrum)
How he or she tries to escape the humdrum ____________________ ____________________ ____________________ ____________________ ____________________ ____________________ ____________________
Outcome

A Pair of Silk Stockings

Kate Chopin

'ORDS TO OWN

dicious (jo͞o·dish'əs) *adj.:* utious; wise.

ppreciable (ə·prē'shə·bəl) *dj.:* measurable.

eritable (ver'i·tə·bəl) *adj.:* enuine; true.

EVALUATE

'hat kind of mother is rs. Sommers?

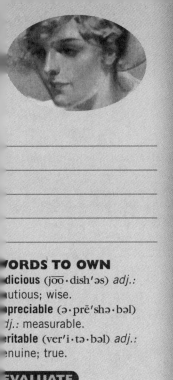

Little Mrs. Sommers one day found herself the unexpected possessor of fifteen dollars. It seemed to her a very large amount of money, and the way in which it stuffed and bulged her worn old *porte-monnaie*[1] gave her a feeling of importance such as she had not enjoyed for years.

The question of investment was one that occupied her greatly. For a day or two she walked about apparently in a dreamy state, but really absorbed in speculation and calculation. She did not wish to act hastily, to do anything she might afterward regret. But it was during the still hours of the night when she lay awake revolving plans in her mind that she seemed to see her way clearly toward a proper and judicious use of the money.

A dollar or two should be added to the price usually paid for Janie's shoes, which would ensure their lasting an appreciable time longer than they usually did. She would buy so-and-so many yards of percale[2] for new shirtwaists for the boys and Janie and Mag. She had intended to make the old ones do by skillful patching. Mag should have another gown. She had seen some beautiful patterns, veritable bargains in the shop windows. And still there would be left enough for new stockings—two pairs apiece—and what darning that would save for a while! She would get caps for the boys and sailor hats for the girls. The vision of her little brood looking fresh and dainty and new for once in their lives excited her and made her restless and wakeful with anticipation.

The neighbors sometimes talked of certain "better days" that little Mrs. Sommers had known before she had ever thought of being Mrs. Sommers. She herself indulged in no such morbid retrospection.[3] She had no time—no second of time to devote to the past. The needs of the present absorbed her every faculty. A vision of the future like some dim, gaunt monster sometimes appalled her, but luckily tomorrow never comes.

Mrs. Sommers was one who knew the value of bargains; who could stand for hours making her way inch by inch toward the desired object that was selling below cost. She could elbow her way if need be; she had learned to clutch a piece of goods and hold it and stick to it with persistence and determination till her turn came to be served, no matter when it came.

But that day she was a little faint and tired. She had swallowed a light luncheon—no! when she came to think of it, between getting the children fed and the place righted, and preparing herself for the shopping bout, she had actually forgotten to eat any luncheon at all!

She sat herself upon a revolving stool before a counter that was comparatively deserted, trying to gather strength and courage to charge

1. ***porte-monnaie*** (pôrt·mô·nā'): French for "purse."
2. **percale:** finely woven cotton cloth.
3. **morbid retrospection:** brooding on things in the past.

through an eager multitude that was besieging breastworks[4] of shirting and figured lawn. An all-gone limp feeling had come over her and she rested her hand aimlessly upon the counter. She wore no gloves. By degrees she grew aware that her hand had encountered something very soothing, very pleasant to touch. She looked down to see that her hand lay upon a pile of silk stockings. A placard nearby announced that they had been reduced in price from two dollars and fifty cents to one dollar and ninety-eight cents; and a young girl who stood behind the counter asked her if she wished to examine their line of silk hosiery. She smiled, just as if she had been asked to inspect a tiara of diamonds with the ultimate view of purchasing it. But she went on feeling the soft, sheeny luxurious things—with both hands now, holding them up to see them glisten, and to feel them glide serpentlike through her fingers.

Two hectic blotches came suddenly into her pale cheeks. She looked up at the girl.

"Do you think there are any eights-and-a-half among these?"

There were any number of eights-and-a-half. In fact, there were more of that size than any other. Here was a light blue pair; there were some lavender, some all black, and various shades of tan and gray. Mrs. Sommers selected a black pair and looked at them very long and closely. She pretended to be examining their texture, which the clerk assured her was excellent.

"A dollar and ninety-eight cents," she mused aloud. "Well, I'll take this pair." She handed the girl a five-dollar bill and waited for her change and for her parcel. What a very small parcel it was! It seemed lost in the depths of her shabby old shopping bag.

Mrs. Sommers after that did not move in the direction of the bargain counter. She took the elevator, which carried her to an upper floor into the region of the ladies' waiting rooms. Here, in a retired corner, she exchanged her cotton stockings for the new silk ones which she had just bought. She was not going through any acute mental process or reasoning with herself, nor was she striving to explain to her satisfaction the motive of her action. She was not thinking at all. She seemed for the time to be taking a rest from that laborious and fatiguing function and to have abandoned herself to some mechanical impulse that directed her actions and freed her of responsibility.

How good was the touch of the raw silk to her flesh! She felt like lying back in the cushioned chair and reveling for a while in the luxury of it. She did for a little while. Then she replaced her shoes, rolled the cotton stockings together, and thrust them into her bag. After doing this she crossed straight over to the shoe department and took her seat to be fitted.

4. **breastworks:** low walls put up as barricades. The bolts of shirting material and fine patterned cotton, or "figured lawn," are compared to barricades being stormed by shoppers.

IDENTIFY

Circle the sensory words and images in lines 50–54.

WORDS TO OWN

acute (ə·kyo͞ot′) *adj.:* keen; sharp.
laborious (lə·bôr′ē·əs) *adj.:* difficult; involving much hard work.
reveling (rev′əl·iŋ) *v.:* taking pleasure.

BUILD FLUENCY

The pace of the story picks up notably in lines 68–83 as Mrs. Sommers gets swept up in the act of spending money she doesn't normally have. Read the passage aloud, trying to capture this narrative movement in your voice.

'ORDS TO OWN
stidious (fas·tid′ē·əs) *adj.:* fficult to please; critical.

EVALUATE
as your opinion of rs. Sommers changed? 'hy or why not?

'ORDS TO OWN
reposterous (prē·päs′tər·əs) *dj.:* ridiculous.

INFER
'hat do you imagine rs. Sommers's life was nce like?

INFER
'hat might Mrs. Sommers ave been hungry for other ıan food?

She was fastidious. The clerk could not make her out; he could not reconcile her shoes with her stockings, and she was not too easily pleased. She held back her skirts and turned her feet one way and her head another way as she glanced down at the polished, pointed-tipped boots. Her foot and ankle looked very pretty. She could not realize that they belonged to her and were a part of herself. She wanted an excellent and stylish fit, she told the young fellow who served her, and she did not mind the difference of a dollar or two more in the price so long as she got what she desired.

It was a long time since Mrs. Sommers had been fitted with gloves. On rare occasions when she had bought a pair they were always "bargains," so cheap that it would have been preposterous and unreasonable to have expected them to be fitted to the hand.

Now she rested her elbow on the cushion of the glove counter, and a pretty, pleasant young creature, delicate and deft of touch, drew a long-wristed "kid" over Mrs. Sommers's hand. She smoothed it down over the wrist and buttoned it neatly, and both lost themselves for a second or two in admiring contemplation of the little symmetrical gloved hand. But there were other places where money might be spent.

There were books and magazines piled up in the window of a stall a few paces down the street. Mrs. Sommers bought two high-priced magazines such as she had been accustomed to read in the days when she had been accustomed to other pleasant things. She carried them without wrapping. As well as she could she lifted her skirts at the crossings. Her stockings and boots and well-fitting gloves had worked marvels in her bearing—had given her a feeling of assurance, a sense of belonging to the well-dressed multitude.

She was very hungry. Another time she would have stilled the cravings for food until reaching her own home, where she would have brewed herself a cup of tea and taken a snack of anything that was available. But the impulse that was guiding her would not suffer her to entertain any such thought.

There was a restaurant at the corner. She had never entered its doors; from the outside she had sometimes caught glimpses of spotless damask and shining crystal, and soft-stepping waiters serving people of fashion.

When she entered, her appearance created no surprise, no consternation, as she had half feared it might. She seated herself at a small table alone, and an attentive waiter at once approached to take her order. She did not want a profusion; she craved a nice and tasty bite—a half dozen bluepoints,[5] a plump chop with cress, a something sweet—a crème-frappé,[6] for instance; a glass of Rhine wine, and after all a small cup of black coffee.

5. **bluepoints:** small oysters.
6. **crème-frappé** (krem·fra·pā′): dessert similar to ice cream.

While waiting to be served she removed her gloves very leisurely and laid them beside her. Then she picked up a magazine and glanced through it, cutting the pages with a blunt edge of her knife.[7] It was all very agreeable. The damask was even more spotless than it had seemed through the window, and the crystal more sparkling. There were quiet ladies and gentlemen, who did not notice her, lunching at the small tables like her own. A soft, pleasing strain of music could be heard, and a gentle breeze was blowing through the window. She tasted a bite, and she read a word or two, and she sipped the amber wine and wiggled her toes in the silk stockings. The price of it made no difference. She counted the money out to the waiter and left an extra coin on his tray, whereupon he bowed before her as before a princess of royal blood.

There was still money in her purse, and her next temptation presented itself in the shape of a matinée poster.

It was a little later when she entered the theater, the play had begun, and the house seemed to her to be packed. But there were vacant seats here and there, and into one of them she was ushered, between brilliantly dressed women who had gone there to kill time and eat candy and display their gaudy attire. There were many others who were there solely for the play and acting. It is safe to say there was no one present who bore quite the attitude which Mrs. Sommers did to her surroundings. She gathered in the whole—stage and players and people in one wide impression, and absorbed it and enjoyed it. She laughed at the comedy and wept—she and the gaudy woman next to her wept over the tragedy. And they talked a little together over it. And the gaudy woman wiped her eyes and sniffled on a tiny square of filmy, perfumed lace and passed little Mrs. Sommers her box of candy.

The play was over, the music ceased, the crowd filed out. It was like a dream ended. People scattered in all directions. Mrs. Sommers went to the corner and waited for the cable car.

A man with keen eyes, who sat opposite her, seemed to like the study of her small, pale face. It puzzled him to decipher what he saw there. In truth, he saw nothing—unless he were wizard enough to detect a poignant wish, a powerful longing that the cable car would never stop anywhere, but go on and on with her forever.

7. **cutting . . . knife:** At one time, magazines and books were often sold with folded, untrimmed pages. These outer edges had to be cut apart before one could read them.

PREDICT

What do you think Mrs. Sommers will do with the rest of the money?

WORDS TO OWN

gaudy (gôd′ē) *adj.:* showy, but lacking in good taste.

WORDS TO OWN

poignant (poin′yənt) *adj.:* emotionally moving.

EVALUATE

Has the day changed Mrs. Sommers permanently? Explain.

Indirect Characterization

The process by which a writer reveals the personality of a character is called **characterization.** One way to reveal character is **direct characterization,** in which the writer tells the reader directly what a character is like. More often, writers reveal character through **indirect characterization,** in which the reader must exercise judgment and put clues together to infer what a character is like. Indirect characterization is created through the character's appearance, words, thoughts and feelings, actions, and others' reactions.

In the chart below, pick a quotation from "A Pair of Silk Stockings," identify which method of indirect characterization it represents, and describe what it reveals about Mrs. Sommers. More than one method can be represented by a single quotation, but be sure that each method is represented at least once.

Quotation	Method of Indirect Characterization	What It Reveals About Mrs. Sommers
"The clerk could not make her out; he could not reconcile her shoes with her stockings, and she was not too easily pleased." (lines 84–86)	others' reactions	Mrs. Sommers's mixture of worn shoes and elegant stockings puzzles the clerk. By not being "easily pleased," she shows herself to be decisive and a good judge of quality.

Vocabulary: How to Own a Word

Related Meanings

Word Bank
judicious
appreciable
veritable
acute
laborious
reveling
fastidious
preposterous
gaudy
poignant

For each group of words below, cross out the unrelated word. The Words to Own are listed first.

1. **a.** judicious **b.** thoughtful **c.** reasonable **d.** reckless
2. **a.** appreciable **b.** negligible **c.** perceptible **d.** tangible
3. **a.** veritable **b.** authentic **c.** false **d.** actual
4. **a.** acute **b.** astute **c.** excruciating **d.** intuitive
5. **a.** laborious **b.** effortless **c.** onerous **d.** strenuous
6. **a.** reveling **b.** disliking **c.** celebrating **d.** relishing
7. **a.** fastidious **b.** indifferent **c.** demanding **d.** strict
8. **a.** preposterous **b.** bizarre **c.** sensible **d.** outrageous
9. **a.** gaudy **b.** plain **c.** ostentatious **d.** showy
10. **a.** poignant **b.** evocative **c.** affecting **d.** bitter

From Life on the Mississippi

Make the Connection

Losing Its Luster

As a youth, Mark Twain was so fascinated by riverboats that he persuaded Horace Bixby, the locally famous pilot of the *Paul Jones,* to teach him how to navigate the Mississippi River between New Orleans and St. Louis (a distance of about seven hundred miles) for five hundred dollars. Twain was not alone in his dream; every boy along the Mississippi, black or white, yearned to work on a steamboat. It didn't matter whether the job was clerk, engineer, mate, or pilot; life on the river meant adventure—at least, until the realities of the work set in.

Getting something we want isn't always as pleasurable as the anticipation of getting it. A person who wants to be an actor might imagine the glamorous trappings of that profession, but the reality of becoming an actor has more to do with hard work, discipline, and daily repetition than it does with fame. Experience brings its own rewards, but it also breeds familiarity; what once seemed mysterious becomes ordinary.

Think about a goal—a skill or an honor—that you successfully attained. Using the graphic below, examine how striving for that goal and then reaching it changed your outlook on it.

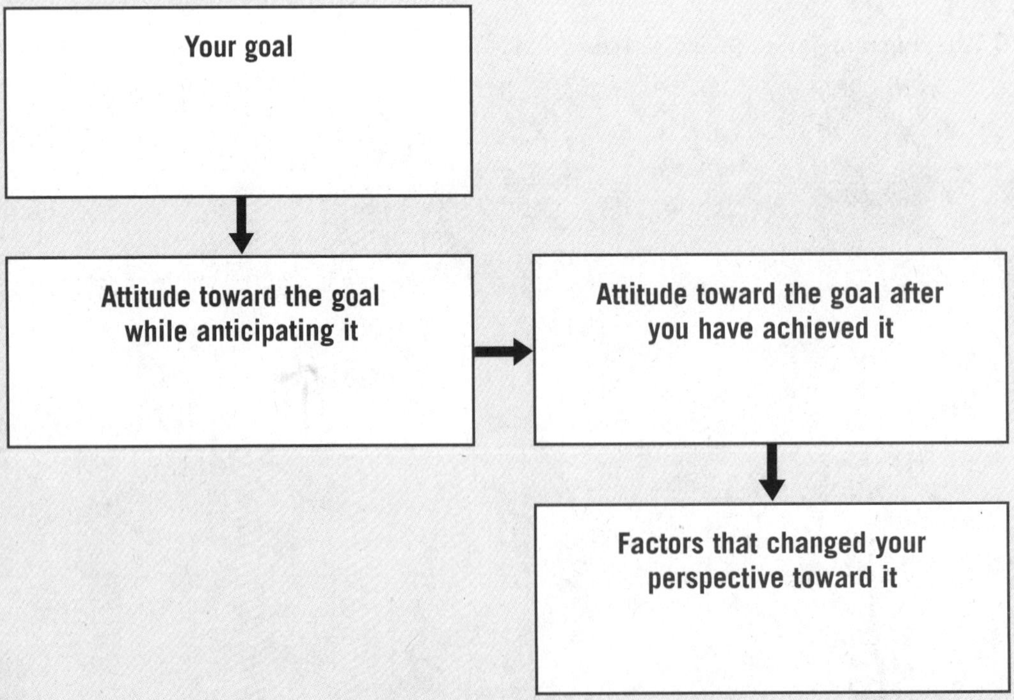

FROM LIFE ON THE MISSISSIPPI

Mark Twain

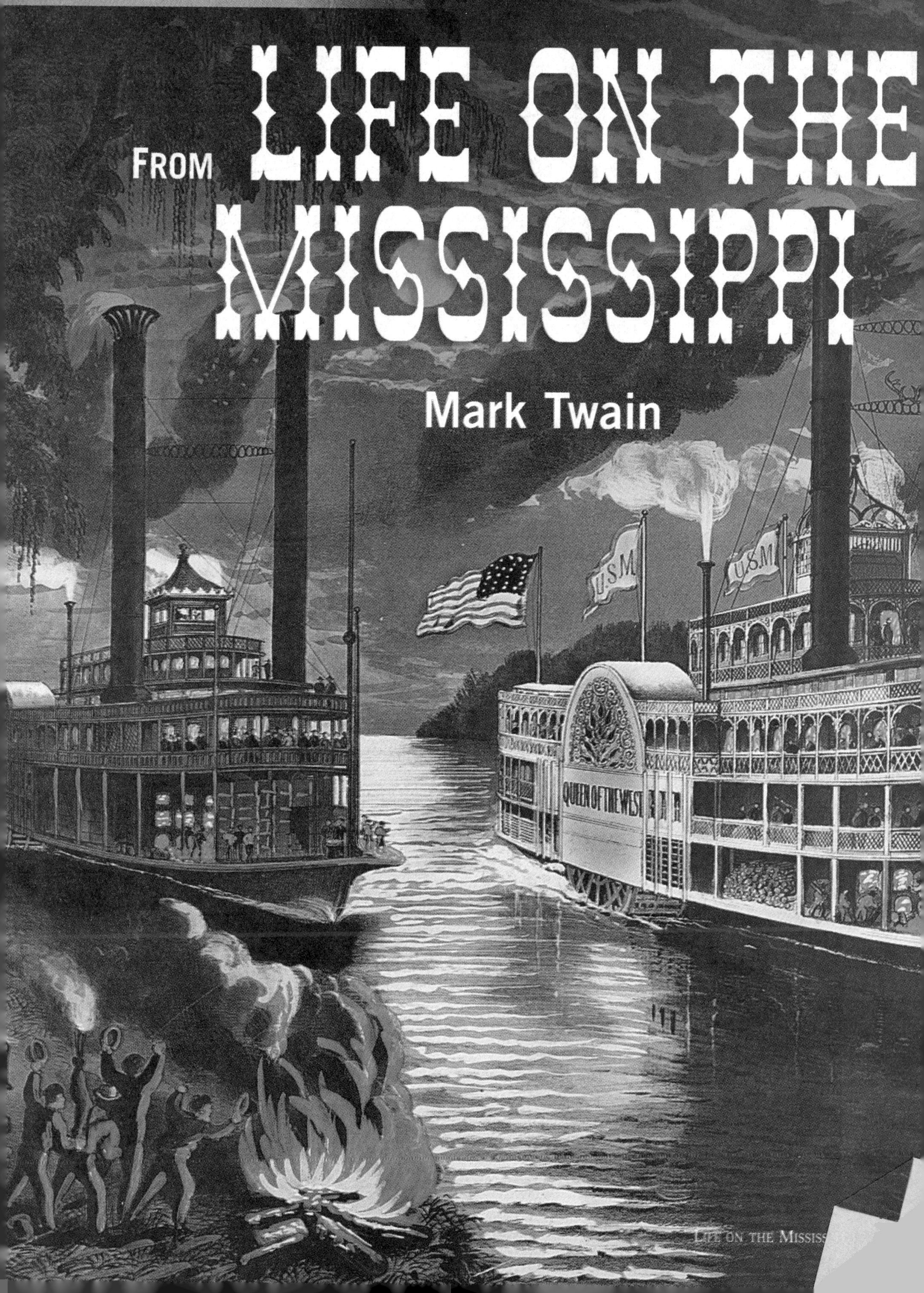

ORDS TO OWN
animate (in·an′ə·mit) *adj.:* eless.
omplacency (kəm·plā′sən·sē) .: self-satisfaction.
ıbside (səb·sīd′) *v.:* to settle own.

DENTIFY
/hat does Twain compare ixby to in lines 15–20?

WORDS TO OWN
nterminable (in·tur′mi·nə·bəl) *adj.:* endless.

Perplexing Lessons

At the end of what seemed a tedious while, I had managed to pack my head full of islands, towns, bars, "points," and bends;[1] and a curiously inanimate mass of lumber it was, too. However, inasmuch as I could shut my eyes and reel off a good long string of these names without leaving out more than ten miles of river in every fifty, I began to feel that I could take a boat down to New Orleans if I could make her skip those little gaps. But of course my complacency could hardly get start enough to lift my nose a trifle into the air, before Mr. Bixby would think of something to fetch it down again. One day he turned on me suddenly with this settler[2]—

"What is the shape of Walnut Bend?"

He might as well have asked me my grandmother's opinion of protoplasm.[3] I reflected respectfully, and then said I didn't know it had any particular shape. My gunpowdery chief went off with a bang, of course, and then went on loading and firing until he was out of adjectives.

I had learned long ago that he only carried just so many rounds of ammunition, and was sure to subside into a very placable and even remorseful old smoothbore[4] as soon as they were all gone. That word "old" is merely affectionate; he was not more than thirty-four. I waited. By and by he said—

"My boy, you've got to know the *shape* of the river perfectly. It is all there is left to steer by on a very dark night. Everything else is blotted out and gone. But mind you, it hasn't the same shape in the night that it has in the daytime."

"How on earth am I ever going to learn it, then?"

"How do you follow a hall at home in the dark? Because you know the shape of it. You can't see it."

"Do you mean to say that I've got to know all the million trifling variations of shape in the banks of this interminable river as well as I know the shape of the front hall at home?"

"On my honor, you've got to know them *better* than any man ever did know the shapes of the halls in his own house."

"I wish I was dead!"

"Now I don't want to discourage you, but"—

"Well, pile it on me; I might as well have it now as another time."

1. **islands . . . bends:** geographic features used in river navigation. Each numbered point was a landmark on a curve or bend in the river.
2. **settler:** colloquial for "something [such as Bixby's question] that does a person in."
3. **protoplasm:** living matter basic to all plant and animal cells.
4. **smoothbore:** gun with no grooves inside its barrel.

"You see, this has got to be learned; there isn't any getting around it. A clear starlight night throws such heavy shadows that if you didn't know the shape of a shore perfectly you would claw away from every bunch of timber, because you would take the black shadow of it for a solid cape;[5] and you see you would be getting scared to death every fifteen minutes by the watch.[6] You would be fifty yards from shore all the time when you ought to be within fifty feet of it. You can't see a snag[7] in one of those shadows, but you know exactly where it is, and the shape of the river tells you when you are coming to it. Then there's your pitch-dark night; the river is a very different shape on a pitch-dark night from what it is on a starlight night. All shores seem to be straight lines, then, and mighty dim ones, too; and you'd *run* them for straight lines only you know better. You boldly drive your boat right into what seems to be a solid, straight wall (you knowing very well that in reality there is a curve there), and that wall falls back and makes way for you. Then there's your gray mist. You take a night when there's one of these grisly, drizzly, gray mists, and then there isn't *any* particular shape to a shore. A gray mist would tangle the head of the oldest man that ever lived. Well, then, different kinds of *moonlight* change the shape of the river in different ways. You see"—

"Oh, don't say anymore, please! Have I got to learn the shape of the river according to all these five hundred thousand different ways? If I tried to carry all that cargo in my head it would make me stoop-shouldered."

"*No!* you only learn *the* shape of the river; and you learn it with such absolute certainty that you can always steer by the shape that's *in your head,* and never mind the one that's before your eyes."

"Very well, I'll try it; but after I have learned it can I depend on it? Will it keep the same form and not go fooling around?"

Before Mr. Bixby could answer, Mr. W—— came in to take the watch, and he said—

"Bixby, you'll have to look out for President's Island and all that country clear away up above the Old Hen and Chickens. The banks are caving and the shape of the shores changing like everything. Why, you wouldn't know the point above 40.[8] You can go up inside the old sycamore snag,[9] now."

So that question was answered. Here were leagues[10] of shore changing shape. My spirits were down in the mud again. Two things

5. **cape:** land projecting into water.
6. **by the watch:** The workday on a steamboat was divided into three four-hour periods, or watches, every twelve hours: two watches for work and one off-watch for rest.
7. **snag:** tree trunk dangerous to navigation because it is partly or completely underwater.
8. **point above 40:** numbered navigational point on the river beyond the landmark numbered 40.
9. **inside . . . snag:** It may not be necessary but still can do no harm to explain that "inside" means between the snag and the shore. [Twain's note]
10. **leagues:** One league equals about 3 miles.

IDENTIFY

How does the shoreline "change" on the three different types of nights? Underline the answers.

RETELL

In lines 61–63, what does Bixby mean?

INFER

What do lines 64–65 reveal about young Twain's personality?

WORDS TO OWN

serenely (sə·rēn′lē) *adv.:* calmly.

INFER

What do the clichés "the salt of the earth" (line 108) and "lord it over" (line 109) mean? Use context clues to help you answer.

seemed pretty apparent to me. One was, that in order to be a pilot a man had got to learn more than any one man ought to be allowed to know; and the other was, that he must learn it all over again in a different way every twenty-four hours.

That night we had the watch until twelve. Now it was an ancient river custom for the two pilots to chat a bit when the watch changed. While the relieving pilot put on his gloves and lit his cigar, his partner, the retiring pilot, would say something like this—

"I judge the upper bar is making down a little at Hale's Point; had quarter twain with the lower lead and mark twain[11] with the other."

"Yes, I thought it was making down a little, last trip. Meet any boats?"

"Met one abreast the head of 21,[12] but she was away over hugging the bar, and I couldn't make her out entirely. I took her for the 'Sunny South'—hadn't any skylights forward of the chimneys."

And so on. And as the relieving pilot took the wheel his partner[13] would mention that we were in such and such a bend, and say we were abreast of such and such a man's woodyard or plantation. This was courtesy; I supposed it was *necessity*. But Mr. W—— came on watch full twelve minutes late on this particular night—a tremendous breach of etiquette; in fact, it is the unpardonable sin among pilots. So Mr. Bixby gave him no greeting whatever, but simply surrendered the wheel and marched out of the pilothouse without a word. I was appalled; it was a villainous night for blackness, we were in a particularly wide and blind part of the river, where there was no shape or substance to anything, and it seemed incredible that Mr. Bixby should have left that poor fellow to kill the boat trying to find out where he was. But I resolved that I would stand by him anyway. He should find that he was not wholly friendless. So I stood around, and waited to be asked where we were. But Mr. W—— plunged on serenely through the solid firmament of black cats that stood for an atmosphere, and never opened his mouth. Here is a proud devil, thought I; here is a limb of Satan that would rather send us all to destruction than put himself under obligations to me, because I am not yet one of the salt of the earth and privileged to snub captains and lord it over everything dead and alive in a steamboat. I presently climbed up on the bench; I did not think it was safe to go to sleep while this lunatic was on watch.

However, I must have gone to sleep in the course of time, because the next thing I was aware of was the fact that day was breaking,

---

11. **quarter . . . mark twain:** Two fathoms. Quarter twain is $2\frac{1}{4}$ fathoms, [or] $13\frac{1}{2}$ feet. Mark three is three fathoms. [Twain's note] These measures of water depth are calculated by using a lead weight attached to a rope. One fathom, or "mark one," equals 6 feet. Two fathoms, or "mark twain," equals 12 feet.
12. **abreast . . . 21:** beside landmark, or point, 21.
13. **partner:** "Partner" is technical for "the other pilot." [Twain's note]

Mr. W—— gone, and Mr. Bixby at the wheel again. So it was four o'clock and all well—but me; I felt like a skinful of dry bones and all of them trying to ache at once.

Mr. Bixby asked me what I had stayed up there for. I confessed that it was to do Mr. W—— a benevolence—tell him where he was. It took five minutes for the entire preposterousness of the thing to filter into Mr. Bixby's system, and then I judge it filled him nearly up to the chin; because he paid me a compliment—and not much of a one either. He said—

"Well, taking you by and large, you do seem to be more different kinds of an ass than any creature I ever saw before. What did you suppose he wanted to know for?"

I said I thought it might be a convenience to him.

"Convenience! D-nation! Didn't I tell you that a man's got to know the river in the night the same as he'd know his own front hall?"

"Well, I can follow the front hall in the dark if I know it *is* the front hall; but suppose you set me down in the middle of it in the dark and not tell me which hall it is; how am *I* to know?"

"Well, you've *got* to, on the river!"

"All right. Then I'm glad I never said anything to Mr. W——"

"I should say so. Why, he'd have slammed you through the window and utterly ruined a hundred dollars' worth of window sash[14] and stuff."

I was glad this damage had been saved, for it would have made me unpopular with the owners. They always hated anybody who had the name of being careless, and injuring things.

I went to work now to learn the shape of the river; and of all the eluding and ungraspable objects that ever I tried to get mind or hands on, that was the chief. I would fasten my eyes upon a sharp, wooded point that projected far into the river some miles ahead of me, and go to laboriously photographing its shape upon my brain; and just as I was beginning to succeed to my satisfaction, we would draw up toward it and the exasperating thing would begin to melt away and fold back into the bank! If there had been a conspicuous dead tree standing upon the very point of the cape, I would find that tree inconspicuously merged into the general forest, and occupying the middle of a straight shore, when I got abreast of it! No prominent hill would stick to its shape long enough for me to make up my mind what its form really was, but it was as dissolving and changeful as if it had been a mountain of butter in the hottest corner of the tropics. Nothing ever had the same shape when I was coming downstream that it had borne when I went up. I mentioned these little difficulties to Mr. Bixby. He said—

"That's the very main virtue of the thing. If the shapes didn't change every three seconds they wouldn't be of any use. Take this place where

14. **window sash:** frame that holds window glass.

WORDS TO OWN

benevolence (bə·nev′ə·ləns) *n.:* kindness.

INTERPRET

What is the **irony** in Bixby's statement in lines 134–135?

BUILD FLUENCY

As narrator, Twain uses somewhat elevated diction, whereas Bixby uses slang. Read lines 139–166 aloud, trying to capture the vocal differences between both modes of speech.

EVALUATE

ines 157–187 contain a umber of nautical terms, uch as *larboard, keelson,* and *hoal soundings.* What effect o they have on the **tone** of the arrative?

we are now, for instance. As long as that hill over yonder is only one hill, I can boom right along the way I'm going; but the moment it splits at the top and forms a V, I know I've got to scratch to starboard[15] in a hurry, or I'll bang this boat's brains out against a rock; and then the moment one of the prongs of the V swings behind the other, I've got to waltz to larboard[16] again, or I'll have a misunderstanding with a snag that would snatch the keelson[17] out of this steamboat as neatly as if it were a sliver in your hand. If that hill didn't change its shape on bad nights there would be an awful steamboat graveyard around here inside of a year."

It was plain that I had got to learn the shape of the river in all the different ways that could be thought of—upside down, wrong end first, inside out, fore-and-aft, and "thort-ships"[18]—and then know what to do on gray nights when it hadn't any shape at all. So I set about it. In the course of time I began to get the best of this knotty lesson, and my self-complacency moved to the front once more. Mr. Bixby was all fixed, and ready to start it to the rear again. He opened on me after this fashion—

"How much water did we have in the middle crossing at Hole-in-the-Wall, trip before last?"

I considered this an outrage. I said—

"Every trip, down and up, the leadsmen[19] are singing through that tangled place for three quarters of an hour on a stretch. How do you reckon I can remember such a mess as that?"

"My boy, you've got to remember it. You've got to remember the exact spot and the exact marks the boat lay in when we had the shoalest[20] water, in every one of the five hundred shoal places between St. Louis and New Orleans; and you mustn't get the shoal soundings and marks[21] of one trip mixed up with the shoal soundings and marks of another, either, for they're not often twice alike. You must keep them separate."

When I came to myself again, I said—

"When I get so that I can do that, I'll be able to raise the dead, and then I won't have to pilot a steamboat to make a living. I want to retire from this business. I want a slush-bucket and a brush; I'm only fit for a roustabout.[22] I haven't got brains enough to be a pilot; and if I had I

---

15. **scratch to starboard:** move quickly to the right side of the boat.
16. **larboard:** the left side of the boat.
17. **keelson:** wood or metal beams fastened along a boat's keel to strengthen it. The keel is the timber along the boat's bottom that supports the frame.
18. **fore-and-aft, and "thort-ships":** end to end and shore to shore.
19. **leadsmen:** workers who use a lead line to measure the water's depth.
20. **shoalest:** most shallow.
21. **soundings and marks:** measurements of water depth.
22. **roustabout:** deckhand; laborer on a boat.

wouldn't have strength enough to carry them around, unless I went on crutches."

"Now drop that! When I say I'll learn[23] a man the river, I mean it. And you can depend on it, I'll learn him or kill him."

Continued Perplexities

There was no use in arguing with a person like this. I promptly put such a strain on my memory that by and by even the shoal water and the countless crossing marks[24] began to stay with me. But the result was just the same. I never could more than get one knotty thing learned before another presented itself. Now I had often seen pilots gazing at the water and pretending to read it as if it were a book; but it was a book that told me nothing. A time came at last, however, when Mr. Bixby seemed to think me far enough advanced to bear a lesson on water-reading. So he began—

"Do you see that long slanting line on the face of the water? Now, that's a reef. Moreover, it's a bluff reef.[25] There is a solid sandbar under it that is nearly as straight up and down as the side of a house. There is plenty of water close up to it, but mighty little on top of it. If you were to hit it you would knock the boat's brains out. Do you see where the line fringes out at the upper end and begins to fade away?"

"Yes, sir."

"Well, that is a low place; that is the head of the reef. You can climb over there, and not hurt anything. Cross over, now, and follow along close under the reef—easy water there—not much current."

I followed the reef along till I approached the fringed end. Then Mr. Bixby said—

"Now get ready. Wait till I give the word. She won't want to mount the reef: a boat hates shoal water. Stand by—wait—*wait*—keep her well in hand. *Now* cramp her down![26] Snatch her![27] Snatch her!"

He seized the other side of the wheel and helped to spin it around until it was hard down, and then we held it so. The boat resisted, and refused to answer for a while, and next she came surging to starboard, mounted the reef, and sent a long, angry ridge of water foaming away from her bows.[28]

"Now watch her; watch her like a cat, or she'll get away from you. When she fights strong and the tiller slips a little, in a jerky, greasy sort of way, let up on her a trifle; it is the way she tells you at night that the water is too shoal; but keep edging her up, little by little, toward the

---

23. learn: "Teach" is not in the river vocabulary. [Twain's note]
24. crossing marks: points on the river where a boat could cross safely.
25. bluff reef: hidden sandbar with a high, steep front. Its position is indicated by lines or ripples on the water.
26. cramp her down: turn the wheel sharply.
27. Snatch her: Act quickly.
28. bows: front part of a boat.

IDENTIFY
Underline each word or phrase that makes up the **extended metaphor** of lines 202–205.

INTERPRET
Ships are traditionally referred to as female, as Bixby does here. Why do you think this is so?

point. You are well up on the bar, now; there is a bar under every point, because the water that comes down around it forms an eddy and allows the sediment to sink. Do you see those fine lines on the face of the water that branch out like the ribs of a fan? Well, those are little reefs; you want to just miss the ends of them, but run them pretty close. Now look out—look out! Don't you crowd that slick, greasy-looking place; there ain't nine feet there; she won't stand it. She begins to smell it; look sharp, I tell you! Oh blazes, there you go! Stop the starboard wheel! Quick! Ship up to back! Set her back!"[29]

The engine bells jingled and the engines answered promptly, shooting white columns of steam far aloft out of the 'scape pipes, but it was too late. The boat had "smelt"[30] the bar in good earnest; the foamy ridges that radiated from her bows suddenly disappeared, a great dead swell[31] came rolling forward and swept ahead of her, she careened far over to larboard, and went tearing away toward the other shore as if she were about scared to death. We were a good mile from where we ought to have been, when we finally got the upper hand of her again.

During the afternoon watch the next day, Mr. Bixby asked me if I knew how to run the next few miles. I said—

"Go inside the first snag above the point, outside the next one, start out from the lower end of Higgins's woodyard, make a square crossing[32] and"—

"That's all right. I'll be back before you close up on the next point."

But he wasn't. He was still below when I rounded it and entered upon a piece of river which I had some misgivings about. I did not know that he was hiding behind a chimney to see how I would perform. I went gaily along, getting prouder and prouder, for he had never left the boat in my sole charge such a length of time before. I even got to "setting" her and letting the wheel go, entirely, while I vaingloriously turned my back and inspected the stern marks[33] and hummed a tune, a sort of easy indifference which I had prodigiously admired in Bixby and other great pilots. Once I inspected rather long, and when I faced to the front again my heart flew into my mouth so suddenly that if I hadn't clapped my teeth together I should have lost it. One of those frightful bluff reefs was stretching its deadly length right across our bows! My head was gone in a moment; I did not know which end I stood on; I gasped and could not get my breath; I spun the wheel down with such rapidity that it wove itself together like a spider's web; the boat answered and turned square away from the reef, but the reef followed her! I fled, and still it followed still it kept—right across my bows! I never looked to see where I was

EVALUATE

low does the **personification** f the boat in lines 240–247 hange your opinion of the kill young Twain is learning?

WORDS TO OWN

misgivings (mis'giv'iŋz) *n. pl.:* doubts; worries.

IDENTIFY

Circle the verbs that help to heighten tension in lines 265–272.

29. **Ship . . . back:** Put it in reverse.
30. **smelt:** dialect for "smelled." That is, the boat recognized water too shallow for safety.
31. **great dead swell:** huge wave.
32. **make a square crossing:** go directly between crossing marks.
33. **stern marks:** landmarks already passed and thus astern of, or behind, the boat.

going, I only fled. The awful crash was imminent—why didn't that villain come! If I committed the crime of ringing a bell, I might get thrown overboard. But better that than kill the boat. So in blind desperation I started such a rattling "shivaree"[34] down below as never had astounded an engineer in this world before, I fancy. Amidst the frenzy of the bells the engines began to back and fill in a furious way, and my reason forsook its throne—we were about to crash into the woods on the other side of the river. Just then Mr. Bixby stepped calmly into view on the hurricane deck.[35] My soul went out to him in gratitude. My distress vanished; I would have felt safe on the brink of Niagara, with Mr. Bixby on the hurricane deck. He blandly and sweetly took his toothpick out of his mouth between his fingers, as if it were a cigar—we were just in the act of climbing an overhanging big tree, and the passengers were scudding astern[36] like rats—and lifted up these commands to me ever so gently—

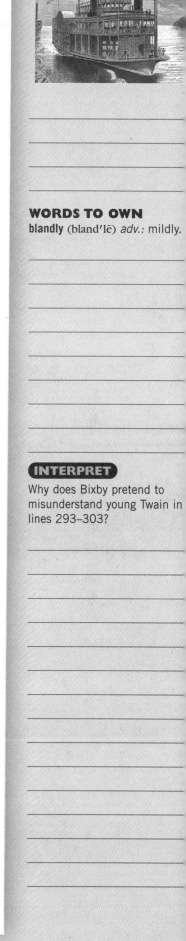

"Stop the starboard. Stop the larboard. Set her back on both."[37]

The boat hesitated, halted, pressed her nose among the boughs a critical instant, then reluctantly began to back away.

"Stop the larboard. Come ahead on it. Stop the starboard. Come ahead on it. Point her for the bar."

I sailed away as serenely as a summer's morning. Mr. Bixby came in and said, with mock simplicity—

"When you have a hail,[38] my boy, you ought to tap the big bell three times before you land, so that the engineers can get ready."

I blushed under the sarcasm, and said I hadn't had any hail.

"Ah! Then it was for wood, I suppose. The officer of the watch will tell you when he wants to wood up."

I went on consuming, and said I wasn't after wood.

"Indeed? Why, what could you want over here in the bend, then? Did you ever know of a boat following a bend upstream at this stage of the river?"

"No, sir—and *I* wasn't trying to follow it. I was getting away from a bluff reef."

"No, it wasn't a bluff reef; there isn't one within three miles of where you were."

"But I saw it. It was as bluff as that one yonder."

"Just about. Run over it!"

"Do you give it as an order?"

"Yes. Run over it."

---

34. "shivaree" (shiv'ə·rē'): noisy celebration.
35. hurricane deck: topmost deck of a steamboat.
36. scudding astern: running to the back of the boat.
37. Stop . . . both: Halt the forward motion of the boat by stopping both the right and left paddle wheels, and put both wheels in reverse.
38. hail: call to land.

WORDS TO OWN
blandly (bland'lē) *adv.:* mildly.

INTERPRET
Why does Bixby pretend to misunderstand young Twain in lines 293–303?

INFER

Why does Twain say that he was now "anxious to kill the boat"?

WORDS TO OWN

void (void) *adj.:* empty.

INFER

What had sapped the grace, beauty, and poetry from the river for Twain?

"If I don't, I wish I may die."

"All right; I am taking the responsibility."

I was just as anxious to kill the boat, now, as I had been to save her before. I impressed my orders upon my memory, to be used at the inquest,[39] and made a straight break for the reef. As it disappeared under our bows I held my breath; but we slid over it like oil.

"Now don't you see the difference? It wasn't anything but a *wind* reef. The wind does that."

"So I see. But it is exactly like a bluff reef. How am I ever going to tell them apart?"

"I can't tell you. It is an instinct. By and by you will just naturally *know* one from the other, but you never will be able to explain why or how you know them apart."

It turned out to be true. The face of the water, in time, became a wonderful book—a book that was a dead language to the uneducated passenger, but which told its mind to me without reserve, delivering its most cherished secrets as clearly as if it uttered them with a voice. And it was not a book to be read once and thrown aside, for it had a new story to tell every day. Throughout the long twelve hundred miles there was never a page that was void of interest, never one that you could leave unread without loss, never one that you would want to skip, thinking you could find higher enjoyment in some other thing. There never was so wonderful a book written by man; never one whose interest was so absorbing, so unflagging, so sparklingly renewed with every reperusal. The passenger who could not read it was charmed with a peculiar sort of faint dimple on its surface (on the rare occasions when he did not overlook it altogether); but to the pilot that was an *italicized* passage; indeed, it was more than that, it was a legend[40] of the largest capitals, with a string of shouting exclamation points at the end of it; for it meant that a wreck or a rock was buried there that could tear the life out of the strongest vessel that ever floated. It is the faintest and simplest expression the water ever makes, and the most hideous to a pilot's eye. In truth, the passenger who could not read this book saw nothing but all manner of pretty pictures in it, painted by the sun and shaded by the clouds, whereas to the trained eye these were not pictures at all, but the grimmest and most dead earnest of reading matter.

Now when I had mastered the language of this water and had come to know every trifling feature that bordered the great river as familiarly as I knew the letters of the alphabet, I had made a valuable acquisition. But I had lost something, too. I had lost something which could never be restored to me while I lived. All the grace, the beauty, the poetry had gone out of the majestic river! I still keep in mind a certain wonderful

39. **inquest:** inquiry by a jury or panel investigating a crime.
40. **legend:** inscription.

sunset which I witnessed when steamboating was new to me. A broad expanse of the river was turned to blood; in the middle distance the red hue brightened into gold, through which a solitary log came floating, black and conspicuous; in one place a long, slanting mark lay sparkling upon the water; in another the surface was broken by boiling, tumbling rings, that were as many-tinted as an opal; where the ruddy flush was faintest, was a smooth spot that was covered with graceful circles and radiating lines, ever so delicately traced; the shore on our left was densely wooded, and the somber shadow that fell from this forest was broken in one place by a long, ruffled trail that shone like silver; and high above the forest wall a clean-stemmed dead tree waved a single leafy bough that glowed like a flame in the unobstructed splendor that was flowing from the sun. There were graceful curves, reflected images, woody heights, soft distances; and over the whole scene, far and near, the dissolving lights drifted steadily, enriching it, every passing moment, with new marvels of coloring.

I stood like one bewitched. I drank it in, in a speechless rapture. The world was new to me, and I had never seen anything like this at home. But as I have said, a day came when I began to cease from noting the glories and the charms which the moon and the sun and the twilight wrought upon the river's face; another day came when I ceased altogether to note them. Then, if that sunset scene had been repeated, I should have looked upon it without rapture, and should have commented upon it, inwardly, after this fashion: This sun means that we are going to have wind tomorrow; that floating log means that the river is rising, small thanks to it; that slanting mark on the water refers to a bluff reef which is going to kill somebody's steamboat one of these nights, if it keeps on stretching out like that; those tumbling "boils" show a dissolving bar and a changing channel there; the lines and circles in the slick water over yonder are a warning that that troublesome place is shoaling up dangerously; that silver streak in the shadow of the forest is the "break" from a new snag,[41] and he has located himself in the very best place he could have found to fish for steamboats; that tall dead tree, with a single living branch, is not going to last long, and then how is a body ever going to get through this blind place at night without the friendly old landmark?

No, the romance and the beauty were all gone from the river. All the value any feature of it had for me now was the amount of usefulness it could furnish toward compassing the safe piloting of a steamboat. Since those days, I have pitied doctors from my heart. What does the lovely flush in a beauty's cheek mean to a doctor but a "break" that ripples above some deadly disease? Are not all her visible charms sown thick with what are to him the signs and symbols of hidden decay? Does he

41. **"break" . . . snag:** ripple or line in the water indicating a newly fallen tree.

WORDS TO OWN

somber (säm′bər) *adj.:* gloomy; dark.

COMPARE AND CONTRAST

Compare the Twain you met at the beginning of this selection with the Twain you meet in lines 388–398. Use descriptive adjectives to mark the difference between "before" and "after."

ever see her beauty at all, or doesn't he simply view her professionally, and comment upon her unwholesome condition all to himself? And doesn't he sometimes wonder whether he has gained most or lost most by learning his trade?

Extended Metaphor

An **extended metaphor** is a **figure of speech** that draws a comparison between two seemingly unlike things and then, often over the course of several sentences of prose or lines of poetry, extends the comparison as far as the writer wants to take it.

Much of Twain's humor comes from the surprise of two very unlike things joined to create an extended—and often hilarious—metaphor. However, he doesn't always use extended metaphor comically. For example, the most prominent extended metaphor in this selection is his comparison between the surface of the water and a book.

In the T-chart below, list characteristics of the water surface that Twain states directly or suggests in his descriptions. For each characteristic, write in the next column the corresponding characteristic to be found in a book.

Water Surface	Book
marks on surface must be interpreted by boat's pilot to understand best way to guide the boat	marks on page must be interpreted by reader to understand the story or idea the writer is trying to convey

Comic Devices

Humor is hard to explain, but we do know that certain comic devices are used in humorous writings; and when they are used by a genius like Twain, they make us laugh.

- **Hyperbole:** outrageous exaggeration made for effect: ". . . when I faced to the front again my heart flew into my mouth so suddenly that if I hadn't clapped my teeth together I should have lost it" (lines 262–264).
- **Comic metaphors:** comparisons between two unlike things that create colorful, hilarious images. Twain's metaphors often involve **incongruity**—two seemingly mismatched or even opposite images, events, or elements are unexpectedly joined: "My gunpowdery chief went off with a bang . . . and then went on loading and firing until he was out of adjectives" (lines 15–17). Many of Twain's funniest comparisons are **extended metaphors.**
- **Understatement:** saying less than what is meant, usually for ironic purposes: "I was glad this damage had been saved, for it would have made me unpopular with the owners" (lines 136–137).

Review the excerpt and locate at least one more example of each of the three comic devices listed below.

Hyperbole	
Comic metaphor	
Understatement	

Vocabulary: How to Own a Word

Word Maps

Word Bank
inanimate
complacency
subside
interminable
serenely
benevolence
misgivings
blandly
void
somber

Using your own paper, complete a word map for each of the Words to Own. Each word map should include a synonym, an antonym, and a dictionary definition of the word, as well as the word's connotation (positive, negative, or neutral) and a sentence that uses the word correctly and reflects its connotation. If the word has no antonym, write *none*. A sample map has been partially completed below as an example.

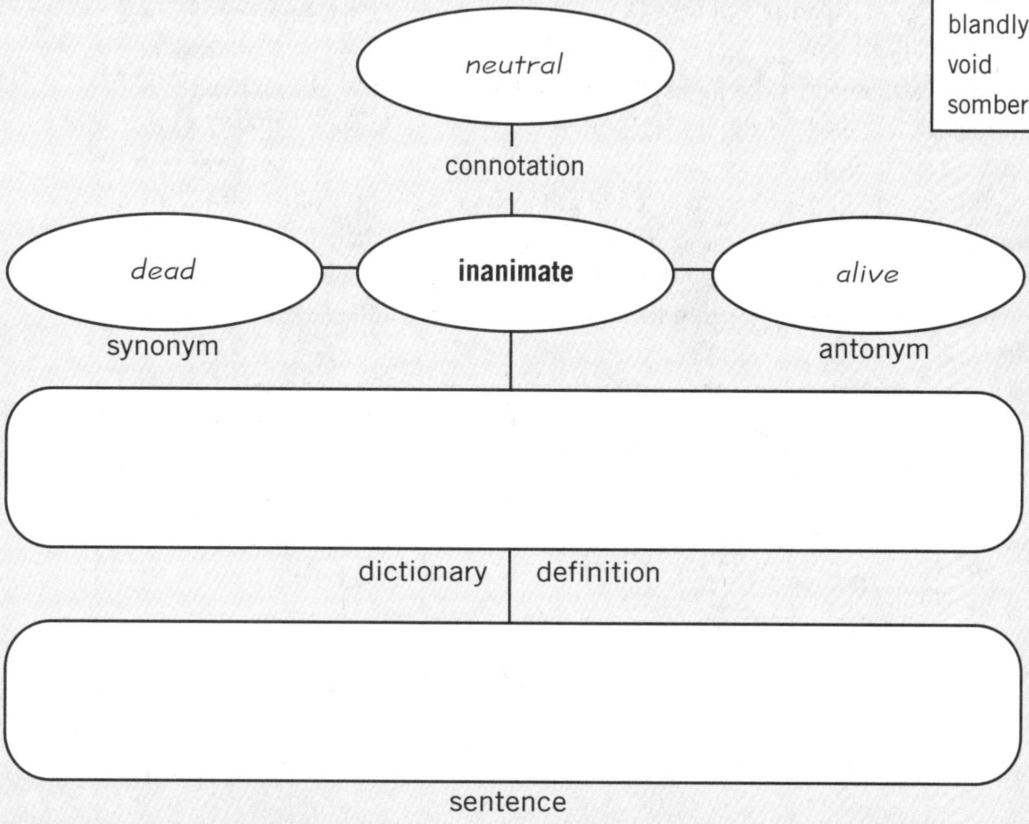

A Mystery of Heroism

Make the Connection

The Hero and the Coward

The Red Badge of Courage, our greatest novel of the American Civil War, is packed both with realistic details of the battlefield and penetrating insight into the minds of men at war. Yet the author, Stephen Crane, wasn't even born until six years after the war ended. But throughout his youth he immersed himself in accounts of the war that was still, in the 1870s and '80s, a national obsession. "I have never been in a battle, of course," he wrote later, "and I believe that I got my sense of the rage of conflict on the football field. The psychology is the same. The opposing team is an enemy tribe."

Instead of glorifying heroism and bravery in the manner of traditional war stories, *The Red Badge of Courage* and the story that follows, "A Mystery of Heroism," vividly depict war's brutality, horror, and confusion. Crane was especially interested in the psychology of heroism—what really causes soldiers in battle to be brave or not, and how reasons that might seem quite trivial and accidental can make one a coward or a hero.

What motivations (pride, concern for others, and so on) do you associate with acts of heroism? Which ones do you associate with cowardice? List them in two columns. Circle any motivations that occur in both columns.

Heroism	Cowardice

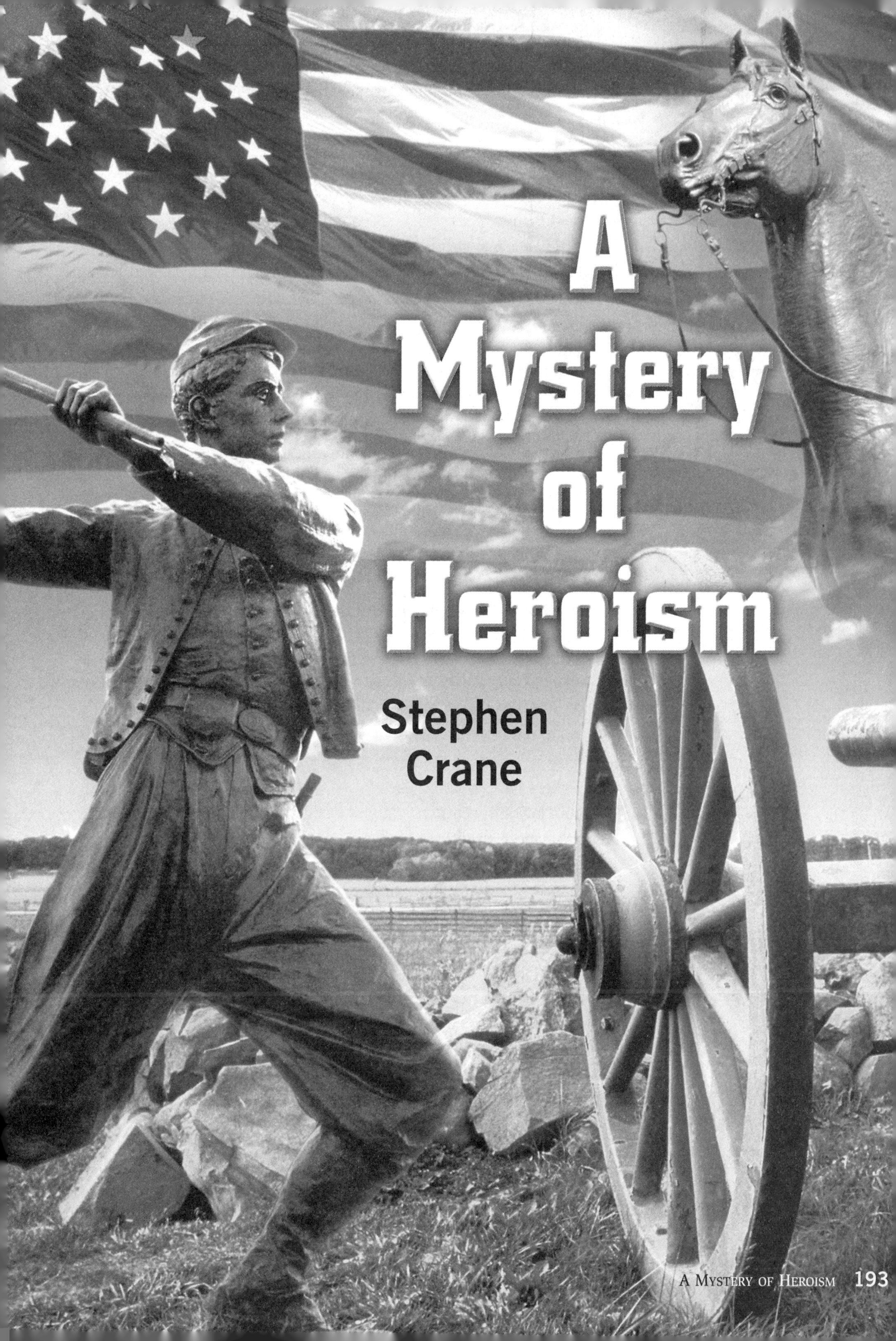

A Mystery of Heroism

Stephen Crane

VISUALIZE

otice the wealth of descriptive
agery that characterizes
ane's **realistic** style. Underline
e specific sensory details that
ake this opening paragraph so
vid.

ORDS TO OWN
onflagration (kän′flə·grā′shən)
.: huge fire.

IDENTIFY

nderline words or phrases in
is paragraph that indicate
hat has been damaged by the
helling.

ORDS TO OWN
tolidity (stə·lid′ə·tē) *n.:*
howing no emotion.

The dark uniforms of the men were so coated with dust from the incessant wrestling of the two armies that the regiment almost seemed a part of the clay bank which shielded them from the shells. On the top of the hill a battery[1] was arguing in tremendous roars with some other guns, and to the eye of the infantry, the artillerymen, the guns, the caissons,[2] the horses, were distinctly outlined upon the blue sky. When a piece was fired, a red streak as round as a log flashed low in the heavens, like a monstrous bolt of lightning. The men of the battery wore white duck trousers, which somehow emphasized their legs, and when they ran and crowded in little groups at the bidding of the shouting officers, it was more impressive than usual to the infantry.

Fred Collins of A Company was saying: "Thunder, I wisht I had a drink. Ain't there any water round here?" Then somebody yelled: "There goes th' bugler!"

As the eyes of half of the regiment swept in one machine-like movement, there was an instant's picture of a horse in a great convulsive leap of a death wound and a rider leaning back with a crooked arm and spread fingers before his face. On the ground was the crimson terror of an exploding shell, with fibers of flame that seemed like lances. A glittering bugle swung clear of the rider's back as fell headlong the horse and the man. In the air was an odor as from a conflagration.

Sometimes they of the infantry looked down at a fair little meadow which spread at their feet. Its long, green grass was rippling gently in a breeze. Beyond it was the gray form of a house half torn to pieces by shells and by the busy axes of soldiers who had pursued firewood. The line of an old fence was now dimly marked by long weeds and by an occasional post. A shell had blown the well house to fragments. Little lines of gray smoke ribboning upward from some embers indicated the place where had stood the barn.

From beyond a curtain of green woods there came the sound of some stupendous scuffle as if two animals of the size of islands were fighting. At a distance there were occasional appearances of swift-moving men, horses, batteries, flags, and, with the crashing of infantry, volleys were heard, often, wild and frenzied cheers. In the midst of it all, Smith and Ferguson, two privates of A Company, were engaged in a heated discussion, which involved the greatest questions of the national existence.

The battery on the hill presently engaged in a frightful duel. The white legs of the gunners scampered this way and that way and the officers redoubled their shouts. The guns, with their demeanors of stolidity and courage, were typical of something infinitely self-possessed in this clamor of death that swirled around the hill.

1. **battery:** set of heavy guns.
2. **caissons** (kā′sənz): ammunition wagons.

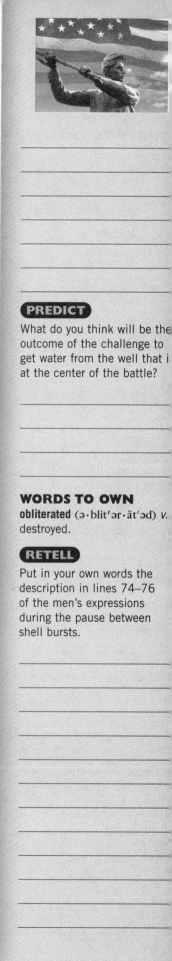

One of a "swing" team was suddenly smitten quivering to the ground and his maddened brethren dragged his torn body in their struggle to escape from this turmoil and danger. A young soldier astride one of the leaders swore and fumed in his saddle and furiously jerked at the bridle. An officer screamed out an order so violently that his voice broke and ended the sentence in a falsetto[3] shriek.

The leading company of the infantry regiment was somewhat exposed and the colonel ordered it moved more fully under the shelter of the hill. There was the clank of steel against steel.

A lieutenant of the battery rode down and passed them, holding his right arm carefully in his left hand. And it was as if this arm was not at all a part of him, but belonged to another man. His sober and reflective charger went slowly. The officer's face was grimy and perspiring and his uniform was tousled as if he had been in direct grapple with an enemy. He smiled grimly when the men stared at him. He turned his horse toward the meadow.

Collins of A Company said: "I wisht I had a drink. I bet there's water in that there ol' well yonder!"

"Yes; but how you goin' to git it?"

For the little meadow which intervened was now suffering a terrible onslaught of shells. Its green and beautiful calm had vanished utterly. Brown earth was being flung in monstrous handfuls. And there was a massacre of the young blades of grass. They were being torn, burned, obliterated. Some curious fortune of the battle had made this gentle little meadow the object of the red hate of the shells and each one as it exploded seemed like an imprecation[4] in the face of a maiden.

The wounded officer who was riding across this expanse said to himself: "Why, they couldn't shoot any harder if the whole army was massed here!"

A shell struck the gray ruins of the house and as, after the roar, the shattered wall fell in fragments, there was a noise which resembled the flapping of shutters during a wild gale of winter. Indeed the infantry paused in the shelter of the bank, appeared as men standing upon a shore contemplating a madness of the sea. The angel of calamity had under its glance the battery upon the hill. Fewer white-legged men labored about the guns. A shell had smitten one of the pieces, and after the flare, the smoke, the dust, the wrath of this blow was gone, it was possible to see white legs stretched horizontally upon the ground. And at that interval to the rear, where it is the business of battery horses to stand with their noses to the fight awaiting the command to drag their guns out of the destruction or into it or wheresoever these incomprehensible humans demanded with whip and spur—in this line

3. **falsetto:** artificially high.
4. **imprecation:** curse.

PREDICT
What do you think will be the outcome of the challenge to get water from the well that i at the center of the battle?

WORDS TO OWN
obliterated (ə·blit′ər·āt′əd) *v.* destroyed.

RETELL
Put in your own words the description in lines 74–76 of the men's expressions during the pause between shell bursts.

ORDS TO OWN
strate (präs′trāt′) *adj.:* lying
t on the ground.

ORDS TO OWN
ninous (äm′ə·nəs) *adj.:*
nister; foreboding.

of passive and dumb spectators, whose fluttering hearts yet would not let them forget the iron laws of man's control of them—in this rank of brute soldiers there had been relentless and hideous carnage. From the ruck[5] of bleeding and prostrate horses, the men of the infantry could see one animal raising its stricken body with its forelegs and turning its nose with mystic and profound eloquence toward the sky.

Some comrades joked Collins about his thirst. "Well, if yeh want a drink so bad, why don't yeh go git it?"

"Well, I will in a minnet if yeh don't shut up."

A lieutenant of artillery floundered his horse straight down the hill with as great concern as if it were level ground. As he galloped past the colonel of the infantry, he threw up his hand in swift salute. "We've got to get out of that," he roared angrily. He was a black-bearded officer, and his eyes, which resembled beads, sparkled like those of an insane man. His jumping horse sped along the column of infantry.

The fat major standing carelessly with his sword held horizontally behind him and with his legs far apart, looked after the receding horseman and laughed. "He wants to get back with orders pretty quick or there'll be no batt'ry left," he observed.

The wise young captain of the second company hazarded[6] to the lieutenant colonel that the enemy's infantry would probably soon attack the hill, and the lieutenant colonel snubbed him.

A private in one of the rear companies looked out over the meadow and then turned to a companion and said: "Look there, Jim." It was the wounded officer from the battery, who some time before had started to ride across the meadow, supporting his right arm carefully with his left hand. This man had encountered a shell apparently at a time when no one perceived him and he could now be seen lying face downward with a stirruped foot stretched across the body of his dead horse. A leg of the charger extended slantingly upward precisely as stiff as a stake. Around this motionless pair the shells still howled.

There was a quarrel in A Company. Collins was shaking his fist in the faces of some laughing comrades. "Dern yeh! I ain't afraid t' go. If yeh say much, I will go!"

"Of course, yeh will! Yeh'll run through that there medder, won't yeh?"

Collins said, in a terrible voice: "You see, now!" At this ominous threat his comrades broke into renewed jeers.

Collins gave them a dark scowl and went to find his captain. The latter was conversing with the colonel of the regiment.

"Captain," said Collins, saluting and standing at attention. In those days all trousers bagged at the knees. "Captain, I want t' git permission to go git some water from that there well over yonder!"

---

5. **ruck:** mass; crowd.
6. **hazarded:** risked saying.

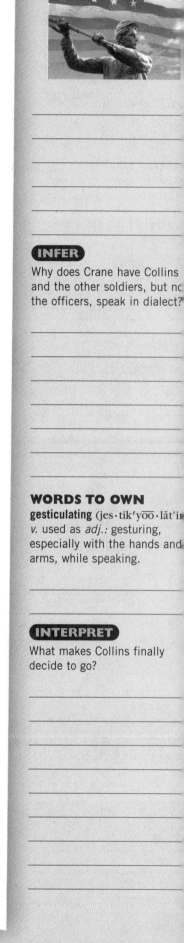

The colonel and the captain swung about simultaneously and stared across the meadow. The captain laughed. "You must be pretty thirsty, Collins?"

"Yes, sir; I am."

"Well—ah," said the captain. After a moment he asked: "Can't you wait?"

"No, sir."

The colonel was watching Collins's face. "Look here, my lad," he said, in a pious sort of a voice. "Look here, my lad." Collins was not a lad. "Don't you think that's taking pretty big risks for a little drink of water?"

"I dunno," said Collins, uncomfortably. Some of the resentment toward his companions, which perhaps had forced him into this affair, was beginning to fade. "I dunno wether 'tis."

The colonel and the captain contemplated him for a time.

"Well," said the captain finally.

"Well," said the colonel, "if you want to go, why go."

Collins saluted. "Much obliged t' yeh."

As he moved away the colonel called after him. "Take some of the other boys' canteens with you an' hurry back now."

"Yes, sir. I will."

The colonel and the captain looked at each other then, for it had suddenly occurred that they could not for the life of them tell whether Collins wanted to go or whether he did not.

They turned to regard Collins and as they perceived him surrounded by gesticulating comrades the colonel said: "Well, by thunder! I guess he's going."

Collins appeared as a man dreaming. In the midst of the questions, the advice, the warnings, all the excited talk of his company mates, he maintained a curious silence.

They were very busy in preparing him for his ordeal. When they inspected him carefully it was somewhat like the examination that grooms give a horse before a race; and they were amazed, staggered by the whole affair. Their astonishment found vent in strange repetitions.

"Are yeh sure a-goin'?" they demanded again and again.

"Certainly I am," cried Collins, at last furiously.

He strode sullenly away from them. He was swinging five or six canteens by their cords. It seemed that his cap would not remain firmly on his head, and often he reached and pulled it down over his brow.

There was a general movement in the compact column. The long animal-like thing moved slightly. Its four hundred eyes were turned upon the figure of Collins.

"Well, sir, if that ain't th' derndest thing. I never thought Fred Collins had the blood in him for that kind of business."

INFER

Why does Crane have Collins and the other soldiers, but no the officers, speak in dialect?

WORDS TO OWN

gesticulating (jes·tik′yo͞o·lāt′in *v.* used as *adj.:* gesturing, especially with the hands and arms, while speaking.

INTERPRET

What makes Collins finally decide to go?

ORDS TO OWN

ovisional (prō·vizh′ə·nəl) *lj.:* temporary; for the time ing.

traction (ri·trak′shən) *n.:* thdrawal.

EVALUATE

t this point in the story, would u call Collins heroic?

"What's he goin' to do, anyhow?"

"He's goin' to that well there after water."

"We ain't dyin' of thirst, are we? That's foolishness."

"Well, somebody put him up to it an' he's doin' it."

"Say, he must be a desperate cuss."

When Collins faced the meadow and walked away from the regiment, he was vaguely conscious that a chasm, the deep valley of all prides, was suddenly between him and his comrades. It was provisional, but the provision was that he return as a victor. He had blindly been led by quaint emotions and laid himself under an obligation to walk squarely up to the face of death.

But he was not sure that he wished to make a retraction even if he could do so without shame. As a matter of truth he was sure of very little. He was mainly surprised.

It seemed to him supernaturally strange that he had allowed his mind to maneuver his body into such a situation. He understood that it might be called dramatically great.

However, he had no full appreciation of anything excepting that he was actually conscious of being dazed. He could feel his dulled mind groping after the form and color of this incident.

Too, he wondered why he did not feel some keen agony of fear cutting his sense like a knife. He wondered at this because human expression had said loudly for centuries that men should feel afraid of certain things and that all men who did not feel this fear were phenomena, heroes.

He was then a hero. He suffered that disappointment which we would all have if we discovered that we were ourselves capable of those deeds which we most admire in history and legend. This, then, was a hero. After all, heroes were not much.

No, it could not be true. He was not a hero. Heroes had no shames in their lives and, as for him, he remembered borrowing fifteen dollars from a friend and promising to pay it back the next day, and then avoiding that friend for ten months. When at home his mother had aroused him for the early labor of his life on the farm, it had often been his fashion to be irritable, childish, diabolical, and his mother had died since he had come to the war.

He saw that in this matter of the well, the canteens, the shells, he was an intruder in the land of fine deeds.

He was now about thirty paces from his comrades. The regiment had just turned its many faces toward him.

From the forest of terrific noises there suddenly emerged a little uneven line of men. They fired fiercely and rapidly at distant foliage on which appeared little puffs of white smoke. The spatter of skirmish firing was added to the thunder of the guns on the hill. The little line of men ran forward. A color sergeant fell flat with his flag as if he had slipped on ice. There was hoarse cheering from this distant field.

Collins suddenly felt that two demon fingers were pressed into his ears. He could see nothing but flying arrows, flaming red. He lurched from the shock of this explosion, but he made a mad rush for the house, which he viewed as a man submerged to the neck in a boiling surf might view the shore. In the air, little pieces of shell howled and the earthquake explosions drove him insane with the menace of their roar. As he ran the canteens knocked together with a rhythmical tinkling.

As he neared the house, each detail of the scene became vivid to him. He was aware of some bricks of the vanished chimney lying on the sod. There was a door which hung by one hinge.

Rifle bullets called forth by the insistent skirmishers came from the far-off bank of foliage. They mingled with the shells and the pieces of shells until the air was torn in all directions by hootings, yells, howls. The sky was full of fiends who directed all their wild rage at his head.

When he came to the well he flung himself face downward and peered into its darkness. There were furtive silver glintings some feet from the surface. He grabbed one of the canteens and, unfastening its cap, swung it down by the cord. The water flowed slowly in with an indolent gurgle.

And now as he lay with his face turned away he was suddenly smitten with the terror. It came upon his heart like the grasp of claws. All the power faded from his muscles. For an instant he was no more than a dead man.

The canteen filled with a maddening slowness in the manner of all bottles. Presently he recovered his strength and addressed a screaming oath to it. He leaned over until it seemed as if he intended to try to push water into it with his hands. His eyes as he gazed down into the well shone like two pieces of metal and in their expression was a great appeal and a great curse. The stupid water derided him.

There was the blaring thunder of a shell. Crimson light shone through the swift-boiling smoke and made a pink reflection on part of the wall of the well. Collins jerked out his arm and canteen with the same motion that a man would use in withdrawing his head from a furnace.

He scrambled erect and glared and hesitated. On the ground near him lay the old well bucket, with a length of rusty chain. He lowered it swiftly into the well. The bucket struck the water and then turning lazily over, sank. When, with hand reaching tremblingly over hand, he hauled it out, it knocked often against the walls of the well and spilled some of its contents.

COMPARE AND CONTRAST

Before he ventured into the meadow, Collins felt "dazed"; now the scene is "vivid" to him. How do you account for the difference?

WORDS TO OWN

indolent (in′də·lənt) *adj.:* lazy

NTERPRET

ıderline the **metaphor** that ane uses to describe the anner of Collins's retreat from e well. Why, at this moment real heroism, does Crane ıploy a metaphor that makes llins appear ridiculous?

ORDS TO OWN

anched (blancht) *v.* used as *dj.*: drained of color.

BUILD FLUENCY

e-read this passage aloud, onouncing each word clearly ıd expressively.

In running with a filled bucket, a man can adopt but one kind of gait. So through this terrible field over which screamed practical angels of death Collins ran in the manner of a farmer chased out of a dairy by a bull.

His face went staring white with anticipation—anticipation of a blow that would whirl him around and down. He would fall as he had seen other men fall, the life knocked out of them so suddenly that their knees were no more quick to touch the ground than their heads. He saw the long blue line of the regiment, but his comrades were standing looking at him from the edge of an impossible star. He was aware of some deep wheel ruts and hoof prints in the sod beneath his feet.

The artillery officer who had fallen in this meadow had been making groans in the teeth of the tempest of sound. These futile cries, wrenched from him by his agony, were heard only by shells, bullets. When wild-eyed Collins came running, this officer raised himself. His face contorted and blanched from pain, he was about to utter some great beseeching cry. But suddenly his face straightened and he called: "Say, young man, give me a drink of water, will you?"

Collins had no room amid his emotions for surprise. He was mad from the threats of destruction.

"I can't," he screamed, and in this reply was a full description of his quaking apprehension. His cap was gone and his hair was riotous. His clothes made it appear that he had been dragged over the ground by the heels. He ran on.

The officer's head sank down and one elbow crooked. His foot in its brass-bound stirrup still stretched over the body of his horse and the other leg was under the steed.

But Collins turned. He came dashing back. His face had now turned gray and in his eyes was all terror. "Here it is! Here it is!"

The officer was as a man gone in drink. His arm bended like a twig. His head drooped as if his neck was of willow. He was sinking to the ground, to lie face downward.

Collins grabbed him by the shoulder. "Here it is. Here's your drink. Turn over! Turn over, man, for God's sake!"

With Collins hauling at his shoulder, the officer twisted his body and fell with his face turned toward that region where lived the unspeakable noises of the swirling missiles. There was the faintest shadow of a smile on his lips as he looked at Collins. He gave a sigh, a little primitive breath like that from a child.

Collins tried to hold the bucket steadily, but his shaking hands caused the water to splash all over the face of the dying man. Then he jerked it away and ran on.

The regiment gave him a welcoming roar. The grimed faces were wrinkled in laughter.

His captain waved the bucket away. "Give it to the men!"

The two genial, skylarking young lieutenants were the first to gain possession of it. They played over it in their fashion.

When one tried to drink, the other teasingly knocked his elbow. "Don't, Billie! You'll make me spill it," said the one. The other laughed.

Suddenly there was an oath, the thud of wood on the ground, and a swift murmur of astonishment from the ranks. The two lieutenants glared at each other. The bucket lay on the ground empty.

EVALUATE

After this **ironic** twist at the end of the story, what do you think has been the value of Collins's heroism?

Situational Irony

Situational irony occurs when what actually happens differs from what one expects will happen. Such irony is at the heart of this story: Collins risks his life to fetch water from the well, only to have the water spilled by the careless horseplay of the two young lieutenants.

To better understand the nature of situational irony, complete the following chart. In the left-hand column are traditional expectations of the sort of thing that will occur in a story of heroism in wartime. In the right-hand column, fill in what actually occurs in "A Mystery of Heroism" that differs from these expectations.

What We Expect	What Actually Happens
Courage comes through sacrificing one's personal desires for the greater good of a group of people.	Collins's initial motivation is simply thirst, and then vanity when he fears shaming himself by not living up to his boast.
The hero is a loner who is not influenced by other people's opinions of him but does only what he thinks is right.	
The hero has a clear sense of purpose in what he does.	
Things achieved through sacrifice are highly valued by those whom they benefit.	

Vocabulary: How to Own a Word

Bases, Prefixes, and Suffixes

Word Bank
conflagration
stolidity
obliterated
prostrate
ominous
gesticulating
provisional
retraction
indolent
blanched

English words are made up of various word parts. These may include base words, prefixes that are added to the beginning of words, and suffixes that are added to the end of words.

For each Word to Own, select the correct base, prefix (if any), and suffix(es) (if any) from the chart below and fill them in on the chart that follows. Some of the word parts have been filled in for you as an example.

Bases	Prefixes	Suffixes
blanc, white *dolere*, to suffer *flagrare*, to burn *gesticulatus*, to make mimicking gestures *littera*, letter *ominosus*, of or serving as an omen *stolid*, firm *stratus*, to stretch out *tract*, to draw *vis*, to see	*con-*, with *in-*, not *ob-*, against *pro-*, before *re-*, back	*-al*, pertaining to *-ate*, having *-ed*, past tense *-ing*, present participle *-ion*, action *-ity*, condition *-ly*, in the manner of *-tion*, action

Word to Own	Base	Prefix	Suffix
conflagration	*flagrare*, to burn		
stolidity			
obliterated			*-ed*, past tense
prostrate			
ominous			
gesticulating			
provisional	*vis*, to see		
retraction			
indolent		*in-*, not	
blanched			

To Build a Fire

Make the Connection

Cold, Cruel World

Jack London was an unknown young writer from San Francisco when he joined the Yukon gold rush in 1897. The time he spent in this bleak, remote region of northwestern Canada gave him an intimate knowledge of the wilderness and the people who inhabit it. He had seen nature in its harshest form and human nature at its most primal—struggling for survival. London soon put his experience to good account: Within a few years books like *The Call of the Wild* and *White Fang* made him one of the most popular writers in the world.

In the chart below, outline your own scenario for a survival story. Begin by describing an extreme environment or condition, such as heat, cold, hunger, or thirst. Then, place that environment or condition in an appropriate setting. Next, describe your main character, focusing on one or two personality traits that may help or hurt the character's chances for survival. Explore some possible causes and effects in your scenario: for example, what led the character into the situation, how he or she prepared or failed to prepare for what happens, what unexpected event occurs that determines the main character's fate.

Environmental or Conditional Extreme:
Setting:
Main Character:
Cause and Effect:

To Build a Fire

Jack London

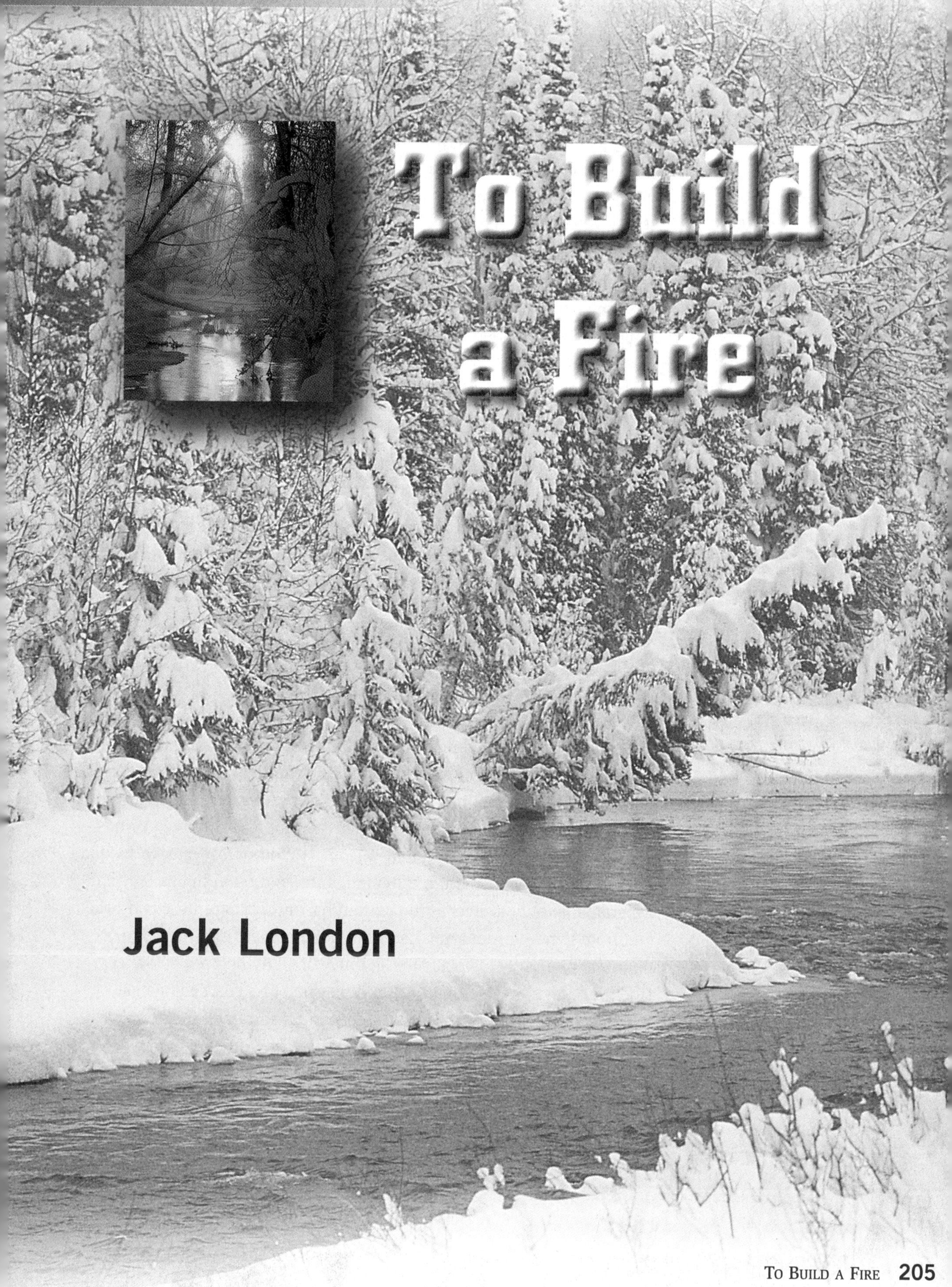

DENTIFY

rcle the images in es 1–6 that create threatening, dreary mosphere.

ORDS TO OWN

tangible (in·tan′jə·bəl) *adj.:* fficult to define; vague.

ORDS TO OWN

dulations (un′dyoo·lā′shənz) *pl.:* wavelike motions.

INTERPRET

hy is the lack of imagination "trouble" for the main haracter?

Day had broken cold and gray, exceedingly cold and gray, when the man turned aside from the main Yukon trail and climbed the high earth bank, where a dim and little-traveled trail led eastward through the fat spruce timberland. It was a steep bank, and he paused for breath at the top, excusing the act to himself by looking at his watch. It was nine o'clock. There was no sun or hint of sun, though there was not a cloud in the sky. It was a clear day, and yet there seemed an intangible pall over the face of things, a subtle gloom that made the day dark, and that was due to the absence of sun. This fact did not worry the man. He was used to the lack of sun. It had been days since he had seen the sun, and he knew that a few more days must pass before that cheerful orb, due south, would just peep above the skyline and dip immediately from view.

The man flung a look back along the way he had come. The Yukon lay a mile wide and hidden under three feet of ice. On top of this ice were as many feet of snow. It was all pure white, rolling in gentle undulations where the ice jams of the freeze-up had formed. North and south, as far as his eye could see, it was unbroken white, save for a dark hairline that curved and twisted from around the spruce-covered island to the south, and that curved and twisted away into the north, where it disappeared behind another spruce-covered island. This dark hairline was the trail—the main trail—that led south five hundred miles to the Chilkoot Pass, Dyea, and salt water; and that led north seventy miles to Dawson, and still on to the north a thousand miles to Nulato, and finally to St. Michael on the Bering Sea, a thousand miles and half a thousand more.

But all this—the mysterious, far-reaching hairline trail, the absence of sun from the sky, the tremendous cold, and the strangeness and weirdness of it all—made no impression on the man. It was not because he was long used to it. He was a newcomer in the land, a *cheechako*,[1] and this was his first winter. The trouble with him was that he was without imagination. He was quick and alert in the things of life, but only in the things, and not in the significances. Fifty degrees below zero meant eighty-odd degrees of frost. Such fact impressed him as being cold and uncomfortable, and that was all. It did not lead him to meditate upon his frailty as a creature of temperature, and upon man's frailty in general, able only to live within certain narrow limits of heat and cold, and from there on it did not lead him to the conjectural[2] field of immortality and man's place in the universe. Fifty degrees below zero stood for a bite of frost that hurt and that must be guarded against by the use of mittens, earflaps, warm moccasins, and thick socks. Fifty degrees below zero was to him just precisely fifty degrees below zero. That there should be anything more to it than that was a thought that never entered his head.

1. ***cheechako*** (chē·chä′kō): Chinook jargon for "newcomer" or "tenderfoot."
2. **conjectural:** based on guesswork or uncertain evidence.

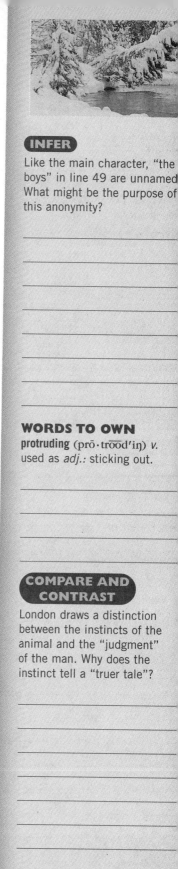

As he turned to go on, he spat speculatively. There was a sharp, explosive crackle that startled him. He spat again. And again, in the air, before it could fall to the snow, the spittle crackled. He knew that at fifty below, spittle crackled on the snow, but this spittle had crackled in the air. Undoubtedly it was colder than fifty below—how much colder he did not know. But the temperature did not matter. He was bound for the old claim on the left fork of Henderson Creek, where the boys were already. They had come over across the divide from the Indian Creek country, while he had come the roundabout way to take a look at the possibilities of getting out logs in the spring from the islands in the Yukon. He would be into camp by six o'clock; a bit after dark, it was true, but the boys would be there, a fire would be going, and a hot supper would be ready. As for lunch, he pressed his hand against the protruding bundle under his jacket. It was also under his shirt, wrapped up in a handkerchief and lying against the naked skin. It was the only way to keep the biscuits from freezing. He smiled agreeably to himself as he thought of those biscuits, each cut open and sopped in bacon grease, and each enclosing a generous slice of fried bacon.

He plunged in among the big spruce trees. The trail was faint. A foot of snow had fallen since the last sled had passed over, and he was glad he was without a sled, traveling light. In fact, he carried nothing but the lunch wrapped in the handkerchief. He was surprised, however, at the cold. It certainly was cold, he concluded, as he rubbed his numb nose and cheekbones with his mittened hand. He was a warm-whiskered man, but the hair on his face did not protect the high cheekbones and the eager nose that thrust itself aggressively into the frosty air.

At the man's heels trotted a dog, a big native husky, the proper wolf dog, gray-coated and without any visible or temperamental difference from its brother, the wild wolf. The animal was depressed by the tremendous cold. It knew that it was no time for traveling. Its instinct told it a truer tale than was told to the man by the man's judgment. In reality, it was not merely colder than fifty below zero; it was colder than sixty below, than seventy below. It was seventy-five below zero. Since the freezing point is thirty-two above zero, it meant that one hundred and seven degrees of frost obtained. The dog did not know anything about thermometers. Possibly in its brain there was no sharp consciousness of a condition of very cold such as was in the man's brain. But the brute had its instinct. It experienced a vague but menacing apprehension that subdued it and made it slink along at the man's heels, and that made it question eagerly every unwonted[3] movement of the man, as if expecting him to go into camp or to seek shelter somewhere and build a fire. The dog had learned fire, and it wanted fire, or else to burrow under the snow and cuddle its warmth away from the air.

3. **unwonted:** unusual.

INFER

Like the main character, "the boys" in line 49 are unnamed. What might be the purpose of this anonymity?

WORDS TO OWN

protruding (prō·tro͞od′iŋ) *v.* used as *adj.:* sticking out.

COMPARE AND CONTRAST

London draws a distinction between the instincts of the animal and the "judgment" of the man. Why does the instinct tell a "truer tale"?

/ORDS TO OWN

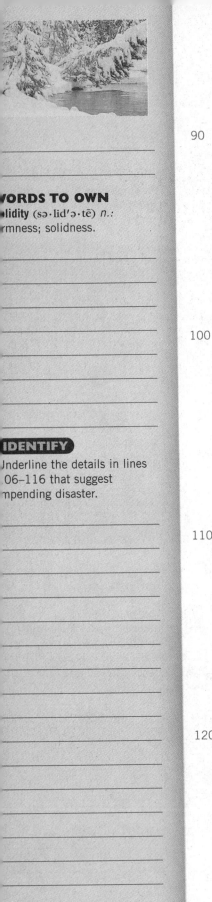

lidity (sə·lid′ə·tē) *n.:* rmness; solidness.

IDENTIFY

Jnderline the details in lines 06–116 that suggest npending disaster.

The frozen moisture of its breathing had settled on its fur in a fine powder of frost, and especially were its jowls, muzzle, and eyelashes whitened by its crystaled breath. The man's red beard and moustache were likewise frosted, but more solidly, the deposit taking the form of ice and increasing with every warm, moist breath he exhaled. Also, the man was chewing tobacco, and the muzzle of ice held his lips so rigidly that he was unable to clear his chin when he expelled the juice. The result was that a crystal beard of the color and solidity of amber was increasing its length on his chin. If he fell down it would shatter itself, like glass, into brittle fragments. But he did not mind the appendage. It was the penalty all tobacco chewers paid in that country, and he had been out before in two cold snaps. They had not been so cold as this, he knew, but by the spirit thermometer[4] at Sixty Mile he knew they had been registered at fifty below and at fifty-five.

He held on through the level stretch of woods for several miles, crossed a wide flat, and dropped down a bank to the frozen bed of a small stream. This was Henderson Creek, and he knew he was ten miles from the forks. He looked at his watch. It was ten o'clock. He was making four miles an hour, and he calculated that he would arrive at the forks at half past twelve. He decided to celebrate that event by eating his lunch there.

The dog dropped in again at his heels, with a tail drooping discouragement, as the man swung along the creek bed. The furrow of the old sled trail was plainly visible, but a dozen inches of snow covered the marks of the last runners. In a month no man had come up or down that silent creek. The man held steadily on. He was not much given to thinking, and just then particularly, he had nothing to think about save that he would eat lunch at the forks and that at six o'clock he would be in camp with the boys. There was nobody to talk to; and, had there been, speech would have been impossible because of the ice muzzle on his mouth. So he continued monotonously to chew tobacco and to increase the length of his amber beard.

Once in a while the thought reiterated itself that it was very cold and that he had never experienced such cold. As he walked along he rubbed his cheekbones and nose with the back of his mittened hand. He did this automatically, now and again changing hands. But rub as he would, the instant he stopped his cheekbones went numb, and the following instant the end of his nose went numb. He was sure to frost his cheeks; he knew that, and experienced a pang of regret that he had not devised a nose strap of the sort Bud wore in the cold snaps. Such a strap passed across the cheeks, as well, and saved them. But it didn't matter much, after all. What were frosted cheeks? A bit painful, that was all; they were never serious.

---

4. **spirit thermometer:** alcohol thermometer. In places where the temperature often drops below the freezing point of mercury, alcohol is used in thermometers.

Empty as the man's mind was of thought, he was keenly observant, and he noticed the changes in the creek, the curves and bends and timber jams, and always he sharply noted where he placed his feet. Once, coming around a bend, he shied abruptly, like a startled horse, curved away from the place where he had been walking, and retreated several paces back along the trail. The creek, he knew, was frozen clear to the bottom—no creek could contain water in that arctic winter—but he knew also that there were springs that bubbled out from the hillsides and ran along under the snow and on top of the ice of the creek. He knew that the coldest snaps never froze these springs, and he knew likewise their danger. They were traps. They hid pools of water under the snow that might be three inches deep, or three feet. Sometimes a skin of ice half an inch thick covered them, and in turn was covered by the snow. Sometimes there were alternate layers of water and ice skin, so that when one broke through he kept on breaking through for a while, sometimes wetting himself to the waist.

That was why he had shied in such panic. He had felt the give under his feet and heard the crackle of a snow-hidden ice skin. And to get his feet wet in such a temperature meant trouble and danger. At the very least it meant delay, for he would be forced to stop and build a fire, and under its protection to bare his feet while he dried his socks and moccasins. He stood and studied the creek bed and its banks, and decided that the flow of water came from the right. He reflected awhile, rubbing his nose and cheeks, then skirted to the left, stepping gingerly and testing the footing for each step. Once clear of the danger, he took a fresh chew of tobacco and swung along at his four-mile gait.

In the course of the next two hours he came upon several similar traps. Usually the snow above the hidden pools had a sunken, candied appearance that advertised the danger. Once again, however, he had a close call; and once, suspecting danger, he compelled the dog to go on in front. The dog did not want to go. It hung back until the man shoved it forward, and then it went quickly across the white, unbroken surface. Suddenly it broke through, floundered to one side, and got away to firmer footing. It had wet its forefeet and legs, and almost immediately the water that clung to it turned to ice. It made quick efforts to lick the ice off its legs, then dropped down in the snow and began to bite out the ice that had formed between the toes. This was a matter of instinct. To permit the ice to remain would mean sore feet. It did not know this. It merely obeyed the mysterious prompting that arose from the deep crypts[5] of its being. But the man knew, having achieved a judgment on the subject, and he removed the mitten from his right hand and helped tear out the ice particles. He did not expose his fingers more than a minute, and was astonished at the swift numbness that

---

5. crypts: hidden recesses.

VISUALIZE

Notice that the man's concern here is to visualize what he cannot see—the hidden pools of water that may or may not li beneath the snow. Why do you think London describes this danger in such great detail?

EVALUATE

Do you think the man was justified in forcing the dog to test the ice's surface?

NFER

'hy does the man beat his and "savagely across his nest"?

INTERPRET

he comment "it certainly vas cold" has occurred several imes in the story. What is he point of repeating this nderstatement?

smote[6] them. It certainly was cold. He pulled on the mitten hastily, and beat the hand savagely across his chest.

At twelve o'clock the day was at its brightest. Yet the sun was too far south on its winter journey to clear the horizon. The bulge of the earth intervened between it and Henderson Creek, where the man walked under a clear sky at noon and cast no shadow. At half past twelve, to the minute, he arrived at the forks of the creek. He was pleased at the speed he had made. If he kept it up, he would certainly be with the boys by six. He unbuttoned his jacket and shirt and drew forth his lunch. The action consumed no more than a quarter of a minute, yet in that brief moment the numbness laid hold of the exposed fingers. He did not put the mitten on, but instead struck the fingers a dozen sharp smashes against his leg. Then he sat down on a snow-covered log to eat. The sting that followed upon the striking of his fingers against his leg ceased so quickly that he was startled. He had had no chance to take a bite of biscuit. He struck the fingers repeatedly and returned them to the mitten, baring the other hand for the purpose of eating. He tried to take a mouthful, but the ice muzzle prevented. He had forgotten to build a fire and thaw out. He chuckled at his foolishness, and as he chuckled he noted the numbness creeping into the exposed fingers. Also, he noted that the stinging which had first come to his toes when he sat down was already passing away. He wondered whether the toes were warm or numb. He moved them inside the moccasins and decided that they were numb.

He pulled the mitten on hurriedly and stood up. He was a bit frightened. He stamped up and down until the stinging returned into the feet. It certainly was cold, was his thought. That man from Sulfur Creek had spoken the truth when telling how cold it sometimes got in the country. And he had laughed at him at the time! That showed one must not be too sure of things. There was no mistake about it, it *was* cold. He strode up and down, stamping his feet and threshing his arms, until reassured by the returning warmth. Then he got out matches and proceeded to make a fire. From the undergrowth, where high water of the previous spring had lodged a supply of seasoned twigs, he got his firewood. Working carefully from a small beginning, he soon had a roaring fire, over which he thawed the ice from his face and in the protection of which he ate his biscuits. For the moment the cold of space was outwitted. The dog took satisfaction in the fire, stretching out close enough for warmth and far enough away to escape being singed.

When the man had finished, he filled his pipe and took his comfortable time over a smoke. Then he pulled on his mittens, settled the earflaps of his cap firmly about his ears, and took the creek trail up the left fork. The dog was disappointed and yearned back toward the fire.

6. **smote:** powerfully struck; past tense of *smite*.

This man did not know cold. Possibly all the generations of his ancestry had been ignorant of cold, of real cold, of cold one hundred and seven degrees below freezing point. But the dog knew; all its ancestry knew, and it had inherited the knowledge. And it knew that it was not good to walk abroad in such fearful cold. It was the time to lie snug in a hole in the snow and wait for a curtain of cloud to be drawn across the face of outer space whence this cold came. On the other hand, there was no keen intimacy between the dog and the man. The one was the toil slave of the other, and the only caresses it had ever received were the caresses of the whiplash and of harsh and menacing throat sounds that threatened the whiplash. So the dog made no effort to communicate its apprehension to the man. It was not concerned in the welfare of the man; it was for its own sake that it yearned back toward the fire. But the man whistled, and spoke to it with the sound of whiplashes, and the dog swung in at the man's heels and followed after.

The man took a chew of tobacco and proceeded to start a new amber beard. Also, his moist breath quickly powdered with white his moustache, eyebrows, and lashes. There did not seem to be so many springs on the left fork of the Henderson, and for half an hour the man saw no signs of any. And then it happened. At a place where there were no signs, where the soft, unbroken snow seemed to advertise solidity beneath, the man broke through. It was not deep. He wet himself halfway to the knees before he floundered out to the firm crust.

He was angry, and cursed his luck aloud. He had hoped to get into camp with the boys at six o'clock, and this would delay him an hour, for he would have to build a fire and dry out his footgear. This was imperative at that low temperature—he knew that much; and he turned aside to the bank, which he climbed. On top, tangled in the underbrush about the trunks of several small spruce trees, was a high-water deposit of dry firewood—sticks and twigs, principally, but also larger portions of seasoned branches and fine, dry, last year's grasses. He threw down several large pieces on top of the snow. This served for a foundation and prevented the young flame from drowning itself in the snow it otherwise would melt. The flame he got by touching a match to a small shred of birch bark that he took from his pocket. This burned even more readily than paper. Placing it on the foundation, he fed the young flame with wisps of dry grass and with the tiniest dry twigs.

He worked slowly and carefully, keenly aware of his danger. Gradually, as the flame grew stronger, he increased the size of the twigs with which he fed it. He squatted in the snow, pulling the twigs out from their entanglement in the brush and feeding directly to the flame. He knew there must be no failure. When it is seventy-five below zero, a man must not fail in his first attempt to build a fire—that is, if his feet are wet. If his feet are dry, and he fails, he can run along the trail for a

INTERPRET

In lines 213–228, the dog becomes a fuller character in the story. What narrative purpose does this serve?

WORDS TO OWN

imperative (im·per′ə·tiv) *adj.:* absolutely necessary; compulsory.

BUILD FLUENCY

As the man's danger becomes more pivotal in the story, the amount of detail increases. Re-read lines 237–250 aloud to understand the increasing importance of small details.

half a mile and restore his circulation. But the circulation of wet and freezing feet cannot be restored by running when it is seventy-five below. No matter how fast he runs, the wet feet will freeze the harder.

All this the man knew. The old-timer on Sulfur Creek had told him about it the previous fall, and now he was appreciating the advice. Already all sensation had gone out of his feet. To build the fire, he had been forced to remove his mittens, and the fingers had quickly gone numb. His pace of four miles an hour had kept his heart pumping blood to the surface of his body and to all the extremities. But the instant he stopped, the action of the pump eased down. The cold of space smote the unprotected tip of the planet, and he, being on that unprotected tip, received the full force of the blow. The blood of his body recoiled before it. The blood was alive, like the dog, and like the dog it wanted to hide away and cover itself up from the fearful cold. So long as he walked four miles an hour, he pumped that blood, willy-nilly, to the surface; but now it ebbed away and sank down into the recesses of his body. The extremities were the first to feel its absence. His wet feet froze the faster, and his exposed fingers numbed the faster, though they had not yet begun to freeze. Nose and cheeks were already freezing, while the skin of all his body chilled as it lost its blood.

But he was safe. Toes and nose and cheeks would be only touched by the frost, for the fire was beginning to burn with strength. He was feeding it twigs the size of his finger. In another minute he would be able to feed it with branches the size of his wrist, and then he could remove his wet footgear, and, while it dried, he could keep his naked feet warm by the fire, rubbing them at first, of course, with snow. The fire was a success. He was safe. He remembered the advice of the old-timer on Sulfur Creek, and smiled. The old-timer had been very serious in laying down the law that no man must travel alone in the Klondike after fifty below. Well, here he was; he had had the accident; he was alone; and he had saved himself. Those old-timers were rather womanish, some of them, he thought. All a man had to do was to keep his head and he was all right. Any man who was a man could travel alone. But it was surprising, the rapidity with which his cheeks and nose were freezing. And he had not thought his fingers could go lifeless in so short a time. Lifeless they were, for he could scarcely make them move together to grip a twig, and they seemed remote from his body and from him. When he touched a twig, he had to look and see whether or not he had hold of it. The wires were pretty well down between him and his finger ends.

All of which counted for little. There was the fire, snapping and crackling and promising life with every dancing flame. He started to untie his moccasins. They were coated with ice; the thick German socks were like sheaths of iron halfway to the knees; and the moccasin strings

WORDS TO OWN

extremities (ek·strem′ə·tēz) *n. pl.:* limbs of the body, especially hands and feet.

recoiled (ri′koild′) *v.:* shrank away; drew back.

INTERPRET

The dog represents instinct. What does the old man **symbolize**—not to the man remembering him, but to London?

were like rods of steel all twisted and knotted as by some conflagration. For a moment he tugged with his numb fingers, then, realizing the folly of it, he drew his sheath knife.

But before he could cut the strings it happened. It was his own fault, or, rather, his mistake. He should not have built the fire under the spruce tree. He should have built it in the open. But it had been easier to pull the twigs from the bush and drop them directly on the fire. Now the tree under which he had done this carried a weight of snow on its boughs. No wind had blown for weeks, and each bough was fully freighted. Each time he had pulled a twig he had communicated a slight agitation to the tree—an imperceptible agitation, so far as he was concerned, but an agitation sufficient to bring about the disaster. High up in the tree one bough capsized its load of snow. This fell on the boughs beneath, capsizing them. This process continued, spreading out and involving the whole tree. It grew like an avalanche, and it descended without warning upon the man and the fire, and the fire was blotted out! Where it had burned was a mantle of fresh and disordered snow.

The man was shocked. It was as though he had just heard his own sentence of death. For a moment he sat and stared at the spot where the fire had been. Then he grew very calm. Perhaps the old-timer on Sulfur Creek was right. If he had only had a trail mate, he would have been in no danger now. The trail mate could have built the fire. Well, it was up to him to build the fire over again, and this second time there must be no failure. Even if he succeeded, he would most likely lose some toes. His feet must be badly frozen by now, and there would be some time before the second fire was ready.

Such were his thoughts, but he did not sit and think them. He was busy all the time they were passing through his mind. He made a new foundation for a fire, this time in the open, where no treacherous tree could blot it out. Next he gathered dry grasses and tiny twigs from the high-water flotsam.[7] He could not bring his fingers together to pull them out, but he was able to gather them by the handful. In this way he got many rotten twigs and bits of green moss that were undesirable, but it was the best he could do. He worked methodically, even collecting an armful of the larger branches to be used later when the fire gathered strength. And all the while the dog sat and watched him, a certain yearning wistfulness in its eyes, for it looked upon him as the fire provider, and the fire was slow in coming.

When all was ready, the man reached in his pocket for a second piece of birch bark. He knew the bark was there, and, though he could not feel it with his fingers, he could hear its crisp rustling as he fumbled for it. Try as he would, he could not clutch hold of it. And all the time,

7. **high-water flotsam:** branches and debris washed ashore by a stream or river during the warm months when the water is high.

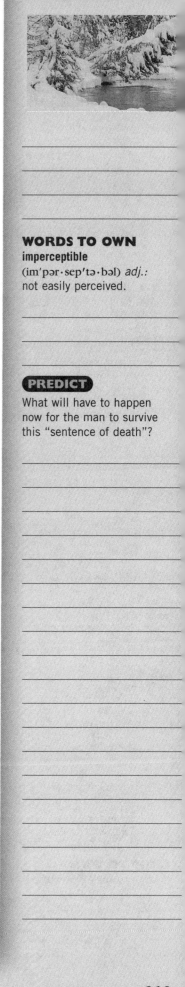

WORDS TO OWN
imperceptible
(im′pər·sep′tə·bəl) *adj.:* not easily perceived.

PREDICT
What will have to happen now for the man to survive this "sentence of death"?

in his consciousness, was the knowledge that each instant his feet were freezing. This thought tended to put him in a panic, but he fought against it and kept calm. He pulled on his mittens with his teeth, and threshed his arms back and forth, beating his hands with all his might against his sides. He did this sitting down, and he stood up to do it; and all the while the dog sat in the snow, its wolf brush of a tail curled around warmly over its forefeet, its sharp wolf ears pricked forward intently as it watched the man. And the man, as he beat and threshed with his arms and hands, felt a great surge of envy as he regarded the creature that was warm and secure in its natural covering.

After a time he was aware of the first faraway signals of sensation in his beaten fingers. The faint tingling grew stronger till it evolved into a stinging ache that was excruciating, but which the man hailed with satisfaction. He stripped the mitten from his right hand and fetched forth the birch bark. The exposed fingers were quickly going numb again. Next he brought out his bunch of sulfur matches. But the tremendous cold had already driven the life out of his fingers. In his effort to separate one match from the others, the whole bunch fell in the snow. He tried to pick it out of the snow, but failed. The dead fingers could neither touch nor clutch. He was very careful. He drove the thought of his freezing feet, and nose, and cheeks, out of his mind, devoting his whole soul to the matches. He watched, using the sense of vision in place of that of touch, and when he saw his fingers on each side of the bunch, he closed them—that is, he willed to close them, for the wires were down, and the fingers did not obey. He pulled the mitten on the right hand, and beat it fiercely against his knee. Then, with both mittened hands, he scooped the bunch of matches, along with much snow, into his lap. Yet he was no better off.

After some manipulation he managed to get the bunch between the heels of his mittened hands. In this fashion he carried it to his mouth. The ice crackled and snapped when by a violent effort he opened his mouth. He drew the lower jaw in, curled the upper lip out of the way, and scraped the bunch with his upper teeth in order to separate a match. He succeeded in getting one, which he dropped on his lap. He was no better off. He could not pick it up. Then he devised a way. He picked it up in his teeth and scratched it on his leg. Twenty times he scratched before he succeeded in lighting it. As it flamed he held it with his teeth to the birch bark. But the burning brimstone went up his nostrils and into his lungs, causing him to cough spasmodically. The match fell into the snow and went out.

The old-timer on Sulfur Creek was right, he thought in the moment of controlled despair that ensued: After fifty below, a man should travel with a partner. He beat his hands, but failed in exciting any sensation. Suddenly he bared both hands, removing the mittens with his teeth.

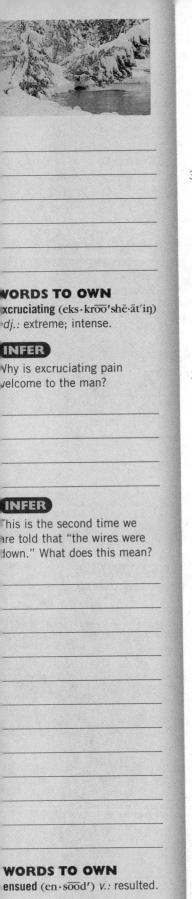

VORDS TO OWN
xcruciating (eks·kro͞o′shē·āt′iŋ) *dj.:* extreme; intense.

INFER
Vhy is excruciating pain velcome to the man?

INFER
This is the second time we are told that "the wires were down." What does this mean?

WORDS TO OWN
ensued (en·so͞od′) *v.:* resulted.

He caught the whole bunch between the heels of his hands. His arm muscles, not being frozen, enabled him to press the hand heels tightly against the matches. Then he scratched the bunch along his leg. It flared into flame, seventy sulfur matches at once! There was no wind to blow them out. He kept his head to one side to escape the strangling fumes, and held the blazing bunch to the birch bark. As he so held it, he became aware of sensation in his hand. His flesh was burning. He could smell it. Deep down below the surface he could feel it. The sensation developed into pain that grew acute. And still he endured it, holding the flame of matches clumsily to the bark that would not light readily because his own burning hands were in the way, absorbing most of the flame.

At last, when he could endure no more, he jerked his hands apart. The blazing matches fell sizzling into the snow, but the birch bark was alight. He began laying dry grass and the tiniest twigs on the flame. He could not pick and choose, for he had to lift the fuel between the heels of his hands. Small pieces of rotten wood and green moss clung to the twigs, and he bit them off as well as he could with his teeth. He cherished the flame carefully and awkwardly. It meant life, and it must not perish. The withdrawal of blood from the surface of his body now made him begin to shiver, and he grew more awkward. A large piece of green moss fell squarely on the little fire. He tried to poke it out with his fingers, but his shivering frame made him poke too far, and he disrupted the nucleus of the little fire, the burning grasses and tiny twigs separating and scattering. He tried to poke them together again, but in spite of the tenseness of the effort, his shivering got away with him, and the twigs were hopelessly scattered. Each twig gushed a puff of smoke and went out. The fire provider had failed. As he looked apathetically about him, his eyes chanced on the dog, sitting across the ruins of the fire from him, in the snow, making restless, hunching movements, slightly lifting one forefoot and then the other, shifting its weight back and forth on them with wistful eagerness.

The sight of the dog put a wild idea into his head. He remembered the tale of the man, caught in a blizzard, who killed a steer and crawled inside the carcass, and so was saved. He would kill the dog and bury his hands in the warm body until the numbness went out of them. Then he could build another fire. He spoke to the dog, calling it to him; but in his voice was a strange note of fear that frightened the animal, who had never known the man to speak in such a way before. Something was the matter, and its suspicious nature sensed danger—it knew not what danger, but somewhere, somehow, in its brain arose an apprehension of the man. It flattened its ears down at the sound of the man's voice, and its restless, hunching movements and the liftings and shiftings of its forefeet became more pronounced; but it would not come to the man.

INTERPRET

Does London express any sympathy for the man's suffering? Explain.

NTERPRET

ow does the phrase
truggled for calmness"
nbody the man's plight?

IDENTIFY

Vhat reaction to the fear
f death is the first sign of
nstinct in the man?

He got on his hands and knees and crawled toward the dog. This unusual posture again excited suspicion, and the animal sidled mincingly away.

The man sat up in the snow for a moment and struggled for calmness. Then he pulled on his mittens, by means of his teeth, and got up on his feet. He glanced down at first in order to assure himself that he was really standing up, for the absence of sensation in his feet left him unrelated to the earth. His erect position in itself started to drive the webs of suspicion from the dog's mind; and when he spoke peremptorily,[8] with the sound of whiplashes in his voice, the dog rendered its customary allegiance and came to him. As it came within reaching distance, the man lost his control. His arms flashed out to the dog, and he experienced genuine surprise when he discovered that his hands could not clutch, that there was neither bend nor feeling in the fingers. He had forgotten for the moment that they were frozen and that they were freezing more and more. All this happened quickly, and before the animal could get away, he encircled its body with his arms. He sat down in the snow, and in this fashion held the dog, while it snarled and whined and struggled.

But it was all he could do, hold its body encircled in his arms and sit there. He realized that he could not kill the dog. There was no way to do it. With his helpless hands he could neither draw nor hold his sheath knife nor throttle the animal. He released it, and it plunged wildly away, its tail between its legs and still snarling. It halted forty feet away and surveyed him curiously, with ears sharply pricked forward. The man looked down at his hands in order to locate them, and found them hanging on the ends of his arms. It struck him as curious that one should have to use his eyes in order to find out where his hands were. He began threshing his arms back and forth, beating the mittened hands against his sides. He did this for five minutes, violently, and his heart pumped enough blood up to the surface to put a stop to his shivering. But no sensation was aroused in his hands. He had an impression that they hung like weights on the ends of his arms, but when he tried to run the impression down, he could not find it.

A certain fear of death, dull and oppressive, came to him. This fear quickly became poignant as he realized that it was no longer a mere matter of freezing his fingers and toes, or of losing his hands and feet, but that it was a matter of life and death, with the chances against him. This threw him into a panic, and he turned and ran up the creek bed along the old, dim trail. The dog joined in behind and kept up with him. He ran blindly, without intention, in fear such as he had never known in his life. Slowly, as he plowed and floundered through the snow, he began to see things again—the banks of the creek, the old timber jams, the leafless aspens, and the sky. The running made him feel better. He did

8. **peremptorily** (pər·emp′tə·ri·lē): in a commanding way.

not shiver. Maybe, if he ran on, his feet would thaw out; and, anyway, if he ran far enough, he would reach the camp and the boys. Without doubt he would lose some fingers and toes and some of his face; but the boys would take care of him, and save the rest of him when he got there. And, at the same time, there was another thought in his mind that said he would never get to the camp and the boys; that it was too many miles away, that the freezing had too great a start on him, and that he would soon be stiff and dead. This thought he kept in the background and refused to consider. Sometimes it pushed itself forward and demanded to be heard, but he thrust it back and strove to think of other things.

It struck him as curious that he could run at all on feet so frozen that he could not feel them when they struck the earth and took the weight of his body. He seemed to himself to skim along above the surface, and to have no connection with the earth. Somewhere he had once seen a winged Mercury,[9] and he wondered if Mercury felt as he felt when skimming over the earth.

His theory of running until he reached camp and the boys had one flaw in it: He lacked the endurance. Several times he stumbled, and finally he tottered, crumpled up, and fell. When he tried to rise, he failed. He must sit and rest, he decided, and next time he would merely walk and keep on going. As he sat and regained his breath, he noted that he was feeling quite warm and comfortable. He was not shivering, and it even seemed that a warm glow had come to his chest and trunk. And yet, when he touched his nose or cheeks, there was no sensation. Running would not thaw them out. Nor would it thaw out his hands and feet. Then the thought came to him that the frozen portions of his body must be extending. He tried to keep this thought down, to forget it, to think of something else; he was aware of the panicky feeling that it caused, and he was afraid of the panic. But the thought asserted itself, and persisted, until it produced a vision of his body totally frozen. This was too much, and he made another wild run along the trail. Once he slowed down to a walk, but the thought of the freezing extending itself made him run again.

And all the time the dog ran with him, at his heels. When he fell down a second time, it curled its tail over its forefeet and sat in front of him, facing him, curiously eager and intent. The warmth and security of the animal angered him, and he cursed it till it flattened down its ears appeasingly. This time the shivering came more quickly upon the man. He was losing in this battle with the frost. It was creeping into his body from all sides. The thought of it drove him on, but he ran no more than a hundred feet when he staggered and pitched headlong. It was his last panic. When he had recovered his breath and control, he sat up

9. **Mercury:** messenger of the gods in Roman mythology. He wears winged sandals and a winged hat.

INTERPRET

Why is this allusion to the Roman god Mercury **ironic**?

EVALUATE

riters almost always void clichés. Yet London onspicuously uses one in lines 19–520. What is the cliché, nd why is it appropriate to his place in the story?

INFER

he man has already resigned imself to death. Why, then, is e thinking about how he'll tell his story when he gets back to is home?

EVALUATE

s this an effective ending for he story? Explain.

INTERPRET

How does this story reflect key naturalist beliefs?

and entertained in his mind the conception of meeting death with dignity. However, the conception did not come to him in such terms. His idea of it was that he had been making a fool of himself, running around like a chicken with its head cut off—such was the simile that occurred to him. Well, he was bound to freeze anyway, and he might as well take it decently. With this newfound peace of mind came the first glimmerings of drowsiness. A good idea, he thought, to sleep off to death. It was like taking an anesthetic. Freezing was not so bad as people thought. There were lots worse ways to die.

He pictured the boys finding his body next day. Suddenly he found himself with them, coming along the trail and looking for himself. And, still with them, he came around a turn in the trail and found himself lying in the snow. He did not belong with himself anymore, for even then he was out of himself, standing with the boys and looking at himself in the snow. It certainly was cold, was his thought. When he got back to the States, he could tell the folks what real cold was. He drifted on from this to a vision of the old-timer on Sulfur Creek. He could see him quite clearly, warm and comfortable, and smoking a pipe.

"You were right, old hoss; you were right," the man mumbled to the old-timer of Sulfur Creek.

Then the man drowsed off into what seemed to him the most comfortable and satisfying sleep he had ever known. The dog sat facing him and waiting. The brief day drew to a close in a long, slow twilight. There were no signs of a fire to be made, and, besides, never in the dog's experience had it known a man to sit like that in the snow and make no fire. As the twilight drew on, its eager yearning for the fire mastered it, and with a great lifting and shifting of forefeet, it whined softly, then flattened its ears down in anticipation of being chidden[10] by the man. But the man remained silent. Later, the dog whined loudly. And still later it crept close to the man and caught the scent of death. This made the animal bristle and back away. A little longer it delayed, howling under the stars that leaped and danced and shone brightly in the cold sky. Then it turned and trotted up the trail in the direction of the camp it knew, where were the other food providers and fire providers.

---

10. chidden: scolded; past participle of *chide*.

Naturalism

The naturalists were a group of nineteenth-century writers who sought to portray life exactly as it is. Naturalist writers believed human behavior is determined by heredity and environment. Relying on new theories in sociology and psychology, the naturalists dissected human behavior with detachment and, they believed, the objectivity of scientists dissecting laboratory specimens. **Naturalism** presents human beings as subject to forces beyond their control.

Some scientists and philosophers believe imagination to be a distinctly human trait. We can conceive of ideas that are not concrete. However, the personality of the main character in "To Build a Fire" is defined by a lack of imagination that ultimately leads to his demise. For each part of the story listed in the chart below, record the main character's attitude and consider how he could have acted differently to save himself.

Action or Thought	Main Character's Attitude or Reaction	How He Could Have Changed His Fate
walking in fifty-below-zero weather		
planning to arrive at destination after dark		
feeling numbness in his extremities		
recalling old-timer's advice not to travel alone		
building his fire under a tree		

Vocabulary: How to Own a Word

Related Meanings

Word Bank
intangible
undulations
protruding
solidity
imperative
extremities
recoiled
imperceptible
excruciating
ensued

For each group of words below, cross out the unrelated word. Then, on the line below each item, briefly tell why the word you chose is unrelated to the others. The Word to Own is listed first and may be one of the unrelated words.

EXAMPLE: **a.** exceedingly **b.** ~~excessive~~ **c.** extremely **d.** extraordinarily

Though all four words have similar meanings, excessive is an adjective and the others are adverbs.

1. **a.** intangible **b.** elusive **c.** imperceptible **d.** palpable

2. **a.** undulations **b.** oscillations **c.** rotations **d.** pulsations

3. **a.** protruding **b.** intruding **c.** obtruding **d.** extending

4. **a.** solidity **b.** fluidity **c.** insubstantiality **d.** instability

5. **a.** imperative **b.** crucial **c.** unnecessary **d.** obligatory

6. **a.** extremities **b.** abdomen **c.** chest **d.** torso

7. a. recoiled b. balked c. confronted d. demurred

8. a. imperceptible b. evident c. noticeable d. distinct

9. a. excruciating b. torturous c. painful d. endurable

10. a. ensued b. preceded c. proceeded d. followed

The Moderns 1900–1950

World War I (1914–1918) was one of the events that changed the American voice in fiction. Before that clash of armies from the old and new worlds, American fiction had spoken in youthful tones—brash, but not fully original, and at times as uncertain as an adolescent's. Then, in 1917, the United States entered the so-called Great War, a conflict that was fought under the bright banners of humanity and democratic righteousness, but that, in fact, became a bloodbath. In 1916, more than a half-million soldiers were killed in a single, month-long battle near the town of Verdun in northeastern France.

CONNECT
/hat are some events that ave had this effect during our own lifetime or your arents' lifetime?

Although America emerged from the war as a victor, something was beginning to change. The country seemed to have lost its innocence. Idealism was turning into cynicism, and a few American writers began to question the authority and tradition that had seemed to be America's bedrock. The war introduced new moral codes, as well as short skirts, bobbed hair, and even new slang expressions. Americans' sense of a connection to their past seemed to be deteriorating.

There were other reasons for this change in outlook. The Great Depression that followed the crash of the New York stock market in 1929 brought suffering to millions of Americans—to those same hard-working people who had put their faith in the boundless capacity of America to provide them with jobs and their children with brighter futures.

CONNECT
Vhat well-known paintings or ieces of music do you know hat date from the early wentieth century?

American writers, like their European counterparts, were also profoundly affected by the **modernist** movement. This movement in literature, painting, music, and the other arts—swept along by disillusionment with traditions that seemed to have become spiritually empty—called for bold experimentation and a wholesale rejection of traditional themes and styles.

World War I and the Great Depression were turning points in American life, marking a loss of innocence and a strong disillusionment with tradition.

The American Dream: Pursuit of a Promise

If **modernism** meant questioning or reinterpreting some of the most deeply held European values, then Americans had been "modern" all along. America had inherited many age-old European traditions and then attached them to an entirely new set of ideals and hopes that grew out of America's frontier experience.

Still, the shock of World War I and then the Great Depression affected everyone; in the global atmosphere of disillusion, it was natural that Americans would reexamine their ideals from their own perspective. These ideals, taken together, have become known as the **American dream.** They emerge out of three central beliefs.

First, there is admiration for America as a new Eden: a land of beauty, bounty, and unlimited promise. In one of the greatest American novels, *The Great Gatsby* (1925), F. Scott Fitzgerald (1896–1940) describes how the New World might have looked to the first European explorers: ". . . for a transitory enchanted moment man must have held his breath in the presence of this continent, compelled into an aesthetic contemplation he neither understood nor desired, face to face for the last time in history with something commensurate to his capacity for wonder." This is the vision of America that attracted the Jamestown settlers and the *Mayflower* Pilgrims and countless millions of immigrants ever since. Benjamin Franklin followed this vision to Philadelphia; farmers and gold-seekers followed it relentlessly westward across the continent.

The second element in the American dream is optimism, justified by the ever-expanding opportunity and abundance that many people have come to expect. Most of the time, Americans have believed in progress—that life keeps getting better and that we are moving toward an era of prosperity, justice, and joy that always seems just around the corner.

Finally, the third important element in the American dream has been the importance and ultimate triumph of the individual—the independent, self-reliant person. This ideal was championed by Ralph Waldo Emerson, who probably deserves most of the credit for defining the essence of the American dream, including its roots in the promise of the "new Eden" and its faith that "things are getting better all the time." Trust the universe and trust yourself, Emerson wrote. "If the single man plant himself indomitable on his instincts, and there abide, the huge world will come round to him."

The three underpinnings of the American dream are a belief in the land as a bountiful new Eden, an unwavering faith in progress, and a confidence in the ultimate triumph of the individual.

The Tenets of the American Dream

- America is a new Eden, a "promised land" of beauty, unlimited resources, and endless opportunities.
- The American birthright is one of ever-expanding opportunity. Progress is a good thing, and we can optimistically expect life to keep getting better and better.

BUILD FLUENCY

Re-read this passage aloud, taking care to pronounce the words clearly and expressively.

CONNECT

Does America seem optimistic today? Explain your answer.

RETELL

Restate Emerson's claim abou "a single man" in your own words.

IDENTIFY

In each of the three tenets, circle one or two words that best sum up the **main idea.**

- The independent, self-reliant individual will triumph. Everything is possible for the person who places trust in his or her own powers and potential.

A Crack in the World: Breakdown of Beliefs and Traditions

The cannonades of World War I and the economic crash a decade later severely damaged these inherited ideas of an Edenic land, an optimism in the future, and faith in individualism. Postwar writers became skeptical of the New England Puritan tradition and the gentility that had been central to the literary ideal. In fact, the center of American literary life now finally started to shift away from New England, which had been the native region of America's most brilliant writers during the nineteenth century. Many modernist writers, in fact, were born in the South, the Midwest, or the West.

In the postwar period, two new intellectual trends or movements, **Marxism** and **psychoanalysis,** combined to increase the pressure on traditional beliefs and values. In Russia during World War I, a Marxist revolution had toppled and even murdered an anointed ruler, the czar. The socialistic beliefs of Karl Marx that had powered the Russian Revolution in 1917 were in direct opposition to the American system of capitalism and free enterprise, and Marxists threatened to export their revolution everywhere. From Moscow, the American journalist John Reed sent back the alarming message: "I have seen the future and it works."

INFER

What do you think Reed meant by "it works"—what is "it," and in what way does it "work"?

In Vienna, there was another unsettling development. Sigmund Freud, the founder of psychoanalysis, had opened the workings of the unconscious mind to scrutiny and called for a new understanding of human sexuality and the role it plays in our unconscious thoughts. Throughout America, there was a growing interest in this new field of psychology, and a resultant anxiety about the degree of freedom an individual really had. If our actions were influenced by our subconscious, and if we had no control over our subconscious, there seemed to be little room left for "free will."

One literary result of this interest in the psyche was the narrative technique called **stream of consciousness.** This writing style abandoned chronology and attempted to imitate the moment-by-moment flow of a character's perceptions and memories. The Irish writer James Joyce (1882–1941) radically changed the very concept of the novel by using stream of consciousness in *Ulysses* (1922), his monumental "odyssey" set in Dublin. Soon afterward, the American writers Katherine Anne Porter (1890–1980) and William Faulkner (1897–1962) used the stream-of-consciousness technique in their works.

Two important trends, Marxism and psychoanalysis, were noteworthy factors in the breakdown of traditional beliefs and values. Psychoanalysis led to the literary technique of stream-of-consciousness narration.

At Home and Abroad: The Jazz Age

In 1919, the Constitution was amended to prohibit the manufacture and sale of alcohol, which was singled out as a central social evil. But far from shoring up traditional values, Prohibition ushered in an age characterized by the bootlegger, the speakeasy, the cocktail, the short-skirted flapper, the new rhythms of jazz, and the dangerous but lucrative profession of the gangster. Recording the Roaring Twenties and making the era a vivid chapter in our history, F. Scott Fitzgerald gave it its name: the Jazz Age.

As energetic as the Roaring Twenties were in America, the pursuit of pleasure abroad was even more attractive to some than its enjoyment at home. F. Scott Fitzgerald was among the many American writers and artists who abandoned their own shores for the expatriate life in France. After World War I, living was not only cheap in Paris and on the sunny French Riviera but also somehow better; it was more exotic, it seemed more filled with grace and luxury, and there was no need to go down a cellar stairway to get a drink. This wave of expatriates was another signal that something had gone wrong with the American dream—with the idea that America was Eden, with our notion of inherent virtue, and especially with the conviction that America was a land of heroes.

The Jazz Age at home was racy and unconventional. The same decade of the 1920s witnessed the flight of many American authors to an expatriate life abroad, especially in France.

Grace Under Pressure: The New American Hero

Disillusionment was a major theme in the fiction of the time. In 1920, Sinclair Lewis (1885–1951) lashed out satirically at the narrow-mindedness of small-town life in his immensely popular novel, *Main Street.* In 1925, Theodore Dreiser (1871–1945) produced a literary landmark with his prototype of the realistic novel, *An American Tragedy,* the story of an ambitious but luckless man who takes a path that leads him not to the success he seeks, but to the execution chamber.

The most influential of all the post–World War I writers, however, was Ernest Hemingway (1899–1961). Hemingway is perhaps most

IDENTIFY

Which word in lines 124–12 refers to an alcoholic drink?

Which word refers to someon who sold illegal alcohol?

Which word refers to an illeg saloon?

Which word means "party girl"?

INFER

In one sentence, tell why the 1920s were called "the Jazz Age."

IDENTIFY

Circle the names of three major American writers of the 1920s.

famous for his literary style, which affected the style of American prose fiction for several generations. Like the Puritans who strove for a "plain style" centuries earlier, Hemingway reduced the flamboyance of literary language to a minimum, to the bare bones of the truth it must express.

Hemingway also introduced a new kind of hero to American fiction, a character type that many readers embraced as a protagonist and a role model. This Hemingway hero is a man of action, a warrior, and a tough competitor; he has a code of honor, courage, and endurance. He shows, in Hemingway's own words, "grace under pressure." But the most important trait of this Hemingway hero is that he is thoroughly disillusioned, a quality that reflected the author's own outlook. For Hemingway feared, a little like Herman Melville, that at the inscrutable center of creation lay nothing at all.

Hemingway found his own answer to this crisis of faith in a belief in the self and in such qualities as decency, bravery, competence, and skill. He clung to this conviction in spite of what he saw as the absolutely unbeatable odds ranged against us all. A further part of the Hemingway code was the importance of recognizing and snatching up the rare, good, rich moments that life offers before those moments elude us.

Hemingway summed up the values of many post–World War I writers, both in his spare, plain style and in his creation of a new kind of hero, disillusioned but also honorable and courageous.

Modernist Voices in Poetry: A Dazzling Period

After the deaths of Emily Dickinson and Walt Whitman, American poetry went into something of a decline. But time would show that the comparatively uneventful period between 1890 and 1910 was but the trough of a wave that was about to break. The force of this wave, when it arrived, would be strong enough to wash away the last traces of British influence on American poetry and to carry our poets into their most dazzling period of variety and experimentation.

During this period, many poets began to explore the artistic life of Europe, especially Paris. With other writers, artists, and composers from all over the world, they absorbed the lessons of modernist painters like Henri Matisse and Pablo Picasso, who were exploring new ways to see and represent reality. In the same way, poets sought to create poems that invited new ways of seeing and thinking. Ezra Pound (1885–1972) and T. S. Eliot (1888–1965) used the suggestive techniques of **Symbolism** to fashion a new, modernist poetry. Pound also spearheaded a related poetic movement called **Imagism.** Exemplified by brilliant poets like

OMPARE AND CONTRAST

) you think the heroes of day's movies and novels are cynical and disillusioned modernist heroes of the 920s? Explain your answer.

DENTIFY

nderline the names of three ajor American modernist oets.

William Carlos Williams (1883–1963), the Imagist and Symbolist styles would prevail in poetry until midway into the twentieth century.

After an uneventful period between 1890 and 1910, developments in Europe helped trigger an explosion of modernist poetry. Ezra Pound and T. S. Eliot, associated with the Symbolist and Imagist movements, were especially important in charting a modernist direction for American poetry.

The Elements of Modernism in American Literature

- Emphasis on bold experimentation in style and form, reflecting the fragmentation of society
- Rejection of traditional themes and subjects
- Sense of disillusionment and loss of faith in the American dream
- Rejection of the ideal of a hero as infallible in favor of a hero who is flawed and disillusioned but shows "grace under pressure"
- Interest in the inner workings of the human mind sometimes expressed through new narrative techniques such as stream of consciousness

Voices of American Character: Poets of Tradition

Meanwhile, other American poets rejected modernist trends. While their colleagues found inspiration in Paris, these poets stayed at home, ignoring or defying the revolution of modernism. Poets like Edwin Arlington Robinson (1869–1935) of Maine, Edgar Lee Masters (1869–1950) of Kansas, Robinson Jeffers (1887–1962) of California, and John Crowe Ransom (1888–1974) of Tennessee preferred to say what they had to say in plain American speech filtered through traditional poetic forms.

The greatest poetic voice in New England was that of Robert Frost (1874–1963). Frost's independence was grounded in his ability to handle ordinary New England speech and in his surprising skill at taking the most conventional poetic forms and giving them a twist all his own. In an era when "good" was being equated by many artists with "new," the only new thing about Robert Frost was old: individual poetic genius. Using this gift to impose his own personality on the iambic line in verse, Frost created a poetic voice that was unique and impossible to imitate.

Poets like Robert Frost continued to use traditional verse forms to produce a uniquely American voice.

IDENTIFY

Underline the names of four major American traditionalist poets.

The Harlem Renaissance: Voices of the African American Experience

African American culture found expression in poetry in two different ways. The works of black poets who wrote in conventional forms, like Paul Laurence Dunbar (1872–1906), were most quickly accepted by white readers. A second group of black poets focused directly on the unique contributions of African American culture to America. Their poetry based its rhythms on spirituals and jazz, its lyrics on songs known as the blues, and its diction on the street talk of the ghettos.

DENTIFY

nderline the names of four ajor poets of the Harlem enaissance.

Foremost among African American lyric poets were James Weldon Johnson (1871–1938), Claude McKay (1890–1948), Countee Cullen (1903–1946), and especially Langston Hughes (1902–1967), who brought literary distinction to the broad movement of artists known as the **Harlem Renaissance.** The geographical center of the movement was Harlem, the section of New York City north of 110th Street in Manhattan. But its spiritual center was a place in the consciousness of African Americans—a people too long ignored, patronized, or otherwise pushed to the margins of American art. When African American poetry, hand in hand with the music echoing from New Orleans, Memphis, and Chicago, became part of the Jazz Age, it was a catalyst for a new appreciation of the role of black talent in American culture.

The poets of the Harlem Renaissance revolutionized the African American contribution to American literature by introducing colloquial speech and the rhythms of jazz and blues into their verse.

The American Dream Revised

Even though the modernists rejected Emerson's optimism, a belief in self-reliance persisted as did the old idea of America as Eden. Hemingway is really telling us about Eden in his *Up in Michigan* stories, where he describes the lakes and streams and woods he knew as a boy and where he extols the restorative power of nature in a way that Emerson might have recognized. This is the same Edenic America that has come down to us through Mark Twain's Mississippi, through Faulkner's Yoknapatawpha County, and through John Steinbeck's Salinas Valley.

As we explore this period of American writing—in some respects, the richest period since the flowering of New England in the first half of the nineteenth century—we stand at the threshold of our own time. Though this period has seen major changes in American attitudes, you'll recognize many concerns that are consistent with concerns of the past. These writers—some of the best that America has produced—experimented boldly with forms and subject matter. But they were also still trying to find the answers to the basic human questions: Who are we? Where are we going? And what values should guide us on that search for our human identity?

American modernist writers both echoed and challenged the American dream. They constituted a broader, more resonant voice than ever before, resulting in a second American renaissance. With all the changes, however, writers continued to ask fundamental questions about the meaning and purpose of human existence.

INTERPRET
What still seems "modern" about modernism?

Design

Make the Connection

Design of Darkness

Robert Frost, by far the most popular American poet of the twentieth century, presented himself as a simple man—a farmer and schoolteacher who expressed life's deepest truths in the plain, honest language of rural New England. But Frost, in fact a native San Franciscan whose education included studies at Dartmouth and Harvard, knew very well how to veil a complex idea with a seemingly simple exterior.

Frost's **sonnet** "Design," for example, is a masterpiece in the subtle way it presents the stark beauty of the natural world without sentimentality. Sometimes we are uplifted and inspired by the beauty of nature; sometimes we are shocked or appalled by nature's potential for danger and violence. Anyone in direct contact with nature knows that sudden violence and grisly death are facts of life. The strong prey on the weak; the swift hunt down the slow; and the healthy ultimately die and decay. By human standards, nature can be cold and merciless.

Use the lines below to explore your connections with and feelings about nature. In the left-hand column, use brief phrases to describe experiences that have impressed you with nature's beauty or consoling power. On the right, list observations or experiences that have highlighted the destructive side of nature.

Beauty in Nature	Destructiveness in Nature

DESIGN

Robert Frost

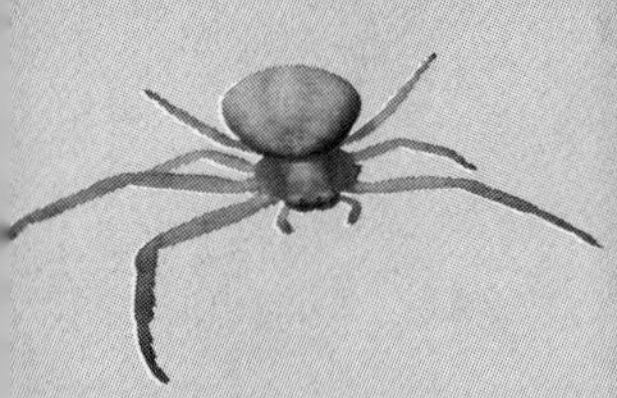

DENTIFY

nderline four **similes** that cur in the first eight lines this sonnet. How do these niles affect the poem's tone?

NFER

hy do you think Frost chose heal-all rather than some her white flower?

INTERPRET

ook up the word *design* in dictionary. Which meanings ight apply to the title of ne poem?

BUILD FLUENCY

Read the poem aloud as xpressively as you can. Use he punctuation as a guide to nits of meaning. At the ends f which lines in the octave the first eight lines) would ou *not* pause?

I found a dimpled spider, fat and white,
On a white heal-all,[1] holding up a moth
Like a white piece of rigid satin cloth—
Assorted characters of death and blight
Mixed ready to begin the morning right,
Like the ingredients of a witches' broth—
A snowdrop spider, a flower like a froth,[2]
And dead wings carried like a paper kite.

What had that flower to do with being white,
The wayside blue and innocent heal-all?
What brought the kindred spider to that height,
Then steered the white moth thither[3] in the night?
What but design of darkness to appall?—
If design govern in a thing so small.

1. **heal-all:** flowering plant of the mint family. The flowers, leaves, and stems are used in folk medicine to treat sore throats and other minor ailments.
2. **froth:** foam.
3. **thither:** archaic for "there."

The Sonnet

A **sonnet** is a fourteen-line, lyric poem, usually written in iambic pentameter, that has one of two basic structures. The form known as the **English, Elizabethan,** or **Shakespearean sonnet** has three four-line units, known as **quatrains,** and it concludes with a pair of lines called a **couplet.**

Frost's poem "Design," however, is an example of the **Petrarchan** or **Italian sonnet,** which is named after the fourteenth-century Italian poet Petrarch. This type of sonnet is typically divided into an **octave** (the first eight lines) and a **sestet** (the last six lines). The octave often asks a question or poses a problem, while the sestet responds to the question, problem, or conflict—often presenting a resolution. The rhyme scheme of the octave is typically *abba, abba,* while the sestet rhymes *cde, cde.*

Frost handles this demanding form with great skill and originality. Consider how he departs from the traditional conventions by answering the following questions.

1. Instead of five rhymes, how many rhymes does the poet use in "Design"? What is the effect of this technique, in your opinion?

   ____

   ____

   ____

2. Where do the speaker's questions occur in the poem? How does this placement depart from the usual pattern of an Italian sonnet?

   ____

   ____

   ____

3. How does the last line affect the whole tone and meaning of the poem?

   ____

   ____

   ____

Once by the Pacific

Make the Connection

The End of It All

In the Biblical story of creation, God says, "Let there be light" (Genesis 1:3). In many religious and cultural traditions, creation is balanced by a prophecy of doomsday, when all things in the universe will pass away.

In "Once by the Pacific," Robert Frost uses an everyday scene—a strong ocean surf pounding on the beach—to summon up a doomsday vision. You've probably seen waves pounding against the shore, in person or on film. Use the space below to write a few sentences describing your thoughts as you watched the oncoming waves. Then, see how your reactions compare and contrast with the feelings of the speaker in Frost's poem.

Once by the Pacific

Robert Frost

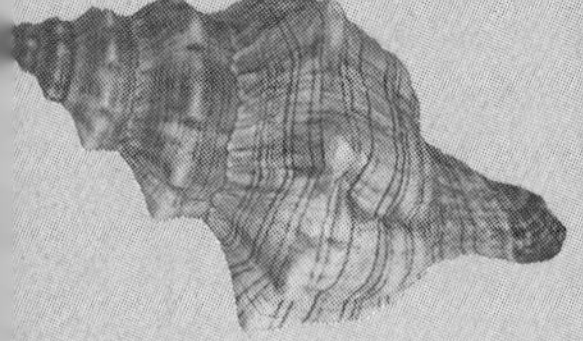

NFER

›st **personifies** the waves in
es 2–4. What do these lines
ggest?

NTERPRET

nat is the "night of dark
:ent" (line 10)?

NTERPRET

hat words and phrases in the
›em create an ominous **tone**?

EVALUATE

the final line, Frost reverses
e words of God's command
: the creation in Genesis 1:3,
_et there be light." How
fective do you think this
lusion is, given the whole
›ntext of Frost's poem?

BUILD FLUENCY

:ead the poem aloud as
xpressively as you can.
se the punctuation as a
uide to units of meaning.

IDENTIFY

low many different rhymes
oes Frost use in this poem?

The shattered water made a misty din.
Great waves looked over others coming in,
And thought of doing something to the shore
That water never did to land before.
The clouds were low and hairy in the skies,
Like locks blown forward in the gleam of eyes.
You could not tell, and yet it looked as if
The shore was lucky in being backed by cliff,
The cliff in being backed by continent;
It looked as if a night of dark intent
Was coming, and not only a night, an age.
Someone had better be prepared for rage.
There would be more than ocean-water broken
Before God's last *Put out the Light* was spoken.

Personification

Personification is a special type of metaphor that attributes human feelings, thoughts, or attitudes to something nonhuman. Frost uses this technique in "Once by the Pacific," as in line 3, where the waves "thought of doing something to the shore."

Re-read "Once by the Pacific," and write down, in the left-hand column of the chart, three examples of personification in the poem. Then, use the right-hand column to describe the two things that each example compares.

Example of Personification	Explanation
"Great waves . . . thought of doing something to the shore. . . ." (lines 2–3)	

Birches

Make the Connection

Stages of Growth

As spindly and awkward as a giraffe's legs, the birch trees of Robert Frost's New England have white bark ringed with black. Their trunks are remarkably pliable—a fact that gives "Birches" its realistic base for Frost to tell a parable in verse about how we may grow and mature throughout life. A **parable** is a short story in which an ordinary event from everyday life is used to teach a much wider moral or religious lesson. In this poem, Frost draws a lesson from nature—from the sight of the bent branches of birch trees and from the thought of a boy swinging on them. An important part of Frost's theme is the instinctively human willingness to accept challenges and to strive toward fulfillment or accomplishment.

How would you evaluate your own feelings about achievement? Compare your accomplishments and attitudes three years ago with your feelings now by filling out the chart below.

Three Years Ago	Today
Hobbies and Special Interests: ______ ______ ______	______ ______ ______
Honors or Achievements: ______ ______ ______	______ ______ ______
Goals for the Future: ______ ______ ______	______ ______ ______

Birches

Robert Frost

UILD FLUENCY

ad lines 1–9 aloud. Where
the major pauses occur?

VISUALIZE

nderline the details in lines
-10 that help you to visualize
e scene Frost describes.

INFER

'hat does the speaker admire
the boy?

INTERPRET

/hat do you think is meant
ymbolically in lines 32–38
y the phrases "not launching
ut too soon," keeping one's
poise," and "climbing
arefully"?

INTERPRET

Vhat does the **metaphor** of
he cup filled up to the brim
lines 37–38) add to the
neaning of this passage?

When I see birches bend to left and right
Across the lines of straighter darker trees,
I like to think some boy's been swinging them.
But swinging doesn't bend them down to stay
As ice storms do. Often you must have seen them
Loaded with ice a sunny winter morning
After a rain. They click upon themselves
As the breeze rises, and turn many-colored
As the stir cracks and crazes their enamel.
Soon the sun's warmth makes them shed crystal shells
Shattering and avalanching on the snow crust—
Such heaps of broken glass to sweep away
You'd think the inner dome of heaven had fallen.
They are dragged to the withered bracken[1] by the load,
And they seem not to break; though once they are bowed
So low for long, they never right themselves:
You may see their trunks arching in the woods
Years afterwards, trailing their leaves on the ground
Like girls on hands and knees that throw their hair
Before them over their heads to dry in the sun.
But I was going to say when Truth broke in
With all her matter of fact about the ice storm,
I should prefer to have some boy bend them
As he went out and in to fetch the cows—
Some boy too far from town to learn baseball,
Whose only play was what he found himself,
Summer or winter, and could play alone.
One by one he subdued his father's trees
By riding them down over and over again
Until he took the stiffness out of them,
And not one but hung limp, not one was left
For him to conquer. He learned all there was
To learn about not launching out too soon
And so not carrying the tree away
Clear to the ground. He always kept his poise[2]
To the top branches, climbing carefully
With the same pains you use to fill a cup
Up to the brim, and even above the brim.
Then he flung outward, feet first, with a swish,
Kicking his way down through the air to the ground.
So was I once myself a swinger of birches.
And so I dream of going back to be.

1. **bracken:** large, coarse fern.
2. **poise:** balance.

It's when I'm weary of considerations,
And life is too much like a pathless wood
Where your face burns and tickles with the cobwebs
Broken across it, and one eye is weeping
From a twig's having lashed across it open.
I'd like to get away from earth awhile
And then come back to it and begin over.
May no fate willfully misunderstand me
And half grant what I wish and snatch me away
Not to return. Earth's the right place for love:
I don't know where it's likely to go better.
I'd like to go by climbing a birch tree,
And climb black branches up a snow-white trunk
Toward heaven, till the tree could bear no more,
But dipped its top and set me down again.
That would be good both going and coming back.
One could do worse than be a swinger of birches.

EVALUATE

What is the **simile** that Frost uses in lines 44–47, and why is this comparison especially effective?

BUILD FLUENCY

Read lines 50–53 aloud, accenting the words naturally as if the passage were in prose

RETELL

Summarize the **theme** or underlying message of this poem. What complex, conflicting attitudes about life does the poem reveal?

Blank Verse

Blank verse is poetry written in unrhymed iambic pentameter. When you read blank verse, take careful note of the punctuation. When you come to a period at the end of a line or in the middle of a line, make a major pause or a full stop. When you come to a comma, semicolon, or dash, pause slightly. If there is no punctuation mark at the end of a line, read right on to the next line without pausing.

- In lines 1–20, how many major pauses occur in the middle of a line? Write the answer in the space provided, and then identify the lines in which these pauses occur.

  ____

  ____

- In lines 1–20, at the end of which lines should you read right on to the next line without pausing?

  ____

  ____

Vocabulary: How to Own a Word

Related Meanings

Word Bank
withered
subdued
poise
swish
willfully

In each of the following groups of words, cross out the unrelated word. The unrelated word may have a different meaning or may be a different part of speech than the others. The words from the poem are shown in boldface type.

EXAMPLE: **a. shattering** **b.** ~~conforming~~ **c.** breaking **d.** fragmenting

1. **a.** shriveled **b.** dried up **c. withered** **d.** pampered
2. **a.** conquered **b. subdued** **c.** feared **d.** vanquished
3. **a. poise** **b.** analysis **c.** balance **d.** composure
4. **a.** hiss **b.** rustle **c.** bang **d. swish**
5. **a.** savage **b.** deliberately **c. willfully** **d.** intentionally

Winter Dreams

Make the Connection

Dream and Disillusionment

"Let me tell you about the very rich," wrote F. Scott Fitzgerald in one of the many short stories in which he chronicled the 1920s. "They are different from you and me. They possess and enjoy early, and it does something to them, makes them soft where we are hard, and cynical where we are trustful." Fitzgerald's fascination with the "very rich" began early, and when sudden literary success made him the most celebrated writer of the Jazz Age, it seemed for a time that all the dreams of his Minnesota boyhood had come true. But he remained, somehow, the born outsider; the glittering world of wealth and privilege always seemed to recede just beyond his frustrated grasp.

Fitzgerald may be America's greatest poet of longing. He wrote about the elusiveness of dreams and the disillusionment that can ensnare those whose dreams seem to come true. Have you ever been forced to the painful realization that something you want can never be yours? Have you ever gotten something you wanted—and then felt disappointed to discover that the reality didn't measure up to the hope? Explore this pattern of dream and disillusionment by filling out the chart below with two examples from literature, films, or your own experience.

Description of Ideal or Dream	Description of Disillusionment	Key Events Leading to Disillusionment

Winter Dreams

F. Scott Fitzgerald

INFER

/hat does the **simile** in the xpression "poor as sin" uggest about the characters' ossible motivation in this ociety?

WORDS TO OWN

:lation (ē·lā′shən) *n.:* :elebration.

INTERPRET

/Vhat do you think Dexter is 'eally longing for, besides his vague daydreams of success on the golf course?

Some of the caddies were poor as sin and lived in one-room houses with a neurasthenic[1] cow in the front yard, but Dexter Green's father owned the second best grocery-store in Black Bear—the best one was "The Hub," patronized by the wealthy people from Sherry Island—and Dexter caddied only for pocket-money.

In the fall when the days became crisp and gray, and the long Minnesota winter shut down like the white lid of a box, Dexter's skis moved over the snow that hid the fairways[2] of the golf course. At these times the country gave him a feeling of profound melancholy—it offended him that the links should lie in enforced fallowness, haunted by ragged sparrows for the long season. It was dreary, too, that on the tees where the gay colors fluttered in summer there were now only the desolate sand-boxes knee-deep in crusted ice. When he crossed the hills the wind blew cold as misery, and if the sun was out he tramped with his eyes squinted up against the hard dimensionless glare.

In April the winter ceased abruptly. The snow ran down into Black Bear Lake scarcely tarrying[3] for the early golfers to brave the season with red and black balls. Without elation, without an interval of moist glory, the cold was gone.

Dexter knew that there was something dismal about this Northern spring, just as he knew there was something gorgeous about the fall. Fall made him clinch his hands and tremble and repeat idiotic sentences to himself, and make brisk abrupt gestures of command to imaginary audiences and armies. October filled him with hope which November raised to a sort of ecstatic triumph, and in this mood the fleeting brilliant impressions of the summer at Sherry Island were ready grist to his mill.[4] He became a golf champion and defeated Mr. T. A. Hedrick in a marvellous match played a hundred times over the fairways of his imagination, a match each detail of which he changed about untiringly—sometimes he won with almost laughable ease, sometimes he came up magnificently from behind. Again, stepping from a Pierce-Arrow automobile, like Mr. Mortimer Jones, he strolled frigidly into the lounge of the Sherry Island Golf Club—or perhaps, surrounded by an admiring crowd, he gave an exhibition of fancy diving from the spring-board of the club raft. . . . Among those who watched him in open-mouthed wonder was Mr. Mortimer Jones.

And one day it came to pass that Mr. Jones—himself and not his ghost—came up to Dexter with tears in his eyes and said that Dexter was the——best caddy in the club, and wouldn't he decide not to quit

1. **neurasthenic** (no͞o′ras·then′ik): thin and weak, as though suffering from a nervous disorder.
2. **fairways:** mowed parts of a golf course. The fairway of most holes starts at the tee and ends near the green.
3. **tarrying:** waiting.
4. **grist to his mill:** something that can be used to advantage.

if Mr. Jones made it worth his while, because every other——caddy in the club lost one ball a hole for him—regularly——

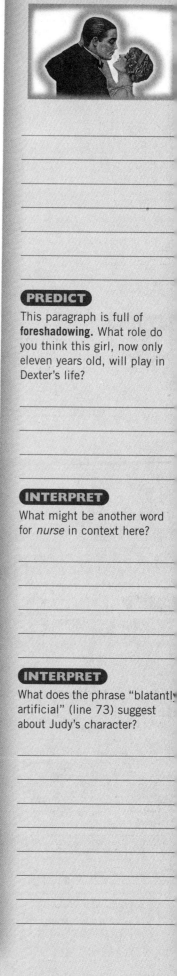

"No, sir," said Dexter decisively, "I don't want to caddy any more." Then, after a pause: "I'm too old."

"You're not more than fourteen. Why the devil did you decide just this morning that you wanted to quit? You promised that next week you'd go over to the State tournament with me."

"I decided I was too old."

Dexter handed in his "A Class" badge, collected what money was due him from the caddy master, and walked home to Black Bear Village.

"The best——caddy I ever saw," shouted Mr. Mortimer Jones over a drink that afternoon. "Never lost a ball! Willing! Intelligent! Quiet! Honest! Grateful!"

The little girl who had done this was eleven—beautifully ugly as little girls are apt to be who are destined after a few years to be inexpressibly lovely and bring no end of misery to a great number of men. The spark, however, was perceptible. There was a general ungodliness in the way her lips twisted down at the corners when she smiled, and in the—Heaven help us!—in the almost passionate quality of her eyes. Vitality is born early in such women. It was utterly in evidence now, shining through her thin frame in a sort of glow.

She had come eagerly out on to the course at nine o'clock with a white linen nurse and five small new golf-clubs in a white canvas bag which the nurse was carrying. When Dexter first saw her she was standing by the caddy house, rather ill at ease and trying to conceal the fact by engaging her nurse in an obviously unnatural conversation graced by startling and irrelevant grimaces from herself.

"Well, it's certainly a nice day, Hilda," Dexter heard her say. She drew down the corners of her mouth, smiled, and glanced furtively around, her eyes in transit falling for an instant on Dexter.

Then to the nurse:

"Well, I guess there aren't very many people out here this morning, are there?"

The smile again—radiant, blatantly artificial—convincing.

"I don't know what we're supposed to do now," said the nurse, looking nowhere in particular.

"Oh, that's all right. I'll fix it up."

Dexter stood perfectly still, his mouth slightly ajar. He knew that if he moved forward a step his stare would be in her line of vision—if he moved backward he would lose his full view of her face. For a moment he had not realized how young she was. Now he remembered having seen her several times the year before—in bloomers.

Suddenly, involuntarily, he laughed, a short abrupt laugh—then, startled by himself, he turned and began to walk quickly away.

"Boy!"

PREDICT

This paragraph is full of **foreshadowing.** What role do you think this girl, now only eleven years old, will play in Dexter's life?

INTERPRET

What might be another word for *nurse* in context here?

INTERPRET

What does the phrase "blatantly artificial" (line 73) suggest about Judy's character?

IDENTIFY

ircle the "bad grammar" that eveals Dexter's social class as eing lower than that of the irl.

INFER

Vhy do you think Dexter feels his "monstrous conviction"?

Dexter stopped.

"Boy——"

Beyond question he was addressed. Not only that, but he was treated to that absurd smile, that preposterous smile—the memory of which at least a dozen men were to carry into middle age.

"Boy, do you know where the golf teacher is?"

"He's giving a lesson."

"Well, do you know where the caddy-master is?"

"He isn't here yet this morning."

"Oh." For a moment this baffled her. She stood alternately on her right and left foot.

"We'd like to get a caddy," said the nurse. "Mrs. Mortimer Jones sent us out to play golf, and we don't know how without we get a caddy."

Here she was stopped by an ominous glance from Miss Jones, followed immediately by the smile.

"There aren't any caddies here except me," said Dexter to the nurse, "and I got to stay here in charge until the caddy-master gets here."

"Oh."

Miss Jones and her retinue[5] now withdrew, and at a proper distance from Dexter became involved in a heated conversation, which was concluded by Miss Jones taking one of the clubs and hitting it on the ground with violence. For further emphasis she raised it again and was about to bring it down smartly upon the nurse's bosom, when the nurse seized the club and twisted it from her hands.

"You damn little mean old *thing!*" cried Miss Jones wildly.

Another argument ensued. Realizing that the elements of the comedy were implied in the scene, Dexter several times began to laugh, but each time restrained the laugh before it reached audibility. He could not resist the monstrous conviction that the little girl was justified in beating the nurse.

The situation was resolved by the fortuitous[6] appearance of the caddy-master, who was appealed to immediately by the nurse.

"Miss Jones is to have a little caddy, and this one says he can't go."

"Mr. McKenna said I was to wait here till you came," said Dexter quickly.

"Well, he's here now." Miss Jones smiled cheerfully at the caddy-master. Then she dropped her bag and set off at a haughty mince[7] toward the first tee.

"Well?" the caddy-master turned to Dexter. "What you standing there like a dummy for? Go pick up the young lady's clubs."

"I don't think I'll go out to-day," said Dexter.

5. **retinue** (ret′'n·yo͞o′): group of followers or servants attending to a person of rank.
6. **fortuitous** (fôr·to͞o′ə·təs): fortunate.
7. **mince:** prim, affected walk.

"You don't——"

"I think I'll quit."

The enormity of his decision frightened him. He was a favorite caddy, and the thirty dollars a month he earned through the summer were not to be made elsewhere around the lake. But he had received a strong emotional shock, and his perturbation required a violent and immediate outlet.

It is not so simple as that, either. As so frequently would be the case in the future, Dexter was unconsciously dictated to by his winter dreams.

II

Now, of course, the quality and the seasonability of these winter dreams varied, but the stuff of them remained. They persuaded Dexter several years later to pass up a business course at the State university—his father, prospering now, would have paid his way—for the precarious[8] advantage of attending an older and more famous university in the East, where he was bothered by his scanty funds. But do not get the impression, because his winter dreams happened to be concerned at first with musings on the rich, that there was anything merely snobbish in the boy. He wanted not association with glittering things and glittering people—he wanted the glittering things themselves. Often he reached out for the best without knowing why he wanted it—and sometimes he ran up against the mysterious denials and prohibitions in which life indulges. It is with one of those denials and not with his career as a whole that this story deals.

He made money. It was rather amazing. After college he went to the city from which Black Bear Lake draws its wealthy patrons. When he was only twenty-three and had been there not quite two years, there were already people who liked to say: "Now *there's* a boy—" All about him rich men's sons were peddling bonds precariously, or investing patrimonies[9] precariously, or plodding through the two dozen volumes of the "George Washington Commercial Course," but Dexter borrowed a thousand dollars on his college degree and his confident mouth, and bought a partnership in a laundry.

It was a small laundry when he went into it but Dexter made a specialty of learning how the English washed fine woolen golf-stockings without shrinking them, and within a year he was catering to the trade that wore knickerbockers. Men were insisting that their Shetland hose and sweaters go to his laundry just as they had insisted on a caddy who could find golf-balls. A little later he was doing their wives' lingerie as well—and running five branches in different parts of the city. Before he was twenty-seven he owned the largest string of laundries in his section

8. **precarious** (prē·ker'ē·əs): uncertain.
9. **patrimonies** (pa'trə·mō'nēz): inheritances.

WORDS TO OWN
perturbation (pur'tər·bā'shən) *n.:* feeling of alarm or agitatio

INFER
What does this passage suggest about Dexter's **motivation** for seeking to possess "the glittering things themselves"?

of the country. It was then that he sold out and went to New York. But the part of his story that concerns us goes back to the days when he was making his first big success.

When he was twenty-three Mr. Hart—one of the gray-haired men who like to say "Now there's a boy"—gave him a guest card to the Sherry Island Golf Club for a week-end. So he signed his name one day on the register, and that afternoon played golf in a foursome with Mr. Hart and Mr. Sandwood and Mr. T. A. Hedrick. He did not consider it necessary to remark that he had once carried Mr. Hart's bag over this same links, and that he knew every trap and gully with his eyes shut—but he found himself glancing at the four caddies who trailed them, trying to catch a gleam or gesture that would remind him of himself, that would lessen the gap which lay between his present and his past.

INFER
hy do you think Dexter might e anxious to "lessen the gap hich lay between his present ıd his past"?

It was a curious day, slashed abruptly with fleeting, familiar impressions. One minute he had the sense of being a trespasser—in the next he was impressed by the tremendous superiority he felt toward Mr. T. A. Hedrick, who was a bore and not even a good golfer any more.

Then, because of a ball Mr. Hart lost near the fifteenth green, an enormous thing happened. While they were searching the stiff grasses of the rough there was a clear call of "Fore!"[10] from behind a hill in their rear. And as they all turned abruptly from their search a bright new ball sliced abruptly over the hill and caught Mr. T. A. Hedrick in the abdomen.

"By Gad!" cried Mr. T. A. Hedrick, "they ought to put some of these crazy women off the course. It's getting to be outrageous."

A head and a voice came up together over the hill:

"Do you mind if we go through?"

"You hit me in the stomach!" declared Mr. Hedrick wildly.

"Did I?" The girl approached the group of men. "I'm sorry. I yelled 'Fore!'"

Her glance fell casually on each of the men—then scanned the fairway for her ball.

"Did I bounce into the rough?"

It was impossible to determine whether this question was ingenuous[11] or malicious. In a moment, however, she left no doubt, for as her partner came up over the hill she called cheerfully:

VORDS TO OWN
alicious (mə·lish′əs) *adj.*: ntentionally hurtful.

INTERPRET
Vhat does Judy's behavior ere suggest about her **haracter**?

"Here I am! I'd have gone on the green except that I hit something."

As she took her stance for a short mashie[12] shot, Dexter looked at her closely. She wore a blue gingham dress, rimmed at throat and shoulders with a white edging that accentuated her tan. The quality of exaggeration, of thinness, which had made her passionate eyes and

---

10. **fore:** warning cry that a golfer gives before hitting a ball down the fairway.
11. **ingenuous** (in·jen′yo͞o·əs): innocent; without guile.
12. **mashie:** a number 5 iron golf club.

downturning mouth absurd at eleven, was gone now. She was arrestingly beautiful. The color in her cheeks was centered like the color in a picture—it was not a "high" color, but a sort of fluctuating and feverish warmth, so shaded that it seemed at any moment it would recede and disappear. This color and the mobility of her mouth gave a continual impression of flux, of intense life, of passionate vitality—balanced only partially by the sad luxury of her eyes.

She swung her mashie impatiently and without interest, pitching the ball into a sand-pit on the other side of the green. With a quick, insincere smile and a careless "Thank you!" she went on after it.

"That Judy Jones!" remarked Mr. Hedrick on the next tee, as they waited—some moments—for her to play on ahead. "All she needs is to be turned up and spanked for six months and then to be married off to an old-fashioned cavalry captain."

"My God, she's good-looking!" said Mr. Sandwood, who was just over thirty.

"Good-looking!" cried Mr. Hedrick contemptuously, "she always looks as if she wanted to be kissed! Turning those big cow-eyes on every calf in town!"

It was doubtful if Mr. Hedrick intended a reference to the maternal instinct.

"She'd play pretty good golf if she'd try," said Mr. Sandwood.

"She has no form," said Mr. Hedrick solemnly.

"She has a nice figure," said Mr. Sandwood.

"Better thank the Lord she doesn't drive a swifter ball," said Mr. Hart, winking at Dexter.

Later in the afternoon the sun went down with a riotous swirl of gold and varying blues and scarlets, and left the dry, rustling night of Western summer. Dexter watched from the veranda of the Golf Club, watched the even overlap of the waters in the little wind, silver molasses under the harvest-moon. Then the moon held a finger to her lips and the lake became a clear pool, pale and quiet. Dexter put on his bathing-suit and swam out to the farthest raft, where he stretched dripping on the wet canvas of the springboard.

There was a fish jumping and a star shining and the lights around the lake were gleaming. Over on a dark peninsula a piano was playing the songs of last summer and of summers before that—songs from "Chin-Chin" and "The Count of Luxemburg" and "The Chocolate Soldier"—and because the sound of a piano over a stretch of water had always seemed beautiful to Dexter he lay perfectly quiet and listened.

The tune the piano was playing at that moment had been gay and new five years before when Dexter was a sophomore at college. They had played it at a prom once when he could not afford the luxury of proms, and he had stood outside the gymnasium and listened. The sound of the tune precipitated in him a sort of ecstasy and it was with

INTERPRET

The phrase "sad luxury" (line 213) contains an apparent contradiction. What **connotations** or associations does the phrase suggest to you?

INFER

In the eyes of these men, what kind of young woman is Judy?

INTERPRET

What kind of **mood** is created by the language (lines 233–238)?

INFER
ow does the song help waken Dexter's "winter eams"?

that ecstasy he viewed what happened to him now. It was a mood of intense appreciation, a sense that, for once, he was magnificently attuned to life and that everything about him was radiating a brightness and a glamour he might never know again.

A low, pale oblong detached itself suddenly from the darkness of the Island, spitting forth the reverberate sound of a racing motor-boat. Two white streamers of cleft water rolled themselves out behind it and almost immediately the boat was beside him, drowning out the hot tinkle of the piano in the drone of its spray. Dexter raising himself on his arms was aware of a figure standing at the wheel, of two dark eyes regarding him over the lengthening space of water—then the boat had gone by and was sweeping in an immense and purposeless circle of spray round and round in the middle of the lake. With equal eccentricity one of the circles flattened out and headed back toward the raft.

"Who's that?" she called, shutting off her motor. She was so near now that Dexter could see her bathing-suit, which consisted apparently of pink rompers.

The nose of the boat bumped the raft, and as the latter tilted rakishly, he was precipitated[13] toward her. With different degrees of interest they recognized each other.

"Aren't you one of those men we played through this afternoon?" she demanded.

He was.

"Well, do you know how to drive a motor-boat? Because if you do I wish you'd drive this one so I can ride on the surf-board behind. My name is Judy Jones"—she favored him with an absurd smirk—rather, what tried to be a smirk, for, twist her mouth as she might, it was not grotesque, it was merely beautiful—"and I live in a house over there on the Island, and in that house there is a man waiting for me. When he drove up at the door I drove out of the dock because he says I'm his ideal."

INFER
Vhy does Judy leave the man vaiting at her house?

There was a fish jumping and a star shining and the lights around the lake were gleaming. Dexter sat beside Judy Jones and she explained how her boat was driven. Then she was in the water, swimming to the floating surf-board with a sinuous[14] crawl. Watching her was without effort to the eye, watching a branch waving or a sea-gull flying. Her arms, burned to butternut, moved sinuously among the dull platinum ripples, elbow appearing first, casting the forearm back with a cadence of falling water, then reaching out and down, stabbing a path ahead.

They moved out into the lake; turning, Dexter saw that she was kneeling on the low rear of the now uptilted surf-board.

"Go faster," she called, "fast as it'll go."

---

13. **precipitated:** thrown headlong.
14. **sinuous:** curving back and forth; snakelike.

Obediently he jammed the lever forward and the white spray mounted at the bow. When he looked around again the girl was standing up on the rushing board, her arms spread wide, her eyes lifted toward the moon.

"It's awful cold," she shouted. "What's your name?"

He told her.

"Well, why don't you come to dinner to-morrow night?"

His heart turned over like the fly-wheel[15] of the boat, and, for the second time, her casual whim gave a new direction to his life.

III

Next evening while he waited for her to come down-stairs, Dexter peopled the soft deep summer room and the sun-porch that opened from it with the men who had already loved Judy Jones. He knew the sort of men they were—the men who when he first went to college had entered from the great prep schools with graceful clothes and the deep tan of healthy summers. He had seen that, in one sense, he was better than these men. He was newer and stronger. Yet in acknowledging to himself that he wished his children to be like them he was admitting that he was but the rough, strong stuff from which they eternally sprang.

When the time had come for him to wear good clothes, he had known who were the best tailors in America, and the best tailors in America had made him the suit he wore this evening. He had acquired that particular reserve peculiar to his university, that set it off from other universities. He recognized the value to him of such a mannerism and he had adopted it; he knew that to be careless in dress and manner required more confidence than to be careful. But carelessness was for his children. His mother's name had been Krimslich. She was a Bohemian of the peasant class and she had talked broken English to the end of her days. Her son must keep to the set patterns.

At a little after seven Judy Jones came down-stairs. She wore a blue silk afternoon dress, and he was disappointed at first that she had not put on something more elaborate. This feeling was accentuated when, after a brief greeting, she went to the door of a butler's pantry and pushing it open called: "You can serve dinner, Martha." He had rather expected that a butler would announce dinner, that there would be a cocktail. Then he put these thoughts behind him as they sat down side by side on a lounge and looked at each other.

"Father and mother won't be here," she said thoughtfully.

He remembered the last time he had seen her father, and he was glad the parents were not to be here to-night—they might wonder who he was. He had been born in Keeble, a Minnesota village fifty miles

15. **fly-wheel:** wheel that regulates the speed of a machine.

INFER

Why does Judy invite Dexter to dinner the following evening?

INFER

According to this passage, what kind of man does Dexter represent?

WORDS TO OWN

reserve (ri·zurv′) *n.:* self-restraint.

INTERPRET

Krimslich is an Eastern European name, and Dexter's mother speaks broken English because she is an immigrant. What does Dexter believe he must do in order to move in higher social circles?

farther north, and he always gave Keeble as his home instead of Black Bear Village. Country towns were well enough to come from if they weren't inconveniently in sight and used as footstools by fashionable lakes.

They talked of his university, which she had visited frequently during the past two years, and of the near-by city which supplied Sherry Island with its patrons, and whither Dexter would return next day to his prospering laundries.

During dinner she slipped into a moody depression which gave Dexter a feeling of uneasiness. Whatever petulance she uttered in her throaty voice worried him. Whatever she smiled at—at him, at a chicken liver, at nothing—it disturbed him that her smile could have no root in mirth, or even in amusement. When the scarlet corners of her lips curved down, it was less a smile than an invitation to a kiss.

Then, after dinner, she led him out on the dark sun-porch and deliberately changed the atmosphere.

"Do you mind if I weep a little?" she said.

"I'm afraid I'm boring you," he responded quickly.

"You're not. I like you. But I've just had a terrible afternoon. There was a man I cared about, and this afternoon he told me out of a clear sky that he was poor as a church-mouse. He'd never even hinted it before. Does this sound horribly mundane?"[16]

"Perhaps he was afraid to tell you."

"Suppose he was," she answered. "He didn't start right. You see, if I'd thought of him as poor—well, I've been mad about loads of poor men, and fully intended to marry them all. But in this case, I hadn't thought of him that way, and my interest in him wasn't strong enough to survive the shock. As if a girl calmly informed her fiancé that she was a widow. He might not object to widows, but——

"Let's start right," she interrupted herself suddenly. "Who are you, anyhow?"

For a moment Dexter hesitated. Then:

"I'm nobody," he announced. "My career is largely a matter of futures."

"Are you poor?"

"No," he said frankly, "I'm probably making more money than any man my age in the Northwest. I know that's an obnoxious remark, but you advised me to start right."

There was a pause. Then she smiled and the corners of her mouth drooped and an almost imperceptible sway brought her closer to him, looking up into his eyes. A lump rose in Dexter's throat, and he waited breathless for the experiment, facing the unpredictable compound that would form mysteriously from the elements of their lips. Then he saw—

---

16. mundane: ordinary; everyday.

/ORDS TO OWN

etulance (pech'ə·ləns) *n.:* ritability; impatience.

irth (murth) *n.:* joyfulness.

DENTIFY

his is the second reference to udy's wanting to be kissed. /hat was the first?

INFER

/hy does Judy paint such a rivolous picture of herself to)exter?

INTERPRET

Vhat does Dexter mean when e says that his career is "a natter of futures"?

she communicated her excitement to him, lavishly, deeply, with kisses that were not a promise but a fulfillment. They aroused in him not hunger demanding renewal but surfeit that would demand more surfeit . . . kisses that were like charity, creating want by holding back nothing at all.

It did not take him many hours to decide that he had wanted Judy Jones ever since he was a proud, desirous little boy.

IV

It began like that—and continued, with varying shades of intensity, on such a note right up to the dénouement.[17] Dexter surrendered a part of himself to the most direct and unprincipled personality with which he had ever come in contact. Whatever Judy wanted, she went after with the full pressure of her charm. There was no divergence of method, no jockeying for position or premeditation of effects—there was a very little mental side to any of her affairs. She simply made men conscious to the highest degree of her physical loveliness. Dexter had no desire to change her. Her deficiencies were knit up with a passionate energy that transcended and justified them.

When, as Judy's head lay against his shoulder that first night, she whispered, "I don't know what's the matter with me. Last night I thought I was in love with a man and to-night I think I'm in love with you——" —it seemed to him a beautiful and romantic thing to say. It was the exquisite excitability that for the moment he controlled and owned. But a week later he was compelled to view this same quality in a different light. She took him in her roadster to a picnic supper, and after supper she disappeared, likewise in her roadster, with another man. Dexter became enormously upset and was scarcely able to be decently civil to the other people present. When she assured him that she had not kissed the other man, he knew she was lying—yet he was glad that she had taken the trouble to lie to him.

He was, as he found before the summer ended, one of a varying dozen who circulated about her. Each of them had at one time been favored above all others—about half of them still basked in the solace of occasional sentimental revivals. Whenever one showed signs of dropping out through long neglect, she granted him a brief honeyed hour, which encouraged him to tag along for a year or so longer. Judy made these forays[18] upon the helpless and defeated without malice, indeed half unconscious that there was anything mischievous in what she did.

When a new man came to town every one dropped out—dates were automatically cancelled.

17. **dénouement** (dā'no͞o·män'): final outcome.
18. **forays** (fôr'āz): raids.

INFER
What does the kiss **symbolize** for Dexter?

WORDS TO OWN
divergence (dī·vur'jəns) *n.*: variance; difference.

INFER
There are elements of Judy's character that Dexter does not like, yet he doesn't want to change her. How do you explain his feelings?

EVALUATE
Does Judy's character seem realistic to you? Why or why not?

RETELL

'hat does it mean that Judy ıad come, in self-defense, nourish herself wholly from ithin"?

The helpless part of trying to do anything about it was that she did it all herself. She was not a girl who could be "won" in the kinetic[19] sense—she was proof against[20] cleverness, she was proof against charm; if any of these assailed her too strongly she would immediately resolve the affair to a physical basis, and under the magic of her physical splendor the strong as well as the brilliant played her game and not their own. She was entertained only by the gratification of her desires and by the direct exercise of her own charm. Perhaps from so much youthful love, so many youthful lovers, she had come, in self-defense, to nourish herself wholly from within.

Succeeding Dexter's first exhilaration came restlessness and dissatisfaction. The helpless ecstasy of losing himself in her was opiate rather than tonic.[21] It was fortunate for his work during the winter that those moments of ecstasy came infrequently. Early in their acquaintance it had seemed for a while that there was a deep and spontaneous mutual attraction—that first August, for example—three days of long evenings on her dusky veranda, of strange wan kisses through the late afternoon, in shadowy alcoves or behind the protecting trellises of the garden arbors, of mornings when she was fresh as a dream and almost shy at meeting him in the clarity of the rising day. There was all the ecstasy of an engagement about it, sharpened by his realization that there was no engagement. It was during those three days that, for the first time, he had asked her to marry him. She said "maybe some day," she said "kiss me," she said "I'd like to marry you," she said "I love you"—she said—nothing.

The three days were interrupted by the arrival of a New York man who visited at her house for half September. To Dexter's agony, rumor engaged them. The man was the son of the president of a great trust company. But at the end of a month it was reported that Judy was yawning. At a dance one night she sat all evening in a motor-boat with a local beau, while the New Yorker searched the club for her frantically. She told the local beau that she was bored with her visitor, and two days later he left. She was seen with him at the station, and it was reported that he looked very mournful indeed.

On this note the summer ended. Dexter was twenty-four, and he found himself increasingly in a position to do as he wished. He joined two clubs in the city and lived at one of them. Though he was by no means an integral part of the stag-lines[22] at these clubs, he managed to be on hand at dances where Judy Jones was likely to appear. He could have gone out socially as much as he liked—he was an eligible young man, now, and popular with down-town fathers. His confessed devotion

19. **kinetic** (ki·net′ik): coming about through action or energy.
20. **proof against:** able to withstand.
21. **opiate . . . tonic:** calming rather than stimulating.
22. **stag-lines:** lines of unaccompanied men at a dance, waiting for available dance partners.

to Judy Jones had rather solidified his position. But he had no social aspirations and rather despised the dancing men who were always on tap for the Thursday or Saturday parties and who filled in at dinners with the younger married set. Already he was playing with the idea of going East to New York. He wanted to take Judy Jones with him. No disillusion as to the world in which she had grown up could cure his illusion as to her desirability.

Remember that—for only in the light of it can what he did for her be understood.

Eighteen months after he first met Judy Jones he became engaged to another girl. Her name was Irene Scheerer, and her father was one of the men who had always believed in Dexter. Irene was light-haired and sweet and honorable, and a little stout, and she had two suitors whom she pleasantly relinquished when Dexter formally asked her to marry him.

Summer, fall, winter, spring, another summer, another fall—so much he had given of his active life to the incorrigible[23] lips of Judy Jones. She had treated him with interest, with encouragement, with malice, with indifference, with contempt. She had inflicted on him the innumerable little slights and indignities possible in such a case—as if in revenge for having ever cared for him at all. She had beckoned him and yawned at him and beckoned him again and he had responded often with bitterness and narrowed eyes. She had brought him ecstatic happiness and intolerable agony of spirit. She had caused him untold inconvenience and not a little trouble. She had insulted him, and she had ridden over him, and she had played his interest in her against his interest in his work—for fun. She had done everything to him except to criticize him—this she had not done—it seemed to him only because it might have sullied the utter indifference she manifested and sincerely felt toward him.

When autumn had come and gone again it occurred to him that he could not have Judy Jones. He had to beat this into his mind but he convinced himself at last. He lay awake at night for a while and argued it over. He told himself the trouble and the pain she had caused him, he enumerated her glaring deficiences as a wife. Then he said to himself that he loved her, and after a while he fell asleep. For a week, lest he imagined her husky voice over the telephone or her eyes opposite him at lunch, he worked hard and late, and at night he went to his office and plotted out his years.

At the end of a week he went to a dance and cut in on her once. For almost the first time since they had met he did not ask her to sit out with him or tell her that she was lovely. It hurt him that she did not miss these things—that was all. He was not jealous when he saw that there was a new man to-night. He had been hardened against jealousy long before.

---

23. incorrigible: incapable of correction or reform.

INTERPRET

Have Dexter's dreams change
Explain why or why not.

INFER

What do you think is Dexter's **motivation** to become engage
to Irene?

EVALUATE

Is Judy a worthy object of Dexter's idealism? Explain your answer.

He stayed late at the dance. He sat for an hour with Irene Scheerer and talked about books and about music. He knew very little about either. But he was beginning to be master of his own time now, and he had a rather priggish[24] notion that he—the young and already fabulously successful Dexter Green—should know more about such things.

That was in October, when he was twenty-five. In January, Dexter and Irene became engaged. It was to be announced in June, and they were to be married three months later.

The Minnesota winter prolonged itself interminably, and it was almost May when the winds came soft and the snow ran down into Black Bear Lake at last. For the first time in over a year Dexter was enjoying a certain tranquility of spirit. Judy Jones had been in Florida, and afterward in Hot Springs, and somewhere she had been engaged, and somewhere she had broken it off. At first, when Dexter had definitely given her up, it had made him sad that people still linked them together and asked for news of her, but when he began to be placed at dinner next to Irene Scheerer people didn't ask him about her any more—they told him about her. He ceased to be an authority on her.

May at last. Dexter walked the streets at night when the darkness was damp as rain, wondering that so soon, with so little done, so much of ecstasy had gone from him. May one year back had been marked by Judy's poignant, unforgivable, yet forgiven turbulence—it had been one of those rare times when he fancied she had grown to care for him. That old penny's worth of happiness he had spent for this bushel of content. He knew that Irene would be no more than a curtain spread behind him, a hand moving among gleaming tea-cups, a voice calling to children . . . fire and loveliness were gone, the magic of nights and the wonder of the varying hours and seasons . . . slender lips, down-turning, dropping to his lips and bearing him up into a heaven of eyes. . . . The thing was deep in him. He was too strong and alive for it to die lightly.

In the middle of May when the weather balanced for a few days on the thin bridge that led to deep summer he turned in one night at Irene's house. Their engagement was to be announced in a week now—no one would be surprised at it. And to-night they would sit together on the lounge at the University Club and look on for an hour at the dancers. It gave him a sense of solidity to go with her—she was so sturdily popular, so intensely "great."

He mounted the steps of the brownstone house and stepped inside.

"Irene," he called.

Mrs. Scheerer came out of the living-room to meet him.

"Dexter," she said, "Irene's gone up-stairs with a splitting headache. She wanted to go with you but I made her go to bed."

"Nothing serious, I——"

24. **priggish:** annoyingly precise and proper.

'ORDS TO OWN

'bulence (tur'byə·ləns) *n.:* egular behavior.

NTERPRET

line 523, Fitzgerald alludes an **aphorism**—a concise, overbial saying. What does e aphorism mean in context?

NFER

ho do you think calls Irene great," and what do they ean by it?

"Oh, no. She's going to play golf with you in the morning. You can spare her for just one night, can't you, Dexter?"

Her smile was kind. She and Dexter liked each other. In the living-room he talked for a moment before he said good-night.

Returning to the University Club, where he had rooms, he stood in the doorway for a moment and watched the dancers. He leaned against the door-post, nodded at a man or two—yawned.

"Hello, darling."

The familiar voice at his elbow startled him. Judy Jones had left a man and crossed the room to him—Judy Jones, a slender enamelled doll in cloth of gold: gold in a band at her head, gold in two slipper points at her dress's hem. The fragile glow of her face seemed to blossom as she smiled at him. A breeze of warmth and light blew through the room. His hands in the pockets of his dinner-jacket tightened spasmodically. He was filled with a sudden excitement.

"When did you get back?" he asked casually.

"Come here and I'll tell you about it."

She turned and he followed her. She had been away—he could have wept at the wonder of her return. She had passed through enchanted streets, doing things that were like provocative music. All mysterious happenings, all fresh and quickening hopes, had gone away with her, come back with her now.

She turned in the doorway.

"Have you a car here? If you haven't, I have."

"I have a coupé."

In then, with a rustle of golden cloth. He slammed the door. Into so many cars she had stepped—like this—like that—her back against the leather, so—her elbow resting on the door—waiting. She would have been soiled long since had there been anything to soil her—except herself—but this was her own self outpouring.

With an effort he forced himself to start the car and back into the street. This was nothing, he must remember. She had done this before, and he had put her behind him, as he would have crossed a bad account from his books.

He drove slowly down-town and, affecting abstraction, traversed the deserted streets of the business section, peopled here and there where a movie was giving out its crowd or where consumptive[25] or pugilistic[26] youth lounged in front of pool halls. The clink of glasses and the slap of hands on the bars issued from saloons, cloisters of glazed glass and dirty yellow light.

She was watching him closely and the silence was embarrassing, yet in this crisis he could find no casual word with which to profane the

25. **consumptive:** destructive; wasteful.
26. **pugilistic** (pyo͞o′jil·is′tik): eager to fight.

INTERPRET
Judy is pictured in gold. Why might this description be **symbolic** in context?

INTERPRET
Why do you think Dexter is so overcome with emotion here?

INTERPRET
What does the narrator mean by saying that Judy "would have been soiled long since had there been anything to so her—except herself"?

NFER

tween the lines, what do you nk Judy and Dexter are ving to each other?

NFER

hy does Judy make a newed play for Dexter?

hour. At a convenient turning he began to zigzag back toward the University Club.

"Have you missed me?" she asked suddenly.

"Everybody missed you."

He wondered if she knew of Irene Scheerer. She had been back only a day—her absence had been almost contemporaneous with his engagement.

"What a remark!" Judy laughed sadly—without sadness. She looked at him searchingly. He became absorbed in the dashboard.

"You're handsomer than you used to be," she said thoughtfully. "Dexter, you have the most rememberable eyes."

He could have laughed at this, but he did not laugh. It was the sort of thing that was said to sophomores. Yet it stabbed at him.

"I'm awfully tired of everything, darling." She called every one darling, endowing the endearment with careless, individual comraderie. "I wish you'd marry me."

The directness of this confused him. He should have told her now that he was going to marry another girl, but he could not tell her. He could as easily have sworn that he had never loved her.

"I think we'd get along," she continued, on the same note, "unless probably you've forgotten me and fallen in love with another girl."

Her confidence was obviously enormous. She had said, in effect, that she found such a thing impossible to believe, that if it were true he had merely committed a childish indiscretion—and probably to show off. She would forgive him, because it was not a matter of any moment but rather something to be brushed aside lightly.

"Of course you could never love anybody but me," she continued. "I like the way you love me. Oh, Dexter, have you forgotten last year?"

"No, I haven't forgotten."

"Neither have I!"

Was she sincerely moved—or was she carried along by the wave of her own acting?

"I wish we could be like that again," she said, and he forced himself to answer:

"I don't think we can."

"I suppose not. . . . I hear you're giving Irene Scheerer a violent rush."

There was not the faintest emphasis on the name, yet Dexter was suddenly ashamed.

"Oh, take me home," cried Judy suddenly; "I don't want to go back to that idiotic dance—with those children."

Then, as he turned up the street that led to the residence district, Judy began to cry quietly to herself. He had never seen her cry before.

The dark street lightened, the dwellings of the rich loomed up around them, he stopped his coupé in front of the great white bulk of the

Mortimer Joneses house, somnolent,[27] gorgeous, drenched with the splendor of the damp moonlight. Its solidity startled him. The strong walls, the steel of the girders, the breadth and beam and pomp of it were there only to bring out the contrast with the young beauty beside him. It was sturdy to accentuate her slightness—as if to show what a breeze could be generated by a butterfly's wing.

He sat perfectly quiet, his nerves in wild clamor, afraid that if he moved he would find her irresistibly in his arms. Two tears had rolled down her wet face and trembled on her upper lip.

"I'm more beautiful than anybody else," she said brokenly, "why can't I be happy?" Her moist eyes tore at his stability—her mouth turned slowly downward with an exquisite sadness: "I'd like to marry you if you'll have me, Dexter. I suppose you think I'm not worth having, but I'll be so beautiful for you, Dexter."

A million phrases of anger, pride, passion, hatred, tenderness fought on his lips. Then a perfect wave of emotion washed over him, carrying off with it a sediment of wisdom, of convention,[28] of doubt, of honor. This was his girl who was speaking, his own, his beautiful, his pride.

"Won't you come in?" He heard her draw in her breath sharply.

Waiting.

"All right," his voice was trembling, "I'll come in."

V

It was strange that neither when it was over nor a long time afterward did he regret that night. Looking at it from the perspective of ten years, the fact that Judy's flare for him endured just one month seemed of little importance. Nor did it matter that by his yielding he subjected himself to a deeper agony in the end and gave serious hurt to Irene Scheerer and to Irene's parents, who had befriended him. There was nothing sufficiently pictorial about Irene's grief to stamp itself on his mind.

Dexter was at bottom hard-minded. The attitude of the city on his action was of no importance to him, not because he was going to leave the city, but because any outside attitude on the situation seemed superficial. He was completely indifferent to popular opinion. Nor, when he had seen that it was no use, that he did not possess in himself the power to move fundamentally or to hold Judy Jones, did he bear any malice toward her. He loved her, and he would love her until the day he was too old for loving—but he could not have her. So he tasted the deep pain that is reserved only for the strong, just as he had tasted for a little while the deep happiness.

Even the ultimate falsity of the grounds upon which Judy terminated the engagement, that she did not want to "take him away" from Irene—

27. somnolent: sleepy.
28. convention: accepted practices of social behavior.

INTERPRET

How is Judy's proposal **ironic**? What is ironic about the fact that Dexter thinks of Judy as "his own"?

EVALUATE

Do you think the narrator sympathizes with Dexter, or does the narrator think Dexter is a fool to fall for Judy?

PREDICT

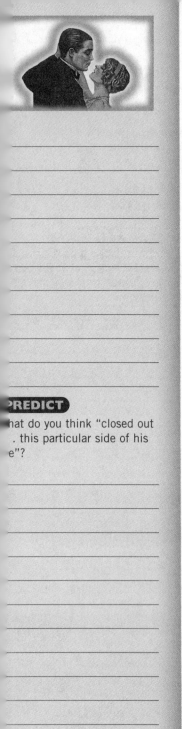

hat do you think "closed out . this particular side of his e"?

Judy, who had wanted nothing else—did not revolt him. He was beyond any revulsion or any amusement.

He went East in February with the intention of selling out his laundries and settling in New York—but the war came to America in March and changed his plans. He returned to the West, handed over the management of the business to his partner, and went into the first officers' training-camp in late April. He was one of those young thousands who greeted the war with a certain amount of relief, welcoming the liberation from webs of tangled emotion.

VI

This story is not his biography, remember, although things creep into it which have nothing to do with those dreams he had when he was young. We are almost done with them and with him now. There is only one more incident to be related here, and it happens seven years farther on.

It took place in New York, where he had done well—so well that there were no barriers too high for him. He was thirty-two years old, and, except for one flying trip immediately after the war, he had not been West in seven years. A man named Devlin from Detroit came into his office to see him in a business way, and then and there this incident occurred, and closed out, so to speak, this particular side of his life.

"So you're from the Middle West," said the man Devlin with careless curiosity. "That's funny—I thought men like you were probably born and raised on Wall Street. You know—wife of one of my best friends in Detroit came from your city. I was an usher at the wedding."

Dexter waited with no apprehension of what was coming.

"Judy Simms," said Devlin with no particular interest; "Judy Jones she was once."

"Yes, I knew her." A dull impatience spread over him. He had heard, of course, that she was married—perhaps deliberately he had heard no more.

"Awfully nice girl," brooded Devlin meaninglessly, "I'm sort of sorry for her."

"Why?" Something in Dexter was alert, receptive, at once.

"Oh, Lud Simms has gone to pieces in a way. I don't mean he ill-uses her, but he drinks and runs around——"

"Doesn't she run around?"

"No. Stays at home with her kids."

"Oh."

"She's a little too old for him," said Devlin.

"Too old!" cried Dexter. "Why, man, she's only twenty-seven."

He was possessed with a wild notion of rushing out into the streets and taking a train to Detroit. He rose to his feet spasmodically.

"I guess you're busy," Devlin apologized quickly. "I didn't realize——"

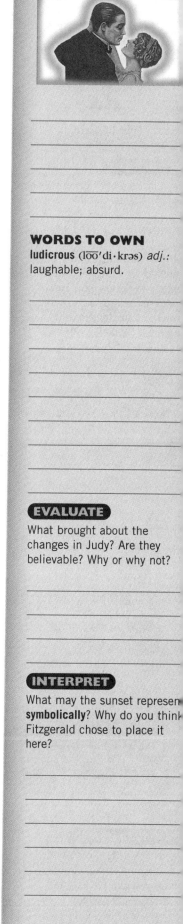

"No, I'm not busy," said Dexter, steadying his voice. "I'm not busy at all. Not busy at all. Did you say she was—twenty-seven? No, I said she was twenty-seven."

"Yes, you did," agreed Devlin dryly.

"Go on, then. Go on."

"What do you mean?"

"About Judy Jones."

Devlin looked at him helplessly.

"Well, that's—I told you all there is to it. He treats her like the devil. Oh, they're not going to get divorced or anything. When he's particularly outrageous she forgives him. In fact, I'm inclined to think she loves him. She was a pretty girl when she first came to Detroit."

A pretty girl! The phrase struck Dexter as ludicrous.

"Isn't she—a pretty girl, any more?"

"Oh, she's all right."

"Look here," said Dexter, sitting down suddenly, "I don't understand. You say she was a 'pretty girl' and now you say she's 'all right.' I don't understand what you mean—Judy Jones wasn't a pretty girl, at all. She was a great beauty. Why, I knew her, I knew her. She was——"

Devlin laughed pleasantly.

"I'm not trying to start a row," he said. "I think Judy's a nice girl and I like her. I can't understand how a man like Lud Simms could fall madly in love with her, but he did." Then he added: "Most of the women like her."

Dexter looked closely at Devlin, thinking wildly that there must be a reason for this, some insensitivity in the man or some private malice.

"Lots of women fade just like *that,*" Devlin snapped his fingers. "You must have seen it happen. Perhaps I've forgotten how pretty she was at her wedding. I've seen her so much since then, you see. She has nice eyes."

A sort of dullness settled down upon Dexter. For the first time in his life he felt like getting very drunk. He knew that he was laughing loudly at something Devlin had said, but he did not know what it was or why it was funny. When, in a few minutes, Devlin went, he lay down on his lounge and looked out the window at the New York sky-line into which the sun was sinking in dull lovely shades of pink and gold.

He had thought that having nothing else to lose he was invulnerable at last—but he knew that he had just lost something more, as surely as if he had married Judy Jones and seen her fade away before his eyes.

The dream was gone. Something had been taken from him. In a sort of panic he pushed the palms of his hands into his eyes and tried to bring up a picture of the waters lapping on Sherry Island and the moonlit veranda, and gingham on the golf-links and the dry sun and the gold color of her neck's soft down. And her mouth damp to his kisses and her

WORDS TO OWN

ludicrous (lo͞o′di·krəs) *adj.:* laughable; absurd.

EVALUATE

What brought about the changes in Judy? Are they believable? Why or why not?

INTERPRET

What may the sunset represen **symbolically**? Why do you thin Fitzgerald chose to place it here?

eyes plaintive with melancholy and her freshness like new fine linen in the morning. Why, these things were no longer in the world! They had existed and they existed no longer.

For the first time in years the tears were streaming down his face. But they were for himself now. He did not care about mouth and eyes and moving hands. He wanted to care, and he could not care. For he had gone away and he could never go back any more. The gates were closed, the sun was gone down, and there was no beauty but the gray beauty of steel that withstands all time. Even the grief he could have borne was left behind in the country of illusion, of youth, of the richness of life, where his winter dreams had flourished.

"Long ago," he said, "long ago, there was something in me, but now that thing is gone. Now that thing is gone, that thing is gone. I cannot cry. I cannot care. That thing will come back no more."

ORDS TO OWN

aintive (plān′tiv) *adj.:* pressing sadness.

NTERPRET

e conclusion of Fitzgerald's vel *The Great Gatsby* scribes the dream that otivated Gatsby: "Gatsby lieved in the . . . future that ar by year recedes before us. eluded us then, but that's no atter—tomorrow we'll run ster, stretch out our arms rther . . . and one fine orning—" Would Dexter gree with Gatsby? Why or hy not?

INFER

/hat "thing" does Dexter ean—is this the same thing" that had been "deep him" before?

BUILD FLUENCY

Read lines 751–769 aloud. In our reading, concentrate on itch, volume, pacing, and xpressive emphasis.

Motivation

Motivation refers to the reasons for a character's behavior. In "Winter Dreams," F. Scott Fitzgerald presents two very complex characters, Dexter Green and Judy Jones, whose motivations are often tangled and paradoxical, or contradictory.

Explore your understanding of what makes these characters "tick" by filling out the chart below. Use details and events from the story to compile a list of entries for each character. The first entry in each column has been done for you.

Dexter's Motivations	Judy's Motivations
dreams of success and glamour	enjoys being adored by men

Vocabulary: How to Own a Word

Synonyms and Antonyms

Word Bank
elation
perturbation
malicious
reserve
petulance
mirth
divergence
turbulence
ludicrous
plaintive

Ten word pairs follow. The first word in each pair is a Word to Own. On the line provided, write **S** if the second word in the pair is a synonym for the Word to Own, or **A** if the word is an antonym. You may need a dictionary or a thesaurus for this activity.

_____ **1.** elation: melancholy

_____ **2.** perturbation: alarm

_____ **3.** malicious: vicious

_____ **4.** reserve: boldness

_____ **5.** petulance: peevishness

_____ **6.** mirth: merriment

_____ **7.** divergence: similarity

_____ **8.** turbulence: agitation

_____ **9.** ludicrous: sensible

_____ **10.** plaintive: exuberant

Context Clues

Using context clues and definitions from your Words to Own, circle the word that correctly completes each sentence.

1. Judy Jones caused great (*elation, reserve*) among the men in town when she accepted their dates.

2. She had many dates because she wanted to have fun, not because she was (*malicious, ludicrous*).

3. If you kept Judy waiting for a date, her (*petulance, mirth*) could spoil the evening.

4. When Dexter met Judy, his (*turbulence, reserve*) melted because he wanted so badly to date her.

5. Only a fool would be so (*ludicrous, plaintive*) as to forget a date with the beautiful Judy.

The Secret Life of Walter Mitty

Make the Connection

Daydreamer

James Thurber enjoyed a long career as a writer and cartoonist for *The New Yorker* magazine, where he established himself as the foremost American humorist of the twentieth century. Like so many cartoonists, Thurber loved to play with **stereotypes,** such as the stock figure of the henpecked husband who cannot quite assert himself in a confusing world where women seem surer of their way.

Walter Mitty, the antihero of Thurber's most famous story, seeks release in fantasy from a wife who overwhelms him. Thurber was so successful in capturing this character, in fact, that the term "Walter Mitty" is found in *Webster's Third New International Dictionary,* where it is defined as "a commonplace unadventurous person who seeks escape from reality through daydreaming and typically imagines himself leading a glamorous life and becoming famous."

Popular culture bombards us with so many images of extraordinary people—politicians, actors, athletes, musicians, soldiers, scientists—that it's almost impossible *not* to daydream ourselves into dramas that are much more interesting than our ordinary lives. In the left-hand column below, list a few stock types (for example, "nerd" or "wallflower") and in the right-hand column, suggest a daydream for each—the more outlandish, the better.

Stereotypical Character	Daydream
nerd	winning the Nobel Prize in chemistry

The Secret Life of Walter Mitty

James Thurber

ORDS TO OWN

kishly (rāk′·ish·lē) *adv.*: shingly; jauntily.

DENTIFY

parody is a work that makes n of another work by itating some aspect of its yle or content. Circle at least o details of this scene that veal the parody.

NTERPRET

hat feeling is conveyed by e use of "Old Man" in this assage?

NTERPRET

/hat shocks Mitty out of his aydream?

INFER

Vhy does Mitty race the ngine—but just a little?

"We're going through!" The commander's voice was like thin ice breaking. He wore his full-dress uniform, with the heavily braided white cap pulled down rakishly over one cold gray eye. "We can't make it, sir. It's spoiling for[1] a hurricane, if you ask me." "I'm not asking you, Lieutenant Berg," said the commander. "Throw on the power lights! Rev her up to 8,500! We're going through!" The pounding of the cylinders increased: ta-pocketa-pocketa-pocketa-*pocketa-pocketa*. The commander stared at the ice forming on the pilot window. He walked over and twisted a row of complicated dials. "Switch on No. 8 auxiliary!" he shouted. "Switch on No. 8 auxiliary!" repeated Lieutenant Berg. "Full strength in No. 3 turret!" shouted the commander. "Full strength in No. 3 turret!" The crew, bending to their various tasks in the huge, hurtling eight-engined navy hydroplane, looked at each other and grinned. "The Old Man'll get us through," they said to one another. "The Old Man ain't afraid of Hell!" . . .

"Not so fast! You're driving too fast!" said Mrs. Mitty. "What are you driving so fast for?"

"Hmm?" said Walter Mitty. He looked at his wife, in the seat beside him, with shocked astonishment. She seemed grossly unfamiliar, like a strange woman who had yelled at him in a crowd. "You were up to fifty-five," she said. "You know I don't like to go more than forty. You were up to fifty-five." Walter Mitty drove on toward Waterbury in silence, the roaring of the SN202 through the worst storm in twenty years of navy flying fading in the remote, intimate airways of his mind. "You're tensed up again," said Mrs. Mitty. "It's one of your days. I wish you'd let Dr. Renshaw look you over."

Walter Mitty stopped the car in front of the building where his wife went to have her hair done. "Remember to get those overshoes while I'm having my hair done," she said. "I don't need overshoes," said Mitty. She put her mirror back into her bag. "We've been all through that," she said, getting out of the car. "You're not a young man any longer." He raced the engine a little. "Why don't you wear your gloves? Have you lost your gloves?" Walter Mitty reached in a pocket and brought out the gloves. He put them on, but after she had turned and gone into the building and he had driven on to a red light, he took them off again. "Pick it up, brother!" snapped a cop as the light changed, and Mitty hastily pulled on his gloves and lurched ahead. He drove around the streets aimlessly for a time, and then he drove past the hospital on his way to the parking lot.

. . . "It's the millionaire banker, Wellington McMillan," said the pretty nurse. "Yes?" said Walter Mitty, removing his gloves slowly. "Who has the case?" "Dr. Renshaw and Dr. Benbow, but there are two specialists here, Dr. Remington from New York and Mr. Pritchard-Mitford from London. He

1. **it's spoiling for:** slang for "conditions are right for."

flew over." A door opened down a long, cool corridor and Dr. Renshaw came out. He looked distraught and haggard. "Hello, Mitty," he said. "We're having the devil's own time with McMillan, the millionaire banker and close personal friend of Roosevelt. Obstreosis of the ductal tract. Tertiary. Wish you'd take a look at him." "Glad to," said Mitty.

In the operating room there were whispered introductions: "Dr. Remington, Dr. Mitty. Mr. Pritchard-Mitford, Dr. Mitty." "I've read your book on streptothricosis," said Pritchard-Mitford, shaking hands. "A brilliant performance, sir." "Thank you," said Walter Mitty. "Didn't know you were in the States, Mitty," grumbled Remington. "Coals to Newcastle,[2] bringing Mitford and me up here for a tertiary." "You are very kind," said Mitty. A huge, complicated machine, connected to the operating table, with many tubes and wires, began at this moment to go pocketa-pocketa-pocketa. "The new anesthetizer is giving way!" shouted an intern. "There is no one in the East who knows how to fix it!" "Quiet, man!" said Mitty, in a low, cool voice. He sprang to the machine, which was now going pocketa-pocketa-queep-pocketa-queep. He began fingering delicately a row of glistening dials. "Give me a fountain pen!" he snapped. Someone handed him a fountain pen. He pulled a faulty piston out of the machine and inserted the pen in its place. "That will hold for ten minutes," he said. "Get on with the operation." A nurse hurried over and whispered to Renshaw, and Mitty saw the man turn pale. "Coreopsis has set in," said Renshaw nervously. "If you would take over, Mitty?" Mitty looked at him and at the craven figure of Benbow, who drank, and at the grave, uncertain faces of the two great specialists. "If you wish," he said. They slipped a white gown on him; he adjusted a mask and drew on thin gloves; nurses handed him shining . . .

"Back it up, Mac! Look out for that Buick!" Walter Mitty jammed on the brakes. "Wrong lane, Mac," said the parking-lot attendant, looking at Mitty closely. "Gee. Yeh," muttered Mitty. He began cautiously to back out of the lane marked "Exit Only." "Leave her sit there," said the attendant. "I'll put her away." Mitty got out of the car. "Hey, better leave the key." "Oh," said Mitty, handing the man the ignition key. The attendant vaulted into the car, backed it up with insolent skill, and put it where it belonged.

They're so damn cocky, thought Walter Mitty, walking along Main Street; they think they know everything. Once he had tried to take his chains[3] off, outside New Milford, and he had got them wound around the axles. A man had had to come out in a wrecking car and unwind them, a young, grinning garageman. Since then Mrs. Mitty always made him drive to a garage to have the chains taken off. The next time, he

2. **coals to Newcastle:** an unnecessary effort. Newcastle, England, was a major coal-producing city.
3. **chains:** chains attached to automobile tires to increase traction in snow and ice.

WORDS TO OWN
distraught (di·strôt′) *adj.:* troubled.
haggard (hag′ərd) *adj.:* waste or worn in appearance.

INTERPRET
What medical stereotypes doe Thurber **parody** in this scene?

WORDS TO OWN
craven (krā′vən) *adj.:* very fearful; cowardly.

WORDS TO OWN
insolent (in′sə·lənt) *adj.:* arrogant.

INTERPRET
What is **ironic** about the scene in the parking lot?

NFER

ıderline the words that don't long on the shopping list. ıy do you think Mitty thinks them?

NFER

hat is the connection etween events in real life and itty's dramatic courtroom ntasy?

VORDS TO OWN

ısinuatingly (in·sin′yōō·āt′iŋ·ē) *adv.:* suggestively.

andemonium (pan′də·mō′nē·m) *n.:* wild confusion.

edlam (bed′ləm) *n.:* place r condition of noise and onfusion.

INTERPRET

Vhat is the link between Aitty's fantasy and the puppy ıiscuit?

thought, I'll wear my right arm in a sling; they won't grin at me then. I'll have my right arm in a sling, and they'll see I couldn't possibly take the chains off myself. He kicked at the slush on the sidewalk. "Overshoes," he said to himself, and he began looking for a shoe store.

When he came out into the street again, with the overshoes in a box under his arm, Walter Mitty began to wonder what the other thing was his wife had told him to get. She had told him, twice, before they set out from their house for Waterbury. In a way he hated these weekly trips to town—he was always getting something wrong. Kleenex, he thought, Squibb's,[4] razor blades? No. Toothpaste, toothbrush, bicarbonate, carborundum, initiative and referendum? He gave it up. But she would remember it. "Where's the what's-its-name?" she would ask. "Don't tell me you forgot the what's-its-name." A newsboy went by shouting something about the Waterbury trial.

. . . "Perhaps this will refresh your memory." The district attorney suddenly thrust a heavy automatic at the quiet figure on the witness stand. "Have you ever seen this before?" Walter Mitty took the gun and examined it expertly. "This is my Webley-Vickers 50.80," he said calmly. An excited buzz ran around the courtroom. The judge rapped for order. "You are a crack shot with any sort of firearms, I believe?" said the district attorney, insinuatingly. "Objection!" shouted Mitty's attorney. "We have shown that the defendant could not have fired the shot. We have shown that he wore his right arm in a sling on the night of the fourteenth of July." Walter Mitty raised his hand briefly and the bickering attorneys were stilled. "With any known make of gun," he said evenly, "I could have killed Gregory Fitzhurst at three hundred feet *with my left hand.*" Pandemonium broke loose in the courtroom. A woman's scream rose above the bedlam and suddenly a lovely, dark-haired girl was in Walter Mitty's arms. The district attorney struck at her savagely. Without rising from his chair, Mitty let the man have it on the point of the chin. "You miserable cur!"[5] . . .

"Puppy biscuit," said Walter Mitty. He stopped walking and the buildings of Waterbury rose up out of the misty courtroom and surrounded him again. A woman who was passing laughed. "He said 'Puppy biscuit,'" she said to her companion. "That man said 'Puppy biscuit' to himself." Walter Mitty hurried on. He went into an A & P, not the first one he came to but a smaller one farther up the street. "I want some biscuit for small, young dogs," he said to the clerk. "Any special brand, sir?" The greatest pistol shot in the world thought a moment. "It says 'Puppies Bark for It' on the box," said Walter Mitty.

4. **Squibb's:** Squibb (now part of Bristol-Myers Squibb) was a U.S. pharmaceutical company, established in 1858, that manufactured a variety of prescription drugs and health-care products, such as cough and cold medicines and vitamins. It is not clear which product Mitty is thinking about.

5. **cur:** a cowardly or contemptible person; also, a mongrel dog.

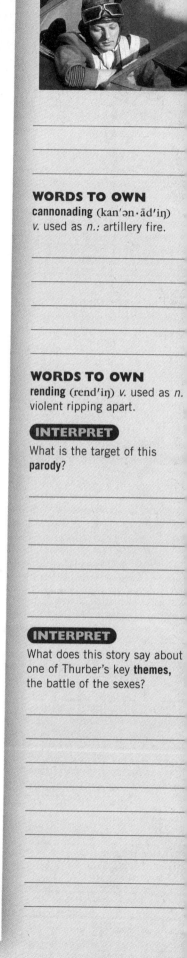

His wife would be through at the hairdresser's in fifteen minutes, Mitty saw in looking at his watch, unless they had trouble drying it; sometimes they had trouble drying it. She didn't like to get to the hotel first; she would want him to be there waiting for her as usual. He found a big leather chair in the lobby, facing a window, and he put the overshoes and the puppy biscuit on the floor beside it. He picked up an old copy of *Liberty* and sank down into the chair. "Can Germany Conquer the World Through the Air?" Walter Mitty looked at the pictures of bombing planes and of ruined streets.

. . . "The cannonading has got the wind up in young Raleigh, sir," said the sergeant. Captain Mitty looked up at him through tousled hair. "Get him to bed," he said wearily. "With the others. I'll fly alone." "But you can't, sir," said the sergeant anxiously. "It takes two men to handle that bomber and the Archies[6] are pounding hell out of the air. Von Richtman's circus[7] is between here and Saulier." "Somebody's got to get to that ammunition dump," said Mitty. "I'm going over. Spot of brandy?" He poured a drink for the sergeant and one for himself. War thundered and whined around the dugout and battered at the door. There was a rending of wood and splinters flew through the room. "A bit of a near thing," said Captain Mitty carelessly. "The box barrage is closing in," said the sergeant. "We only live once, Sergeant," said Mitty, with his faint, fleeting smile. "Or do we?" He poured another brandy and tossed it off. "I never see a man could hold his brandy like you, sir," said the sergeant. "Begging your pardon, sir." Captain Mitty stood up and strapped on his huge Webley-Vickers automatic. "It's forty kilometers through hell, sir," said the sergeant. Mitty finished one last brandy. "After all," he said softly, "what isn't?" The pounding of the cannon increased; there was the rat-tat-tatting of machine guns, and from somewhere came the menacing pocketa-pocketa-pocketa of the new flamethrowers. Walter Mitty walked to the door of the dugout humming "Auprès de Ma Blonde."[8] He turned and waved to the sergeant. "Cheerio!" he said. . . .

Something struck his shoulder. "I've been looking all over this hotel for you," said Mrs. Mitty. "Why do you have to hide in this old chair? How did you expect me to find you?" "Things close in," said Walter Mitty vaguely. "What?" Mrs. Mitty said. "Did you get the what's-its-name? The puppy biscuit? What's in that box?" "Overshoes," said Mitty. "Couldn't you have put them on in the store?" "I was thinking," said Walter Mitty. "Does it ever occur to you that I am sometimes thinking?" She looked at him. "I'm going to take your temperature when I get you home," she said.

---

6. **Archies:** German antiaircraft guns or gunners in World War I.
7. **circus:** squadron of planes.
8. **Auprès de Ma Blonde** (ō·prā′ də mä blônd): French song. The title means "Near My Blonde."

WORDS TO OWN
cannonading (kan′ən·ād′iŋ) *v.* used as *n.*: artillery fire.

WORDS TO OWN
rending (rend′iŋ) *v.* used as *n.* violent ripping apart.

INTERPRET
What is the target of this **parody**?

INTERPRET
What does this story say about one of Thurber's key **themes,** the battle of the sexes?

EVALUATE

o you think the ending is umorous or tragic? Explain our answer.

They went out through the revolving doors that made a faintly derisive whistling sound when you pushed them. It was two blocks to the parking lot. At the drugstore on the corner she said, "Wait here for me. I forgot something. I won't be a minute." She was more than a minute. Walter Mitty lighted a cigarette. It began to rain, rain with sleet in it. He stood up against the wall of the drugstore, smoking. . . . He put his shoulders back and his heels together. "To hell with the handkerchief," said Walter Mitty scornfully. He took one last drag on his cigarette and snapped it away. Then, with that faint, fleeting smile playing about his lips, he faced the firing squad; erect and motionless, proud and disdainful, Walter Mitty the Undefeated, inscrutable[9] to the last.

9. **inscrutable** (in·skro͞ot′ə·bəl): mysterious.

Parody

Much of the comic effect of "The Secret Life of Walter Mitty" depends on Thurber's use of **parody.** A parody is a work that makes fun of another work by imitating some aspect of its style or content. A writer of parody is often like a cartoonist, playfully exaggerating some prominent feature out of proportion.

You've probably encountered parodies (or "spoofs") of shows, songs, and movies. For a parody to "work," the audience has to be familiar with the target of the parody. A spoof of horror movies, for example, will have all the outward features we associate with "serious" horror movies—a dark night, spooky music, unexpected noises, a cast of teenagers who mysteriously disappear one by one—and make them ridiculous through exaggeration. The night will be *too* dark, the noises too loud to be anything but silly, the cast too self-conscious in their overacting to let the audience forget that it's all for fun.

Explore James Thurber's use of parody in "The Secret Life of Walter Mitty" by filling out the chart below. On the left-hand side of the chart, list the five roles that Walter Mitty plays in his fantasies. On the right-hand side, identify who or what are the targets of Thurber's satire. (Clue: Pay special attention to the **jargon,** or specialized terminology, being bandied about in each daydream.)

Mitty's Fantasy Roles	Who/What Is Being Parodied
1.	
2.	
3.	
4.	
5.	

Jargon

Jargon has several different meanings. It is often used for the specialized terminology of a profession or group. Bureaucratic jargon, for example, is the language that appears on official government forms. Scientists have their own jargon. So do lawyers, doctors, and sportswriters.

Sometimes the word *jargon* has a negative connotation. It is applied to speech or writing that is characterized by unfamiliar or pretentious language.

In "The Secret Life of Walter Mitty," James Thurber uses jargon humorously to parody certain stereotypes. Look at the jargon that is bandied about in Mitty's daydreams. Choose one of the daydreams and list examples of jargon that Thurber uses.

Vocabulary: How to Own a Word

Column Match

Word Bank
rakishly
distraught
haggard
craven
insolent
insinuatingly
pandemonium
bedlam
cannonading
rending

In the space provided, write the letter of the word or phrase in Column B that best defines each word in Column A.

	Column A	Column B
____	**1.** insolent	**a.** suggestively
____	**2.** rakishly	**b.** place of confusion
____	**3.** bedlam	**c.** troubled
____	**4.** haggard	**d.** jauntily
____	**5.** cannonading	**e.** boldly disrespectful
____	**6.** pandemonium	**f.** worn in appearance
____	**7.** insinuatingly	**g.** wild disorder
____	**8.** craven	**h.** artillery fire
____	**9.** rending	**i.** cowardly
____	**10.** distraught	**j.** tearing apart

A Worn Path

Make the Connection

An Eventful Journey

Eudora Welty lived nearly all of her very long life in her hometown of Jackson, Mississippi, and her many short stories depict the Southern life she knew so well. In particular, she is noted for capturing colloquial speech—that is, the way people really talk—with painstaking accuracy and a musician's ear for the right word, the right phrase.

Welty's fiction seems so perfectly a reflection of her surroundings and her times that it is easy to overlook her sophisticated artistry. She was a master at adapting the particularities of real life to the timeless **archetypes** of storytelling—patterns for plots and characters that transcend any one place or time. One such archetype, the perilous journey, has long been used by storytellers as a metaphor for life. When we think of a perilous journey, we might conjure up images of a steely, larger-than-life hero or heroine who endures incredible hardships and faces monstrous adversaries. But a perilous journey can be a much more ordinary—even everyday—affair, on a road as modest and simple as a worn path.

Think of some "perilous journeys" you know from books or movies—or even your own life. What basic features do they have in common? Consider the fundamental elements of any "perilous journey" story by completing the boxes below.

Characteristics of the Heroine or Hero

Characteristics of the Journey

Characteristics of the Dangers

Characteristics of the Goal or Reward

A Worn Path

Eudora Welty

PREDICT

ɔok up the word *phoenix* in a ictionary. What do you expect ill happen to a character with ıat name?

VORDS TO OWN

endulum (pen′dyo͞o·ləm) ·.: freely swinging weight uspended from a fixed ·oint to regulate a clock's ıovement.

ersistent (pər·sist′ənt) *adj.:* ontinuing.

ıeditative (med′ə·tāt′iv) *adj.:* leeply thoughtful; reflective.

llumined (i·lo͞o′mənd) *v.:* ighted up.

BUILD FLUENCY

Read lines 14–31 aloud as xpressively as you can. In our reading, be sure that your one reflects the distinction ɔetween Phoenix's lines and he narrative portions of the ext.

WORDS TO OWN

intent (in·tent′) *adj.:* purposeful.

appointed (ə·point′id) *v.* used as *adj.:* assigned.

It was December—a bright frozen day in the early morning. Far out in the country there was an old Negro woman with her head tied in a red rag, coming along a path through the pinewoods. Her name was Phoenix Jackson. She was very old and small and she walked slowly in the dark pine shadows, moving a little from side to side in her steps, with the balanced heaviness and lightness of a pendulum in a grandfather clock. She carried a thin, small cane made from an umbrella, and with this she kept tapping the frozen earth in front of her. This made a grave and persistent noise in the still air, that seemed meditative like the chirping of a solitary little bird.

She wore a dark striped dress reaching down to her shoe tops, and an equally long apron of bleached sugar sacks, with a full pocket: all neat and tidy, but every time she took a step she might have fallen over her shoelaces, which dragged from her unlaced shoes. She looked straight ahead. Her eyes were blue with age. Her skin had a pattern all its own of numberless branching wrinkles and as though a whole little tree stood in the middle of her forehead, but a golden color ran underneath, and the two knobs of her cheeks were illumined by a yellow burning under the dark. Under the red rag her hair came down on her neck in the frailest of ringlets, still black, and with an odor like copper.

Now and then there was a quivering in the thicket. Old Phoenix said, "Out of my way, all you foxes, owls, beetles, jack rabbits, coons, and wild animals! . . . Keep out from under these feet, little bobwhites. . . . Keep the big wild hogs out of my path. Don't let none of those come running in my direction. I got a long way." Under her small black-freckled hand her cane, limber as a buggy whip, would switch at the brush as if to rouse up any hiding things.

On she went. The woods were deep and still. The sun made the pine needles almost too bright to look at, up where the wind rocked. The cones dropped as light as feathers. Down in the hollow was the mourning dove—it was not too late for him.

The path ran up a hill. "Seem like there is chains about my feet, time I get this far," she said, in the voice of argument old people keep to use with themselves. "Something always take a hold of me on this hill—pleads I should stay."

After she got to the top she turned and gave a full, severe look behind her where she had come. "Up through pines," she said at length. "Now down through oaks."

Her eyes opened their widest, and she started down gently. But before she got to the bottom of the hill a bush caught her dress.

Her fingers were busy and intent, but her skirts were full and long, so that before she could pull them free in one place they were caught in another. It was not possible to allow the dress to tear. "I in the thorny bush," she said. "Thorns, you doing your appointed work. Never want to let folks pass, no sir. Old eyes thought you was a pretty little *green* bush."

Finally, trembling all over, she stood free, and after a moment dared to stoop for her cane.

"Sun so high!" she cried, leaning back and looking, while the thick tears went over her eyes. "The time getting all gone here."

At the foot of this hill was a place where a log was laid across the creek.

"Now comes the trial," said Phoenix.

Putting her right foot out, she mounted the log and shut her eyes. Lifting her skirt, leveling her cane fiercely before her, like a festival figure in some parade, she began to march across. Then she opened her eyes and she was safe on the other side.

"I wasn't as old as I thought," she said.

But she sat down to rest. She spread her skirts on the bank around her and folded her hands over her knees. Up above her was a tree in a pearly cloud of mistletoe. She did not dare to close her eyes, and when a little boy brought her a plate with a slice of marble cake on it she spoke to him. "That would be acceptable," she said. But when she went to take it there was just her own hand in the air.

So she left that tree, and had to go through a barbed-wire fence. There she had to creep and crawl, spreading her knees and stretching her fingers like a baby trying to climb the steps. But she talked loudly to herself: She could not let her dress be torn now, so late in the day, and she could not pay for having her arm or her leg sawed off if she got caught fast where she was.

At last she was safe through the fence and risen up out in the clearing. Big dead trees, like black men with one arm, were standing in the purple stalks of the withered cotton field. There sat a buzzard.

"Who you watching?"

In the furrow she made her way along.

"Glad this not the season for bulls," she said, looking sideways, "and the good Lord made his snakes to curl up and sleep in the winter. A pleasure I don't see no two-headed snake coming around that tree, where it come once. It took a while to get by him, back in the summer."

She passed through the old cotton and went into a field of dead corn. It whispered and shook and was taller than her head. "Through the maze now," she said, for there was no path.

Then there was something tall, black, and skinny there, moving before her.

At first she took it for a man. It could have been a man dancing in the field. But she stood still and listened, and it did not make a sound. It was as silent as a ghost.

"Ghost," she said sharply, "who be you the ghost of? For I have heard of nary death close by."

But there was no answer—only the ragged dancing in the wind.

VISUALIZE

What **simile** does Welty use to describe Phoenix's progress across the log? Based on this simile, how do you visualize the character?

WORDS TO OWN

furrow (fur′ō) *n.:* groove in the land made by a plow.

RETELL

In rural Southern dialect, the word *nary* means "not one" or "not any." **Paraphrase** Phoenix's dialogue here in standard English.

She shut her eyes, reached out her hand, and touched a sleeve. She found a coat and inside that an emptiness, cold as ice.

"You scarecrow," she said. Her face lighted. "I ought to be shut up for good," she said with laughter. "My senses is gone. I too old. I the oldest people I ever know. Dance, old scarecrow," she said, "while I dancing with you."

She kicked her foot over the furrow, and with mouth drawn down, shook her head once or twice in a little strutting way. Some husks blew down and whirled in streamers about her skirts.

VISUALIZE
nderline the details that help
ou imagine the **setting.**

Then she went on, parting her way from side to side with the cane, through the whispering field. At last she came to the end, to a wagon track where the silver grass blew between the red ruts. The quail were walking around like pullets, seeming all dainty and unseen.

"Walk pretty," she said. "This the easy place. This the easy going."

She followed the track, swaying through the quiet bare fields, through the little strings of trees silver in their dead leaves, past cabins silver from weather, with the doors and windows boarded shut, all like old women under a spell sitting there. "I walking in their sleep," she said, nodding her head vigorously.

In a ravine she went where a spring was silently flowing through a hollow log. Old Phoenix bent and drank. "Sweet gum makes the water sweet," she said, and drank more. "Nobody know who made this well, for it was here when I was born."

The track crossed a swampy part where the moss hung as white as lace from every limb. "Sleep on, alligators, and blow your bubbles." Then the track went into the road.

Deep, deep the road went down between the high green-colored banks. Overhead the live oaks met, and it was as dark as a cave.

A black dog with a lolling tongue came up out of the weeds by the ditch. She was meditating, and not ready, and when he came at her she only hit him a little with her cane. Over she went in the ditch, like a little puff of milkweed.

INFER
Vhat kind of social
elationship is implied by
he way that Phoenix and
he young white man address
ach other?

Down there, her senses drifted away. A dream visited her, and she reached her hand up, but nothing reached down and gave her a pull. So she lay there and presently went to talking. "Old woman," she said to herself, "that black dog come up out of the weeds to stall you off, and now there he sitting on his fine tail, smiling at you."

A white man finally came along and found her—a hunter, a young man, with his dog on a chain. "Well, Granny!" he laughed. "What are you doing there?"

"Lying on my back like a June bug waiting to be turned over, mister," she said, reaching up her hand.

He lifted her up, gave her a swing in the air, and set her down. "Anything broken, Granny?"

"No sir, them old dead weeds is springy enough," said Phoenix, when she had got her breath. "I thank you for your trouble."

"Where do you live, Granny?" he asked, while the two dogs were growling at each other.

"Away back yonder, sir, behind the ridge. You can't even see it from here."

"On your way home?"

"No sir, I going to town."

"Why, that's too far! That's as far as I walk when I come out myself, and I get something for my trouble." He patted the stuffed bag he carried, and there hung down a little closed claw. It was one of the bobwhites, with its beak hooked bitterly to show it was dead. "Now you go on home, Granny!"

"I bound to go to town, mister," said Phoenix. "The time come around."

He gave another laugh, filling the whole landscape. "I know you old colored people! Wouldn't miss going to town to see Santa Claus!"

But something held old Phoenix very still. The deep lines in her face went into a fierce and different radiation. Without warning, she had seen with her own eyes a flashing nickel fall out of the man's pocket onto the ground.

"How old are you, Granny?" he was saying.

"There is no telling, mister," she said, "no telling."

Then she gave a little cry and clapped her hands and said, "Git on away from here, dog! Look! Look at that dog!" She laughed as if in admiration. "He ain't scared of nobody. He a big black dog." She whispered, "Sic him!"

"Watch me get rid of that cur," said the man. "Sic him, Pete! Sic him!"

Phoenix heard the dogs fighting, and heard the man running and throwing sticks. She even heard a gunshot. But she was slowly bending forward by that time, further and further forward, the lids stretched down over her eyes, as if she were doing this in her sleep. Her chin was lowered almost to her knees. The yellow palm of her hand came out from the fold of her apron. Her fingers slid down and along the ground under the piece of money with the grace and care they would have in lifting an egg from under a setting hen. Then she slowly straightened up, she stood erect, and the nickel was in her apron pocket. A bird flew by. Her lips moved. "God watching me the whole time. I come to stealing."

The man came back, and his own dog panted about them. "Well, I scared him off that time," he said, and then he laughed and lifted his gun and pointed it at Phoenix.

She stood straight and faced him.

"Doesn't the gun scare you?" he said, still pointing it.

INTERPRET
In a few words, characterize the hunter's response to Phoenix.

WORDS TO OWN
radiation (rā′dē·ā′shən) *n.:* pattern; arrangement.

INFER
What can you infer about Phoenix from her actions and words in this passage?

INTERPRET
Do you think that the man dropped the nickel accidentally, or deliberately? Why?

INTERPRET

'hat does Phoenix's etermination to continue her urney imply thematically?

INTERPRET

ow does Phoenix's reliance n her feet emphasize the title nd **theme** of the story?

WORDS TO OWN

ceremonial (ser′ə·mō′nē·əl) *adj.:* formal.

"No, sir, I seen plenty go off closer by, in my day, and for less than what I done," she said holding utterly still.

He smiled, and shouldered the gun. "Well, Granny," he said, "you must be a hundred years old, and scared of nothing. I'd give you a dime if I had any money with me. But you take my advice and stay home, and nothing will happen to you."

"I bound to go on my way, mister," said Phoenix. She inclined her head in the red rag. Then they went in different directions, but she could hear the gun shooting again and again over the hill.

She walked on. The shadows hung from the oak trees to the road like curtains. Then she smelled woodsmoke, and smelled the river, and she saw a steeple and the cabins on their steep steps. Dozens of little black children whirled around her. There ahead was Natchez shining. Bells were ringing. She walked on.

In the paved city it was Christmas time. There were red and green electric lights strung and crisscrossed everywhere, and all turned on in the daytime. Old Phoenix would have been lost if she had not distrusted her eyesight and depended on her feet to know where to take her.

She paused quietly on the sidewalk where people were passing by. A lady came along in the crowd, carrying an armful of red-, green-, and silver-wrapped presents; she gave off perfume like the red roses in hot summer, and Phoenix stopped her.

"Please, missy, will you lace up my shoe?" She held up her foot.

"What do you want, Grandma?"

"See my shoe," said Phoenix. "Do all right for out in the country, but wouldn't look right to go in a big building."

"Stand still then, Grandma," said the lady. She put her packages down on the sidewalk beside her and laced and tied both shoes tightly.

"Can't lace 'em with a cane," said Phoenix. "Thank you, missy. I doesn't mind asking a nice lady to tie up my shoe, when I gets out on the street."

Moving slowly and from side to side, she went into the big building, and into a tower of steps, where she walked up and around and around until her feet knew to stop.

She entered a door, and there she saw nailed up on the wall the document that had been stamped with the gold seal and framed in the gold frame, which matched the dream that was hung up in her head.

"Here I be," she said. There was a fixed and ceremonial stiffness over her body.

"A charity case, I suppose," said an attendant who sat at the desk before her.

But Phoenix only looked above her head. There was sweat on her face, the wrinkles in her skin shone like a bright net.

"Speak up, Grandma," the woman said. "What's your name? We must have your history, you know. Have you been here before? What seems to be the trouble with you?"

Old Phoenix only gave a twitch to her face as if a fly were bothering her.

"Are you deaf?" cried the attendant.

But then the nurse came in.

"Oh, that's just old Aunt Phoenix," she said. "She doesn't come for herself—she has a little grandson. She makes these trips just as regular as clockwork. She lives away back off the Old Natchez Trace." She bent down. "Well, Aunt Phoenix, why don't you just take a seat? We won't keep you standing after your long trip." She pointed.

The old woman sat down, bolt upright in the chair.

"Now, how is the boy?" asked the nurse.

Old Phoenix did not speak.

"I said, how is the boy?"

But Phoenix only waited and stared straight ahead, her face very solemn and withdrawn into rigidity.

"Is his throat any better?" asked the nurse. "Aunt Phoenix, don't you hear me? Is your grandson's throat any better since the last time you came for the medicine?"

With her hands on her knees, the old woman waited, silent, erect and motionless, just as if she were in armor.

"You mustn't take up our time this way, Aunt Phoenix," the nurse said. "Tell us quickly about your grandson, and get it over. He isn't dead, is he?"

At last there came a flicker and then a flame of comprehension across her face, and she spoke.

"My grandson. It was my memory had left me. There I sat and forgot why I made my long trip."

"Forgot?" The nurse frowned. "After you came so far?"

Then Phoenix was like an old woman begging a dignified forgiveness for waking up frightened in the night. "I never did go to school, I was too old at the Surrender," she said in a soft voice. "I'm an old woman without an education. It was my memory fail me. My little grandson, he is just the same, and I forgot it in the coming."

"Throat never heals, does it?" said the nurse, speaking in a loud, sure voice to old Phoenix. By now she had a card with something written on it, a little list. "Yes. Swallowed lye. When was it?—January—two-three years ago—"

Phoenix spoke unasked now. "No, missy, he not dead, he just the same. Every little while his throat begin to close up again, and he not able to swallow. He not get his breath. He not able to help himself. So the time come around, and I go on another trip for the soothing medicine."

INTERPRET
Why is the reason for Phoenix journey not revealed earlier?

WORDS TO OWN
solemn (säl′əm) *adj.:* serious.

DENTIFY

hy is the situation of oenix's grandson so esperate?

INTERPRET

ow does Phoenix's gift for her randson contribute to the ory's **theme**?

EVALUATE

low well does the **metaphor** f a "worn path" work in this tory?

"All right. The doctor said as long as you came to get it, you could have it," said the nurse. "But it's an obstinate case."

"My little grandson, he sit up there in the house all wrapped up, waiting by himself," Phoenix went on. "We is the only two left in the world. He suffer and it don't seem to put him back at all. He got a sweet look. He going to last. He wear a little patch quilt and peep out holding his mouth open like a little bird. I remembers so plain now. I not going to forget him again, no, the whole enduring time. I could tell him from all the others in creation."

"All right." The nurse was trying to hush her now. She brought her a bottle of medicine. "Charity," she said, making a check mark in a book.

Old Phoenix held the bottle close to her eyes, and then carefully put it into her pocket.

"I thank you," she said.

"It's Christmas time, Grandma," said the attendant. "Could I give you a few pennies out of my purse?"

"Five pennies is a nickel," said Phoenix stiffly.

"Here's a nickel," said the attendant.

Phoenix rose carefully and held out her hand. She received the nickel and then fished the other nickel out of her pocket and laid it beside the new one. She stared at her palm closely, with her head on one side.

Then she gave a tap with her cane on the floor.

"This is what come to me to do," she said. "I going to the store and buy my child a little windmill they sells, made out of paper. He going to find it hard to believe there such a thing in the world. I'll march myself back where he waiting, holding it straight up in this hand."

She lifted her free hand, gave a little nod, turned around, and walked out of the doctor's office. Then her slow step began on the stairs, going down.

Theme

The **theme** of a literary work is its main idea or insight into life. Sometimes an author will state a work's theme directly; such a statement is called an **explicit theme.** Far more often, however, a reader has to infer the theme of a work after considerable thought. The author allows the reader to identify the **implicit theme** after considering elements such as **character, plot, setting, mood, symbol,** and **tone.**

Keep in mind that a work's theme is not the same as its **subject.** A story's subject might be stated in a word or phrase such as "growing up," "love," "a special journey," "heroism," or "fear." A story's theme, however, like the **thesis** of a persuasive essay, is the statement or conclusion that a writer wants to make about that subject: for example, "For most young people, growing up is a process that involves the pain of achieving self-knowledge." Theme must be stated in at least one sentence, and some themes are complex enough to require several sentences, or even an essay.

In the space provided below, write a sentence or two in which you identify Eudora Welty's most important theme in "A Worn Path."

Vocabulary: How to Own a Word

Antonyms

Word Bank
pendulum
persistent
meditative
illumined
intent
appointed
furrow
radiation
ceremonial
solemn

Read each sentence below carefully. Each word in boldface type is a Word to Own. Choose the word that is the antonym of the Word to Own, and write its letter in the space provided.

_____ **1.** Phoenix's cane made a **persistent** tapping sound on the earth.

a. unattractive **b.** inconstant **c.** soft **d.** quiet

_____ **2.** When she arrived at her destination, Phoenix stood with **ceremonial** rigidity.

a. unnecessary **b.** painless **c.** informal **d.** loud

_____ **3.** Her face was **illumined** by a natural golden glow.

a. darkened **b.** soured **c.** unsurpassed **d.** weakened

_____ **4.** Phoenix's attitude was **intent** when she untangled her dress from the thorn bush.

a. slow **b.** thick **c.** confident **d.** purposeless

_____ **5.** While trying to remember the purpose of her visit, the old woman was **solemn.**

a. frivolous **b.** unhappy **c.** sane **d.** regretful

Synonyms

Read each sentence below carefully. For each boldface Word to Own, choose the word or phrase that is similar in meaning and write its letter in the space provided.

_____ **6.** She seemed **meditative** as she continued alone on the path through the forest.

a. confused
b. irritated
c. insolent
d. deeply thoughtful

_____ **7.** Her steps were balanced like the movement of a **pendulum.**

a. a swinging weighted object
b. a bird in flight
c. an ancient coin
d. a windmill

_____ **8.** After speaking to a buzzard, she continued into the **furrow.**

a. a wide opening
b. a groove in the land
c. a wooden tool
d. a small reptile

_____ **9.** As she watched a nickel drop from the hunter's pocket, the lines in her face went into a different **radiation.**

a. sarcastic grin
b. haggard appearance
c. pattern
d. mournful look

_____ **10.** Despite her fatigue, she stayed faithful to her **appointed** task.

a. difficult
b. stressful
c. dreaded
d. assigned

Soldier's Home

Make the Connection

A Hero's Welcome

Throughout most of the twentieth century, there was one man who, for people all over the world, epitomized the American writer—Ernest Hemingway. Hemingway redefined the "American hero" in his fiction, and he seems to have modeled his own life after the characters he had invented. The Hemingway hero is disillusioned by a world that has all but abandoned his own stern code of conduct, which demands courage, a stoical willingness to endure pain, and, above all, "grace under pressure." The only reward in such a world is dignity, and the only victories are the moments of intense pleasure available to those whose senses have been honed on suffering.

This bleak view of life grew from Hemingway's own experience of World War I, which many idealistically believed would be "the war to end all wars." But the war turned out to be a bloodbath. Advances in weaponry made the Great War devastating, both physically and psychologically. Soldiers who returned home were often described as "shellshocked"—suffering from a mental and emotional condition of confusion, exhaustion, anxiety, and depression. Many of them simply couldn't readjust to life back home, which seemed to offer little they could relate to or believe in.

This condition, now known as post-traumatic stress disorder, is not limited to soldiers returning from war. Perhaps you have seen movies or television dramas that depict people who simply cannot cope with life after a terrible experience. What are some of the possible causes of this condition, and what can be done to help? Explore "shell shock" by completing the table below.

Possible Causes of Post-Traumatic Stress Disorder	Possible Treatments

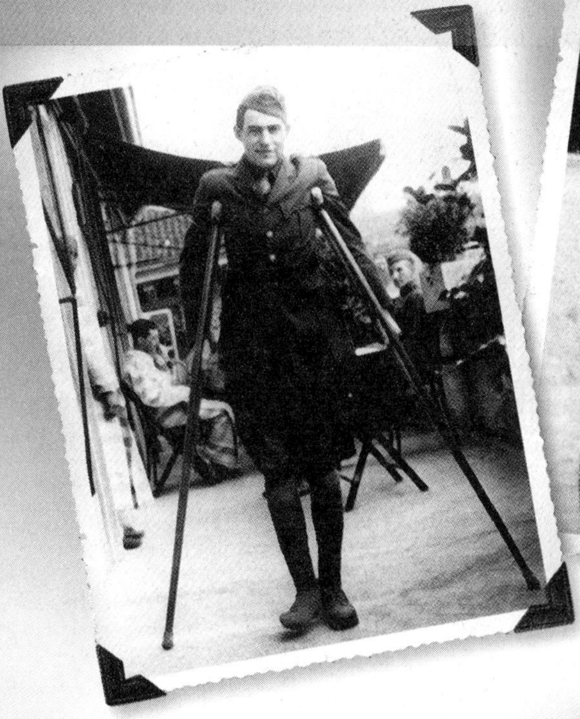

Soldier's Home

Ernest Hemingway

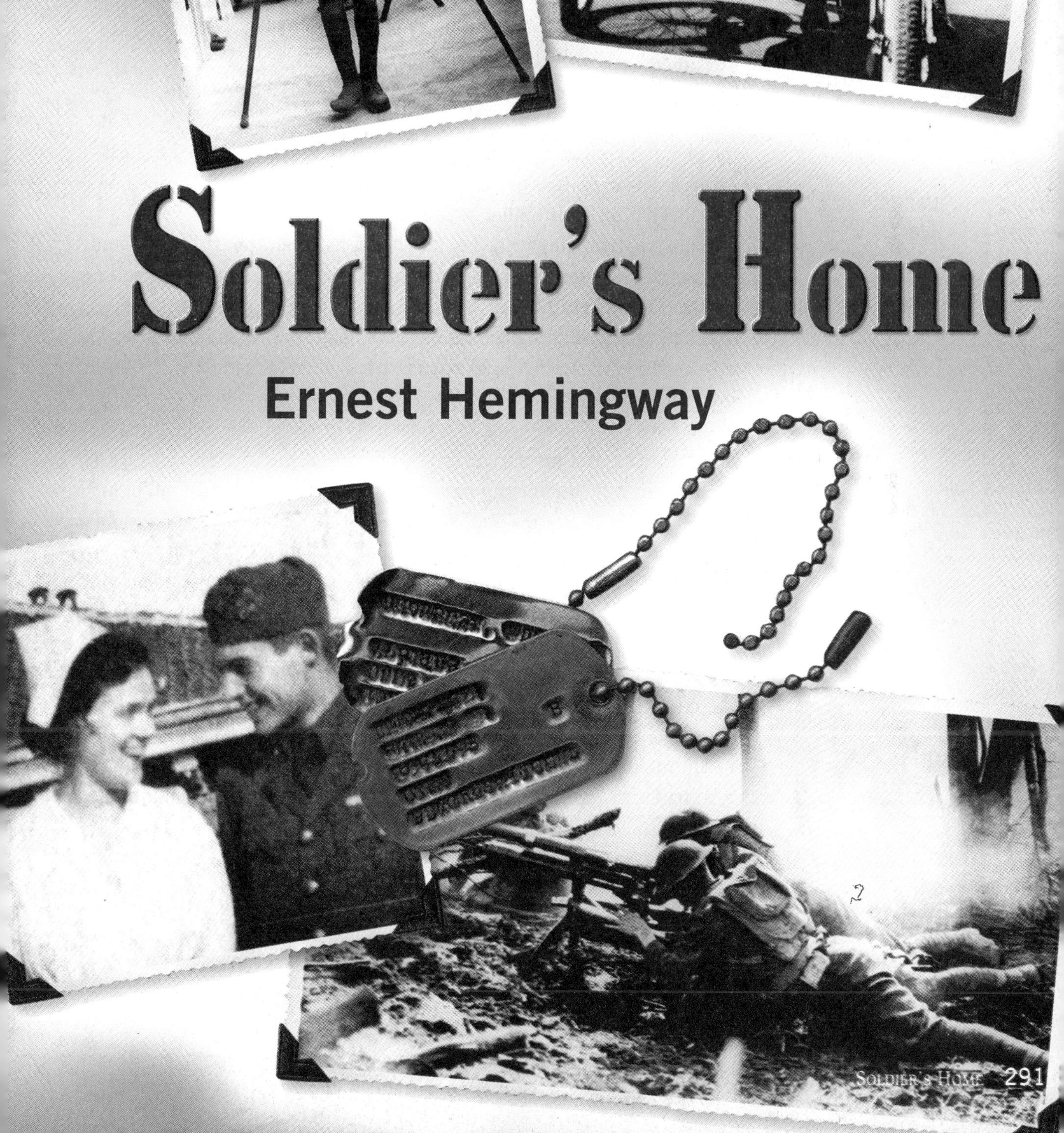

NTERPRET

statement or expression is
ıbiguous when it can mean
o or more different things.
ow is the story's **title**
ıbiguous? (Clue: What two
eanings could the apostrophe
gnal?)

'ORDS TO OWN

aborately (ē·lab′ə·rit·lē)
dv.: with great care.

steria (hi·ster′ē·ə) *n.:*
ıcontrolled excitement.

rocity (ə·träs′ə·tē) *n.* used
adj.: horrible; brutal.

NTERPRET

Hemingway's work, lies
ten have a corrupting
fluence and can poison
ery aspect of an experience.
ow do lies cause a change
Krebs's attitude toward his
vn war experience?

VORDS TO OWN

pocryphal (ə·päk′rə·fəl) *adj.:*
f questionable authority;
ılse.

xaggeration (eg·zaj′ər·ā′shən)
.: overstatement.

Krebs went to the war from a Methodist college in Kansas. There is a picture which shows him among his fraternity brothers, all of them wearing exactly the same height and style collar. He enlisted in the Marines in 1917 and did not return to the United States until the second division returned from the Rhine[1] in the summer of 1919.

There is a picture which shows him on the Rhine with two German girls and another corporal. Krebs and the corporal look too big for their uniforms. The German girls are not beautiful. The Rhine does not show in the picture.

By the time Krebs returned to his home town in Oklahoma the greeting of heroes was over. He came back much too late. The men from the town who had been drafted had all been welcomed elaborately on their return. There had been a great deal of hysteria. Now the reaction had set in. People seemed to think it was rather ridiculous for Krebs to be getting back so late, years after the war was over.

At first Krebs, who had been at Belleau Wood, Soissons, the Champagne, St. Mihiel and in the Argonne[2] did not want to talk about the war at all. Later he felt the need to talk but no one wanted to hear about it. His town had heard too many atrocity stories to be thrilled by actualities. Krebs found that to be listened to at all he had to lie, and after he had done this twice he, too, had a reaction against the war and against talking about it. A distaste for everything that had happened to him in the war set in because of the lies he had told. All of the times that had been able to make him feel cool and clear inside himself when he thought of them; the times so long back when he had done the one thing, the only thing for a man to do, easily and naturally, when he might have done something else, now lost their cool, valuable quality and then were lost themselves.

His lies were quite unimportant lies and consisted in attributing to himself things other men had seen, done or heard of, and stating as facts certain apocryphal incidents familiar to all soldiers. Even his lies were not sensational at the pool room. His acquaintances, who had heard detailed accounts of German women found chained to machine guns in the Argonne forest and who could not comprehend, or were barred by their patriotism from interest in, any German machine gunners who were not chained, were not thrilled by his stories.

Krebs acquired the nausea in regard to experience that is the result of untruth or exaggeration, and when he occasionally met another man who had really been a soldier and they talked a few minutes in the dressing room at a dance he fell into the easy pose of the old soldier

1. **Rhine:** river that flows through Germany toward the North Sea.
2. **Belleau** (be·lō′) **Wood . . . Argonne** (är′gän′): sites of World War I battles that demonstrated the Allies' superior strength against the Germans.

among other soldiers: that he had been badly, sickeningly frightened all the time. In this way he lost everything.

During this time, it was late summer, he was sleeping late in bed, getting up to walk down town to the library to get a book, eating lunch at home, reading on the front porch until he became bored and then walking down through the town to spend the hottest hours of the day in the cool dark of the pool room. He loved to play pool.

In the evening he practised on his clarinet, strolled down town, read and went to bed. He was still a hero to his two young sisters. His mother would have given him breakfast in bed if he had wanted it. She often came in when he was in bed and asked him to tell her about the war, but her attention always wandered. His father was non-committal.

Before Krebs went away to the war he had never been allowed to drive the family motor car. His father was in the real estate business and always wanted the car to be at his command when he required it to take clients out into the country to show them a piece of farm property. The car always stood outside the First National Bank building where his father had an office on the second floor. Now, after the war, it was still the same car.

Nothing was changed in the town except that the young girls had grown up. But they lived in such a complicated world of already defined alliances and shifting feuds that Krebs did not feel the energy or the courage to break into it. He liked to look at them, though. There were so many good-looking young girls. Most of them had their hair cut short. When he went away only little girls wore their hair like that or girls that were fast. They all wore sweaters and shirt waists with round Dutch collars. It was a pattern. He liked to look at them from the front porch as they walked on the other side of the street. He liked to watch them walking under the shade of the trees. He liked the round Dutch collars above their sweaters. He liked their silk stockings and flat shoes. He liked their bobbed hair and the way they walked.

When he was in town their appeal to him was not very strong. He did not like them when he saw them in the Greek's ice cream parlor. He did not want them themselves really. They were too complicated. There was something else. Vaguely he wanted a girl but he did not want to have to work to get her. He would have liked to have a girl but he did not want to have to spend a long time getting her. He did not want to get into the intrigue and the politics. He did not want to have to do any courting. He did not want to tell any more lies. It wasn't worth it.

He did not want any consequences. He did not want any consequences ever again. He wanted to live along without consequences. Besides he did not really need a girl. The army had taught him that. It was all right to pose as though you had to have a girl. Nearly everybody did that. But it wasn't true. You did not need a girl. That was the funny thing. First a fellow boasted how girls mean nothing to him, that he

INTERPRET

What do these details tell yo about Krebs's relationship with his sisters and with his parents?

WORDS TO OWN

alliances (ə·lī'əns·iz) *n. pl.:* close associations for commo objectives.

intrigue (in'trēg') *n.:* schemin

consequences (kän'si·kwens·iz) *n. pl.:* resu of an action.

INTERPRET

What effect do you think Hemingway seeks to achieve with **repetition** here?

NTERPRET

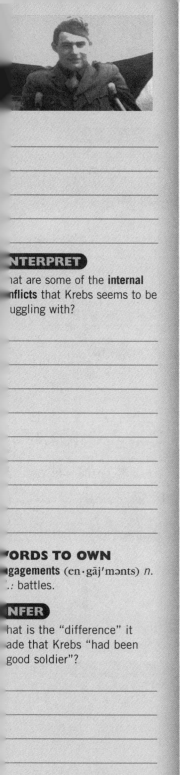

hat are some of the **internal nflicts** that Krebs seems to be uggling with?

ORDS TO OWN

gagements (en·gāj′mənts) *n.* .: battles.

NFER

hat is the "difference" it ade that Krebs "had been good soldier"?

never thought of them, that they could not touch him. Then a fellow boasted that he could not get along without girls, that he had to have them all the time, that he could not go to sleep without them.

That was all a lie. It was all a lie both ways. You did not need a girl unless you thought about them. He learned that in the army. Then sooner or later you always got one. When you were really ripe for a girl you always got one. You did not have to think about it. Sooner or later it would come. He had learned that in the army.

Now he would have liked a girl if she had come to him and not wanted to talk. But here at home it was all too complicated. He knew he could never get through it all again. It was not worth the trouble. That was the thing about French girls and German girls. There was not all this talking. You couldn't talk much and you did not need to talk. It was simple and you were friends. He thought about France and then he began to think about Germany. On the whole he had liked Germany better. He did not want to leave Germany. He did not want to come home. Still, he had come home. He sat on the front porch.

He liked the girls that were walking along the other side of the street. He liked the look of them much better than the French girls or the German girls. But the world they were in was not the world he was in. He would like to have one of them. But it was not worth it. They were such a nice pattern. He liked the pattern. It was exciting. But he would not go through all the talking. He did not want one badly enough. He liked to look at them all, though. It was not worth it. Not now when things were getting good again.

He sat there on the porch reading a book on the war. It was a history and he was reading about all the engagements he had been in. It was the most interesting reading he had ever done. He wished there were more maps. He looked forward with a good feeling to reading all the really good histories when they would come out with good detail maps. Now he was really learning about the war. He had been a good soldier. That made a difference.

One morning after he had been home about a month his mother came into his bedroom and sat on the bed. She smoothed her apron.

"I had a talk with your father last night, Harold," she said, "and he is willing for you to take the car out in the evenings."

"Yeah?" said Krebs, who was not fully awake. "Take the car out? Yeah?"

"Yes. Your father has felt for some time that you should be able to take the car out in the evenings whenever you wished but we only talked it over last night."

"I'll bet you made him," Krebs said.

"No. It was your father's suggestion that we talk the matter over."

"Yeah. I'll bet you made him," Krebs sat up in bed.

"Will you come down to breakfast, Harold?" his mother said.

"As soon as I get my clothes on," Krebs said.

His mother went out of the room and he could hear her frying something downstairs while he washed, shaved and dressed to go down into the dining-room for breakfast. While he was eating breakfast his sister brought in the mail.

"Well, Hare," she said. "You old sleepy-head. What do you ever get up for?"

Krebs looked at her. He liked her. She was his best sister.

"Have you got the paper?" he asked.

She handed him *The Kansas City Star* and he shucked off its brown wrapper and opened it to the sporting page. He folded *The Star* open and propped it against the water pitcher with his cereal dish to steady it, so he could read while he ate.

"Harold," his mother stood in the kitchen doorway, "Harold, please don't muss up the paper. Your father can't read his *Star* if it's been mussed."

"I won't muss it," Krebs said.

His sister sat down at the table and watched him while he read.

"We're playing indoor over at school this afternoon," she said. "I'm going to pitch."

"Good," said Krebs. "How's the old wing?"[3]

"I can pitch better than lots of the boys. I tell them all you taught me. The other girls aren't much good."

"Yeah?" said Krebs.

"I tell them all you're my beau.[4] Aren't you my beau, Hare?"

"You bet."

"Couldn't your brother really be your beau just because he's your brother?"

"I don't know."

"Sure you know. Couldn't you be my beau, Hare, if I was old enough and if you wanted to?"

"Sure. You're my girl now."

"Am I really your girl?"

"Sure."

"Do you love me?"

"Uh, huh."

"Will you love me always?"

"Sure."

"Will you come over and watch me play indoor?"

"Maybe."

"Aw, Hare, you don't love me. If you loved me, you'd want to come over and watch me play indoor."

---

3. **wing:** arm.
4. **beau** (bō): boyfriend.

INFER

Based on this brief interactio
why do you think this sister i
Krebs's favorite?

INTERPRET

What does Mrs. Krebs's statement suggest about Harold's relationship with his father?

NFER

hat does this exchange reveal
out Krebs's relationship with
s mother?

INTERPRET

hat might the hardening
acon fat represent
mbolically? Explain
our answer.

Krebs's mother came into the dining-room from the kitchen. She carried a plate with two fried eggs and some crisp bacon on it and a plate of buckwheat cakes.

"You run along, Helen," she said. "I want to talk to Harold."

She put the eggs and bacon down in front of him and brought in a jug of maple syrup for the buckwheat cakes. Then she sat down across the table from Krebs.

"I wish you'd put down the paper a minute, Harold," she said.

Krebs took down the paper and folded it.

"Have you decided what you are going to do yet, Harold?" his mother said, taking off her glasses.

"No," said Krebs.

"Don't you think it's about time?" His mother did not say this in a mean way. She seemed worried.

"I hadn't thought about it," Krebs said.

"God has some work for every one to do," his mother said. "There can be no idle hands in His Kingdom."

"I'm not in His Kingdom," Krebs said.

"We are all of us in His Kingdom."

Krebs felt embarrassed and resentful as always.

"I've worried about you so much, Harold," his mother went on. "I know the temptations you must have been exposed to. I know how weak men are. I know what your own dear grandfather, my own father, told us about the Civil War and I have prayed for you. I pray for you all day long, Harold."

Krebs looked at the bacon fat hardening on his plate.

"Your father is worried, too," his mother went on. "He thinks you have lost your ambition, that you haven't got a definite aim in life. Charley Simmons, who is just your age, has a good job and is going to be married. The boys are all settling down; they're all determined to get somewhere; you can see that boys like Charley Simmons are on their way to being really a credit to the community."

Krebs said nothing.

"Don't look that way, Harold," his mother said. "You know we love you and I want to tell you for your own good how matters stand. Your father does not want to hamper your freedom. He thinks you should be allowed to drive the car. If you want to take some of the nice girls out riding with you, we are only too pleased. We want you to enjoy yourself. But you are going to have to settle down to work, Harold. Your father doesn't care what you start in at. All work is honorable as he says. But you've got to make a start at something. He asked me to speak to you this morning and then you can stop in and see him at his office."

"Is that all?" Krebs said.

"Yes. Don't you love your mother, dear boy?"

"No," Krebs said.

His mother looked at him across the table. Her eyes were shiny. She started crying.

"I don't love anybody," Krebs said.

It wasn't any good. He couldn't tell her, he couldn't make her see it. It was silly to have said it. He had only hurt her. He went over and took hold of her arm. She was crying with her head in her hands.

"I didn't mean it," he said. "I was just angry at something. I didn't mean I didn't love you."

His mother went on crying. Krebs put his arm on her shoulder.

"Can't you believe me, mother?"

His mother shook her head.

"Please, please, mother. Please believe me."

"All right," his mother said chokily. She looked up at him. "I believe you, Harold."

Krebs kissed her hair. She put her face up to him.

"I'm your mother," she said. "I held you next to my heart when you were a tiny baby."

Krebs felt sick and vaguely nauseated.

"I know, Mummy," he said. "I'll try and be a good boy for you."

"Would you kneel and pray with me, Harold?" his mother asked.

They knelt down beside the dining-room table and Krebs's mother prayed.

"Now, you pray, Harold," she said.

"I can't," Krebs said.

"Try, Harold."

"I can't."

"Do you want me to pray for you?"

"Yes."

So his mother prayed for him and then they stood up and Krebs kissed his mother and went out of the house. He had tried so to keep his life from being complicated. Still, none of it had touched him. He had felt sorry for his mother and she had made him lie. He would go to Kansas City and get a job and she would feel all right about it. There would be one more scene maybe before he got away. He would not go down to his father's office. He would miss that one. He wanted his life to go smoothly. It had just gotten going that way. Well, that was all over now, anyway. He would go over to the schoolyard and watch Helen play indoor baseball.

INTERPRET

Why do you think Krebs says that he does not love anybod

WORDS TO OWN

nauseated (nô′zē·āt′id) *v.* use as *adj.:* feeling sickness or discomfort in the stomach.

INFER

Why do you think Hemingway chose not to include the fathe in the story?

EVALUATE

Is this a good ending for the story, in your opinion? Why or why not?

Style

Style is the distinctive way in which a writer uses language. Style is determined by such factors as sentence length and complexity, syntax, word choice, and the use of figurative language and imagery.

Ernest Hemingway's fame as a writer came as much from his revolutionary handling of language as from the plots and characters in his stories. Most "serious" writers of the generation before the First World War wrote in a richly complex style. Hemingway characteristically wrote in a plain, direct style that often consisted of short, simple sentences that left much unsaid.

There's more to Hemingway's style than just short sentences. He was obsessed with revealing the most truth with the fewest possible words. Read the two passages shown below from the story. Then, in the space provided following each passage, write what you notice about Hemingway's style.

1. He did not want to get into the intrigue and the politics. He did not want to have to do any courting. He did not want to tell any more lies. It wasn't worth it.

____

____

____

____

____

____

2. He did not want any consequences. He did not want any consequences ever again. He wanted to live along without consequences.

____

____

____

____

____

____

Vocabulary: How to Own a Word

Related Meanings

In each of the following groups of words, cross out the unrelated word. The unrelated word may have a different meaning or may be a different part of speech than the others. The Words to Own are shown in boldface type.

Word Bank
elaborately
hysteria
atrocity
apocryphal
exaggeration
alliances
intrigue
consequences
engagements
nauseated

EXAMPLE:	a. **grotesque**	b. ~~conform~~	c. weird	d. strange
1.	a. **apocryphal**	b. lie	c. false	d. fictitious
2.	a. purposes	b. **consequences**	c. results	d. outcomes
3.	a. **engagements**	b. conflicts	c. battles	d. marriages
4.	a. carefully	b. foolishly	c. painstakingly	d. **elaborately**
5.	a. **atrocity**	b. horror	c. unusual	d. brutality
6.	a. scheme	b. **intrigue**	c. question	d. plot
7.	a. excitement	b. commotion	c. **hysteria**	d. joke
8.	a. cooperate	b. associations	c. unions	d. **alliances**
9.	a. fabulous	b. overstatement	c. **exaggeration**	d. hyperbole
10.	a. awful	b. **nauseated**	c. dreadful	d. vile

Before You Read THE POEM

The Love Song of J. Alfred Prufrock

Make the Connection

No More Heroes?

Thomas Stearns Eliot—known to readers as T. S. Eliot—was born in St. Louis to an intellectual family with deep New England roots. After graduating from Harvard, Eliot studied for a time in Paris and then moved to London to begin his career as a poet. In 1915, just a year after the outbreak of World War I, Eliot published "The Love Song of J. Alfred Prufrock," the poem that made him famous.

"Prufrock" captures the mood of helpless paralysis that many Europeans and Americans felt in the face of the modern forces of technology and industrialism. The individual no longer seemed to count for anything; the war in Europe had quickly turned into mechanized slaughter in which millions of young men were losing their lives, it seemed, for nothing.

Joseph Campbell, a noted student of world mythology, has commented, "The hero is today running up against a hard world that is in no way responsive to his spiritual need." Do you agree? On the chart below, explore your thoughts about heroism in contemporary life. On the left-hand side of the chart, list specific aspects of life today that discourage heroism. On the right-hand side, list qualities that you think are essential in a hero, and also list the names of people today whom you regard as heroic. Add a phrase or two to explain your inclusion of each name.

Aspects of Life Discouraging Heroism	Qualities of a Hero/ Names of My Heroes

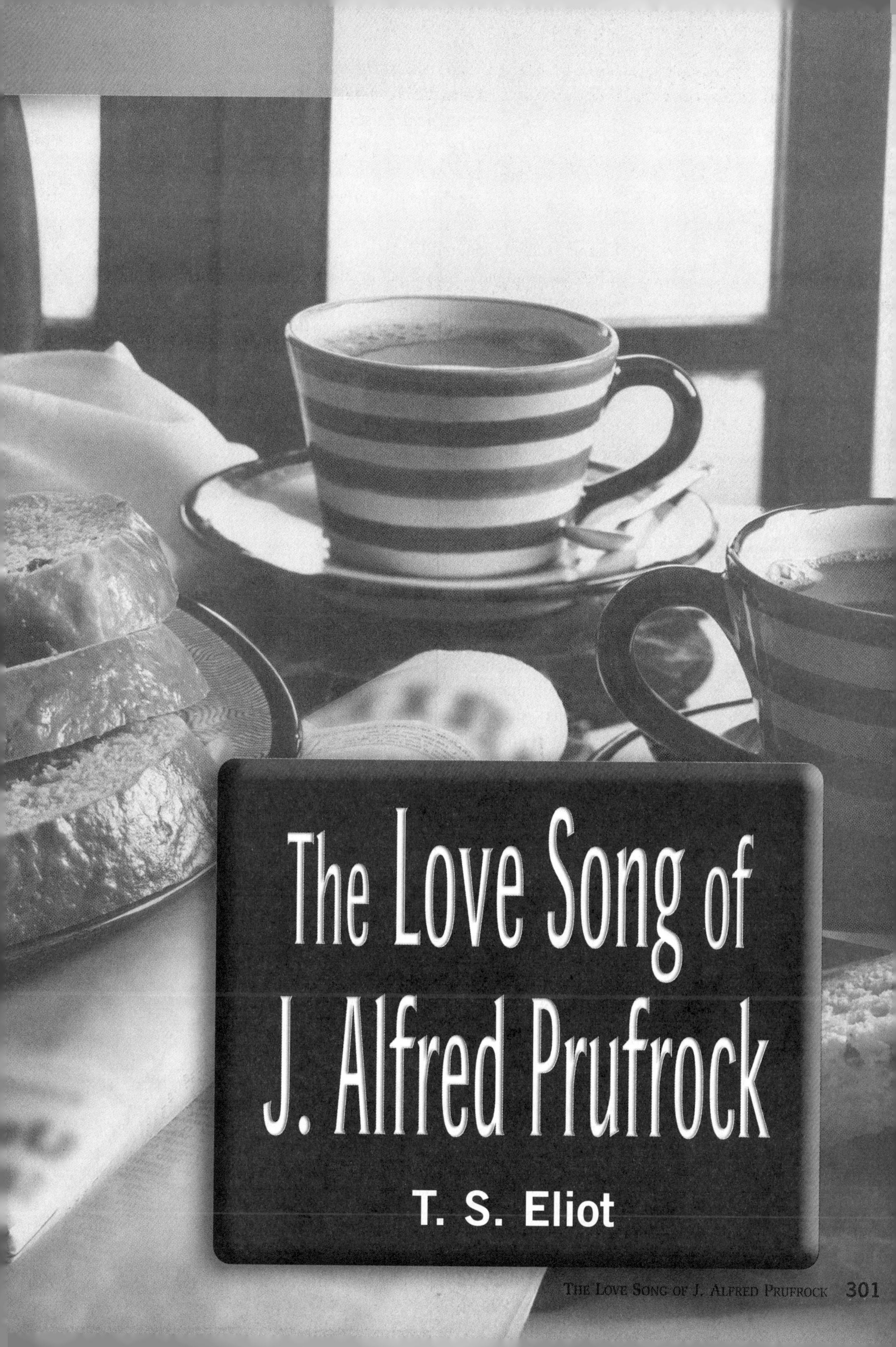

The Love Song of J. Alfred Prufrock

T. S. Eliot

VALUATE

araphrase the **simile** in lines -3. Is the comparison fective? Why or why not?

INFER

hom might the **speaker** be lking to?

INTERPRET

this passage (lines 15–22), hat is the fog compared to? nderline words and phrases hat develop the **metaphor.**

INFER

Vhat effect does repeating the vord *time* have?

S'io credessi che mia risposta fosse
a persona che mai tornasse al mondo,
questa fiamma staria senza più scosse.
Ma per ciò che giammai di questo fondo
non tornò vivo alcun, s'i'odo il vero,
senza tema d'infamia ti rispondo.[1]

Let us go then, you and I,
When the evening is spread out against the sky
Like a patient etherized upon a table;
Let us go, through certain half-deserted streets,
The muttering retreats
Of restless nights in one-night cheap hotels
And sawdust restaurants with oyster-shells:
Streets that follow like a tedious argument
Of insidious intent
To lead you to an overwhelming question . . .
Oh, do not ask, "What is it?"
Let us go and make our visit.

In the room the women come and go
Talking of Michelangelo.[2]

The yellow fog that rubs its back upon the window-panes,
The yellow smoke that rubs its muzzle on the window-panes,
Licked its tongue into the corners of the evening,
Lingered upon the pools that stand in drains,
Let fall upon its back the soot that falls from chimneys,
Slipped by the terrace, made a sudden leap,
And seeing that it was a soft October night,
Curled once about the house, and fell asleep.

And indeed there will be time
For the yellow smoke that slides along the street
Rubbing its back upon the window-panes;
There will be time, there will be time
To prepare a face to meet the faces that you meet;
There will be time to murder and create,

1. **Epigraph:** This quotation is from Dante's epic poem *The Divine Comedy* (1321). The speaker is Guido da Montefeltro, a man consigned to Hell for dispensing evil advice. He speaks from a flame that quivers when he talks: "If I thought my answer were to one who ever could return to the world, this flame should shake no more; but since none ever did return alive from this depth, if what I hear be true, without fear of infamy I answer this." (*Inferno,* Canto 27, lines 61–66) Think of Prufrock as speaking from his own personal hell.
2. **Michelangelo:** Michelangelo Buonarroti (1475–1564), a great artist of the Italian Renaissance.

And time for all the works and days of hands
That lift and drop a question on your plate;
Time for you and time for me,
And time yet for a hundred indecisions,
And for a hundred visions and revisions,
Before the taking of a toast and tea.

In the room the women come and go
Talking of Michelangelo.

And indeed there will be time
To wonder, "Do I dare?" and, "Do I dare?"
Time to turn back and descend the stair,
With a bald spot in the middle of my hair—
(They will say: "How his hair is growing thin!")
My morning coat, my collar mounting firmly to the chin,
My necktie rich and modest, but asserted by a simple pin—
(They will say: "But how his arms and legs are thin!")
Do I dare
Disturb the universe?
In a minute there is time
For decisions and revisions which a minute will reverse.

For I have known them all already, known them all—
Have known the evenings, mornings, afternoons,
I have measured out my life with coffee spoons;
I know the voices dying with a dying fall[3]
Beneath the music from a farther room.
So how should I presume?

And I have known the eyes already, known them all—
The eyes that fix you in a formulated[4] phrase,
And when I am formulated, sprawling on a pin,
When I am pinned and wriggling on the wall,
Then how should I begin
To spit out all the butt-ends of my days and ways?
And how should I presume?

And I have known the arms already, known them all—
Arms that are braceleted and white and bare
(But in the lamplight, downed with light brown hair!)

IDENTIFY

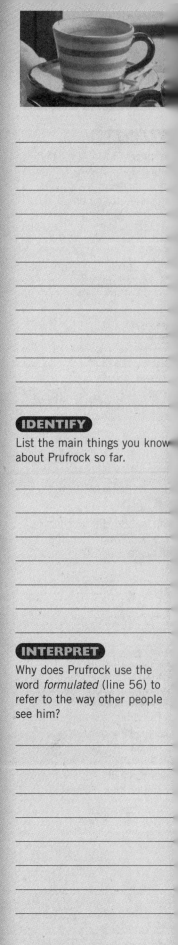

List the main things you know about Prufrock so far.

INTERPRET

Why does Prufrock use the word *formulated* (line 56) to refer to the way other people see him?

---

3. dying fall: in music, notes that fade away.

4. formulated: reduced to a formula and made insignificant.

NTERPRET

alingers (line 77) means retends to be sick." How this **image** of the evening nnected to the one that ens the poem?

INFER

/ho is "the eternal Footman" ine 85)? What does the eference suggest?

INTERPRET

n the Bible, a man named azarus is raised from he dead by Jesus (John 11:38–44). How do these ines connect with the opening uotation from Dante?

Is it perfume from a dress
That makes me so digress?
Arms that lie along a table, or wrap about a shawl.
    And should I then presume?
    And how should I begin?

. . . . .

Shall I say, I have gone at dusk through narrow streets
And watched the smoke that rises from the pipes
Of lonely men in shirt-sleeves, leaning out of windows? . . .

I should have been a pair of ragged claws
Scuttling across the floors of silent seas.

. . . . .

And the afternoon, the evening, sleeps so peacefully!
Smoothed by long fingers,
Asleep . . . tired . . . or it malingers,
Stretched on the floor, here beside you and me.
Should I, after tea and cakes and ices,
Have the strength to force the moment to its crisis?
But though I have wept and fasted, wept and prayed,
Though I have seen my head (grown slightly bald) brought in
    upon a platter,[5]
I am no prophet—and here's no great matter;
I have seen the moment of my greatness flicker,
And I have seen the eternal Footman hold my coat, and snicker,
And in short, I was afraid.

And would it have been worth it, after all,
After the cups, the marmalade, the tea,
Among the porcelain, among some talk of you and me,
Would it have been worth while,
To have bitten off the matter with a smile,
To have squeezed the universe into a ball
To roll it towards some overwhelming question,
To say: "I am Lazarus, come from the dead,
Come back to tell you all, I shall tell you all"—
If one, settling a pillow by her head,
    Should say: "That is not what I meant at all.
    That is not it, at all."

---

5. **my head . . . a platter:** allusion to the execution of John the Baptist (Mark 6:17–28 and Matthew 14:3–11). The dancing of Salome so pleased Herod Antipas, ruler of ancient Galilee, that he offered her any reward she desired. Goaded by her mother, who hated John, Salome asked for John's head. Herod ordered the prophet beheaded and his head delivered on a serving plate.

And would it have been worth it, after all,
Would it have been worth while,
After the sunsets and the dooryards and the sprinkled streets,
After the novels, after the teacups, after the skirts that trail along
the floor—
And this, and so much more?—
It is impossible to say just what I mean!
But as if a magic lantern[6] threw the nerves in patterns on a screen:
Would it have been worth while
If one, settling a pillow or throwing off a shawl,
And turning toward the window, should say:
"That is not it at all,
That is not what I meant, at all."

. . . . .

No! I am not Prince Hamlet, nor was meant to be;
Am an attendant lord, one that will do
To swell a progress,[7] start a scene or two,
Advise the prince; no doubt, an easy tool,
Deferential, glad to be of use,
Politic, cautious, and meticulous;
Full of high sentence,[8] but a bit obtuse;
At times, indeed, almost ridiculous—
Almost, at times, the Fool.

I grow old . . . I grow old . . .
I shall wear the bottoms of my trousers rolled.

Shall I part my hair behind? Do I dare to eat a peach?
I shall wear white flannel trousers, and walk upon the beach.
I have heard the mermaids singing, each to each.

I do not think that they will sing to me.

I have seen them riding seaward on the waves
Combing the white hair of the waves blown back
When the wind blows the water white and black.

We have lingered in the chambers of the sea
By sea-girls wreathed with seaweed red and brown
Till human voices wake us, and we drown.

6. **magic lantern:** early type of projector that could magnify and project opaque photographs or book pages as well as transparent slides.
7. **swell a progress:** fill out a scene in a play or pageant by serving as an extra.
8. **high sentence:** pompous talk.

BUILD FLUENCY

Read lines 99–110 aloud, using as much expression as you can. Be careful to differentiate the speaker from the lines of dialogue.

EVALUATE

Hamlet, a famous character in a play by Shakespeare, is unable to act decisively. How are Hamlet and Prufrock alike?

INFER

The style of the time called for fashionable young men to turn up the cuffs of their trousers. What is Prufrock hoping for here?

INTERPRET

If the mermaids do not sing to him, what will he miss in life?

INTERPRET

What breaks the romantic spell cast by the sight of the mermaids? What could "drown" mean here?

The Voice of the Poem

When discussing the words and ideas of a poem, critics usually refer to the narrative voice as the **speaker** of the poem. If it is clear that the speaker is an invented character, not the poet, addressing one or more listeners, the poem is called a **dramatic monologue.** In this type of poem, we learn everything about the setting, the situation, the other characters, and the speaker's personality through what the speaker tells us. In many modern poems, however, it's impossible to know whether the speaker is a character or simply the poet.

Some critics have classified "The Love Song of J. Alfred Prufrock" as a dramatic monologue, but the greatness of the poem lies in the way it resists any easy interpretation. What do you think? Explore this masterpiece of modernist poetry by completing the following chart.

What evidence do you find in the poem that the speaker is Prufrock, an invented character who is distinct from the poet?

Whom is Prufock addressing throughout the poem—that is, who is the listener?

What evidence do you find in the poem that the speaker may indeed be Eliot?

Vocabulary: How to Own a Word

Word Maps

Word Bank
tedious
insidious
presume
digress
ragged

Create a word map including a synonym, an antonym, and the connotation—positive, negative, or neutral—for each word in the Word Bank. Also, provide the dictionary definition and write a sentence using the word correctly. Be sure that the sentence you write reflects the connotation of the word. If you think an oval does not apply, write "none." An example has been done partially for you.

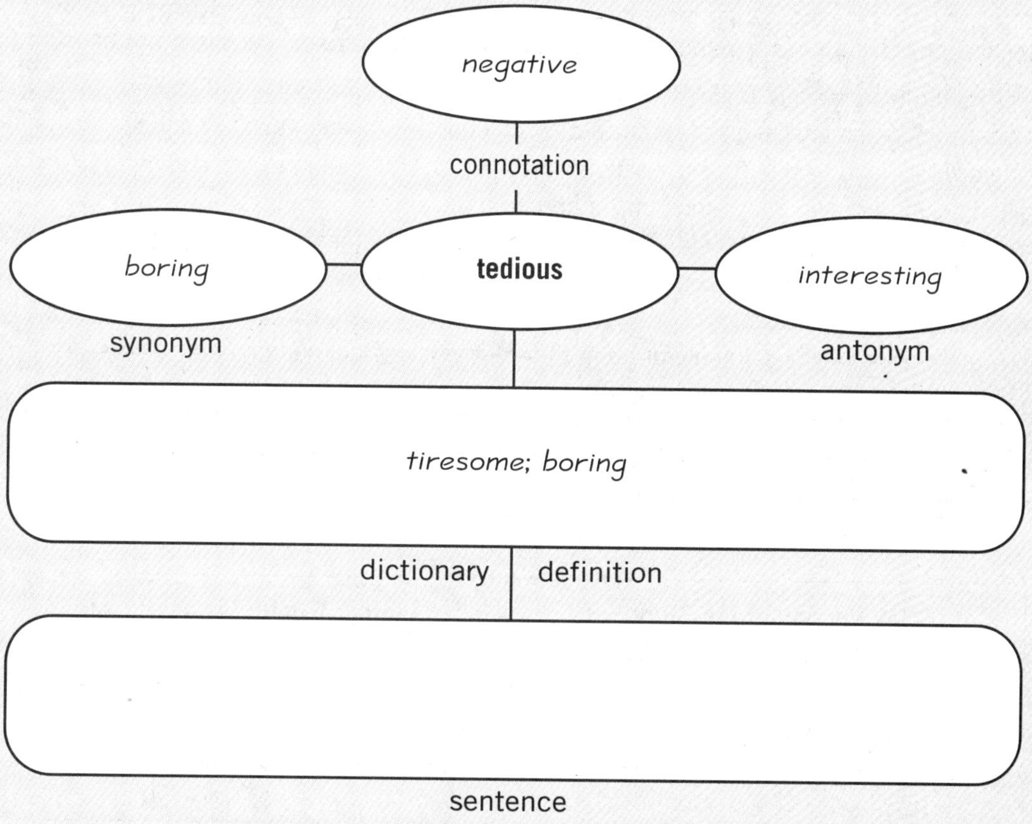

The Jilting of Granny Weatherall

Make the Connection

Memories

Katherine Anne Porter was born in a Texas log cabin. She was raised, mostly by her grandmother, as a member of a sprawling family beset with hardship and deprivation. Her schooling was fragmentary, but her real education may have come from family gatherings with their endlessly retold stories, dense with history. As a writer, Porter became celebrated for tales that grew out of her memories and were then painstakingly crafted into superb works of art.

Porter had an acute understanding of how our memories become our stories. Over time, a memory becomes so shaped by emotion, reconsideration, changes of emphasis, and simple forgetting that it may bear little relation to the original experience. Remembering is one of the human mind's most complex miracles. Who can say why some specific details or sense impressions, sometimes ever so slight, may linger for years in a person's memory, while other details and impressions vanish, never to resurface?

Every family has its stories, often in different versions depending on who tells them. What are some of your family's most vivid stories? Do you have your own version of a story that varies from that of someone else in the family? Use the chart below to record first your own memory of some particular event, and then the version that might be told by another member of your family.

My Version of the Story	Another Family Member's Version

The Jilting of Granny Weatherall

Katherine Anne Porter

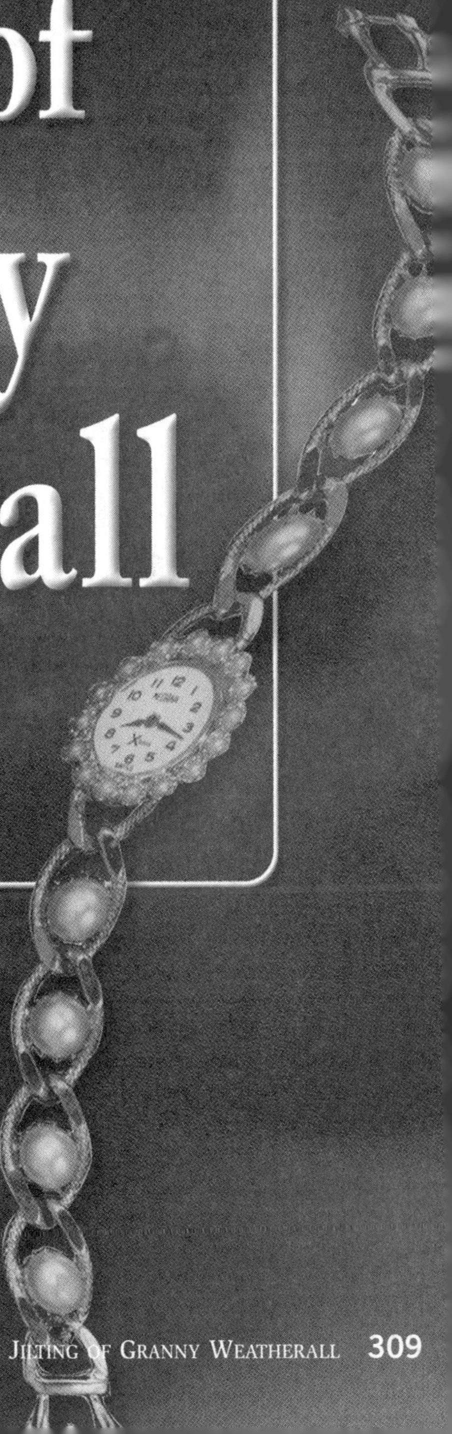

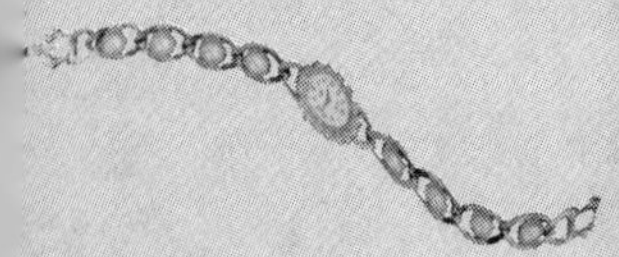

DENTIFY

ircle the word in the first aragraph that hints at a great ge difference between the octor and the woman in the ed.

INTERPRET

Vhat is happening to Granny t this point?

WORDS TO OWN

tactful (takt′fəl) *adj.:* skilled in saying the right thing.

She flicked her wrist neatly out of Doctor Harry's pudgy careful fingers and pulled the sheet up to her chin. The brat ought to be in knee breeches. Doctoring around the country with spectacles on his nose! "Get along now, take your schoolbooks and go. There's nothing wrong with me."

Doctor Harry spread a warm paw like a cushion on her forehead where the forked green vein danced and made her eyelids twitch. "Now, now, be a good girl, and we'll have you up in no time."

"That's no way to speak to a woman nearly eighty years old just because she's down. I'd have you respect your elders, young man."

"Well, Missy, excuse me." Doctor Harry patted her cheek. "But I've got to warn you, haven't I? You're a marvel, but you must be careful or you're going to be good and sorry."

"Don't tell me what I'm going to be. I'm on my feet now, morally speaking. It's Cornelia. I had to go to bed to get rid of her."

Her bones felt loose, and floated around in her skin, and Doctor Harry floated like a balloon around the foot of the bed. He floated and pulled down his waistcoat and swung his glasses on a cord. "Well, stay where you are, it certainly can't hurt you."

"Get along and doctor your sick," said Granny Weatherall. "Leave a well woman alone. I'll call for you when I want you. . . . Where were you forty years ago when I pulled through milk leg[1] and double pneumonia? You weren't even born. Don't let Cornelia lead you on," she shouted, because Doctor Harry appeared to float up to the ceiling and out. "I pay my own bills, and I don't throw my money away on nonsense!"

She meant to wave goodbye, but it was too much trouble. Her eyes closed of themselves, it was like a dark curtain drawn around the bed. The pillow rose and floated under her, pleasant as a hammock in a light wind. She listened to the leaves rustling outside the window. No, somebody was swishing newspapers: No, Cornelia and Doctor Harry were whispering together. She leaped broad awake, thinking they whispered in her ear.

"She was never like this, *never* like this!" "Well, what can we expect?" "Yes, eighty years old. . . ."

Well, and what if she was? She still had ears. It was like Cornelia to whisper around doors. She always kept things secret in such a public way. She was always being tactful and kind. Cornelia was dutiful; that was the trouble with her. Dutiful and good: "So good and dutiful," said Granny, "that I'd like to spank her." She saw herself spanking Cornelia and making a fine job of it.

"What'd you say, Mother?"

Granny felt her face tying up in hard knots.

---

1. **milk leg:** painful swelling of the leg, usually as a result of an infection during childbirth.

"Can't a body think, I'd like to know?"

"I thought you might want something."

"I do. I want a lot of things. First off, go away and don't whisper."

She lay and drowsed, hoping in her sleep that the children would keep out and let her rest a minute. It had been a long day. Not that she was tired. It was always pleasant to snatch a minute now and then. There was always so much to be done, let me see: tomorrow.

Tomorrow was far away and there was nothing to trouble about. Things were finished somehow when the time came; thank God there was always a little margin over for peace: Then a person could spread out the plan of life and tuck in the edges orderly. It was good to have everything clean and folded away, with the hairbrushes and tonic bottles sitting straight on the white embroidered linen: the day started without fuss and the pantry shelves laid out with rows of jelly glasses and brown jugs and white stone-china jars with blue whirligigs and words painted on them: coffee, tea, sugar, ginger, cinnamon, allspice: and the bronze clock with the lion on top nicely dusted off. The dust that lion could collect in twenty-four hours! The box in the attic with all those letters tied up, well, she'd have to go through that tomorrow. All those letters—George's letters and John's letters and her letters to them both—lying around for the children to find afterward made her uneasy. Yes, that would be tomorrow's business. No use to let them know how silly she had been once.

While she was rummaging around she found death in her mind and it felt clammy and unfamiliar. She had spent so much time preparing for death there was no need for bringing it up again. Let it take care of itself now. When she was sixty she had felt very old, finished, and went around making farewell trips to see her children and grandchildren, with a secret in her mind: This is the very last of your mother, children! Then she made her will and came down with a long fever. That was all just a notion like a lot of other things, but it was lucky too, for she had once for all got over the idea of dying for a long time. Now she couldn't be worried. She hoped she had better sense now. Her father had lived to be one hundred and two years old and had drunk a noggin[2] of strong hot toddy[3] on his last birthday. He told the reporters it was his daily habit, and he owed his long life to that. He had made quite a scandal and was very pleased about it. She believed she'd just plague Cornelia a little.

"Cornelia! Cornelia!" No footsteps, but a sudden hand on her cheek. "Bless you, where have you been?"

"Here, Mother."

"Well, Cornelia, I want a noggin of hot toddy."

"Are you cold, darling?"

---

2. noggin: mug.

3. hot toddy: drink made of liquor mixed with hot water, sugar, and spices.

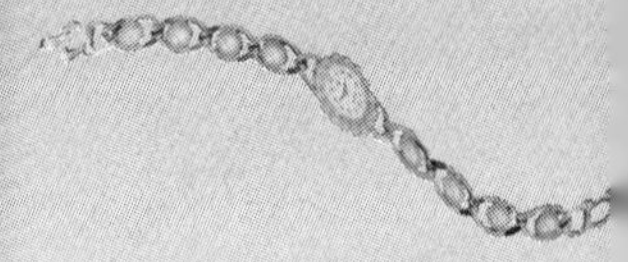

WORDS TO OWN

margin (mär′jən) *n.:* extra amount.

INFER

Who are George and John?

WORDS TO OWN

clammy (klam′ē) *adj.:* cold and damp.

plague (plāg) *v.:* annoy.

EVALUATE

What are your impressions of Granny Weatherall from what you have read so far?

INTERPRET

What do these details add to your knowledge of Granny's character?

IDENTIFY/INFER

What do you think Granny's last name, Weatherall, implies about her character and about the story?

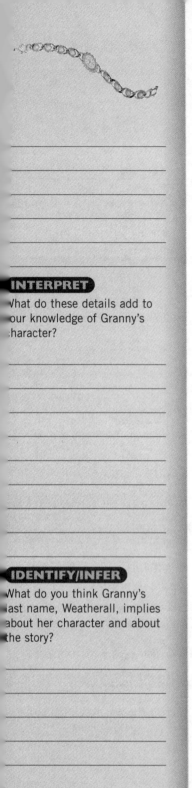

"I'm chilly, Cornelia. Lying in bed stops the circulation. I must have told you that a thousand times."

Well, she could just hear Cornelia telling her husband that Mother was getting a little childish and they'd have to humor her. The thing that most annoyed her was that Cornelia thought she was deaf, dumb, and blind. Little hasty glances and tiny gestures tossed around her and over her head saying, "Don't cross her, let her have her way, she's eighty years old," and she sitting there as if she lived in a thin glass cage. Sometimes Granny almost made up her mind to pack up and move back to her own house where nobody could remind her every minute that she was old. Wait, wait, Cornelia, till your own children whisper behind your back!

In her day she had kept a better house and had got more work done. She wasn't too old yet for Lydia to be driving eighty miles for advice when one of the children jumped the track, and Jimmy still dropped in and talked things over: "Now, Mammy, you've a good business head, I want to know what you think of this? . . ." Old. Cornelia couldn't change the furniture around without asking. Little things, little things! They had been so sweet when they were little. Granny wished the old days were back again with the children young and everything to be done over. It had been a hard pull, but not too much for her. When she thought of all the food she had cooked, and all the clothes she had cut and sewed, and all the gardens she had made—well, the children showed it. There they were, made out of her, and they couldn't get away from that. Sometimes she wanted to see John again and point to them and say, Well, I didn't do so badly, did I? But that would have to wait. That was for tomorrow. She used to think of him as a man, but now all the children were older than their father, and he would be a child beside her if she saw him now. It seemed strange and there was something wrong in the idea. Why, he couldn't possibly recognize her. She had fenced in a hundred acres once, digging the postholes herself and clamping the wires with just a Negro boy to help. That changed a woman. John would be looking for a young woman with the peaked Spanish comb in her hair and the painted fan. Digging postholes changed a woman. Riding country roads in the winter when women had their babies was another thing: sitting up nights with sick horses and sick Negroes and sick children and hardly ever losing one. John, I hardly ever lost one of them! John would see that in a minute, that would be something he could understand, she wouldn't have to explain anything!

It made her feel like rolling up her sleeves and putting the whole place to rights again. No matter if Cornelia was determined to be everywhere at once, there were a great many things left undone on this place. She would start tomorrow and do them. It was good to be strong enough for everything, even if all you made melted and changed and slipped under your hands, so that by the time you finished you almost forgot what you were working for. What was it I set out to do? she asked herself intently, but she could not remember. A fog rose over the valley, she saw it marching across the creek swallowing the trees and moving up the hill like an army of ghosts. Soon it would be at the near edge of the orchard, and then it was time to go in and light the lamps. Come in, children, don't stay out in the night air.

Lighting the lamps had been beautiful. The children huddled up to her and breathed like little calves waiting at the bars in the twilight. Their eyes followed the match and watched the flame rise and settle in a blue curve, then they moved away from her. The lamp was lit, they didn't have to be scared and hang on to mother any more. Never, never, never more. God, for all my life I thank Thee. Without Thee, my God, I could never have done it. Hail, Mary, full of grace.

I want you to pick all the fruit this year and see that nothing is wasted. There's always someone who can use it. Don't let good things rot for want of using. You waste life when you waste good food. Don't let things get lost. It's bitter to lose things. Now, don't let me get to thinking, not when I am tired and taking a little nap before supper. . . .

The pillow rose about her shoulders and pressed against her heart and the memory was being squeezed out of it: Oh, push down the pillow, somebody: It would smother her if she tried to hold it. Such a fresh breeze blowing and such a green day with no threats in it. But he had not come, just the same. What does a woman do when she has put on the white veil and set out the white cake for a man and he doesn't come? She tried to remember. No, I swear he never harmed me but in that. He never harmed me but in that . . . and what if he did? There was the day, the day, but a whirl of dark smoke rose and covered it, crept up and over into the bright field where everything was planted so carefully in orderly rows. That was hell, she knew hell when she saw it. For sixty years she had prayed against remembering him and against losing her soul in the deep pit of hell, and now the two things were mingled in one and the thought of him was a smoky cloud from hell that moved and crept in her head when she had just got rid of Doctor Harry and was trying to rest a minute. Wounded vanity, Ellen, said a sharp voice in the top of her mind. Don't let your wounded vanity get the upper hand of you. Plenty of girls get jilted. You were jilted, weren't you? Then stand up to it. Her eyelids wavered and let in streamers of blue-gray light like tissue paper over her eyes. She must get up and pull the shades down or she'd never sleep. She was in bed again and the shades were not down. How could that happen? Better turn over, hide from the light, sleeping in the light gave you nightmares. "Mother, how do you feel now?" and a stinging wetness on her forehead. But I don't like having my face washed in cold water!

INTERPRET

What do you think the lamp **symbolizes** for Granny Weatherall?

IDENTIFY/INTERPRET

What happened to Granny sixty years ago, when she "put on the white veil"? How has this event affected her?

WORDS TO OWN

vanity (van′ə·tē) *n.:* excessive pride.

jilted (jilt′id) *v.:* rejected (as a lover).

Hapsy? George? Lydia? Jimmy? No, Cornelia, and her features were swollen and full of little puddles. "They're coming, darling, they'll all be here soon." Go wash your face, child, you look funny.

Instead of obeying, Cornelia knelt down and put her head on the pillow. She seemed to be talking but there was no sound. "Well, are you tongue-tied? Whose birthday is it? Are you going to give a party?"

Cornelia's mouth moved urgently in strange shapes. "Don't do that, you bother me, daughter."

"Oh, no, Mother. Oh, no . . ."

Nonsense. It was strange about children. They disputed your every word. "No what, Cornelia?"

"Here's Doctor Harry."

"I won't see that boy again. He just left five minutes ago."

"That was this morning, Mother. It's night now. Here's the nurse."

"This is Doctor Harry, Mrs. Weatherall. I never saw you look so young and happy!"

"Ah, I'll never be young again—but I'd be happy if they'd let me lie in peace and get rested."

She thought she spoke up loudly, but no one answered. A warm weight on her forehead, a warm bracelet on her wrist, and a breeze went on whispering, trying to tell her something. A shuffle of leaves in the everlasting hand of God, He blew on them and they danced and rattled. "Mother, don't mind, we're going to give you a little hypodermic."[4] "Look here, daughter, how do ants get in this bed? I saw sugar ants yesterday." Did you send for Hapsy too?

It was Hapsy she really wanted. She had to go a long way back through a great many rooms to find Hapsy standing with a baby on her arm. She seemed to herself to be Hapsy also, and the baby on Hapsy's arm was Hapsy and himself and herself, all at once, and there was no surprise in the meeting. Then Hapsy melted from within and turned flimsy as gray gauze and the baby was a gauzy shadow, and Hapsy came up close and said, "I thought you'd never come," and looked at her very searchingly and said, "You haven't changed a bit!" They leaned forward to kiss, when Cornelia began whispering from a long way off, "Oh, is there anything you want to tell me? Is there anything I can do for you?"

Yes, she had changed her mind after sixty years and she would like to see George. I want you to find George. Find him and be sure to tell him I forgot him. I want him to know I had my husband just the same and my children and my house like any other woman. A good house too and a good husband that I loved and fine children out of him. Better than I hoped for even. Tell him I was given back everything he took away and more. Oh, no, oh, God, no, there was something else besides the house and the man and the children. Oh, surely they were not all?

4. hypodermic: injection of medicine.

VORDS TO OWN

sputed (di·spyo͞ot′id) *v.:* ontested.

INTERPRET

Vho is Hapsy, and where is he?

EVALUATE

Can you accept Granny's statement about George at ace value? If not, what do ou think she means?

What was it? Something not given back. . . . Her breath crowded down under her ribs and grew into a monstrous frightening shape with cutting edges; it bored up into her head, and the agony was unbelievable: Yes, John, get the Doctor now, no more talk, my time has come.

When this one was born it should be the last. The last. It should have been born first, for it was the one she had truly wanted. Everything came in good time. Nothing left out, left over. She was strong, in three days she would be as well as ever. Better. A woman needed milk in her to have her full health.

"Mother, do you hear me?"

"I've been telling you—"

"Mother, Father Connolly's here."

"I went to Holy Communion only last week. Tell him I'm not so sinful as all that."

"Father just wants to speak to you."

He could speak as much as he pleased. It was like him to drop in and inquire about her soul as if it were a teething baby, and then stay on for a cup of tea and a round of cards and gossip. He always had a funny story of some sort, usually about an Irishman who made his little mistakes and confessed them, and the point lay in some absurd thing he would blurt out in the confessional showing his struggles between native piety and original sin.[5] Granny felt easy about her soul. Cornelia, where are your manners? Give Father Connolly a chair. She had her secret comfortable understanding with a few favorite saints who cleared a straight road to God for her. All as surely signed and sealed as the papers for the new Forty Acres. Forever . . . heirs and assigns forever. Since the day the wedding cake was not cut, but thrown out and wasted. The whole bottom dropped out of the world, and there she was blind and sweating with nothing under her feet and the walls falling away. His hand had caught her under the breast, she had not fallen, there was the freshly polished floor with the green rug on it, just as before. He had cursed like a sailor's parrot and said, "I'll kill him for you." Don't lay a hand on him, for my sake leave something to God. "Now, Ellen, you must believe what I tell you. . . ."

So there was nothing, nothing to worry about any more, except sometimes in the night one of the children screamed in a nightmare, and they both hustled out shaking and hunting for the matches and calling, "There, wait a minute, here we are!" John, get the doctor now, Hapsy's time has come. But there was Hapsy standing by the bed in a white cap. "Cornelia, tell Hapsy to take off her cap. I can't see her plain."

Her eyes opened very wide and the room stood out like a picture she had seen somewhere. Dark colors with the shadows rising toward the

IDENTIFY

What is Granny remembering? (Clues: Note the words *born*, *last*, and *milk* in this passage.)

INTERPRET

Who is "he" in this passage? Explain your view.

5. **original sin:** in Christian theology, the sin of disobedience committed by Adam and Eve, the first man and woman, which is passed on to all persons.

ORDS TO OWN

ppery (frip′ər·ē) *n.:* omething showy, frivolous, unnecessary.

mbus (nim′bəs) *n.:* aura; alo.

INTERPRET

ho is the man, and what is e situation?

INTERPRET

hat is the effect of Granny's epeated, unconvincing rotests that George means othing to her?

ceiling in long angles. The tall black dresser gleamed with nothing on it but John's picture, enlarged from a little one, with John's eyes very black when they should have been blue. You never saw him, so how do you know how he looked? But the man insisted the copy was perfect, it was very rich and handsome. For a picture, yes, but it's not my husband. The table by the bed had a linen cover and a candle and a crucifix. The light was blue from Cornelia's silk lampshades. No sort of light at all, just frippery. You had to live forty years with kerosene lamps to appreciate honest electricity. She felt very strong and she saw Doctor Harry with a rosy nimbus around him.

"You look like a saint, Doctor Harry, and I vow that's as near as you'll ever come to it."

"She's saying something."

"I heard you, Cornelia. What's all this carrying-on?"

"Father Connolly's saying—"

Cornelia's voice staggered and bumped like a cart in a bad road. It rounded corners and turned back again and arrived nowhere. Granny stepped up in the cart very lightly and reached for the reins, but a man sat beside her and she knew him by his hands, driving the cart. She did not look in his face, for she knew without seeing, but looked instead down the road where the trees leaned over and bowed to each other and a thousand birds were singing a Mass. She felt like singing too, but she put her hand in the bosom of her dress and pulled out a rosary, and Father Connolly murmured Latin in a very solemn voice and tickled her feet.[6] My God, will you stop that nonsense? I'm a married woman. What if he did run away and leave me to face the priest by myself? I found another a whole world better. I wouldn't have exchanged my husband for anybody except St. Michael[7] himself, and you may tell him that for me with a thank you in the bargain.

Light flashed on her closed eyelids, and a deep roaring shook her. Cornelia, is that lightning? I hear thunder. There's going to be a storm. Close all the windows. Call the children in. . . . "Mother, here we are, all of us." "Is that you, Hapsy?" "Oh, no, I'm Lydia. We drove as fast as we could." Their faces drifted above her, drifted away. The rosary fell out of her hands and Lydia put it back. Jimmy tried to help, their hands fumbled together, and Granny closed two fingers around Jimmy's thumb. Beads wouldn't do, it must be something alive. She was so amazed her thoughts ran round and round. So, my dear Lord, this is my death and I wasn't even thinking about it. My children have come to see me die. But I can't, it's not time. Oh, I always hated surprises. I wanted to give

6. **murmured . . . feet:** The priest is performing the sacramental last rites of the Roman Catholic Church, which include anointing the dying person's feet with oil.
7. **Michael:** most powerful of the four archangels in Jewish and Christian doctrine. In Christian art, he is usually depicted as a handsome knight in white armor.

Cornelia the amethyst[8] set—Cornelia, you're to have the amethyst set, but Hapsy's to wear it when she wants, and, Doctor Harry, do shut up. Nobody sent for you. Oh, my dear Lord, do wait a minute. I meant to do something about the Forty Acres, Jimmy doesn't need it and Lydia will later on, with that worthless husband of hers. I meant to finish the altar cloth and send six bottles of wine to Sister Borgia for her dyspepsia.[9] I want to send six bottles of wine to Sister Borgia, Father Connolly, now don't let me forget.

Cornelia's voice made short turns and tilted over and crashed. "Oh, Mother, oh, Mother, oh, Mother . . ."

"I'm not going, Cornelia. I'm taken by surprise. I can't go."

You'll see Hapsy again. What about her? "I thought you'd never come." Granny made a long journey outward, looking for Hapsy. What if I don't find her? What then? Her heart sank down and down, there was no bottom to death, she couldn't come to the end of it. The blue light from Cornelia's lampshade drew into a tiny point in the center of her brain, it flickered and winked like an eye, quietly it fluttered and dwindled. Granny lay curled down within herself, amazed and watchful, staring at the point of light that was herself; her body was now only a deeper mass of shadow in an endless darkness and this darkness would curl around the light and swallow it up. God, give a sign!

For the second time there was no sign. Again no bridegroom and the priest in the house. She could not remember any other sorrow because this grief wiped them all away. Oh, no, there's nothing more cruel than this—I'll never forgive it. She stretched herself with a deep breath and blew out the light.

BUILD FLUENCY

Read the boxed passage aloud as expressively as you can, taking careful note of the punctuation, such as question marks, exclamation points, and dashes.

WORDS TO OWN

dwindled (dwin′dəld) *v.:* diminished.

INTERPRET

How do you interpret this final sentence? What does the light **symbolize,** in your opinion?

INTERPRET

How does the end of the story show that Granny has never come to terms with being jilted?

8. **amethyst** (am′i·thist): purple or violet quartz gemstone, used in jewelry.
9. **dyspepsia** (dis·pep′sē·ə): indigestion.

Stream of Consciousness

In "The Jilting of Granny Weatherall," Porter uses a technique called **stream of consciousness** to convey the main character's thoughts and memories. Use the chart below to list some of the important people and events, past and present, that Granny Weatherall recalls as she is dying. Then, answer the questions that follow.

Important People	Important Events

1. Choose one of the people or events that you noted on the chart, and explain why you think this memory is important to Granny Weatherall.

____

____

____

2. Do you find this story believable? Explain why or why not.

____

____

____

Vocabulary: How to Own a Word

Word Bank
tactful
margin
clammy
plague
vanity
jilted
disputed
frippery
nimbus
dwindled

Connotations

For the following Words to Own, decide which has a positive (**P**), negative (**N**), or neutral (**0**) connotation, and write the appropriate letter in the space provided before the number for that word. Then, explain your answer on the lines provided by using examples or personal experiences.

EXAMPLE: ___P___ cheap ___I bought two tapes because they were so cheap.___

_____ **1.** clammy ______________________________

____

_____ **2.** disputed ______________________________

____

_____ **3.** dwindled ______________________________

____

_____ **4.** frippery ______________________________

____

_____ **5.** jilted ______________________________

____

_____ **6.** margin ______________________________

____

_____ **7.** nimbus ______________________________

____

_____ **8.** plague ______________________________

____

_____ **9.** tactful ______________________________

____

_____ **10.** vanity ______________________________

____

Nobel Prize Acceptance Speech, 1950

Make the Connection

The Psychology of Fear

In his first inaugural address, delivered during the Great Depression in March 1933, President Franklin Delano Roosevelt said, "The only thing we have to fear is fear itself." In a similarly eloquent speech when he accepted the Nobel Prize in literature in 1950, the novelist William Faulkner developed the same theme.

Is fear always a bad thing? Are there times when this emotion helps rather than hinders us? Explore your thoughts about the disadvantages and possible advantages of fear by filling out the chart below.

Two Sides of Fear

Disadvantages	Advantages

Nobel Prize Acceptance Speech, 1950

William Faulkner

DENTIFY

ɔw does Faulkner define his ırpose in the first paragraph? ıderline the words giving the ıswer.

DENTIFY

:cording to Faulkner, what fect has the profound anxiety ɔout nuclear war had upon ›ung writers?

DENTIFY

'hat does Faulkner say is the ɔasest of all things"? Circle ıe words giving the answer. 'hat are the "universal uths"? Underline the words ving the answer.

DENTIFY

ı the final paragraph, what 're Faulkner's grounds for elieving that human beings ill not merely endure, but ıso prevail? Underline the ıswer.

EVALUATE

; this an effective piece of **ratory**? Explain your answer.

I feel that this award was not made to me as a man, but to my work—a life's work in the agony and sweat of the human spirit, not for glory and least of all for profit, but to create out of the materials of the human spirit something which did not exist before. So this award is only mine in trust. It will not be difficult to find a dedication for the money part of it commensurate with the purpose and significance of its origin. But I would like to do the same with the acclaim too, by using this moment as a pinnacle from which I might be listened to by the young men and women already dedicated to the same anguish and travail, among whom is already that one who will someday stand here where I am standing.

Our tragedy today is a general and universal physical fear so long sustained by now that we can even bear it. There are no longer problems of the spirit. There is only the question: When will I be blown up? Because of this, the young man or woman writing today has forgotten the problems of the human heart in conflict with itself which alone can make good writing because only that is worth writing about, worth the agony and the sweat.

He must learn them again. He must teach himself that the basest of all things is to be afraid; and, teaching himself that, forget it forever, leaving no room in his workshop for anything but the old verities and truths of the heart, the old universal truths lacking which any story is ephemeral and doomed—love and honor and pity and pride and compassion and sacrifice. Until he does so, he labors under a curse. He writes not of love but of lust, of defeats in which nobody loses anything of value, of victories without hope and, worst of all, without pity or compassion. His griefs grieve on no universal bones, leaving no scars. He writes not of the heart but of the glands.

Until he relearns these things, he will write as though he stood among and watched the end of man. I decline to accept the end of man. It is easy enough to say that man is immortal simply because he will endure: that when the last dingdong of doom has clanged and faded from the last worthless rock hanging tideless in the last red and dying evening, that even then there will still be one more sound: that of his puny inexhaustible voice, still talking. I refuse to accept this. I believe that man will not merely endure: he will prevail. He is immortal, not because he alone among creatures has an inexhaustible voice, but because he has a soul, a spirit capable of compassion and sacrifice and endurance. The poet's, the writer's, duty is to write about these things. It is his privilege to help man endure by lifting his heart, by reminding him of the courage and honor and hope and pride and compassion and pity and sacrifice which have been the glory of his past. The poet's voice need not merely be the record of man, it can be one of the props, the pillars to help him endure and prevail.

Oratory

Oratory is skill or eloquence in public speaking. Orators use a variety of devices and techniques in order to make their words inspiring or persuasive. Some of these techniques are listed on the left-hand side of the chart below. After you read the list, re-read the speech. Then, use the right-hand side of the chart to list a specific example of each technique.

Techniques of Oratory	Example from Faulkner's Speech
Parallelism	
Antithesis (balance of contrasting elements)	
Repetition	
Metaphor	

# of De Witt Williams on his way to Lincoln Cemetery

Make the Connection

An Ordinary Life?

Modern writers have often seen poetry and drama in events that might outwardly seem ordinary or routine. In her poem about De Witt Williams, set in Chicago, Gwendolyn Brooks uses apparently ordinary details to communicate a rich impression of her subject's personality and lifestyle.

What might a poet see in the details of your daily routine? Use the chart below to map your daily schedule during the school year and comment on the special significance that each activity on the chart has for you.

My Routine	
Morning Activities:	Significance:
Afternoon Activities:	Significance:
Evening Activities:	Significance:

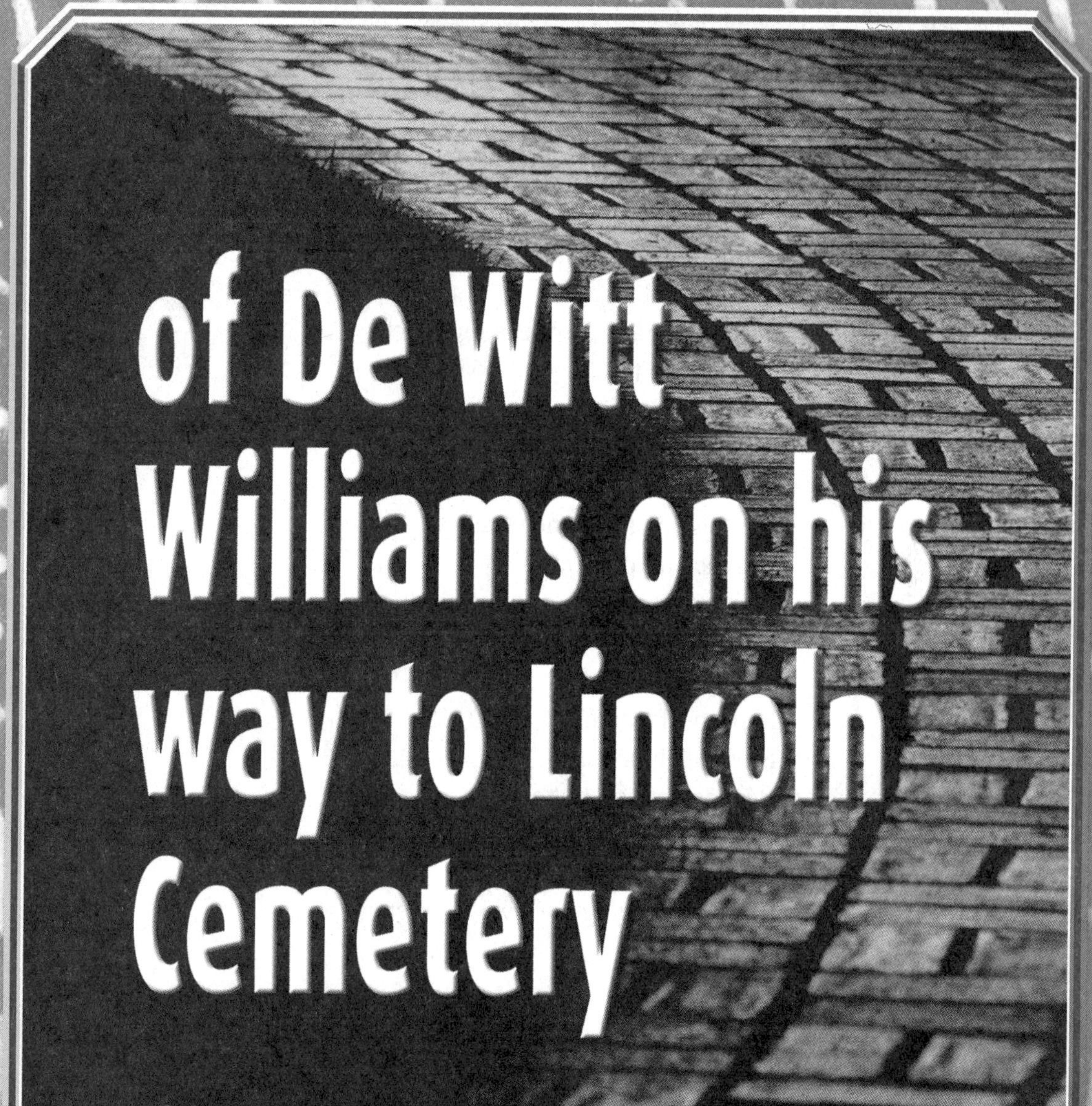

# of De Witt Williams on his way to Lincoln Cemetery

Gwendolyn Brooks

NTERPRET

ıe 5 refers to the spiritual wing Low, Sweet Chariot," which a chariot and a band angels arrive to take a dying rson to heaven. African nericans often sang this song express their desire for eedom from bondage. Why do u think Brooks includes the ıes here?

DENTIFY

nderline the details that tell u about this man's life.

NTERPRET

hat is the effect of the **frain,** which ends the poem ith a repetition of the ɔening lines?

NTERPRET

'hat is the **tone** of the title, nd how does it relate to the ɛst of the poem?

He was born in Alabama.
He was bred in Illinois.
He was nothing but a
Plain black boy.

Swing low swing low sweet sweet chariot.
Nothing but a plain black boy.

Drive him past the Pool Hall.
Drive him past the Show.
Blind within his casket,
But maybe he will know.

Down through Forty-seventh Street:
Underneath the L,
And—Northwest Corner, Prairie,
That he loved so well.

Don't forget the Dance Halls—
Warwick and Savoy,
Where he picked his women, where
He drank his liquid joy.

Born in Alabama.
Bred in Illinois.
He was nothing but a
Plain black boy.

Swing low swing low sweet sweet chariot.
Nothing but a plain black boy.

Tone

Tone is the attitude a writer takes toward the subject of a work, the characters in it, or the audience. In everyday speech, we use voice inflections to show how we feel about what we are saying. Writers manipulate language in an attempt to achieve the same effect. Tone often depends on **diction,** or word choice, and on a writer's **style,** or his or her distinctive way of writing.

1. What tone is suggested by the elaborate title of Brooks's poem?

2. In lines 5 and 23, Brooks makes the tone even more complicated when she uses **repetition** and **alludes** to a famous spiritual, "Swing Low, Sweet Chariot." How would you describe the effect of these lines on the poem's tone?

3. What do the references to the "Pool Hall" (line 7), the "Show" (line 8), a favorite street corner (lines 13–14), and the "Dance Halls" (lines 15–18) suggest about De Witt Williams's life?

4. What is the the tone of the **refrain**? Is it ironic? Explain.

5. How would you describe the speaker's overall attitude toward De Witt Williams and his death?

The Weary Blues

Make the Connection

Sweet Blues

African American music is among the great contributions of American culture to the world. Among the musical expressions you can hear every day are blues, ragtime, jazz, and rap. The kind of music known as blues started to attract attention around 1900. This style became widely popular in the United States and abroad and made stars out of such blues singers as Bessie Smith and Ethel Waters. Blues music has influenced many different types of popular music, from rock and soul to country, folk, and jazz. In his poem, Langston Hughes tries to re-create the experience of a "sad raggy tune" and also to capture some of its rhythms in words.

On the lines provided below, jot down any associations you have with the word *blues*. What do you already know about blues music? Is there any blues influence in the kinds of music you like?

The Weary Blues

Langston Hughes

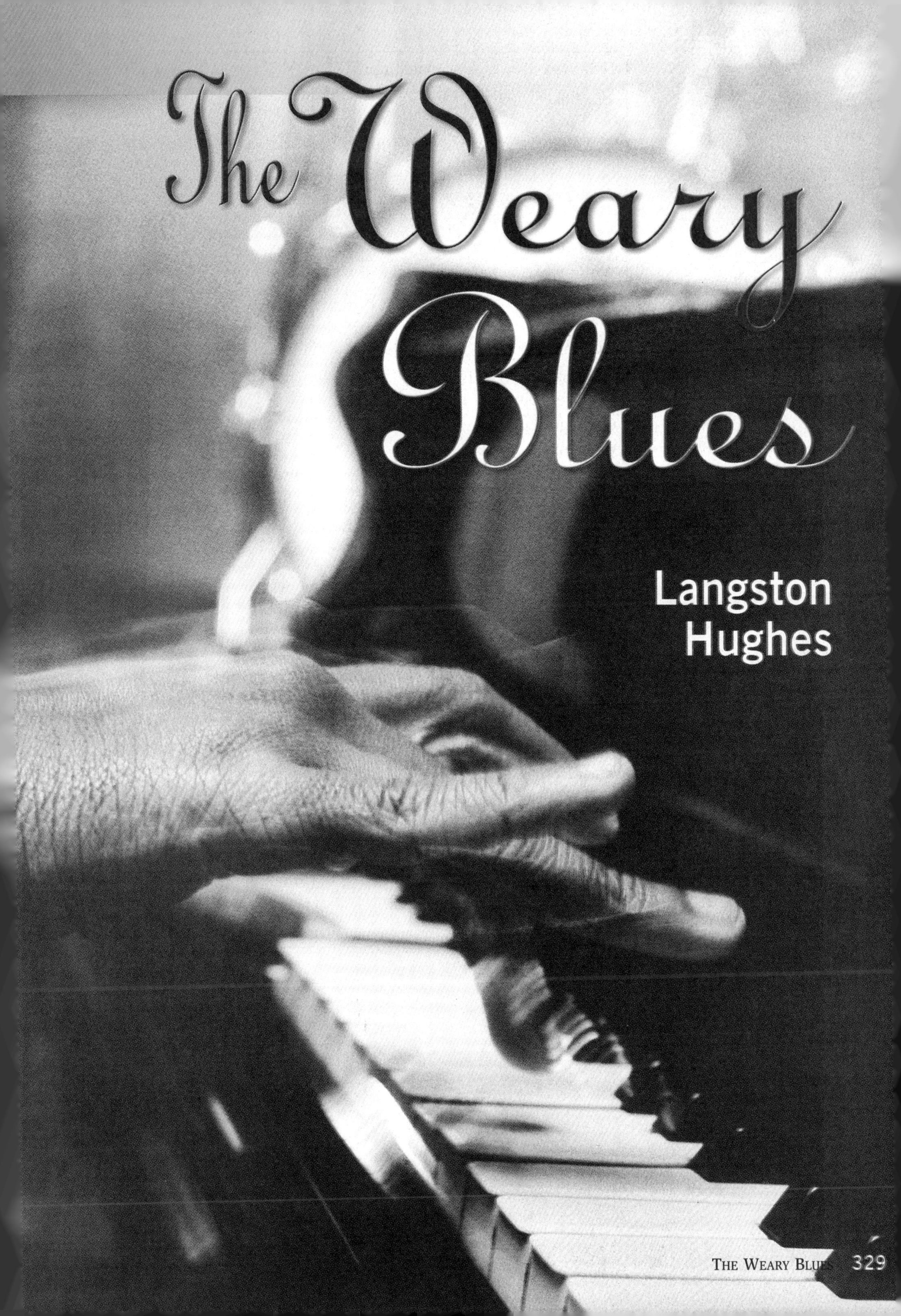

DENTIFY

ıderline words in the poem ıt help to create a sad or ɛlancholy **mood.**

NTERPRET

ıat are some of the **nnotations** of *rickety, raggy,* d *fool?* What general ıpression do the words leave the piano player?

INTERPRET

ow does the language of the ɔng lyric differ from the rest f the poem?

EVALUATE

lughes spent two years ʋorking on the ending of this oem. Do you think his final ersion is effective? Why or ʋhy not?

BUILD FLUENCY

Read the poem aloud, focusing on rhythm and other sound effects.

Droning a drowsy syncopated tune,[1]
Rocking back and forth to a mellow croon,
    I heard a Negro play.
Down on Lenox Avenue[2] the other night
By the pale dull pallor of an old gas light
    He did a lazy sway . . .
    He did a lazy sway . . .
To the tune o' those Weary Blues.
With his ebony hands on each ivory key
He made that poor piano moan with melody.
    O Blues!
Swaying to and fro on his rickety stool
He played that sad raggy tune like a musical fool.
    Sweet Blues!
Coming from a black man's soul.
    O Blues!
In a deep song voice with a melancholy tone
I heard that Negro sing, that old piano moan—
    "Ain't got nobody in all this world,
    Ain't got nobody but ma salf.
    I's gwine to quit ma frownin'
    And put ma troubles on the shelf."
Thump, thump, thump, went his foot on the floor.
He played a few chords then he sang some more—
    "I got the Weary Blues
    And I can't be satisfied.
    Got the Weary Blues
    And can't be satisfied—
    I ain't happy no mo'
    And I wish that I had died."
And far into the night he crooned that tune.
The stars went out and so did the moon.
The singer stopped playing and went to bed
While the Weary Blues echoed through his head.
He slept like a rock or a man that's dead.

1. **syncopated tune:** melody in which accents are placed on normally unaccented beats.
2. **Lenox Avenue:** street in Harlem.

Rhythm

Rhythm is the alternation of stressed and unstressed syllables in language. The most obvious kind of rhythm is produced by meter, or the regular pattern of stressed and unstressed syllables found in some poetry. Writers can also create rhythms by using such devices as rhyme, repetition, pauses, and variations in line length.

On the chart below, you will see a list of techniques Langston Hughes uses to create a highly distinctive rhythm in "The Weary Blues." After you have read the list, re-read the poem carefully. On the right-hand side of the chart, record an example of each technique listed.

Technique	Example
Alternation of long and short lines	
Repetition	
Alliteration	
Assonance	

The Red Wheelbarrow
what if a much of a which of a wind

Make the Connection

Now and Then

In "The Red Wheelbarrow," William Carlos Williams reminds us that there may be elements of both poetry and dignity in the most ordinary objects. In "what if a much of a which of a wind," E. E. Cummings explores the determination of the human spirit to prevail in spite of hardship and even devastation.

On the left-hand side of the graphic below, make a list of at least six objects from your everyday world that might be subjects for a poem. On the right-hand side, jot down some of your predictions about the future of the planet. You might focus your thoughts on "What if . . . ?"

Everyday Objects for a Poem	Predictions for the Planet

The Red Wheelbarrow

William Carlos Williams

what if a much of a which of a wind

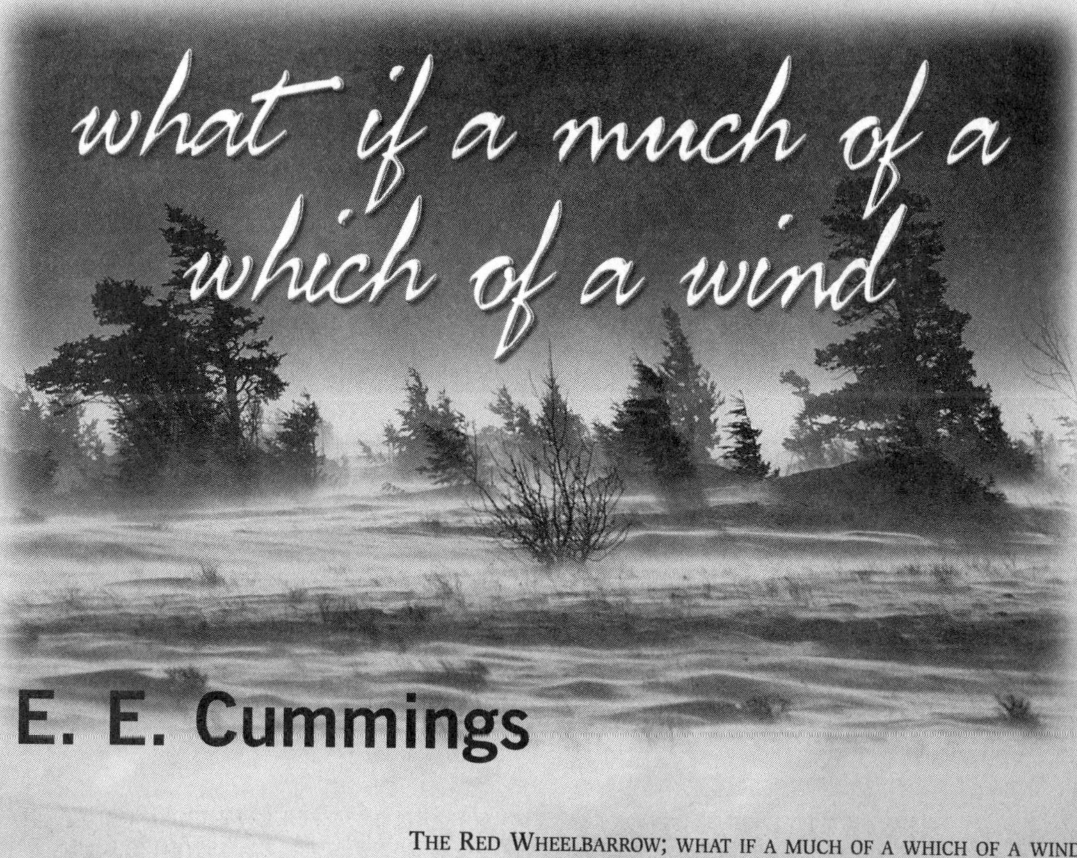

E. E. Cummings

NFER

nat might depend on a red
ieelbarrow?

INTERPRET

a poem this short, **diction,**
word choice, becomes
specially important. Which
ords are crucial to the
nagery?

The Red Wheelbarrow

William Carlos Williams

so much depends
upon

a red wheel
barrow

glazed with rain
water

beside the white
chickens.

what if a much of a which of a wind

E. E. Cummings

what if a much of a which of a wind
gives the truth to summer's lie;
bloodies with dizzying leaves the sun
and yanks immortal stars awry?[1]
Blow king to beggar and queen to seem
(blow friend to fiend:blow space to time)
—when skies are hanged and oceans drowned,
the single secret will still be man

what if a keen of a lean wind flays[2]
screaming hills with sleet and snow:
strangles valleys by ropes of thing
and stifles forests in white ago?
Blow hope to terror;blow seeing to blind
(blow pity to envy and soul to mind)
—whose hearts are mountains,roots are trees,
it's they shall cry hello to the spring

what if a dawn of a doom of a dream
bites this universe in two,
peels forever out of his grave
and sprinkles nowhere with me and you?
Blow soon to never and never to twice
(blow life to isn't:blow death to was)
—all nothing's only our hugest home;
the most who die,the more we live

1. **awry** (ə·rī′): out of place.
2. **flays:** here, whips; lashes.

INFER

What might "summer's lie" be?

IDENTIFY

E. E. Cummings is noted for using verbs, adjectives, and adverbs as nouns. What examples can you find? Circle at least four examples of this technique.

INTERPRET

A **paradox** is a statement that appears self-contradictory but that reveals a kind of truth. How do you explain the paradox developed in the third stanza—in which the universe is reduced to a colossal nothing, yet the "we" of humankind lives on?

BUILD FLUENCY

Read Cummings's poem aloud, focusing on rhythm and units of meaning. Be sure your reading reflects the element of parallel structure in the poem.

Imagery

Imagery is the use of language to evoke a picture or a concrete sensation of a person, a thing, a place, or an experience. Although most images appeal to the sense of sight, they sometimes appeal to the senses of taste, smell, hearing, and touch as well.

1. On the lines below, list three images from "The Red Wheelbarrow." What do these images have in common?

2. On the lines below, list one image from "what if a much of a which of a wind" for each of the senses shown.

Sight:

Hearing:

Touch:

Taste:

Musical Devices

All by himself, E. E. Cummings altered conventional English syntax and made typography part of the shape and meaning of a poem. His poetry, however, is extremely lyrical and is marked by such conventional musical devices as **rhyme, alliteration, assonance,** and **repetition.**

Re-read "what if a much of a which of a wind" and note examples of each of these elements. Then, fill in the chart.

Musical Devices	Examples
End rhyme	
Slant rhyme	
Alliteration	
Assonance	
Repetition	

American Drama

We respond to a play in very much the way we respond to a sports event. Let's assume that one summer evening you go to a professional baseball game. For some reason, you take a liking to one of the pitchers. Then someone sitting next to you says that the pitcher has been out for several weeks with an injured elbow and is trying to make a comeback. If he fails in this game, he is finished. You start rooting for him. He gets some bad calls from the plate umpire, and you boo or whistle. Then your neighbor tells you that the pitcher is not pitching his best. Unless he stops protecting his injured elbow and starts putting more speed into his pitches, he will not win.

Most plays have more psychological complexity than this situation does. With a little imagination, however, we can add to the pitcher's problems. Suppose, for instance, that the pitcher's wife is afraid that if he throws too hard, he will ruin his elbow and be unable to play. She tells him that if he damages his elbow further, she will leave him; but, to him, the glory of winning transcends practical matters. To his wife, he is a ball-playing "boy," careless and immature. And so forth . . . What has happened in this scenario is what happens in almost every play. Early on, the playwright organizes our emotions behind some character or group of characters: We are "for" them. The playwright has placed these characters in a situation involving **conflict** and then has made us understand that it is not just any conflict: The character or characters have something vital at stake. They want to win, and they need to win in order to survive. In the baseball game, the situation is made difficult for the pitcher, who is the **protagonist** (the major character who wants something and who drives the action forward). The pitcher struggles against both **external conflict** (the opposing side) and **internal conflict** (his fears of damaging his arm, his feelings about the pressure from his wife). The fan sitting next to you has given us the background information, or **exposition** (who the pitcher is, what he wants to do, and what he has at stake). The story of a character who, against the odds, wants something meaningful has been set in motion. The tension mounts as the innings pass; we are witnessing, or participating in and enjoying, a drama.

The word *participation* is important. We have all heard ballplayers say how encouraged they are by the response of the spectators. Actors, too, may say as they come offstage after a scene, "That's a wonderful audience out there tonight!" And because of the audience, performances often rise to a higher level. It has often been said that a play exists halfway between the stage and the audience. What an audience

EVALUATE

What two kinds of **conflict** can be represented in drama? Do you think the best plays represent one kind more than the other, or a combination of both? Explain.

gets from a performance is directly related to what it brings to the performance, not only in the way of understanding and feeling, but also in enthusiasm. In successful dramatic performances, a note is sounded onstage, and a chord of recognition or responsiveness echoes back from the audience. A play performed in an empty theater is not a play.

The basic elements of drama include exposition, which gives us information, and a protagonist, the major character who struggles against internal conflict and external conflict.

The History of American Drama: The Caboose of Literature

Eugene O'Neill (1888–1953) is generally considered the first important figure in American drama. It is significant that decades after the 1920 production of his first full-length play, *Beyond the Horizon,* he is still regarded as the most important playwright the United States has produced.

American drama before O'Neill consisted mostly of shows and entertainments. These wildly theatrical spectacles often featured such delights as chariot races and burning cities, staged by means of special effects that dazzled audiences. Melodramas and farces were also written for famous actors, much as television shows today are created to display the personalities and talents of popular performers. In fact, O'Neill's own father, James O'Neill, spent the better part of his life touring in a spectacular melodrama based on Alexandre Dumas's *The Count of Monte Cristo.*

There was great theatrical activity in the United States in the nineteenth century, a time when there were no movies, radio, or television. Every town of any size had its theater or "opera house" in which touring companies performed. Given the hunger for entertainment, one may wonder why no significant American drama was staged in the century that produced, among others, Melville, Emerson, Whitman, Dickinson, and Twain.

One explanation is that theater has usually followed the other arts, rather than pointed the way toward new directions. Robert Sherwood, one of a group of notable American playwrights between 1920 and 1940, once said, "Drama travels in the caboose of literature." Theater seems to take up new attitudes, subject matter, and forms only after they have been explored in the other arts. For the most part, theater tends to dramatize accepted attitudes and values.

The reason for this is that theater is a social art, one we attend as part of a large group; we seem to respond to something new much more slowly as a group than we do as individuals. When you laugh or cry in the theater, your response is noticed. You are, in a sense, giving your approval, and this approval may be subject to criticism or condemnation by those sitting around you who are not laughing or crying. Furthermore, you may not be shocked to *read* about your secret thoughts, dreams, and desires; but if you *see* them shown on stage as you sit among a thousand people, you may refuse to respond, refuse to acknowledge them. You may even rise up and stalk out of the theater.

Thus, the novel and, to some extent, the poetry of the nineteenth and early twentieth centuries were more daring than the theater in giving us a record of experience, in showing us life as it *is* lived rather than as it *should be* lived.

During the period before Eugene O'Neill, American drama tended to be mild and sentimental, rarely questioning the life and attitudes it depicted, almost never challenging the accepted traditions of its times.

The Influence of Europe: Psychology and Taboo Subjects

European drama, which was to influence modern American drama profoundly, matured in the last third of the nineteenth century with the achievements of three playwrights: the Norwegian Henrik Ibsen, the Swede August Strindberg, and the Russian Anton Chekhov. Ibsen deliberately tackled subjects such as guilt, sexuality, and mental illness—subjects that had never before been so realistically and disturbingly portrayed on stage. Strindberg brought to his characterizations an unprecedented level of psychological complexity. And Chekhov, along with Ibsen and Strindberg, shifted the subject matter of drama from wildly theatrical displays of external action to inner action and emotions and the concerns of everyday life. Chekhov once remarked, "People don't go to the North Pole and fall off icebergs. They go to the office and quarrel with their wives and eat cabbage soup."

INFER

Vhat would you guess to be ome of the characteristics of drama these European laywrights of the late nineteenth century were eacting against?

Ibsen, Strindberg, and Chekhov wrote plays about life as it is actually lived. They presented characters and situations more or less realistically, in what has been called the "slice-of-life" dramatic technique.

Realism and Eugene O'Neill: Putting American Drama on the Map

Realistic drama is based on the illusion that when we watch a play, we are looking at life through a "fourth wall" that has been removed so that we can see the action. Soon after the beginning of the twentieth century, realism became the dominant mode of American drama. As with all theatrical revolutions, the movement toward realism began apart from the commercial theater. But very soon after the new drama succeeded in the little theaters off Broadway (about 1916), the commercial theater adopted realism, too.

In 1916 and 1917, two small theater groups in New York—the Provincetown Players and the Washington Square Players—began to produce new American plays. They provided a congenial home for new American playwrights, notably Eugene O'Neill, whose first one-act plays about the sea were produced by the Provincetown Players in Greenwich Village in 1916.

These theater groups seemed to have no program. They were not sure what they were for, but they were sure what they were against: the established commercial theater. They would produce any play, in any style, that commercial theater would not touch.

O'Neill gravitated there naturally. Well aware of Sigmund Freud and his new theories about the complex self, O'Neill tried especially hard to reveal more than realism—or naturalism—could normally reveal. In *The Great God Brown* (1926), O'Neill experimented with using masks to differentiate between two sides of a personality. In *Days Without End* (1934), he had two actors play one character to achieve the same end. And in *Strange Interlude* (1928), characters spoke in asides to the audience, revealing thoughts and feelings that could not be expressed in dialogue to other characters.

INFER
Masks have often been used in theater. What other purposes, besides portraying different sides of a personality, might they have?

With his experimental flair, his enormous output, and his high aspirations for the theater, Eugene O'Neill dominated American drama in his generation. His plays were widely produced abroad, and he was awarded the Nobel Prize in literature in 1936.

Arthur Miller: Playwright of Our Social Conscience

The post–World War II years brought two important figures to prominence in American drama: Arthur Miller (1915–   ) and Tennessee Williams (1911–1983). Miller and Williams represent the two principal movements in modern American drama: realism, and the attempt to break away from realism or to blend it with more poetic expression.

Arthur Miller's best work, *Death of a Salesman,* is one of the most successful in fusing the realistic and the imaginative; in all of his other plays, however, Miller is the master of realism. He is a true disciple of Henrik Ibsen, not only in his realistic technique but also in his concern about society's impact on his characters' lives.

In Miller's plays, the course of the action and the development of characters depend not only on the characters' psychological makeup, but also on the social, philosophical, and economic atmosphere of their times. Miller's most notable character, Willy Loman in *Death of a Salesman,* is a self-deluded man; but he is also a product of the American dream of success and a victim of the American business machine, which disposes of him when he has outlived his usefulness.

Miller is a writer of high moral seriousness, whether he is dealing with personal versus social responsibility, as in *All My Sons* (1947), or with witch hunts past and present, as in *The Crucible* (1953). Miller writes a plain and muscular prose that under the force of emotion often becomes eloquent, as in Linda Loman's famous speech in *Death of a Salesman,* in which she talks to her two sons about their father:

> *I don't say he's a great man. Willy Loman never made a lot of money. His name was never in the paper. He's not the finest character that ever lived. But he's a human being, and a terrible thing is happening to him. So attention must be paid. He's not to be allowed to fall into his grave like an old dog. Attention, attention must finally be paid to such a person.*

Tennessee Williams: Playwright of Our Souls

Tennessee Williams's concern was not with social matters, but with personal ones. If Miller was often the playwright of our social conscience, then Williams was the playwright of our souls. In play after play, he probed the psychological complexities of his characters, especially of his female characters: Amanda and Laura in *The Glass Menagerie* (1944), Blanche in *A Streetcar Named Desire* (1947), and Alma in *Summer and Smoke* (1948).

In contrast to Miller's spare, plain language, Williams's writing is delicate and sensuous; it is often colored with lush imagery and evocative rhythms. Miller's characters are, by and large, ordinary people with whom we identify because they are caught up in the social tensions of our times. Williams's characters are often lost ladies, drowning in their own neuroses, but somehow mirroring a part of our own complex psychological selves.

The actual scenes in Williams's plays are usually purely realistic, even though these scenes may deal with colorful and extreme characters. He always conceived his plays in visually arresting, colorful, theatrical environments.

COMPARE AND CONTRAST

Briefly characterize the different dramatic styles of Arthur Miller and Tennessee Williams.

In the works of Arthur Miller and Tennessee Williams, we see the two strongest strands in American drama: pure realism, and realism blended with an imaginative, poetic sensibility.

The Revolt Against Realism: Theater of Fragmentation

Currently, there is a revolt against realism in American drama. Naturally, the movement is toward theatricalism again, with its emphasis on stage effects and imaginative settings. This revolt does not confine itself to a particular manner of staging; instead, it extends to the texture of language and plot in the scripts themselves.

The moral and religious certainties that once bound people together exert little or no force on many modern audiences. Some people believe that survival itself depends on a willingness to accept life as formless or meaningless.

Some American playwrights found this new outlook on life impossible to express in the orderly "beginning, middle, end" format of realism. They borrowed, again from Europe, a theater of fragmentation, impressions, and stream of consciousness that was called "expressionist." **Expressionist drama** aimed at the revelation of characters' interior consciousness without reference to a logical sequence of surface actions. Many writers, such as the Irish playwright Samuel Beckett (1906–1989) and French writer Eugene Ionesco (1912–1994), who used expressionist techniques in drama, came to be called playwrights of the Theater of the Absurd.

Experimental drama has increased the options that are open to playwrights. Edward Albee (1928–   ) drew freely upon a variety of styles—expressionist, absurdist, realistic—to create the electrifying domestic drama *Who's Afraid of Virginia Woolf* (1962), now an American classic. There are practically no conventions in the theater anymore; there is simply a stage and an audience. Playwrights are free to load the stage with scenery, lights, and special effects; but they are equally free—as the playwright was in the age of Shakespeare—to have an actor gesture toward one side of an utterly bare stage and say, "This is the Forest of Arden."

Dramatists now have the freedom to express their deepest feelings in almost any form they choose—provided that their approach can be made comprehensible to an audience and touch their emotions.

IDENTIFY

Underline the sentences that explain how drama in the late twentieth century broke away from realism.

From The Crucible

Make the Connection

Public Voices, Private Lives

Most people recognize and live with the difference between their public selves and their private selves. Sometimes, however, those selves come into conflict. Then, individuals must make a choice. Which self will triumph? Which self will be sacrificed? Can a compromise be found? These choices can sometimes be matters of life and death.

Arthur Miller has said that he wrote *The Crucible* with the conviction that "there were moments when an individual conscience was all that could keep the world from falling apart." Think of some event in past or recent history that demonstrates a triumph of individual conscience. Briefly describe the circumstances and outcome of the event.

Arthur Miller

FROM The Crucible

The following scene from Act Four is the last scene in the play. The judges have refused to postpone the executions of John Proctor and Rebecca Nurse. The Reverend Hale is trying to persuade the prisoners to confess falsely, rather than throw away the life God gave them. He arranges for Elizabeth to see John, in the hope that she will convince him to confess.

***A** sound—the sibilance of dragging feet on stone. They turn. A pause.* HERRICK *enters with* JOHN PROCTOR. *His wrists are chained. He is another man, bearded, filthy, his eyes misty as though webs had overgrown them. He halts inside the doorway, his eye caught by the sight of* ELIZABETH. *The emotion flowing between them prevents anyone from speaking for an instant. Now* HALE, *visibly affected, goes to* DANFORTH *and speaks quietly.*

Hale: Pray, leave them, Excellency.

Danforth, *pressing* HALE *impatiently aside:* Mr. Proctor, you have been notified, have you not? PROCTOR *is silent, staring at* ELIZABETH. I see light in the sky, Mister; let you counsel with your wife, and may God help you turn your back on Hell. PROCTOR *is silent, staring at* ELIZABETH.

Hale, *quietly:* Excellency, let—

DANFORTH *brushes past* HALE *and walks out.* HALE *follows.* CHEEVER *stands and follows,* HATHORNE *behind.* HERRICK *goes.* PARRIS, *from a safe distance, offers:*

Parris: If you desire a cup of cider, Mr. Proctor, I am sure I— PROCTOR *turns an icy stare at him, and he breaks off.* PARRIS *raises his palms toward* PROCTOR. God lead you now. PARRIS *goes out.*

Alone. PROCTOR *walks to her, halts. It is as though they stood in a spinning world. It is beyond sorrow, above it. He reaches out his hand as though toward an embodiment not quite real, and as he touches her, a strange soft sound, half laughter, half amazement, comes from his throat. He pats her hand. She covers his hand with hers. And then, weak, he sits. Then she sits, facing him.*

Proctor: The child?

Elizabeth: It grows.

Proctor: There is no word of the boys?

Elizabeth: They're well. Rebecca's Samuel keeps them.

Proctor: You have not seen them?

Elizabeth: I have not. *She catches a weakening in herself and downs it.*

Proctor: You are a—marvel, Elizabeth.

Elizabeth: You—have been tortured?

Proctor: Aye. *Pause. She will not let herself be drowned in the sea that threatens her.* They come for my life now.

Elizabeth: I know it.

DENTIFY

nderline the stage directions 1at Miller uses to convey the verwhelming emotion of this ieeting.

Pause.

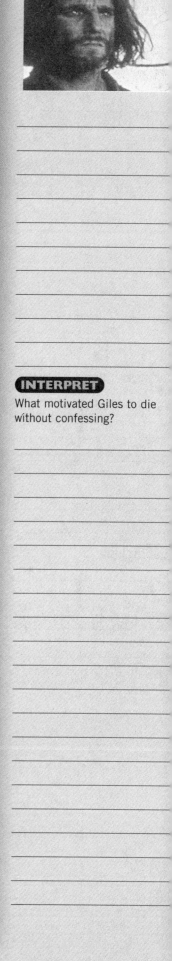

Proctor: None—have yet confessed?

Elizabeth: There be many confessed.

Proctor: Who are they?

Elizabeth: There be a hundred or more, they say. Goody Ballard is one; Isaiah Goodkind is one. There be many.

Proctor: Rebecca?

Elizabeth: Not Rebecca. She is one foot in Heaven now; naught may hurt her more.

Proctor: And Giles?

Elizabeth: You have not heard of it?

Proctor: I hear nothin', where I am kept.

Elizabeth: Giles is dead.

He looks at her incredulously.

Proctor: When were he hanged?

Elizabeth, *quietly, factually:* He were not hanged. He would not answer aye or nay to his indictment; for if he denied the charge they'd hang him surely, and auction out his property. So he stand mute, and died Christian under the law. And so his sons will have his farm. It is the law, for he could not be condemned a wizard without he answer the indictment, aye or nay.

Proctor: Then how does he die?

Elizabeth, *gently:* They press him, John.

Proctor: Press?

Elizabeth: Great stones they lay upon his chest until he plead aye or nay. *With a tender smile for the old man:* They say he give them but two words. "More weight," he says. And died.

Proctor, *numbed—a thread to weave into his agony:* "More weight."

Elizabeth: Aye. It were a fearsome man, Giles Corey.

Pause.

Proctor, *with great force of will, but not quite looking at her:* I have been thinking I would confess to them, Elizabeth. *She shows nothing.* What say you? If I give them that?

Elizabeth: I cannot judge you, John.

Pause.

Proctor, *simply—a pure question:* What would you have me do?

Elizabeth: As you will, I would have it. *Slight pause.* I want you living, John. That's sure.

Proctor—*he pauses, then with a flailing of hope:* Giles' wife? Have she confessed?

Elizabeth: She will not.

INTERPRET

What motivated Giles to die without confessing?

Pause.

Proctor: It is a pretense, Elizabeth.

Elizabeth: What is?

Proctor: I cannot mount the gibbet like a saint. It is a fraud. I am not that man. *She is silent.* My honesty is broke, Elizabeth; I am no good man. Nothing's spoiled by giving them this lie that were not rotten long before.

Elizabeth: And yet you've not confessed till now. That speak goodness in you.

Proctor: Spite only keeps me silent. It is hard to give a lie to dogs. *Pause, for the first time he turns directly to her.* I would have your forgiveness, Elizabeth.

Elizabeth: It is not for me to give, John, I am—

Proctor: I'd have you see some honesty in it. Let them that never lied die now to keep their souls. It is pretense for me, a vanity that will not blind God nor keep my children out of the wind. *Pause.* What say you?

Elizabeth, *upon a heaving sob that always threatens:* John, it come to naught that I should forgive you, if you'll not forgive yourself. *Now he turns away a little, in great agony.* It is not my soul, John, it is yours. *He stands, as though in physical pain, slowly rising to his feet with a great immortal longing to find his answer. It is difficult to say, and she is on the verge of tears.* Only be sure of this, for I know it now: Whatever you will do, it is a good man does it. *He turns his doubting, searching gaze upon her.* I have read my heart this three month, John. *Pause.* I have sins of my own to count. It needs a cold wife to prompt lechery.

Proctor, *in great pain:* Enough, enough—

Elizabeth, *now pouring out her heart:* Better you should know me!

Proctor: I will not hear it! I know you!

Elizabeth: You take my sins upon you, John—

Proctor, *in agony:* No, I take my own, my own!

Elizabeth: John, I counted myself so plain, so poorly made, no honest love could come to me! Suspicion kissed you when I did; I never knew how I should say my love. It were a cold house I kept! *In fright, she swerves, as* HATHORNE *enters.*

Hathorne: What say you, Proctor? The sun is soon up.

PROCTOR, *his chest heaving, stares, turns to* ELIZABETH. *She comes to him as though to plead, her voice quaking.*

Elizabeth: Do what you will. But let none be your judge. There be no higher judge under Heaven than Proctor is! Forgive me, forgive me, John—I never knew such goodness in the world! *She covers her face, weeping.*

PROCTOR *turns from her to* HATHORNE; *he is off the earth, his voice hollow.*

EVALUATE

/hat is your opinion of John nd Elizabeth's relationship at his point in the play?

INTERPRET/EVALUATE

According to Elizabeth, why vas she always suspicious of ohn's love? Do you think her eelings are understandable? Why or why not?

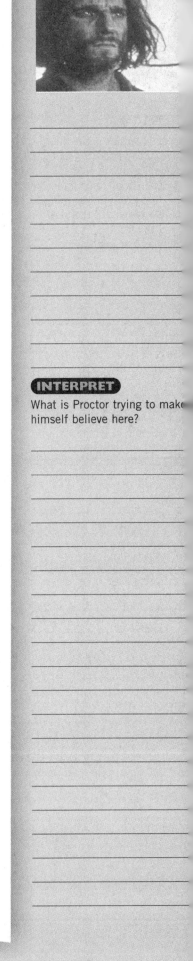

Proctor: I want my life.

Hathorne, *electrified, surprised:* You'll confess yourself?

Proctor: I will have my life.

Hathorne, *with a mystical tone:* God be praised! It is a providence! *He rushes out the door, and his voice is heard calling down the corridor:* He will confess! Proctor will confess!

Proctor, *with a cry, as he strides to the door:* Why do you cry it? *In great pain he turns back to her.* It is evil, is it not? It is evil.

Elizabeth, *in terror, weeping:* I cannot judge you, John, I cannot!

Proctor: Then who will judge me? *Suddenly clasping his hands:* God in Heaven, what is John Proctor, what is John Proctor? *He moves as an animal, and a fury is riding in him, a tantalized search.* I think it is honest, I think so; I am no saint. *As though she had denied this he calls angrily at her:* Let Rebecca go like a saint; for me it is fraud!

Voices are heard in the hall, speaking together in suppressed excitement.

Elizabeth: I am not your judge, I cannot be. *As though giving him release:* Do as you will, do as you will!

Proctor: Would you give them such a lie? Say it. Would you ever give them this? *She cannot answer.* You would not; if tongs of fire were singeing you you would not! It is evil. Good, then—it is evil, and I do it!

HATHORNE *enters with* DANFORTH, *and, with them,* CHEEVER, PARRIS, *and* HALE. *It is a businesslike, rapid entrance, as though the ice had been broken.*

Danforth, *with great relief and gratitude:* Praise to God, man, praise to God; you shall be blessed in Heaven for this. CHEEVER *has hurried to the bench with pen, ink, and paper.* PROCTOR *watches him.* Now then, let us have it. Are you ready, Mr. Cheever?

Proctor, *with a cold, cold horror at their efficiency:* Why must it be written?

Danforth: Why, for the good instruction of the village, Mister; this we shall post upon the church door! *To* PARRIS, *urgently:* Where is the marshal?

Parris, *runs to the door and calls down the corridor:* Marshal! Hurry!

Danforth: Now, then, Mister, will you speak slowly, and directly to the point, for Mr. Cheever's sake. *He is on record now, and is really dictating to* CHEEVER, *who writes.* Mr. Proctor, have you seen the Devil in your life? PROCTOR*'s jaws lock.* Come, man, there is light in the sky; the town waits at the scaffold; I would give out this news. Did you see the Devil?

Proctor: I did.

Parris: Praise God!

Danforth: And when he come to you, what were his demand? PROCTOR *is silent.* DANFORTH *helps.* Did he bid you to do his work upon the earth?

INTERPRET

What is Proctor trying to make himself believe here?

REDICT

thur Miller has argued that ordinary person can be ragic hero, if he or she lieves in something intensely ough to give up everything se. By the end of the play, you think John Proctor will alify as a tragic hero?

NTERPRET

nce people have already stified that they saw ebecca with the Devil, why oes Danforth want John to rify it?

Proctor: He did.

Danforth: And you bound yourself to his service? DANFORTH *turns, as* REBECCA NURSE *enters, with* HERRICK *helping to support her. She is barely able to walk.* Come in, come in, woman!

Rebecca, *brightening as she sees* PROCTOR: Ah, John! You are well, then, eh?

PROCTOR *turns his face to the wall.*

Danforth: Courage, man, courage—let her witness your good example that she may come to God herself. Now hear it, Goody Nurse! Say on, Mr. Proctor. Did you bind yourself to the Devil's service?

Rebecca, *astonished:* Why, John!

Proctor, *through his teeth, his face turned from* REBECCA: I did.

Danforth: Now, woman, you surely see it profit nothin' to keep this conspiracy any further. Will you confess yourself with him?

Rebecca: Oh, John—God send his mercy on you!

Danforth: I say, will you confess yourself, Goody Nurse?

Rebecca: Why, it is a lie, it is a lie; how may I damn myself? I cannot, I cannot.

Danforth: Mr. Proctor. When the Devil came to you did you see Rebecca Nurse in his company? PROCTOR *is silent.* Come, man, take courage—did you ever see her with the Devil?

Proctor, *almost inaudibly:* No.

DANFORTH, *now sensing trouble, glances at* JOHN *and goes to the table, and picks up a sheet—the list of condemned.*

Danforth: Did you ever see her sister, Mary Easty, with the Devil?

Proctor: No, I did not.

Danforth, *his eyes narrow on* PROCTOR: Did you ever see Martha Corey with the Devil?

Proctor: I did not.

Danforth, *realizing, slowly putting the sheet down:* Did you ever see anyone with the Devil?

Proctor: I did not.

Danforth: Proctor, you mistake me. I am not empowered to trade your life for a lie. You have most certainly seen some person with the Devil. PROCTOR *is silent.* Mr. Proctor, a score of people have already testified they saw this woman with the Devil.

Proctor: Then it is proved. Why must I say it?

Danforth: Why "must" you say it! Why, you should rejoice to say it if your soul is truly purged of any love for Hell!

Proctor: They think to go like saints. I like not to spoil their names.

Danforth, *inquiring, incredulous:* Mr. Proctor, do you think they go like saints?

Proctor, *evading:* This woman never thought she done the Devil's work.

Danforth: Look you, sir. I think you mistake your duty here. It matters nothing what she thought—she is convicted of the unnatural murder of children, and you for sending your spirit out upon Mary Warren. Your soul alone is the issue here, Mister, and you will prove its whiteness or you cannot live in a Christian country. Will you tell me now what persons conspired with you in the Devil's company? PROCTOR *is silent.* To your knowledge was Rebecca Nurse ever—

Proctor: I speak my own sins; I cannot judge another. *Crying out, with hatred:* I have no tongue for it.

Hale, *quickly to* DANFORTH: Excellency, it is enough he confess himself. Let him sign it, let him sign it.

Parris, *feverishly:* It is a great service, sir. It is a weighty name; it will strike the village that Proctor confess. I beg you, let him sign it. The sun is up, Excellency!

Danforth, *considers; then with dissatisfaction:* Come, then, sign your testimony. *To* CHEEVER: Give it to him. CHEEVER *goes to* PROCTOR, *the confession and a pen in hand.* PROCTOR *does not look at it.* Come, man, sign it.

Proctor, *after glancing at the confession:* You have all witnessed it—it is enough.

Danforth: You will not sign it?

Proctor: You have all witnessed it; what more is needed?

Danforth: Do you sport with me? You will sign your name or it is no confession, Mister! *His breast heaving with agonized breathing,* PROCTOR *now lays the paper down and signs his name.*

Parris: Praise be to the Lord!

PROCTOR *has just finished signing when* DANFORTH *reaches for the paper. But* PROCTOR *snatches it up, and now a wild terror is rising in him, and a boundless anger.*

Danforth, *perplexed, but politely extending his hand:* If you please, sir.

Proctor: No.

Danforth, *as though* PROCTOR *did not understand:* Mr. Proctor, I must have—

Proctor: No, no. I have signed it. You have seen me. It is done! You have no need for this.

Parris: Proctor, the village must have proof that—

Proctor: Damn the village! I confess to God, and God has seen my name on this! It is enough!

Danforth: No, sir, it is—

Proctor: You came to save my soul, did you not? Here! I have confessed myself; it is enough!

Danforth: You have not con—

INTERPRET

Why is John reluctant to sign his name to the confession? What **symbolic** content does a signature have?

Proctor: I have confessed myself! Is there no good penitence but it be public? God does not need my name nailed upon the church! God sees my name; God knows how black my sins are! It is enough!

Danforth: Mr. Proctor—

Proctor: You will not use me! I am no Sarah Good or Tituba, I am John Proctor! You will not use me! It is no part of salvation that you should use me!

Danforth: I do not wish to—

Proctor: I have three children—how may I teach them to walk like men in the world, and I sold my friends?

Danforth: You have not sold your friends—

Proctor: Beguile me not! I blacken all of them when this is nailed to the church the very day they hang for silence!

Danforth: Mr. Proctor, I must have good and legal proof that you—

Proctor: You are the high court, your word is good enough! Tell them I confessed myself; say Proctor broke his knees and wept like a woman; say what you will, but my name cannot—

Danforth, *with suspicion:* It is the same, is it not? If I report it or you sign to it?

Proctor—*he knows it is insane:* No, it is not the same! What others say and what I sign to is not the same!

Danforth: Why? Do you mean to deny this confession when you are free?

Proctor: I mean to deny nothing!

Danforth: Then explain to me, Mr. Proctor, why you will not let—

Proctor, *with a cry of his whole soul:* Because it is my name! Because I cannot have another in my life! Because I lie and sign myself to lies! Because I am not worth the dust on the feet of them that hang! How may I live without my name? I have given you my soul; leave me my name!

Danforth, *pointing at the confession in* PROCTOR*'s hand:* Is that document a lie? If it is a lie I will not accept it! What say you? I will not deal in lies, Mister! PROCTOR *is motionless.* You will give me your honest confession in my hand, or I cannot keep you from the rope. PROCTOR *does not reply.* Which way do you go, Mister?

His breast heaving, his eyes staring, PROCTOR *tears the paper and crumples it, and he is weeping in fury, but erect.*

Danforth: Marshal!

Parris, *hysterically, as though the tearing paper were his life:* Proctor, Proctor!

Hale: Man, you will hang! You cannot!

Proctor, *his eyes full of tears:* I can. And there's your first marvel, that I can. You have made your magic now, for now I do think I see some

INTERPRET

/hat does Proctor mean when e refers so emphatically to is name? Why is his name so nportant to him?

shred of goodness in John Proctor. Not enough to weave a banner with, but white enough to keep it from such dogs. ELIZABETH, *in a burst of terror, rushes to him and weeps against his hand.* Give them no tear! Tears pleasure them! Show honor now, show a stony heart and sink them with it! *He has lifted her, and kisses her now with great passion.*

Rebecca: Let you fear nothing! Another judgment waits us all!

Danforth: Hang them high over the town! Who weeps for these, weeps for corruption! *He sweeps out past them.* HERRICK *starts to lead* REBECCA, *who almost collapses, but* PROCTOR *catches her, and she glances up at him apologetically.*

Rebecca: I've had no breakfast.

Herrick: Come, man.

HERRICK *escorts them out,* HATHORNE *and* CHEEVER *behind them.* ELIZABETH *stands staring at the empty doorway.*

Parris, *in deadly fear, to* ELIZABETH: Go to him, Goody Proctor! There is yet time!

From outside a drumroll strikes the air. PARRIS *is startled.* ELIZABETH *jerks about toward the window.*

Parris: Go to him! *He rushes out the door, as though to hold back his fate.* Proctor! Proctor!

Again, a short burst of drums.

Hale: Woman, plead with him! *He starts to rush out the door, and then goes back to her.* Woman! It is pride, it is vanity. *She avoids his eyes, and moves to the window. He drops to his knees.* Be his helper! What profit him to bleed? Shall the dust praise him? Shall the worms declare his truth? Go to him, take his shame away!

Elizabeth, *supporting herself against collapse, grips the bars of the window, and with a cry:* He have his goodness now. God forbid I take it from him!

The final drumroll crashes, then heightens violently. HALE *weeps in frantic prayer, and the new sun is pouring in upon her face, and the drums rattle like bones in the morning air.*

The curtain falls

INTERPRET

Why does this act, which so (such as Hale) can only see suicidal, represent for Procto some "shred of goodness" in him?

EVALUATE

Do you agree with Hale that John's decision to die is base on vanity? Or do you agree with Elizabeth that he now h "his goodness"?

BUILD FLUENCY

Together with a partner or a small group, choose a passa from this scene that you think is especially eloquent. Cast the parts, and then rehearse a dramatic reading of the passage. When you are satisfied with your interpretation, perform the passage for an audience of classmates or friends.

Motivation

Motivation refers to the reasons for a character's behavior. For each character's action shown on the chart below, write what you believe to be the motivation.

Character	Action	Motivation
Elizabeth Proctor	She says she will not judge her husband for telling a lie.	
Deputy Governor Danforth	He insists that John Proctor sign the confession.	
John Proctor	He is unwilling to follow through with a lie in order to save his life.	

Vocabulary: How to Own a Word

Synonyms and Antonyms

The first word in each item below appears in the play. The second word or phrase may be a synonym or an antonym for the first word. On the line provided, write **S** if the second word or phrase is a synonym for the first word, or **A** if it is an antonym. You may need a dictionary or a thesaurus for this activity.

_____ **1.** sibilance: hissing

_____ **2.** embodiment: concrete expression

_____ **3.** incredulously: trustingly

_____ **4.** gibbet: gallows

_____ **5.** lechery: purity

_____ **6.** swerves: veers

_____ **7.** providence: blessed event

_____ **8.** tantalized: disenchanted

_____ **9.** singeing: burning slightly

_____ **10.** evading: confronting

ETELL

w did Americans' attitudes
out the war in Vietnam differ
m their attitudes about
rld War II?

CONNECT

iefly note one way
chnology helps you. Then,
te one way technology
eates problems for you.

Contemporary Literature 1950 to Present

On August 6, 1945, an atomic bomb was dropped on the Japanese city of Hiroshima from the U.S. airplane *Enola Gay*. Within seconds, the center of Hiroshima had disappeared. The bomb, in effect, ended World War II, and its mushroom cloud has cast a shadow over each generation since.

Although many Americans disapproved of the use of the atomic bomb, most Americans agreed with the purpose of the war itself. They were fighting against tyranny, against regimes that would destroy the American way of life. Only twenty years later, however, the United States became deeply involved in another overseas war—this time in Vietnam—that would sharply divide the nation. In the 1960s, demonstrations, both peaceful and violent, became commonplace.

The 1970s saw the winding down of the Vietnam War, but another focus of disillusion filled the news: the Watergate scandal that in 1974 forced the resignation of President Richard Nixon. On the other hand, the celebration in 1976 of the bicentennial of the Declaration of Independence witnessed a prideful restatement of fundamental American values.

Then came the 1980s, when individual enjoyment and material success seemed to overshadow other concerns. As the 1980s ended, so did the cold war, the struggle between the United States and the Soviet Union that had dominated international politics since shortly after the end of World War II. The Soviet Union collapsed as its republics and satellite nations declared independence. The end of the cold war reduced but did not end the threat of nuclear warfare.

In many ways, the nuclear bomb is the dramatic symbol of the last half of the twentieth century. Its infamous mushroom cloud represents the proliferation of science and technology, the purpose of which was, ironically enough, to benefit humankind, to make life richer and easier for all. In some ways, science and technology have fulfilled their promise. They have increased life spans and have fed and housed many people better. They have moved us faster from place to place—even allowing a few of us to stroll on the surface of the moon.

But at the same time, poverty and crime persist. Technology has standardized and "assembly-lined" our lives and displaced countless workers. Many people often feel they are only a number on a computer disk or credit card. Our very thoughts seem to be controlled by mass advertising, mass journalism, and mass entertainment. Some people even predict that our new technologies will deliver the planet itself back to lower organisms—to the cockroaches and ants—who may survive the nuclear holocaust that might one day engulf us.

The aftermath of World War II ushered in an age of rapid developments in science and technology. The postwar years have offered many Americans increased opportunities for economic and cultural growth, but the individual person often seems lost in the fast-paced, computerized world.

Contemporary Fiction: Diversity and Vitality

Probably the most common word used to describe American culture at the end of the twentieth century is **postmodern,** a term that, like our age, is still in the process of being defined. Postmodernism sees contemporary culture as a departure from modernism, the dominant movement in the arts from about 1900 to 1950. In literature, such great American modernists as Ezra Pound, T. S. Eliot, William Carlos Williams, Katherine Anne Porter, William Faulkner, and Ernest Hemingway forged new styles and new forms to express the sensibility of the twentieth century. Postmodern writers build with many of the tools provided by the modernists, and they are now constructing a body of literature that is strikingly different from that of the first half of the twentieth century.

Postmodern fiction writers allow for multiple meanings and multiple worlds in their words. Realistic and literal worlds, future worlds, and dreamlike metaphorical worlds may merge; narrators and characters may tell different versions of a story, or a story may deliberately accommodate several valid interpretations. The postmodernist asks, Why choose only one version? Why limit ourselves?

The vitality of contemporary fiction lies in its cultural diversity, in its enthusiasm for blending fiction with nonfiction, and in its extraordinary sense of play. It also demonstrates a typically American ability to invigorate the old with the new.

Contemporary fiction allows for multiple meanings and multiple worlds, uses nontraditional forms, and comments upon itself. But it embraces traditional storytellers as well as postmodern risk-takers. It features cultural diversity, crisscrosses the boundaries between fiction and nonfiction, and uses subjects, images, and themes from the past fearlessly.

CONNECT

Name a movie, TV show, or book that has characteristics of a postmodern work. Briefly explain.

Characteristics of Postmodern Literature

- Allows for multiple meanings and multiple worlds
- Structures works in nontraditional forms
- Comments upon itself
- Features cultural diversity
- Blends and overlaps fiction and nonfiction
- Uses the past fearlessly

Contemporary Nonfiction: Breaking the Barriers

Until fairly recently, "nonfiction" meant whatever was *not* fiction—suggesting that nonfiction was a nonliterary form and a nonart. Nonfiction writers were lumped together with journalists, who were in turn defined as nonliterary folk whose work was quickly written, read, and discarded. Critics tended to concentrate on the search for the elusive Great American Novel, which was thought to be more important than anything a nonfiction writer could produce.

Since the 1970s, however, nonfiction has come into its own; according to author William Zinsser, nonfiction has "crept in and occupied the throne." Featured reviews now discuss the art (not just the factual content) of books on computers, architecture, travel, history, film, and other subjects. Critics, however, are still uncertain about the terminology we should apply to nonfiction. For instance, when discussing fiction, we can talk about point of view, character, plot, theme, and setting; with more complex fiction, we can analyze irony, metaphors, symbols, and levels of meaning. But these traditional literary terms don't always apply to nonfiction.

DENTIFY

hat was the last nonfiction ok you read? Circle the erary terms listed in lines 7–99 that might apply in a view of that book.

More troubling is the problem of accuracy. No one expects a novel to be true, although it may be based on verifiable facts. But truth or accuracy is often a test applied to nonfiction, with frequently unsatisfactory results. A class recently read Peter Matthiessen's *The Snow Leopard* (1978), a travel memoir about wildlife in the Himalayas and the writer's search for the meaning of life. The class praised the book for its penetrating observations, philosophical depth, and narrative technique. Students were then asked if they would like it just as much if they learned that it was fiction, that Matthiessen had done extensive library research but had never gone to the Himalayas at all. (This is, of course, *not* the case.) No, many students said, they would not like the book as well. It would no longer be true.

The New Journalism. In the 1960s, the New Journalism (also called Literary Journalism) began to appear. Writers like Truman Capote, Tom

Wolfe, Joan Didion, and Norman Mailer employed many of the devices of fiction. A New Journalist did not feel obligated to keep personal opinion and his or her presence out of the writing. For example, Truman Capote befriended the murderers he was writing about in his book *In Cold Blood,* which he called a nonfiction novel—a perfect example of the overlapping of genres. Readers wanted to know just what the writer was thinking or feeling about the subject, and so the tone of a book became nearly as important as its facts.

If facts alone do not distinguish nonfiction from fiction, what does? No one is sure. What readers *are* sure about is their interest in nonfiction that uses the traditional attractions of accomplished fiction: characters to care about, suspense, and compelling use of language. Many readers, eager for literature that will illuminate their lives, enrich their knowledge, and entertain them, have become as willing to pursue those goals in nonfiction as they are in fiction.

Contemporary nonfiction has become a field equal to fiction, though questions about terminology and accuracy still give rise to controversy. Literary Journalism has added personal and fictional elements to nonfiction, enhancing its popularity with today's readers.

Contemporary Poetry: The Decline of Modernism

It is difficult to describe the course of American poetry since 1945, because recent trends are still too close to be viewed objectively. Moreover, in recent years, unprecedented numbers of Americans have been writing poetry, so it is a special challenge to determine which poets and which movements will last.

There are a number of clear, significant differences between American poetry written before 1945 and the poetry written in the decades since. The twenty years between World War I and World War II marked the flowering and near monopoly of modernist poetry. This was the kind of poetry defined, by and large, by the theory and practice of T. S. Eliot, Ezra Pound, and, somewhat later, W. H. Auden (1907–1973).

In 1917, Eliot had called for an impersonal, objective poetry that would transcend the subjective emotions of the poet. The poem, said Eliot, should be impersonal, allusive (it should make references, or allusions, to other works), and intellectually challenging. Modernist writers followed Ezra Pound's insistence that the image was all-important and that all unnecessary words should be omitted; but in doing this, they often eliminated material that could have made their poetry more accessible to readers.

IDENTIFY

What was "new" about the journalism of the 1960s? Underline the sentence that gives you the answer.

IDENTIFY

Circle at least three characteristics of modernist poetry, as it was defined by Eliot and Pound.

NFER

hat do you think Lowell eant by characterizing the 50s as "tranquilized"?

NTERPRET

e-read lines 170–174. How oes *Howl* seem to challenge e modernist principles stablished by T. S. Eliot (lines 46–149)?

By the early 1950s, though, there was a growing sense that modernism was somehow becoming played out, that it was no longer appropriate for the times. The era itself may have had something to do with the shift away from modernism. A generation had returned from war to a country where conformity and material success were predominant values. The Soviet Union and the atomic bomb worried Americans in the late 1940s and early 1950s, but acquiring a house and a car and making money were generally of more immediate importance. "These are the tranquilized *Fifties,*" wrote poet Robert Lowell (1917–1977).

By the early 1950s, many writers and readers felt that modernist poetry—impersonal, allusive, difficult—was no longer appropriate. The times called for a more personal and accessible approach that challenged complacency and convention.

The Beat Poets. In 1956, a long poem called *Howl* was published by Allen Ginsberg (1926–1997), who could by no stretch of the imagination be described as dull. A cry of outrage against the conformity of the 1950s, *Howl* was as far removed from the safe confines of modernism as could be imagined. It begins, "I saw the best minds of my generation destroyed by madness, starving hysterical naked," and it continues at the same intense pitch for hundreds of lines.

Together with *On the Road* (1957), Jack Kerouac's novel celebrating the bohemian life, *Howl* quickly became a kind of bible for young nonconformists known as the Beat Generation. Beat poetry and the Beat lifestyle of poetry readings, jazz, and late-night coffeehouses in San Francisco and New York's Greenwich Village had an immediate impact on American popular culture. *Life* magazine even ran illustrated stories about the new bohemians. Many of Ginsberg's concerns—the injustices of modern life, the importance of the imagination—would become the principal themes of poetry a decade later.

Poetry and personal experience. In 1959, Robert Lowell published *Life Studies,* one of the most important and influential volumes of verse to appear since World War II. These poems are about personal experiences that modernist poets had avoided dealing with directly: emotional problems, alcoholism, illness, and depression. In *Life Studies,* Lowell clearly and decisively broke with Eliot's theory that poetry should be impersonal; in doing so, he helped to reunite, both for himself and for other writers, "the man who suffers and the mind which creates."

Shortly after *Life Studies* appeared, a critic described Lowell's poems as "confessional." The label stuck, and the **Confessional School** of poets, mostly friends or students of Lowell, was officially born. These poets—including John Berryman (1914–1972), Anne Sexton (1928–1974), and Sylvia Plath (1932–1963)—wrote frank, sometimes brutal poems about their private lives. Nothing could have been further from Eliot's model.

INFER
How did the poems of the Confessional School differ from Eliot's model?

Landmarks in the revolt against modernist poetry include Allen Ginsberg's* Howl *(1956) and Robert Lowell's* Life Studies *(1959), both of which deal vividly with the poets' personal experience. The Confessional School of poets, which included Lowell, Plath, and Sexton, wrote frank and revealing poems about their private lives.

A time of diversity. Since the 1970s, American poetry has been characterized by diversity. Much contemporary poetry reflects a democratic quality, often influenced by the works of Walt Whitman and William Carlos Williams. Poetry lives in the people, contemporary poets seem to say, and any walk of life, any everyday experience, any style of expression can result in authentic poetry. These poets often write in the vernacular, the language of common speech, and do not hesitate to surprise or even shock with their language, attitudes, and details of their private lives.

Poetry today is anything but impersonal.

Where the Present Meets the Past on the Way to the Future

The literature that captures a wide audience often does so by offering a fresh voice and a new attitude, for these are the powerful needs of each new generation. Yet much of contemporary American literature still deals with the same themes that concerned our greatest writers of the nineteenth century. "The invariable mark of wisdom," Emerson wrote, "is to find the miraculous in the common." But it is more difficult to find transcendent spiritual values in the cheap clutter of modern life than it was in the woods around Emerson's Concord. "I find myself . . . circling back to man's religious nature," novelist John Updike has written of his own work, "and the real loss to man and art alike when that nature has nowhere to plug itself in. . . ." These words could serve to describe the work of a great number of contemporary writers whose intellectual roots can be traced to the Transcendentalists of the nineteenth century, and even further back to those hardy, practical Puritans who braved that two-month voyage in a small wooden boat.

CONNECT
Do you agree or disagree with Updike's assertion that our "religious nature . . . has nowhere to plug itself in" these days? Briefly explain.

The Magic Barrel

Make the Connection

Tell Me Why . . .

Why do people fall in love? Poets, philosophers, popular songwriters, and just about everybody else have been pondering that question for a long time. Do you have an answer of your own? Is love purely emotional? Does it involve the mind as well as the heart? Can deep emotional connections exist between people who, on the surface, inhabit very different worlds? On the lines below, write down some of your ideas about the subject.

Bernard Malamud

The Magic Barrel

ORDS TO OWN

ager (mē′gər) *adj.:* poor, dequate.

DENTIFY

at is Finkle's **motivation** marriage? Underline the swer.

Not long ago there lived in uptown New York, in a small, almost meager room, though crowded with books, Leo Finkle, a rabbinical student in the Yeshivah University.[1] Finkle, after six years of study, was to be ordained in June and had been advised by an acquaintance that he might find it easier to win himself a congregation if he were married. Since he had no present prospects of marriage, after two tormented days of turning it over in his mind, he called in Pinye Salzman, a marriage broker whose two-line advertisement he had read in the *Forward.*[2]

The matchmaker appeared one night out of the dark fourth-floor hallway of the graystone rooming house where Finkle lived, grasping a black, strapped portfolio that had been worn thin with use. Salzman, who had been long in the business, was of slight but dignified build, wearing an old hat, and an overcoat too short and tight for him. He smelled frankly of fish, which he loved to eat, and although he was missing a few teeth, his presence was not displeasing, because of an amiable manner curiously contrasted with mournful eyes. His voice, his lips, his wisp of beard, his bony fingers were animated, but give him a moment of repose and his mild blue eyes revealed a depth of sadness, a characteristic that put Leo a little at ease although the situation, for him, was inherently tense.

He at once informed Salzman why he had asked him to come, explaining that his home was in Cleveland, and that but for his parents, who had married comparatively late in life, he was alone in the world. He had for six years devoted himself almost entirely to his studies, as a result of which, understandably, he had found himself without time for a social life and the company of young women. Therefore he thought it the better part of trial and error—of embarrassing fumbling—to call in an experienced person to advise him on these matters. He remarked in passing that the function of the marriage broker was ancient and honorable, highly approved in the Jewish community, because it made practical the necessary without hindering joy. Moreover, his own parents had been brought together by a matchmaker. They had made, if not a financially profitable marriage—since neither had possessed any worldly goods to speak of—at least a successful one in the sense of their everlasting devotion to each other. Salzman listened in embarrassed surprise, sensing a sort of apology. Later, however, he experienced a glow of pride in his work, an emotion that had left him years ago, and he heartily approved of Finkle.

The two went to their business. Leo had led Salzman to the only clear place in the room, a table near a window that overlooked the lamp-lit city. He seated himself at the matchmaker's side but facing him,

1. **Yeshivah** (ye·shē′və) **University:** prominent New York City school serving both as a general college and as a seminary for Orthodox Jewish rabbis.
2. ***Forward:*** formerly the *Jewish Daily Forward,* a newspaper published in New York City.

attempting by an act of will to suppress the unpleasant tickle in his throat. Salzman eagerly unstrapped his portfolio and removed a loose rubber band from a thin packet of much-handled cards. As he flipped through them, a gesture and sound that physically hurt Leo, the student pretended not to see and gazed steadfastly out the window. Although it was still February, winter was on its last legs, signs of which he had for the first time in years begun to notice. He now observed the round white moon, moving high in the sky through a cloud menagerie, and watched with half-open mouth as it penetrated a huge hen, and dropped out of her like an egg laying itself. Salzman, though pretending through eyeglasses he had just slipped on, to be engaged in scanning the writing on the cards, stole occasional glances at the young man's distinguished face, noting with pleasure the long, severe scholar's nose, brown eyes heavy with learning, sensitive yet ascetic lips, and a certain, almost hollow quality of the dark cheeks. He gazed around at shelves upon shelves of books and let out a soft, contented sigh.

When Leo's eyes fell upon the cards, he counted six spread out in Salzman's hand.

"So few?" he asked in disappointment.

"You wouldn't believe me how much cards I got in my office," Salzman replied. "The drawers are already filled to the top, so I keep them now in a barrel, but is every girl good for a new rabbi?"

Leo blushed at this, regretting all he had revealed of himself in a curriculum vitae[3] he had sent to Salzman. He had thought it best to acquaint him with his strict standards and specifications, but in having done so, felt he had told the marriage broker more than was absolutely necessary.

He hesitantly inquired, "Do you keep photographs of your clients on file?"

"First comes family, amount of dowry, also what kind promises," Salzman replied, unbuttoning his tight coat and settling himself in the chair. "After comes pictures, rabbi."

"Call me Mr. Finkle. I'm not yet a rabbi."

Salzman said he would, but instead called him doctor, which he changed to rabbi when Leo was not listening too attentively.

Salzman adjusted his horn-rimmed spectacles, gently cleared his throat and read in an eager voice the contents of the top card:

"Sophie P. Twenty four year. Widow one year. No children. Educated high school and two years college. Father promises eight thousand dollars. Has wonderful wholesale business. Also real estate. On the mother's side comes teachers, also one actor. Well known on Second Avenue."

---

3. ***curriculum vitae*** (kə·rik′yo͞o·ləm vīt′ē): Latin for "course of life"; that is, a résumé or summary of one's career and qualifications.

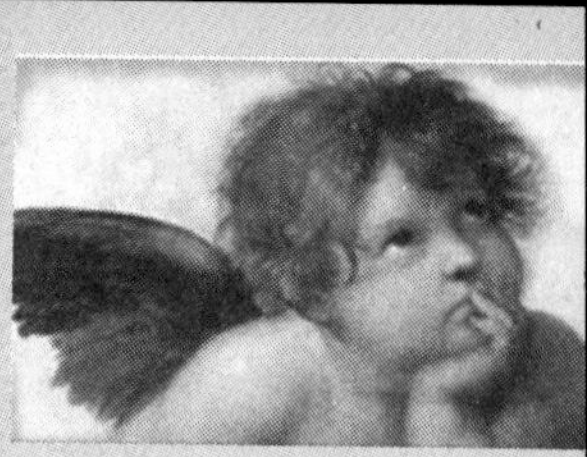

INTERPRET

How does Finkle feel about using a marriage broker to fin a bride? Which details reveal the answer?

WORDS TO OWN

suppress (sə·pres′) *v.:* to restrain; hold back.
ascetic (ə·set′ik) *adj.:* severe; stern.

IDENTIFY

Which detail in this passage helps to explain the story's title? Underline the words giving the answer.

WORDS TO OWN

dowry (dou′rē) *n.:* money or goods that a bride brings with her in a marriage.

INFER

Why does Salzman keep calling Leo "rabbi" and "doctor"?

NTERPRET

hat difference of opinion
oout the bride's qualifications
o you notice between Finkle
nd Salzman?

INFER

/hat does an "Americanized
amily" imply, and why
ould it offer a wonderful
pportunity, according
o Salzman?

RETELL

How would you say, "I know
what I'm talking" (line 124)
in standard English?

Leo gazed up in surprise. "Did you say a widow?"

"A widow don't mean spoiled, rabbi. She lived with her husband maybe four months. He was a sick boy she made a mistake to marry him."

"Marrying a widow has never entered my mind."

"This is because you have no experience. A widow, especially if she is young and healthy like this girl, is a wonderful person to marry. She will be thankful to you the rest of her life. Believe me, if I was looking now for a bride, I would marry a widow."

Leo reflected, then shook his head.

Salzman hunched his shoulders in an almost imperceptible gesture of disappointment. He placed the card down on the wooden table and began to read another:

"Lily H. High school teacher. Regular. Not a substitute. Has savings and new Dodge car. Lived in Paris one year. Father is successful dentist thirty-five years. Interested in professional man. Well Americanized family. Wonderful opportunity.

"I knew her personally," said Salzman. "I wish you could see this girl. She is a doll. Also very intelligent. All day you could talk to her about books and theater and what not. She also knows current events."

"I don't believe you mentioned her age?"

"Her age?" Salzman said, raising his brows. "Her age is thirty-two years."

Leo said after a while, "I'm afraid that seems a little too old."

Salzman let out a laugh. "So how old are you, rabbi?"

"Twenty-seven."

"So what is the difference, tell me, between twenty-seven and thirty-two? My own wife is seven years older than me. So what did I suffer?—Nothing. If a Rothschild's[4] daughter wants to marry you, would you say on account her age, no?"

"Yes," Leo said dryly.

Salzman shook off the no in the yes. "Five years don't mean a thing. I give you my word that when you will live with her for one week you will forget her age. What does it mean five years—that she lived more and knows more than somebody who is younger? On this girl, God bless her, years are not wasted. Each one that it comes makes better the bargain."

"What subject does she teach in high school?"

"Languages. If you heard the way she speaks French, you will think it is music. I am in the business twenty-five years, and I recommend her with my whole heart. Believe me, I know what I'm talking, rabbi."

"What's on the next card?" Leo said abruptly.

Salzman reluctantly turned up the third card:

---

4. **Rothschild's:** The Rothschilds are a wealthy banking family.

"Ruth K. Nineteen years. Honor student. Father offers thirteen thousand cash to the right bridegroom. He is a medical doctor. Stomach specialist with marvelous practice. Brother-in-law owns own garment business. Particular people."

Salzman looked as if he had read his trump card.

"Did you say nineteen?" Leo asked with interest.

"On the dot."

"Is she attractive?" He blushed. "Pretty?"

Salzman kissed his finger tips. "A little doll. On this I give you my word. Let me call the father tonight and you will see what means pretty."

But Leo was troubled. "You're sure she's that young?"

"This I am positive. The father will show you the birth certificate."

"Are you positive there isn't something wrong with her?" Leo insisted.

"Who says there is wrong?"

"I don't understand why an American girl her age should go to a marriage broker."

A smile spread over Salzman's face.

"So for the same reason you went, she comes."

Leo flushed. "I am pressed for time."

Salzman, realizing he had been tactless, quickly explained. "The father came, not her. He wants she should have the best, so he looks around himself. When we will locate the right boy he will introduce him and encourage. This makes a better marriage than if a young girl without experience takes for herself. I don't have to tell you this."

"But don't you think this young girl believes in love?" Leo spoke uneasily.

Salzman was about to guffaw but caught himself and said soberly, "Love comes with the right person, not before."

Leo parted dry lips but did not speak. Noticing that Salzman had snatched a glance at the next card, he cleverly asked, "How is her health?"

"Perfect," Salzman said, breathing with difficulty. "Of course, she is a little lame on her right foot from an auto accident that it happened to her when she was twelve years, but nobody notices on account she is so brilliant and also beautiful."

Leo got up heavily and went to the window. He felt curiously bitter and upbraided himself for having called in the marriage broker. Finally, he shook his head.

"Why not?" Salzman persisted, the pitch of his voice rising.

"Because I detest stomach specialists."

"So what do you care what is his business? After you marry her do you need him? Who says he must come every Friday night in your house?"

INFER

Why does Leo think that a young American girl would not go to a matchmaker?

INTERPRET

What does this question (line 153) reveal about Finkle's character? What does Salzman's response reveal about his character?

WORDS TO OWN

upbraided (up·brād′id) *v.:* severely criticized.

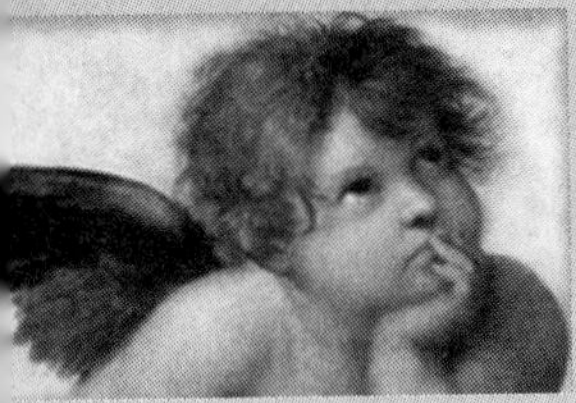

ORDS TO OWN
entele (klī′ən·tel′) *n.:*
stomers.

NTERPRET
nat does the phrase
ommercial cupid" (line 189)
ggest about Salzman?

EVALUATE
ı Yiddish literature, the
atchmaker is a figure who is
artly comic, partly tragic, and
sually teetering at the edge
f destitution. The matchmaker
, often a sufferer nursing a
ecret sorrow. How well does
ne figure of Salzman fit into
nis tradition?

Ashamed of the way the talk was going, Leo dismissed Salzman, who went home with heavy, melancholy eyes.

Though he had felt only relief at the marriage broker's departure, Leo was in low spirits the next day. He explained it as arising from Salzman's failure to produce a suitable bride for him. He did not care for his type of clientele. But when Leo found himself hesitating whether to seek out another matchmaker, one more polished than Pinye, he wondered if it could be—his protestations to the contrary, and although he honored his father and mother—that he did not, in essence, care for the matchmaking institution? This thought he quickly put out of mind yet found himself still upset. All day he ran around in the woods—missed an important appointment, forgot to give out his laundry, walked out of a Broadway cafeteria without paying and had to run back with the ticket in his hand; had even not recognized his landlady in the street when she passed with a friend and courteously called out, "A good evening to you, Doctor Finkle." By nightfall, however, he had regained sufficient calm to sink his nose into a book and there found peace from his thoughts.

Almost at once there came a knock on the door. Before Leo could say enter, Salzman, commercial cupid, was standing in the room. His face was gray and meager, his expression hungry, and he looked as if he would expire on his feet. Yet the marriage broker managed, by some trick of the muscles, to display a broad smile.

"So good evening. I am invited?"

Leo nodded, disturbed to see him again, yet unwilling to ask the man to leave.

Beaming still, Salzman laid his portfolio on the table. "Rabbi, I got for you tonight good news."

"I've asked you not to call me rabbi. I'm still a student."

"Your worries are finished. I have for you a first-class bride."

"Leave me in peace concerning this subject." Leo pretended lack of interest.

"The world will dance at your wedding."

"Please, Mr. Salzman, no more."

"But first must come back my strength," Salzman said weakly. He fumbled with the portfolio straps and took out of the leather case an oily paper bag, from which he extracted a hard, seeded roll and a small, smoked whitefish. With a quick motion of his hand he stripped the fish out of its skin and began ravenously to chew. "All day in a rush," he muttered.

Leo watched him eat.

"A sliced tomato you have maybe?" Salzman hesitantly inquired.

"No."

The marriage broker shut his eyes and ate. When he had finished he carefully cleaned up the crumbs and rolled up the remains of the fish, in the paper bag. His spectacled eyes roamed the room until he discovered, amid some piles of books, a one-burner gas stove. Lifting his hat he humbly asked, "A glass tea you got, rabbi?"

Conscience-stricken, Leo rose and brewed the tea. He served it with a chunk of lemon and two cubes of lump sugar, delighting Salzman.

After he had drunk his tea, Salzman's strength and good spirits were restored.

"So tell me, rabbi," he said amiably, "you considered some more the three clients I mentioned yesterday?"

"There was no need to consider."

"Why not?"

"None of them suits me."

"What then suits you?"

Leo let it pass because he could give only a confused answer.

Without waiting for a reply, Salzman asked, "You remember this girl I talked to you—the high school teacher?"

"Age thirty-two?"

But, surprisingly, Salzman's face lit in a smile. "Age twenty-nine."

Leo shot him a look. "Reduced from thirty-two?"

"A mistake," Salzman avowed. "I talked today with the dentist. He took me to his safety deposit box and showed me the birth certificate. She was twenty-nine years last August. They made her a party in the mountains where she went for her vacation. When her father spoke to me the first time I forgot to write the age and I told you thirty-two, but now I remember this was a different client, a widow."

"The same one you told me about? I thought she was twenty-four?"

"A different. Am I responsible that the world is filled with widows?"

"No, but I'm not interested in them, nor for that matter, in school teachers."

Salzman pulled his clasped hands to his breast. Looking at the ceiling he devoutly exclaimed, "Yiddishe kinder,[5] what can I say to somebody that he is not interested in high school teachers? So what then you are interested?"

Leo flushed but controlled himself.

"In what else will you be interested," Salzman went on, "if you not interested in this fine girl that she speaks four languages and has personally in the bank ten thousand dollars? Also her father guarantees further twelve thousand. Also she has a new car, wonderful clothes, talks on all subjects, and she will give you a first-class home and children. How near do we come in our life to paradise?"

"If she's so wonderful, why wasn't she married ten years ago?"

"Why?" said Salzman with a heavy laugh. "—Why? Because she is *partikiler*. This is why. She wants the *best*."

5. ***Yiddishe kinder:*** Yiddish for "Jewish children."

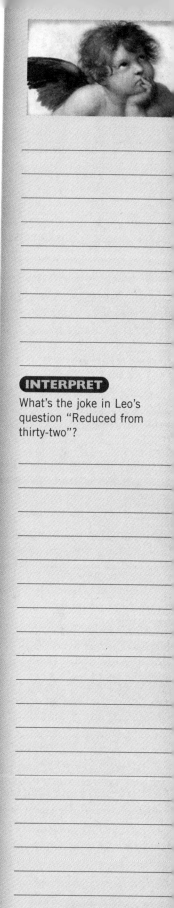

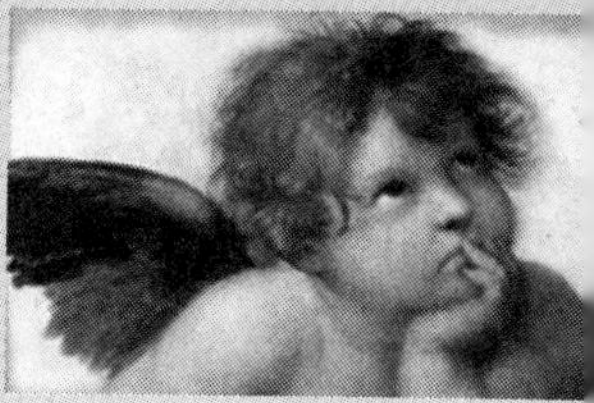

INTERPRET

What's the joke in Leo's question "Reduced from thirty-two"?

ORDS TO OWN
uptial (nup′shəl) *adj.:* related
weddings or marriage.

INTERPRET
hat do you think is
lalamud's purpose in having
eo suspect that Salzman is
atching him?

PREDICT
s lines 282–283 indicate,
ily has arrived at a point
here she chooses to speak
er feelings honestly, without
games or distortions. Can the
same be said of Finkle? If not,
do you think he will change?

WORDS TO OWN
traditional (trə·dish′ə·nəl) *adj.:*
established; customary.

Leo was silent, amused at how he had entangled himself. But Salzman had aroused his interest in Lily H., and he began seriously to consider calling on her. When the marriage broker observed how intently Leo's mind was at work on the facts he had supplied, he felt certain they would soon come to an agreement.

Late Saturday afternoon, conscious of Salzman, Leo Finkle walked with Lily Hirschorn along Riverside Drive. He walked briskly and erectly, wearing with distinction the black fedora he had that morning taken with trepidation out of the dusty hat box on his closet shelf, and the heavy black Saturday coat he had thoroughly whisked clean. Leo also owned a walking stick, a present from a distant relative, but quickly put temptation aside and did not use it. Lily, petite and not unpretty, had on something signifying the approach of spring. She was au courant,[6] animatedly, with all sorts of subjects, and he weighed her words and found her surprisingly sound—score another for Salzman, whom he uneasily sensed to be somewhere around, hiding perhaps high in a tree along the street, flashing the lady signals with a pocket mirror; or perhaps a cloven-hoofed Pan,[7] piping nuptial ditties as he danced his invisible way before them, strewing wild buds on the walk and purple grapes in their path, symbolizing fruit of a union, though there was of course still none.

Lily startled Leo by remarking, "I was thinking of Mr. Salzman, a curious figure, wouldn't you say?"

Not certain what to answer, he nodded.

She bravely went on, blushing, "I for one am grateful for his introducing us. Aren't you?"

He courteously replied, "I am."

"I mean," she said with a little laugh—and it was all in good taste, or at least gave the effect of being not in bad—"do you mind that we came together so?"

He was not displeased with her honesty, recognizing that she meant to set the relationship aright, and understanding that it took a certain amount of experience in life, and courage, to want to do it quite that way. One had to have some sort of past to make that kind of beginning.

He said that he did not mind. Salzman's function was traditional and honorable—valuable for what it might achieve, which, he pointed out, was frequently nothing.

Lily agreed with a sigh. They walked on for a while and she said after a long silence, again with a nervous laugh, "Would you mind if I asked you something a little bit personal? Frankly, I find the subject

---

6. ***au courant*** (ō ko͞o·rän′): French for "in the current," that is, up-to-date on news or events.
7. **Pan:** in Greek mythology, a god associated with forests, pastures, flocks, and shepherds. Pan is usually pictured as having the legs, horns, and ears of a goat, and the head and upper body of a man. He plays music on reed pipes.

fascinating." Although Leo shrugged, she went on half embarrassedly, "How was it that you came to your calling? I mean was it a sudden passionate inspiration?"

Leo, after a time, slowly replied, "I was always interested in the Law."[8]

"You saw revealed in it the presence of the Highest?"

He nodded and changed the subject. "I understand that you spent a little time in Paris, Miss Hirschorn?"

"Oh, did Mr. Salzman tell you, Rabbi Finkle?" Leo winced but she went on, "It was ages ago and almost forgotten. I remember I had to return for my sister's wedding."

And Lily would not be put off. "When," she asked in a trembly voice, "did you become enamored of God?"

He stared at her. Then it came to him that she was talking not about Leo Finkle, but of a total stranger, some mystical figure, perhaps even passionate prophet that Salzman had dreamed up for her—no relation to the living or dead. Leo trembled with rage and weakness. The trickster had obviously sold her a bill of goods, just as he had him, who'd expected to become acquainted with a young lady of twenty-nine, only to behold, the moment he laid eyes upon her strained and anxious face, a woman past thirty-five and aging rapidly. Only his self-control had kept him this long in her presence.

"I am not," he said gravely, "a talented religious person," and in seeking words to go on, found himself possessed by shame and fear. "I think," he said in a strained manner, "that I came to God not because I loved Him, but because I did not."

This confession he spoke harshly because its unexpectedness shook him.

Lily wilted. Leo saw a profusion of loaves of bread go flying like ducks high over his head, not unlike the winged loaves by which he had counted himself to sleep last night. Mercifully, then, it snowed, which he would not put past Salzman's machinations.

He was infuriated with the marriage broker and swore he would throw him out of the room the minute he reappeared. But Salzman did not come that night, and when Leo's anger had subsided, an unaccountable despair grew in its place. At first he thought this was caused by his disappointment in Lily, but before long it became evident that he had involved himself with Salzman without a true knowledge of his own intent. He gradually realized—with an emptiness that seized him with six hands—that he had called in the broker to find him a bride because he was incapable of doing it himself. This terrifying insight he had derived as a result of his meeting and conversation with Lily

8. **Law:** first five books of the Bible, the most sacred texts of Judaism. These books are also called the Torah or the Five Books of Moses.

INTERPRET

What uncomfortable realizatic has just struck Leo?

INTERPRET

Explain why Leo came to be a rabbinical student.

WORDS TO OWN

machinations (mak'ə·nā'shənz) *n. pl.:* plots; schemes.

WORDS TO OWN

evident (ev'ə·dənt) *adj.:* clear; obvious.

Hirschorn. Her probing questions had somehow irritated him into revealing—to himself more than her—the true nature of his relationship to God, and from that it had come upon him, with shocking force, that apart from his parents, he had never loved anyone. Or perhaps it went the other way, that he did not love God so well as he might, because he had not loved man. It seemed to Leo that his whole life stood starkly revealed and he saw himself for the first time as he truly was—unloved and loveless. This bitter but somehow not fully unexpected revelation brought him to a point of panic, controlled only by extraordinary effort. He covered his face with his hands and cried.

The week that followed was the worst of his life. He did not eat and lost weight. His beard darkened and grew ragged. He stopped attending seminars and almost never opened a book. He seriously considered leaving the Yeshivah, although he was deeply troubled at the thought of the loss of all his years of study—saw them like pages torn from a book, strewn over the city—and at the devastating effect of this decision upon his parents. But he had lived without knowledge of himself, and never in the Five Books and all the Commentaries—mea culpa[9]—had the truth been revealed to him. He did not know where to turn, and in all this desolating loneliness there was no *to whom,* although he often thought of Lily but not once could bring himself to go downstairs and make the call. He became touchy and irritable, especially with his landlady, who asked him all manner of personal questions; on the other hand, sensing his own disagreeableness, he waylaid her on the stairs and apologized abjectly, until mortified, she ran from him. Out of this, however, he drew the consolation that he was a Jew and that a Jew suffered. But gradually, as the long and terrible week drew to a close, he regained his composure and some idea of purpose in life: to go on as planned. Although he was imperfect, the ideal was not. As for his quest of a bride, the thought of continuing afflicted him with anxiety and heartburn, yet perhaps with this new knowledge of himself he would be more successful than in the past. Perhaps love would now come to him and a bride to that love. And for this sanctified seeking who needed a Salzman?

The marriage broker, a skeleton with haunted eyes, returned that very night. He looked, withal, the picture of frustrated expectancy—as if he had steadfastly waited the week at Miss Lily Hirschorn's side for a telephone call that never came.

Casually coughing, Salzman came immediately to the point: "So how did you like her?"

Leo's anger rose and he could not refrain from chiding the matchmaker: "Why did you lie to me, Salzman?"

Salzman's pale face went dead white, the world had snowed on him.

INTERPRET

/hat important change ccurs in Leo's character t this point?

IDENTIFY

Vithal, a word often seen in ihakespeare, is rarely used oy contemporary American vriters. What are some neanings of this word? Use a dictionary if necessary.

9. ***mea culpa*** (mā′ä ko͞ol′pä): Latin for "by my fault."

"Did you not state that she was twenty-nine?" Leo insisted.

"I give you my word—"

"She was thirty-five, if a day. *At least* thirty-five."

"Of this don't be too sure. Her father told me—"

"Never mind. The worst of it was that you lied to her."

"How did I lie to her, tell me?"

"You told her things about me that weren't true. You made me out to be more, consequently less than I am. She had in mind a totally different person, a sort of semi-mystical Wonder Rabbi."

"All I said, you was a religious man."

"I can imagine."

Salzman sighed. "This is my weakness that I have," he confessed. "My wife says to me I shouldn't be a salesman, but when I have two fine people that they would be wonderful to be married, I am so happy that I talk too much." He smiled wanly. "This is why Salzman is a poor man."

Leo's anger left him. "Well, Salzman, I'm afraid that's all."

The marriage broker fastened hungry eyes on him.

"You don't want any more a bride?"

"I do," said Leo, "but I have decided to seek her in a different way. I am no longer interested in an arranged marriage. To be frank, I now admit the necessity of premarital love. That is, I want to be in love with the one I marry."

"Love?" said Salzman, astounded. After a moment he remarked, "For us, our love is our life, not for the ladies. In the ghetto they—"

"I know, I know," said Leo. "I've thought of it often. Love, I have said to myself, should be a by-product of living and worship rather than its own end. Yet for myself I find it necessary to establish the level of my need and fulfill it."

Salzman shrugged but answered, "Listen, rabbi, if you want love, this I can find for you also. I have such beautiful clients that you will love them the minute your eyes will see them."

Leo smiled unhappily. "I'm afraid you don't understand."

But Salzman hastily unstrapped his portfolio and withdrew a manila packet from it.

"Pictures," he said, quickly laying the envelope on the table.

Leo called after him to take the pictures away, but as if on the wings of the wind, Salzman had disappeared.

March came. Leo had returned to his regular routine. Although he felt not quite himself yet—lacked energy—he was making plans for a more active social life. Of course it would cost something, but he was an expert in cutting corners; and when there were no corners left he would make circles rounder. All the while Salzman's pictures had lain on the table, gathering dust. Occasionally as Leo sat studying, or enjoying a cup of tea, his eyes fell on the manila envelope, but he never opened it.

INTERPRET

What does "You made me out to be more, consequently less than I am" mean?

EVALUATE

How do Salzman and Finkle differ in their opinion of romantic love? Which perspective do you agree with?

IDENTIFY

What does the idiom "to cut corners" mean?

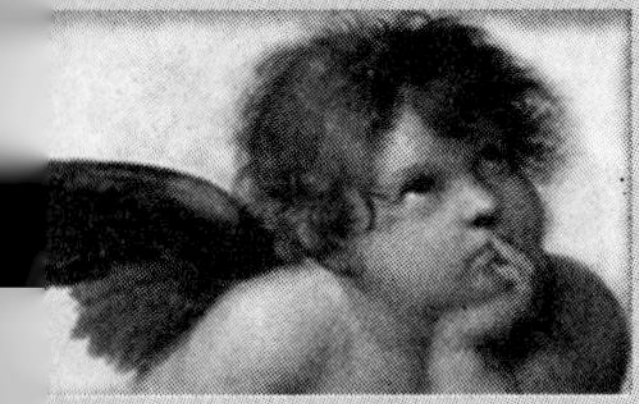

BUILD FLUENCY

ead lines 425–441 aloud as :pressively as you can. As you ·actice your reading, keep in ind that the passage presents crucial event in the plot.

INFER

/here do you think Leo might ave seen the woman in the hotograph or someone esembling her?

INTERPRET

This is a moment of dynamic :hange for Leo. What is he :xperiencing?. Why does he hink this change is somehow evil (line 460)?

The days went by and no social life to speak of developed with a member of the opposite sex—it was difficult, given the circumstances of his situation. One morning Leo toiled up the stairs to his room and stared out the window at the city. Although the day was bright his view of it was dark. For some time he watched the people in the street below hurrying along and then turned with a heavy heart to his little room. On the table was the packet. With a sudden relentless gesture he tore it open. For a half-hour he stood by the table in a state of excitement, examining the photographs of the ladies Salzman had included. Finally, with a deep sigh he put them down. There were six, of varying degrees of attractiveness, but look at them long enough and they all became Lily Hirschorn: all past their prime, all starved behind bright smiles, not a true personality in the lot. Life, despite their frantic yoohooings, had passed them by; they were pictures in a briefcase that stank of fish. After a while, however, as Leo attempted to return the photographs into the envelope, he found in it another, a snapshot of the type taken by a machine for a quarter. He gazed at it a moment and let out a cry.

Her face deeply moved him. Why, he could at first not say. It gave him the impression of youth—spring flowers, yet age—a sense of having been used to the bone, wasted; this came from the eyes, which were hauntingly familiar, yet absolutely strange. He had a vivid impression that he had met her before, but try as he might he could not place her although he could almost recall her name, as if he had read it in her own handwriting. No, this couldn't be; he would have remembered her. It was not, he affirmed, that she had an extraordinary beauty—no, though her face was attractive enough; it was that *something* about her moved him. Feature for feature, even some of the ladies of the photographs could do better; but she leaped forth to his heart—had *lived,* or wanted to—more than just wanted, perhaps regretted how she had lived—had somehow deeply suffered: It could be seen in the depths of those reluctant eyes, and from the way the light enclosed and shone from her, and within her, opening realms of possibility: This was her own. Her he desired. His head ached and eyes narrowed with the intensity of his gazing, then as if an obscure fog had blown up in the mind, he experienced fear of her and was aware that he had received an impression, somehow, of evil. He shuddered, saying softly, it is thus with us all. Leo brewed some tea in a small pot and sat sipping it without sugar, to calm himself. But before he had finished drinking, again with excitement he examined the face and found it good: good for Leo Finkle. Only such a one could understand him and help him seek whatever he was seeking. She might, perhaps, love him. How she had happened to be among the discards in Salzman's barrel he could never guess, but he knew he must urgently go find her.

Leo rushed downstairs, grabbed up the Bronx[10] telephone book, and searched for Salzman's home address. He was not listed, nor was his office. Neither was he in the Manhattan[11] book. But Leo remembered having written down the address on a slip of paper after he had read Salzman's advertisement in the "personals" column of the *Forward.* He ran up to his room and tore through his papers, without luck. It was exasperating. Just when he needed the matchmaker he was nowhere to be found. Fortunately Leo remembered to look in his wallet. There on a card he found his name written and a Bronx address. No phone number was listed, the reason—Leo now recalled—he had originally communicated with Salzman by letter. He got on his coat, put a hat on over his skullcap and hurried to the subway station. All the way to the far end of the Bronx he sat on the edge of his seat. He was more than once tempted to take out the picture and see if the girl's face was as he remembered it, but he refrained, allowing the snapshot to remain in his inside coat pocket, content to have her so close. When the train pulled into the station he was waiting at the door and bolted out. He quickly located the street Salzman had advertised.

The building he sought was less than a block from the subway, but it was not an office building, nor even a loft, nor a store in which one could rent office space. It was a very old tenement house. Leo found Salzman's name in pencil on a soiled tag under the bell and climbed three dark flights to his apartment. When he knocked, the door was opened by a thin, asthmatic, gray-haired woman, in felt slippers.

"Yes?" she said, expecting nothing. She listened without listening. He could have sworn he had seen her, too, before but knew it was an illusion.

"Salzman—does he live here? Pinye Salzman," he said, "the matchmaker?"

She stared at him a long minute. "Of course."

He felt embarrassed. "Is he in?"

"No." Her mouth, though left open, offered nothing more.

"The matter is urgent. Can you tell me where his office is?"

"In the air." She pointed upward.

"You mean he has no office?" Leo asked.

"In his socks."

He peered into the apartment. It was sunless and dingy, one large room divided by a half-open curtain, beyond which he could see a sagging metal bed. The near side of the room was crowded with rickety chairs, old bureaus, a three-legged table, racks of cooking utensils, and all the apparatus of a kitchen. But there was no sign of Salzman or his magic barrel, probably also a figment of the imagination. An odor of

10. **Bronx:** borough of New York City.
11. **Manhattan:** borough of New York City, south of the Bronx.

INTERPRET

What does Mrs. Salzman mean when she says her husband's office is "in the air" and "in his socks"?

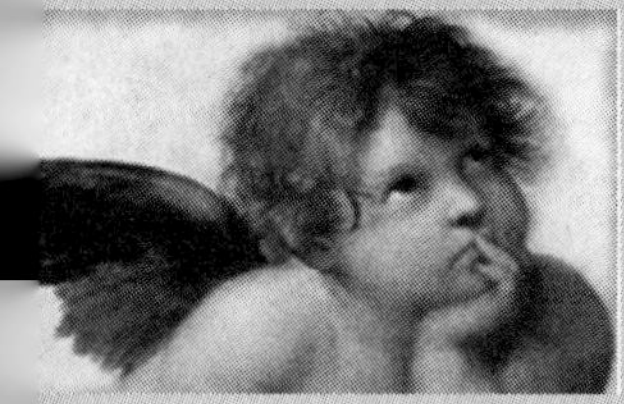

INTERPRET

:alzman tries to steer Leo way from the woman in the hoto. Has Salzman changed, r is this just a new twist on is former character?

frying fish made Leo weak to the knees.

"Where is he?" he insisted. "I've got to see your husband."

At length she answered, "So who knows where he is? Every time he thinks a new thought he runs to a different place. Go home, he will find you."

"Tell him Leo Finkle."

She gave no sign she had heard.

He walked downstairs, depressed.

But Salzman, breathless, stood waiting at his door.

Leo was astounded and overjoyed. "How did you get here before me?"

"I rushed."

"Come inside."

They entered. Leo fixed tea, and a sardine sandwich for Salzman. As they were drinking he reached behind him for the packet of pictures and handed them to the marriage broker.

Salzman put down his glass and said expectantly, "You found somebody you like?"

"Not among these."

The marriage broker turned away.

"Here is the one I want." Leo held forth the snapshot.

Salzman slipped on his glasses and took the picture into his trembling hand. He turned ghastly and let out a groan.

"What's the matter?" cried Leo.

"Excuse me. Was an accident this picture. She isn't for you."

Salzman frantically shoved the manila packet into his portfolio. He thrust the snapshot into his pocket and fled down the stairs.

Leo, after momentary paralysis, gave chase and cornered the marriage broker in the vestibule. The landlady made hysterical outcries but neither of them listened.

"Give me back the picture, Salzman."

"No." The pain in his eyes was terrible.

"Tell me who she is then."

"This I can't tell you. Excuse me."

He made to depart, but Leo, forgetting himself, seized the matchmaker by his tight coat and shook him frenziedly.

"Please," sighed Salzman. "*Please.*"

Leo ashamedly let him go. "Tell me who she is," he begged. "It's very important for me to know."

"She is not for you. She is a wild one—wild, without shame. This is not a bride for a rabbi."

"What do you mean wild?"

"Like an animal. Like a dog. For her to be poor was a sin. This is why to me she is dead now."

"In God's name, what do you mean?"

"Her I can't introduce to you," Salzman cried.

"Why are you so excited?"

"Why, he asks," Salzman said, bursting into tears. "This is my baby, my Stella, she should burn in hell."

Leo hurried up to bed and hid under the covers. Under the covers he thought his life through. Although he soon fell asleep he could not sleep her out of his mind. He woke, beating his breast. Though he prayed to be rid of her, his prayers went unanswered. Through days of torment he endlessly struggled not to love her; fearing success, he escaped it. He then concluded to convert her to goodness, himself to God. The idea alternately nauseated and exalted him.

He perhaps did not know that he had come to a final decision until he encountered Salzman in a Broadway cafeteria. He was sitting alone at a rear table, sucking the bony remains of a fish. The marriage broker appeared haggard, and transparent to the point of vanishing.

Salzman looked up at first without recognizing him. Leo had grown a pointed beard and his eyes were weighted with wisdom.

"Salzman," he said, "love has at last come to my heart."

"Who can love from a picture?" mocked the marriage broker.

"It is not impossible."

"If you can love her, then you can love anybody. Let me show you some new clients that they just sent me their photographs. One is a little doll."

"Just her I want," Leo murmured.

"Don't be a fool, doctor. Don't bother with her."

"Put me in touch with her, Salzman," Leo said humbly. "Perhaps I can be of service."

Salzman had stopped eating and Leo understood with emotion that it was now arranged.

Leaving the cafeteria, he was, however, afflicted by a tormenting suspicion that Salzman had planned it all to happen this way.

Leo was informed by letter that she would meet him on a certain corner, and she was there one spring night, waiting under a street lamp. He appeared, carrying a small bouquet of violets and rosebuds. Stella stood by the lamppost, smoking. She wore white with red shoes, which fitted his expectations, although in a troubled moment he had imagined the dress red, and only the shoes white. She waited uneasily and shyly. From afar he saw that her eyes—clearly her father's—were filled with desperate innocence. He pictured, in her, his own redemption. Violins and lit candles revolved in the sky. Leo ran forward with flowers outthrust.

Around the corner, Salzman, leaning against a wall, chanted prayers for the dead.

INTERPRET

The **ambiguity** of Salzman's motives is deliberate on the author's part. Did Salzman leave Stella's picture with Finkle on purpose or by accident? Is the deep emotio Salzman shows here real or pretended?

EVALUATE

In your opinion, whose view o life is closer to the truth, Leo' or Salzman's? Explain.

INFER

What is the meaning of the last line of the story?

Static and Dynamic Characters

A **static character** does not change much over the course of a story. A **dynamic character** changes in an important way as a result of the story's action.

Using the chart below, compare and contrast Leo Finkle and Pinye Salzman. Which of these characters is static, in your opinion? Which is dynamic? Why?

Leo Finkle	Pinye Salzman

Vocabulary: How to Own a Word

Word Bank
meager
suppress
ascetic
dowry
upbraided
clientele
nuptial
traditional
machinations
evident

Antonyms

For each of the following items, choose the word that is the antonym of the italicized Word to Own. Write the letter of the antonym in the space provided.

_____ **1.** Salzman earns a *meager* salary as a professional matchmaker.

a. inaccurate **b.** plentiful **c.** ludicrous **d.** wonderful

_____ **2.** Leo tried to *suppress* any outward expression of nervousness.

a. ignore **b.** reject **c.** release **d.** assess

_____ **3.** Leo's lips suggested an *ascetic* character.

a. bizarre **b.** introverted **c.** calculating **d.** pleasure-loving

_____ **4.** He *upbraided* himself for his lack of self-knowledge.

a. praised **b.** chided **c.** questioned **d.** searched

_____ **5.** It's *evident* that Leo doesn't have much of a social life.

a. frightening **b.** logical **c.** pleasant **d.** unclear

Completing Sentences

In the space provided, write the Word to Own that best completes each sentence. Choose from the five Words to Own below.

dowry **traditional** **machinations** **nuptial** **clientele**

6. The practice of matchmaking was a very __________ one in their culture.

7. The family of the bride were required to provide a __________ .

8. Salzman is poor because he doesn't have much of a __________ .

9. Will Leo and Stella invite Salzman to the __________ services?

10. Leo is suspicious that everything is a product of Salzman's __________ .

From Black Boy

Make the Connection

Awakenings

Childhood awakenings vary—they can be disappointing, frightening, or delightful. The discoveries we make as children, which awaken us to what the world is really like, depend on the specific circumstances of our lives. In this excerpt from his autobiography, Richard Wright recalls some hard realities of his childhood.

The English poet William Wordsworth once wrote, "The Child is father of the Man." How does this line emphasize the importance of one's childhood experiences? Write your response on the following lines.

From BLACK BOY

Richard Wright

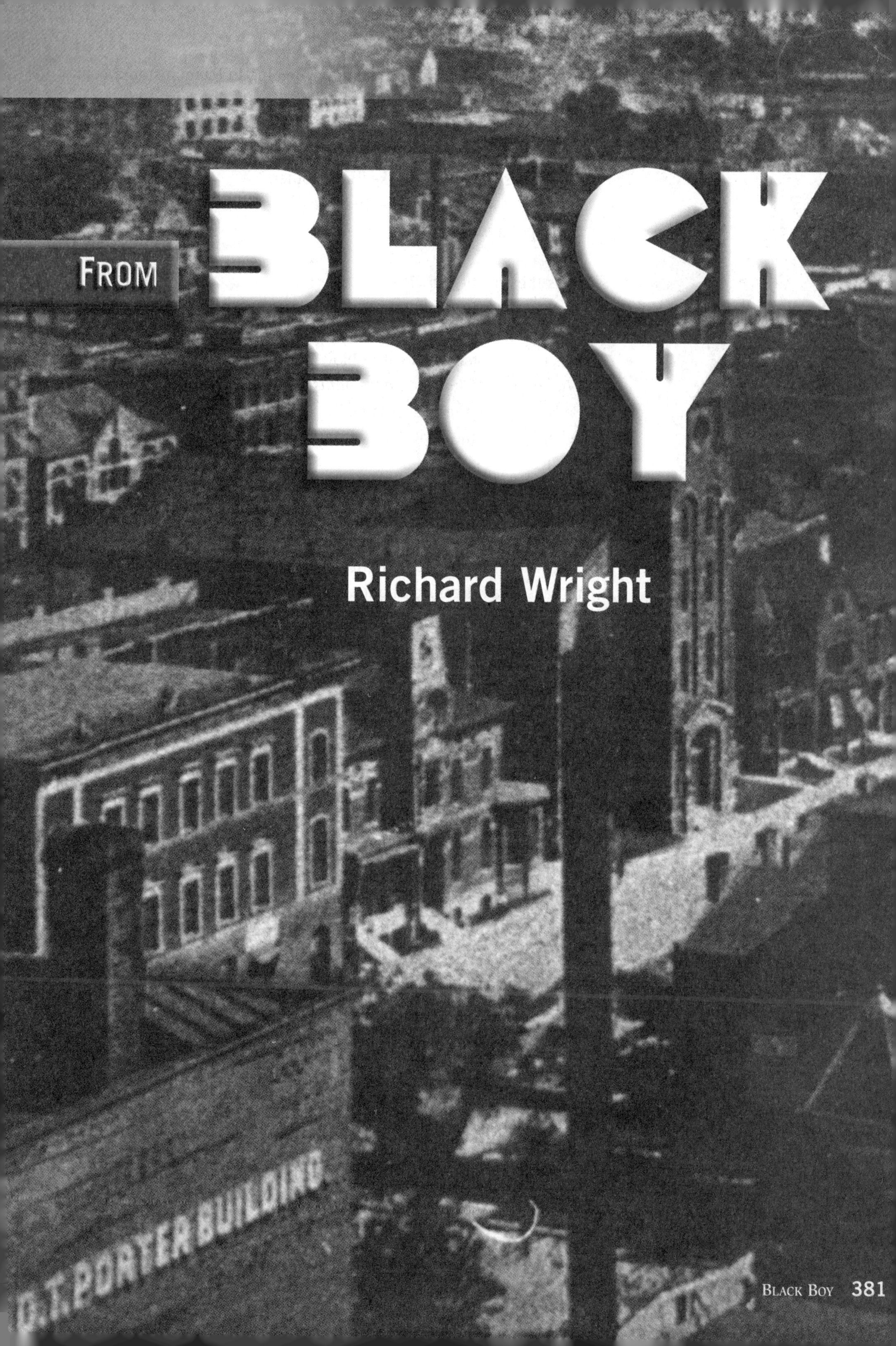

One day my mother told me that we were going to Memphis on a boat, the *Kate Adams,* and my eagerness thereafter made the days seem endless. Each night I went to bed hoping that the next morning would be the day of departure.

"How big is the boat?" I asked my mother.

"As big as a mountain," she said.

"Has it got a whistle?"

"Yes."

"Does the whistle blow?"

"Yes."

"When?"

"When the captain wants it to blow."

"Why do they call it the *Kate Adams*?"

"Because that's the boat's name."

"What color is the boat?"

"White."

"How long will we be on the boat?"

"All day and all night."

"Will we sleep on the boat?"

"Yes, when we get sleepy, we'll sleep. Now, hush."

For days I had dreamed about a huge white boat floating on a vast body of water, but when my mother took me down to the levee on the day of leaving, I saw a tiny, dirty boat that was not at all like the boat I had imagined. I was disappointed and when time came to go on board I cried and my mother thought that I did not want to go with her to Memphis, and I could not tell her what the trouble was. Solace came when I wandered about the boat and gazed at Negroes throwing dice, drinking whiskey, playing cards, lolling on boxes, eating, talking, and singing. My father took me down into the engine room and the throbbing machines enthralled me for hours.

In Memphis we lived in a one-story brick tenement. The stone buildings and the concrete pavements looked bleak and hostile to me. The absence of green, growing things made the city seem dead. Living space for the four of us—my mother, my brother, my father, and me—was a kitchen and a bedroom. In the front and rear were paved areas in which my brother and I could play, but for days I was afraid to go into the strange city streets alone.

It was in this tenement that the personality of my father first came fully into the orbit of my concern. He worked as a night porter in a Beale Street drugstore and he became important and forbidding to me only when I learned that I could not make noise when he was asleep in the daytime. He was the lawgiver in our family and I never laughed in his presence. I used to lurk timidly in the kitchen doorway and watch his huge body sitting slumped at the table. I stared at him with awe as he

NTERPRET

hat evidence is there that right was an imaginative ild?

VORDS TO OWN

nthralled (en·thrôld′) *v.:* ascinated.

INFER

Vhy did Wright find his father forbidding" (line 40)?

VORDS TO OWN

urk (lurk) *v.:* to hide nnoticed.

gulped his beer from a tin bucket, as he ate long and heavily, sighed, belched, closed his eyes to nod on a stuffed belly. He was quite fat and his bloated stomach always lapped over his belt. He was always a stranger to me, always somehow alien and remote. . . .

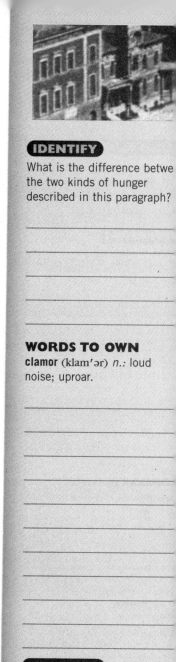

Hunger stole upon me so slowly that at first I was not aware of what hunger really meant. Hunger had always been more or less at my elbow when I played, but now I began to wake up at night to find hunger standing at my bedside, staring at me gauntly. The hunger I had known before this had been no grim, hostile stranger; it had been a normal hunger that had made me beg constantly for bread, and when I ate a crust or two I was satisfied. But this new hunger baffled me, scared me, made me angry and insistent. Whenever I begged for food now my mother would pour me a cup of tea which would still the clamor in my stomach for a moment or two; but a little later I would feel hunger nudging my ribs, twisting my empty guts until they ached. I would grow dizzy and my vision would dim. I became less active in my play, and for the first time in my life I had to pause and think of what was happening to me.

"Mama, I'm hungry," I complained one afternoon.

"Jump up and catch a kungry," she said, trying to make me laugh and forget.

"What's a *kungry*?"

"It's what little boys eat when they get hungry," she said.

"What does it taste like?"

"I don't know."

"Then why do you tell me to catch one?"

"Because you said that you were hungry," she said, smiling.

I sensed that she was teasing me and it made me angry.

"But I'm hungry. I want to eat."

"You'll have to wait."

"But I want to eat now."

"But there's nothing to eat," she told me.

"Why?"

"Just because there's none," she explained.

"But I want to eat," I said, beginning to cry.

"You'll just have to wait," she said again.

"But why?"

"For God to send some food."

"When is He going to send it?"

"I don't know."

"But I'm hungry!"

She was ironing and she paused and looked at me with tears in her eyes.

IDENTIFY

What is the difference betwe the two kinds of hunger described in this paragraph?

WORDS TO OWN

clamor (klam′ər) *n.:* loud noise; uproar.

EVALUATE

What do you think of the way the mother answers her hungr son's questions?

UILD FLUENCY

ad lines 86–104 aloud as pressively as you can. Be re to differentiate the two eakers in the dialogue.

NTERPRET

nat is meant by the phrase eep biological bitterness" ne 104)?

ORDS TO OWN

spirited (di·spir′it·id) *adj.:* scouraged.

PREDICT

ow that his father has left, ow do you think Wright's life ill change?

"Where's your father?" she asked me.

I stared in bewilderment. Yes, it was true that my father had not come home to sleep for many days now and I could make as much noise as I wanted. Though I had not known why he was absent, I had been glad that he was not there to shout his restrictions at me. But it had never occurred to me that his absence would mean that there would be no food.

"I don't know," I said.

"Who brings food into the house?" my mother asked me.

"Papa," I said. "He always brought food."

"Well, your father isn't here now," she said.

"Where is he?"

"I don't know," she said.

"But I'm hungry," I whimpered, stomping my feet.

"You'll have to wait until I get a job and buy food," she said.

As the days slid past, the image of my father became associated with my pangs of hunger, and whenever I felt hunger I thought of him with a deep biological bitterness.

My mother finally went to work as a cook and left me and my brother alone in the flat each day with a loaf of bread and a pot of tea. When she returned at evening she would be tired and dispirited and would cry a lot. Sometimes, when she was in despair, she would call us to her and talk to us for hours, telling us that we now had no father, that our lives would be different from those of other children, that we must learn as soon as possible to take care of ourselves, to dress ourselves, to prepare our own food; that we must take upon ourselves the responsibility of the flat while she worked. Half frightened, we would promise solemnly. We did not understand what had happened between our father and our mother and the most that these long talks did to us was to make us feel a vague dread. Whenever we asked why father had left, she would tell us that we were too young to know.

One evening my mother told me that thereafter I would have to do the shopping for food. She took me to the corner store to show me the way. I was proud; I felt like a grownup. The next afternoon I looped the basket over my arm and went down the pavement toward the store. When I reached the corner, a gang of boys grabbed me, knocked me down, snatched the basket, took the money, and sent me running home in panic. That evening I told my mother what had happened, but she made no comment; she sat down at once, wrote another note, gave me more money, and sent me out to the grocery again. I crept down the steps and saw the same gang of boys playing down the street. I ran back into the house.

"What's the matter?" my mother asked.

"It's those same boys," I said. "They'll beat me."

"You've got to get over that," she said. "Now, go on."

"I'm scared," I said.

"Go on and don't pay any attention to them," she said.

I went out of the door and walked briskly down the sidewalk, praying that the gang would not molest me. But when I came abreast of them someone shouted.

"There he is!"

They came toward me and I broke into a wild run toward home. They overtook me and flung me to the pavement. I yelled, pleaded, kicked, but they wrenched the money out of my hand. They yanked me to my feet, gave me a few slaps, and sent me home sobbing. My mother met me at the door.

"They b-beat m-me," I gasped. "They t-t-took the m-money."

I started up the steps, seeking the shelter of the house.

"Don't you come in here," my mother warned me.

I froze in my tracks and stared at her.

"But they're coming after me," I said.

"You just stay right where you are," she said in a deadly tone. "I'm going to teach you this night to stand up and fight for yourself."

She went into the house and I waited, terrified, wondering what she was about. Presently she returned with more money and another note; she also had a long heavy stick.

"Take this money, this note, and this stick," she said. "Go to the store and buy those groceries. If those boys bother you, then fight."

I was baffled. My mother was telling me to fight, a thing that she had never done before.

"But I'm scared," I said.

"Don't you come into this house until you've gotten those groceries," she said.

"They'll beat me; they'll beat me," I said.

"Then stay in the streets; don't come back here!"

I ran up the steps and tried to force my way past her into the house. A stinging slap came on my jaw. I stood on the sidewalk, crying.

"Please, let me wait until tomorrow," I begged.

"No," she said. "Go now! If you come back into this house without those groceries, I'll whip you!"

She slammed the door and I heard the key turn in the lock. I shook with fright. I was alone upon the dark, hostile streets and gangs were after me. I had the choice of being beaten at home or away from home. I clutched the stick, crying, trying to reason. If I were beaten at home, there was absolutely nothing that I could do about it; but if I were beaten in the streets, I had a chance to fight and defend myself. I walked slowly down the sidewalk, coming closer to the gang of boys, holding the stick tightly. I was so full of fear that I could scarcely breathe. I was almost upon them now.

INFER

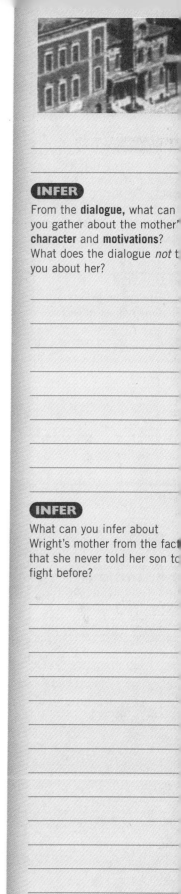

From the **dialogue,** what can you gather about the mother' **character** and **motivations**? What does the dialogue *not* t you about her?

INFER

What can you infer about Wright's mother from the fac that she never told her son tc fight before?

DENTIFY

rcle three vivid words in es 179–187 that describe e action of the fight.

ORDS TO OWN

nzy (fren′zē) *n.:* frantic havior; wildness.

DENTIFY

is passage contains a mber of **colloquial phrases.** hat is the meaning of the lowing: *egging them on, tore t,* and *give them the same?*

ORDS TO OWN

dently (är′dənt·lē) *adv.:* tensely; eagerly.

alled (gôld) *v.:* irritated; ngered.

"There he is again!" the cry went up.

They surrounded me quickly and began to grab for my hand.

"I'll kill you!" I threatened.

They closed in. In blind fear I let the stick fly, feeling it crack against a boy's skull. I swung again, lamming another skull, then another. Realizing that they would retaliate if I let up for but a second, I fought to lay them low, to knock them cold, to kill them so that they could not strike back at me. I flayed with tears in my eyes, teeth clenched, stark fear making me throw every ounce of my strength behind each blow. I hit again and again, dropping the money and the grocery list. The boys scattered, yelling, nursing their heads, staring at me in utter disbelief. They had never seen such frenzy. I stood panting, egging them on, taunting them to come on and fight. When they refused, I ran after them and they tore out for their homes, screaming. The parents of the boys rushed into the streets and threatened me, and for the first time in my life I shouted at grownups, telling them that I would give them the same if they bothered me. I finally found my grocery list and the money and went to the store. On my way back I kept my stick poised for instant use, but there was not a single boy in sight. That night I won the right to the streets of Memphis. . . .

After my father's desertion, my mother's ardently religious disposition dominated the household and I was often taken to Sunday school where I met God's representative in the guise of a tall, black preacher. One Sunday my mother invited the tall, black preacher to a dinner of fried chicken. I was happy, not because the preacher was coming but because of the chicken. One or two neighbors also were invited. But no sooner had the preacher arrived than I began to resent him, for I learned at once that he, like my father, was used to having his own way. The hour for dinner came and I was wedged at the table between talking and laughing adults. In the center of the table was a huge platter of golden-brown fried chicken. I compared the bowl of soup that sat before me with the crispy chicken and decided in favor of the chicken. The others began to eat their soup, but I could not touch mine.

"Eat your soup," my mother said.

"I don't want any," I said.

"You won't get anything else until you've eaten your soup," she said.

The preacher had finished his soup and had asked that the platter of chicken be passed to him. It galled me. He smiled, cocked his head this way and that, picking out choice pieces. I forced a spoonful of soup down my throat and looked to see if my speed matched that of the preacher. It did not. There were already bare chicken bones on his plate, and he was reaching for more. I tried eating my soup faster, but it was no use; the other people were now serving themselves chicken and the platter was more than half empty. I gave up and sat staring in despair at the vanishing pieces of fried chicken.

"Eat your soup or you won't get anything," my mother warned.

I looked at her appealingly and could not answer. As piece after piece of chicken was eaten, I was unable to eat my soup at all. I grew hot with anger. The preacher was laughing and joking and the grownups were hanging on his words. My growing hate of the preacher finally became more important than God or religion and I could no longer contain myself. I leaped up from the table, knowing that I should be ashamed of what I was doing, but unable to stop, and screamed, running blindly from the room.

"That preacher's going to eat *all* the chicken!" I bawled.

The preacher tossed back his head and roared with laughter, but my mother was angry and told me that I was to have no dinner because of my bad manners.

When I awakened one morning my mother told me that we were going to see a judge who would make my father support me and my brother. An hour later all three of us were sitting in a huge crowded room. I was overwhelmed by the many faces and the voices which I could not understand. High above me was a white face which my mother told me was the face of the judge. Across the huge room sat my father, smiling confidently, looking at us. My mother warned me not to be fooled by my father's friendly manner; she told me that the judge might ask me questions, and if he did I must tell him the truth. I agreed, yet I hoped that the judge would not ask me anything.

For some reason the entire thing struck me as being useless; I felt that if my father were going to feed me, then he would have done so regardless of what a judge said to him. And I did not want my father to feed me; I was hungry, but my thoughts of food did not now center about him. I waited, growing restless, hungry. My mother gave me a dry sandwich and I munched and stared, longing to go home. Finally I heard my mother's name called; she rose and began weeping so copiously that she could not talk for a few moments; at last she managed to say that her husband had deserted her and two children, that her children were hungry, that they stayed hungry, that she worked, that she was trying to raise them alone. Then my father was called; he came forward jauntily, smiling. He tried to kiss my mother, but she turned away from him. I only heard one sentence of what he said.

"I'm doing all I can, Your Honor," he mumbled, grinning.

It had been painful to sit and watch my mother crying and my father laughing and I was glad when we were outside in the sunny streets. Back at home my mother wept again and talked complainingly about the unfairness of the judge who had accepted my father's word. After the

INTERPRET
How is this scene related to Wright's experience of hunge described on page 383?

INTERPRET
How has Wright's attitude toward his hunger and his father changed at this point? Why does he feel that way?

INFER
Why does the judge accept th father's word?

court scene, I tried to forget my father; I did not hate him; I simply did not want to think of him. Often when we were hungry my mother would beg me to go to my father's job and ask him for a dollar, a dime, a nickel . . . But I would never consent to go. I did not want to see him.

My mother fell ill and the problem of food became an acute, daily agony. Hunger was with us always. Sometimes the neighbors would feed us or a dollar bill would come in the mail from my grandmother. It was winter and I would buy a dime's worth of coal each morning from the corner coalyard and lug it home in paper bags. For a time I remained out of school to wait upon my mother, then Granny came to visit us and I returned to school.

At night there were long, halting discussions about our going to live with Granny, but nothing came of it. Perhaps there was not enough money for railroad fare. Angered by having been hauled into court, my father now spurned us completely. I heard long, angrily whispered conversations between my mother and grandmother to the effect that "that woman ought to be killed for breaking up a home." What irked me was the ceaseless talk and no action. If someone had suggested that my father be killed, I would perhaps have become interested; if someone had suggested that his name never be mentioned, I would no doubt have agreed; if someone had suggested that we move to another city, I would have been glad. But there was only endless talk that led nowhere and I began to keep away from home as much as possible, preferring the simplicity of the streets to the worried, futile talk at home.

Finally we could no longer pay the rent for our dingy flat; the few dollars that Granny had left us before she went home were gone. Half sick and in despair, my mother made the rounds of the charitable institutions, seeking help. She found an orphan home that agreed to assume the guidance of me and my brother provided my mother worked and made small payments. My mother hated to be separated from us, but she had no choice.

The orphan home was a two-story frame building set amid trees in a wide, green field. My mother ushered me and my brother one morning into the building and into the presence of a tall, gaunt, mulatto woman who called herself Miss Simon. At once she took a fancy to me and I was frightened speechless; I was afraid of her the moment I saw her and my fear lasted during my entire stay in the home.

The house was crowded with children and there was always a storm of noise. The daily routine was blurred to me and I never quite grasped it. The most abiding feeling I had each day was hunger and fear. The meals were skimpy and there were only two of them. Just before we went to bed each night we were given a slice of bread smeared with molasses. The children were silent, hostile, vindictive, continuously complaining of hunger. There was an overall atmosphere of nervousness

NFER

a boy, Wright preferred the nplicity of action to the mplexity of words. As an ult, Wright lived by words. ow might such a change cur in a person?

'ORDS TO OWN

tile (fyo͞ot''l) *adj.*: useless; intless.

NTERPRET

om details in lines 299–307, w would you characterize e care of the children by e orphanage?

and intrigue, of children telling tales upon others, of children being deprived of food to punish them.

The home did not have the money to check the growth of the wide stretches of grass by having it mown, so it had to be pulled by hand. Each morning after we had eaten a breakfast that seemed like no breakfast at all, an older child would lead a herd of us to the vast lawn and we would get to our knees and wrench the grass loose from the dirt with our fingers. At intervals Miss Simon would make a tour of inspection, examining the pile of pulled grass beside each child, scolding or praising according to the size of the pile. Many mornings I was too weak from hunger to pull the grass; I would grow dizzy and my mind would become blank and I would find myself, after an interval of unconsciousness, upon my hands and knees, my head whirling, my eyes staring in bleak astonishment at the green grass, wondering where I was, feeling that I was emerging from a dream . . .

During the first days my mother came each night to visit me and my brother, then her visits stopped. I began to wonder if she, too, like my father, had disappeared into the unknown. I was rapidly learning to distrust everything and everybody. When my mother did come, I asked her why had she remained away so long and she told me that Miss Simon had forbidden her to visit us, that Miss Simon had said that she was spoiling us with too much attention. I begged my mother to take me away; she wept and told me to wait, that soon she would take us to Arkansas. She left and my heart sank.

Miss Simon tried to win my confidence; she asked me if I would like to be adopted by her if my mother consented and I said no. She would take me into her apartment and talk to me, but her words had no effect. Dread and mistrust had already become a daily part of my being and my memory grew sharp, my senses more impressionable; I began to be aware of myself as a distinct personality striving against others. I held myself in, afraid to act or speak until I was sure of my surroundings, feeling most of the time that I was suspended over a void. My imagination soared; I dreamed of running away. Each morning I vowed that I would leave the next morning, but the next morning always found me afraid.

One day Miss Simon told me that thereafter I was to help her in the office. I ate lunch with her and, strangely, when I sat facing her at the table, my hunger vanished. The woman killed something in me. Next she called me to her desk where she sat addressing envelopes.

"Step up close to the desk," she said. "Don't be afraid."

I went and stood at her elbow. There was a wart on her chin and I stared at it.

"Now, take a blotter from over there and blot each envelope after I'm through writing on it," she instructed me, pointing to a blotter that stood about a foot from my hand.

INTERPRET

Compare and contrast this description of hunger's effec with the description on p. 3 that begins, "Hunger stole upon me so slowly. . . ." Ho are these two passages alike How are they different?

I stared and did not move or answer.

"Take the blotter," she said.

I wanted to reach for the blotter and succeeded only in twitching my arm.

"Here," she said sharply, reaching for the blotter and shoving it into my fingers.

She wrote in ink on an envelope and pushed it toward me. Holding the blotter in my hand, I stared at the envelope and could not move.

"Blot it," she said.

I could not lift my hand. I knew what she had said; I knew what she wanted me to do; and I had heard her correctly. I wanted to look at her and say something, tell her why I could not move; but my eyes were fixed upon the floor. I could not summon enough courage while she sat there looking at me to reach over the yawning space of twelve inches and blot the wet ink on the envelope.

"Blot it!" she spoke sharply.

Still I could not move or answer.

"Look at me!"

I could not lift my eyes. She reached her hand to my face and I twisted away.

"What's wrong with you?" she demanded.

I began to cry and she drove me from the room. I decided that as soon as night came I would run away. The dinner bell rang and I did not go to the table, but hid in a corner of the hallway. When I heard the dishes rattling at the table, I opened the door and ran down the walk to the street. Dusk was falling. Doubt made me stop. Ought I go back? No; hunger was back there, and fear. I went on, coming to concrete sidewalks. People passed me. Where was I going? I did not know. The farther I walked the more frantic I became. In a confused and vague way I knew that I was doing more running *away* from than running *toward* something. I stopped. The streets seemed dangerous. The buildings were massive and dark. The moon shone and the trees loomed frighteningly. No, I could not go on. I would go back. But I had walked so far and had turned too many corners and had not kept track of the direction. Which way led back to the orphan home? I did not know. I was lost.

I stood in the middle of the sidewalk and cried. A "white" policeman came to me and I wondered if he was going to beat me. He asked me what was the matter and I told him that I was trying to find my mother. His "white" face created a new fear in me. I was remembering the tale of the "white" man who had beaten the "black" boy. A crowd gathered and I was urged to tell where I lived. Curiously, I was too full of fear to cry now. I wanted to tell the "white" face that I had run off from an orphan home and that Miss Simon ran it, but I was afraid. Finally I was taken to the police station where I was fed. I felt better. I sat in a big chair where

NTERPRET
at are Miss Simon's otions as she keeps telling n to blot the envelope? at are Wright's emotions?

NTERPRET
hat is the crucial thing the licemen do for Wright that ns his trust?

I was surrounded by "white" policemen, but they seemed to ignore me. Through the window I could see that night had completely fallen and that lights now gleamed in the streets. I grew sleepy and dozed. My shoulder was shaken gently and I opened my eyes and looked into a "white" face of another policeman who was sitting beside me. He asked me questions in a quiet, confidential tone, and quite before I knew it he was not "white" any more. I told him that I had run away from an orphan home and that Miss Simon ran it.

It was but a matter of minutes before I was walking alongside a policeman, heading toward the home. The policeman led me to the front gate and I saw Miss Simon waiting for me on the steps. She identified me and I was left in her charge. I begged her not to beat me, but she yanked me upstairs into an empty room and lashed me thoroughly. Sobbing, I slunk off to bed, resolved to run away again. But I was watched closely after that.

My mother was informed upon her next visit that I had tried to run away and she was terribly upset.

"Why did you do it?" she asked.

"I don't want to stay here," I told her.

"But you must," she said. "How can I work if I'm to worry about you? You must remember that you have no father. I'm doing all I can."

"I don't want to stay here," I repeated.

"Then, if I take you to your father . . ."

"I don't want to stay with him either," I said.

"But I want you to ask him for enough money for us to go to my sister's in Arkansas," she said.

Again I was faced with choices I did not like, but I finally agreed. After all, my hate for my father was not so great and urgent as my hate for the orphan home. My mother held to her idea and one night a week or so later I found myself standing in a room in a frame house. My father and a strange woman were sitting before a bright fire that blazed in a grate. My mother and I were standing about six feet away, as though we were afraid to approach them any closer.

"It's not for me," my mother was saying. "It's for your children that I'm asking you for money."

"I ain't got nothing," my father said, laughing.

"Come here, boy," the strange woman called to me.

I looked at her and did not move.

"Give him a nickel," the woman said. "He's cute."

"Come here, Richard," my father said, stretching out his hand.

I backed away, shaking my head, keeping my eyes on the fire.

"He is a cute child," the strange woman said.

"You ought to be ashamed," my mother said to the strange woman. "You're starving my children."

INTERPRET

What is the point of the repeated use of *white* in quotation marks in this paragraph? What does "he w not 'white' any more" mean?

RETELL

Summarize the events that have taken place since Wrigh entered the orphanage.

"Now, don't you-all fight," my father said, laughing.

"I'll take that poker and hit you!" I blurted at my father.

He looked at my mother and laughed louder.

"You told him to say that," he said.

"Don't say such things, Richard," my mother said.

"You ought to be dead," I said to the strange woman.

The woman laughed and threw her arms about my father's neck. I grew ashamed and wanted to leave.

"How can you starve your children?" my mother asked.

"Let Richard stay with me," my father said.

"Do you want to stay with your father, Richard?" my mother asked.

"No," I said.

"You'll get plenty to eat," he said.

"I'm hungry now," I told him. "But I won't stay with you."

"Aw, give the boy a nickel," the woman said.

My father ran his hand into his pocket and pulled out a nickel.

"Here, Richard," he said.

"Don't take it," my mother said.

"Don't teach him to be a fool," my father said. "Here, Richard, take it."

I looked at my mother, at the strange woman, at my father, then into the fire. I wanted to take the nickel, but I did not want to take it from my father.

"You ought to be ashamed," my mother said, weeping. "Giving your son a nickel when he's hungry. If there's a God, He'll pay you back."

"That's all I got," my father said, laughing again and returning the nickel to his pocket.

We left. I had the feeling that I had had to do with something unclean. Many times in the years after that the image of my father and the strange woman, their faces lit by the dancing flames, would surge up in my imagination so vivid and strong that I felt I could reach out and touch it; I would stare at it, feeling that it possessed some vital meaning which always eluded me.

A quarter of a century was to elapse between the time when I saw my father sitting with the strange woman and the time when I was to see him again, standing alone upon the red clay of a Mississippi plantation, a sharecropper,[1] clad in ragged overalls, holding a muddy hoe in his gnarled, veined hands—a quarter of a century during which my mind and consciousness had become so greatly and violently altered that when I tried to talk to him I realized that, though ties of blood made us kin, though I could see a shadow of my face in his face, though there was an echo of my voice in his voice, we were forever strangers,

VALUATE

hat opinions of the **main aracter** did you form during s conversation, and what ecific lines of **dialogue** lped shape those opinions?

ORDS TO OWN

apse (ē·laps′) *v.:* to pass by; ip away.

1. **sharecropper:** farmer who works a piece of land for its owner and gets a small portion of the crop in return.

speaking a different language, living on vastly distant planes of reality. That day a quarter of a century later when I visited him on the plantation—he was standing against the sky, smiling toothlessly, his hair whitened, his body bent, his eyes glazed with dim recollection, his fearsome aspect of twenty-five years ago gone forever from him—I was overwhelmed to realize that he could never understand me or the scalding experiences that had swept me beyond his life and into an area of living that he could never know. I stood before him, poised, my mind aching as it embraced the simple nakedness of his life, feeling how completely his soul was imprisoned by the slow flow of the seasons, by wind and rain and sun, how fastened were his memories to a crude and raw past, how chained were his actions and emotions to the direct, animalistic impulses of his withering body . . .

From the white landowners above him there had not been handed to him a chance to learn the meaning of loyalty, of sentiment, of tradition. Joy was as unknown to him as was despair. As a creature of the earth, he endured, hearty, whole, seemingly indestructible, with no regrets and no hope. He asked easy, drawling questions about me, his other son, his wife, and he laughed, amused, when I informed him of their destinies. I forgave him and pitied him as my eyes looked past him to the unpainted wooden shack. From far beyond the horizons that bound this bleak plantation there had come to me through my living the knowledge that my father was a black peasant who had gone to the city seeking life, but who had failed in the city; a black peasant whose life had been hopelessly snarled in the city, and who had at last fled the city—that same city which had lifted me in its burning arms and borne me toward alien and undreamed-of shores of knowing.

INTERPRET

What changes have happene[d] to Wright's father since they last met? How has Wright changed since he last saw his father?

WORDS TO OWN

withering (wi*th*′ər·iŋ) *v.* used as *adj.:* drying up; weakening

IDENTIFY

Why is Wright able to forgive and pity his father?

INTERPRET

What knowledge has Wright gained from the example of his father's life?

Dialogue

Dialogue is the directly quoted words or conversation between two or more people. In addition to its important role in drama and fiction, dialogue can be significant in nonfiction as well. In this excerpt from his autobiography, Richard Wright uses dialogue to show, rather than describe, his feelings. Dialogue is also an effective method of **indirect characterization.**

For each line of dialogue below, identify the speaker. Then, briefly state how you feel each line contributes to characterization.

1. "Jump up and catch a kungry." (line 64)

2. "It's those same boys. . . . They'll beat me." (line 130)

3. "I'm doing all I can, Your Honor." (line 257)

4. "Blot it." (line 358)

5. "I'll take that poker and hit you!" (line 439)

Vocabulary: How to Own a Word

Connotations

Word Bank
enthralled
lurk
clamor
dispirited
frenzy
ardently
galled
futile
elapse
withering

The words *pushy* and *persistent* have similar meanings but different **connotations.** Most people find it a compliment to be called persistent, but would be offended if they were labeled pushy. Neutral words, such as *hat,* usually do not evoke strong emotions.

For the following Words to Own, decide which has a positive (**P**), negative (**N**), or neutral (**O**) connotation, and write the appropriate letter in the space provided before the number for that word. Then, explain your answer on the lines provided by using examples or personal experiences.

_____ **1.** enthralled ______________________________

____

_____ **2.** lurk ______________________________

____

_____ **3.** clamor ______________________________

____

_____ **4.** dispirited ______________________________

____

_____ **5.** frenzy ______________________________

____

_____ **6.** ardently ______________________________

____

_____ **7.** galled ______________________________

____

_____ **8.** futile ______________________________

____

_____ **9.** elapse ______________________________

____

_____ **10.** withering ______________________________

____

The Fish

Make the Connection

Creature Teachers

Has your pet parrot ever given you the silent treatment? Does your cat flaunt its freedom in front of dogs passing by on a leash?

Sometimes animals seem to exhibit very human qualities. Before you read Elizabeth Bishop's poem about a fish, think of at least two examples in which an animal seems to exhibit human qualities, and write them on the lines below. You could describe a pet or an animal you've observed in a zoo or elsewhere, or you could draw your examples from stories or poems you have read or films you have seen.

Animal: ______________________________

Human Qualities: ______________________________

____

____

____

____

____

____

____

The Fish

Elizabeth Bishop

DENTIFY

ad the first nine lines
efully. What is the **speaker's**
t impression of the fish?
derline the words that give
answer.

VALUATE

ines 10–15, **similes** are
d to describe the skin of
fish. Is the comparison
h wallpaper effective?
plain.

NFER

at does the phrase "terrible
gen" (line 23) mean?

I caught a tremendous fish
and held him beside the boat
half out of water, with my hook
fast in a corner of his mouth.
He didn't fight.
He hadn't fought at all.
He hung a grunting weight,
battered and venerable
and homely. Here and there
his brown skin hung in strips
like ancient wall-paper,
and its pattern of darker brown
was like wall-paper:
shapes like full-blown roses
stained and lost through age.
He was speckled with barnacles,
fine rosettes of lime,
and infested
with tiny white sea-lice,
and underneath two or three
rags of green weed hung down.
While his gills were breathing in
the terrible oxygen
—the frightening gills
fresh and crisp with blood,
that can cut so badly—
I thought of the coarse white flesh
packed in like feathers,
the big bones and the little bones,
the dramatic reds and blacks
of his shiny entrails,
and the pink swim-bladder
like a big peony.
I looked into his eyes
which were far larger than mine
but shallower, and yellowed,
the irises backed and packed
with tarnished tinfoil
seen through the lenses
of old scratched isinglass.[1]
They shifted a little, but not
to return my stare.

---

1. **isinglass** (ī′zin·glas′): mica, glasslike mineral that crystallizes in thin layers.

—It was more like the tipping
of an object toward the light.
I admired his sullen face,
the mechanism of his jaw,
and then I saw
that from his lower lip
—if you could call it a lip—
grim, wet, and weapon-like,
hung five old pieces of fish-line,
or four and a wire leader
with the swivel still attached,
with all their five big hooks
grown firmly in his mouth.
A green line, frayed at the end
where he broke it, two heavier lines,
and a fine black thread
still crimped from the strain and snap
when it broke and he got away.
Like medals with their ribbons
frayed and wavering,
a five-haired beard of wisdom
trailing from his aching jaw.
I stared and stared
and victory filled up
the little rented boat,
from the pool of bilge
where oil had spread a rainbow
around the rusted engine
to the bailer rusted orange,
the sun-cracked thwarts,
the oarlocks on their strings,
the gunnels—until everything
was rainbow, rainbow, rainbow!
And I let the fish go.

INTERPRET

The **speaker** compares the hooks and fish lines to "medals with their ribbons" (line 61). What does this **simile** suggest about the fish?

INTERPRET

Explain the meaning of lines 65–67. What kind of "victory" is referred to?

INTERPRET

What does the **speaker** mean by "rainbow, rainbow, rainbow (line 75)?

EVALUATE

What was your response to the last line?

BUILD FLUENCY

Read the whole poem aloud as expressively as you can. Focus on units of meaning, pacing, volume, and emphasis.

Personification

A metaphor is a direct comparison between two unlike things. **Personification** is a kind of metaphor in which a nonhuman thing or quality is talked about as if it were human. For example, it may be given human feelings, thoughts, or attitudes.

Re-read lines 61–64 of the poem. On the lines below, identify the two figures of speech that personify the fish. Then, briefly describe the type of person that these images suggest.

Personification of the Fish
(lines 61–64)

Figure of Speech 1:

____

____

Figure of Speech 2:

____

____

Type of Person:

____

____

____

____

Vocabulary: How to Own a Word

Column Match

In the space provided, write the letter of the word or phrase in Column B that best defines each word from the poem in Column A.

Column A	Column B
_____ 1. venerable	a. showing resentment; morose
_____ 2. homely	b. breathing organs of fish
_____ 3. speckled	c. aging and worthy of respect
_____ 4. infested	d. intestines; guts
_____ 5. gills	e. dulled the shine of
_____ 6. entrails	f. not good-looking; plain
_____ 7. tarnished	g. seats in a boat for rowers
_____ 8. sullen	h. marked with contrasting colors
_____ 9. frayed	i. overrun in large numbers
_____ 10. thwarts	j. ragged; worn away

From The Way to Rainy Mountain

Make the Connection

Knowledge of the Past

What is it that we honor about the past? Perhaps it is the realization that the generations preceding us built civilizations, gave us life, and served as models because of their knowledge. We search in many ways for the secret of what these forebears knew. We search in history, archaeology, anthropology, art, linguistics, architecture, music, mythology, and literature. In many ways, as we delve into the past, we also search for knowledge of ourselves.

On the lines provided below, write briefly about your own interest in the past. Tell why you believe (or do not believe) that searching for the knowledge of past generations can be valuable and enlightening.

FROM The Way to Rainy Mountain

N. Scott Momaday

A single knoll rises out of the plain in Oklahoma north and west of the Wichita Range. For my people, the Kiowas, it is an old landmark, and they gave it the name Rainy Mountain. The hardest weather in the world is there. Winter brings blizzards, hot tornadic winds arise in the spring, and in summer the prairie is an anvil's edge. The grass turns brittle and brown, and it cracks beneath your feet. There are green belts along the rivers and creeks, linear groves of hickory and pecan, willow and witch hazel. At a distance in July or August the steaming foliage seems almost to writhe in fire. Great green and yellow grasshoppers are everywhere in the tall grass, popping up like corn to sting the flesh, and tortoises crawl about on the red earth, going nowhere in the plenty of time. Loneliness is an aspect of the land. All things in the plain are isolate; there is no confusion of objects in the eye, but *one* hill or *one* tree or *one* man. To look upon that landscape in the early morning, with the sun at your back, is to lose the sense of proportion. Your imagination comes to life, and this, you think, is where Creation was begun.

I returned to Rainy Mountain in July. My grandmother had died in the spring, and I wanted to be at her grave. She had lived to be very old and at last infirm. Her only living daughter was with her when she died, and I was told that in death her face was that of a child.

I like to think of her as a child. When she was born, the Kiowas were living that last great moment of their history. For more than a hundred years they had controlled the open range from the Smoky Hill River to the Red, from the headwaters of the Canadian to the fork of the Arkansas and Cimarron. In alliance with the Comanches, they had ruled the whole of the southern Plains. War was their sacred business, and they were among the finest horsemen the world has ever known. But warfare for the Kiowas was preeminently a matter of disposition rather than of survival, and they never understood the grim, unrelenting advance of the U.S. Cavalry. When at last, divided and ill-provisioned, they were driven onto the Staked Plains in the cold rains of autumn, they fell into panic. In Palo Duro Canyon they abandoned their crucial stores to pillage and had nothing then but their lives. In order to save themselves, they surrendered to the soldiers at Fort Sill and were imprisoned in the old stone corral that now stands as a military museum. My grandmother was spared the humiliation of those high gray walls by eight or ten years, but she must have known from birth the affliction of defeat, the dark brooding of old warriors.

Her name was Aho, and she belonged to the last culture to evolve in North America. Her forebears came down from the high country in western Montana nearly three centuries ago. They were a mountain people, a mysterious tribe of hunters whose language has never been positively classified in any major group. In the late seventeenth

DENTIFY

nderline the **main idea** and e details that support it.

INTERPRET

hat word would you use to escribe the **setting** the author ortrays in this paragraph?

VORDS TO OWN

firm (in·furm′) *adj.:* hysically weak.

VORDS TO OWN

reeminently (prē·em′ə·nənt·lē) *dv.:* above all else.

INFER

n the past, why do you think varfare had not been a matter of survival for the Kiowas?

century they began a long migration to the south and east. It was a journey toward the dawn, and it led to a golden age. Along the way the Kiowas were befriended by the Crows, who gave them the culture and religion of the Plains. They acquired horses, and their ancient nomadic spirit was suddenly free of the ground. They acquired Tai-me, the sacred Sun Dance doll, from that moment the object and symbol of their worship, and so shared in the divinity of the sun. Not least, they acquired the sense of destiny, therefore courage and pride. When they entered upon the southern Plains they had been transformed. No longer were they slaves to the simple necessity of survival; they were a lordly and dangerous society of fighters and thieves, hunters and priests of the sun. According to their origin myth, they entered the world through a hollow log. From one point of view, their migration was the fruit of an old prophecy, for indeed they emerged from a sunless world.

Although my grandmother lived out her long life in the shadow of Rainy Mountain, the immense landscape of the continental interior lay like memory in her blood. She could tell of the Crows, whom she had never seen, and of the Black Hills, where she had never been. I wanted to see in reality what she had seen more perfectly in the mind's eye, and traveled fifteen hundred miles to begin my pilgrimage.

Yellowstone, it seemed to me, was the top of the world, a region of deep lakes and dark timber, canyons and waterfalls. But, beautiful as it is, one might have the sense of confinement there. The skyline in all directions is close at hand, the high wall of the woods and deep cleavages of shade. There is a perfect freedom in the mountains, but it belongs to the eagle and the elk, the badger and the bear. The Kiowas reckoned their stature by the distance they could see, and they were bent and blind in the wilderness.

Descending eastward, the highland meadows are a stairway to the plain. In July the inland slope of the Rockies is luxuriant with flax and buckwheat, stonecrop and larkspur. The earth unfolds and the limit of the land recedes. Clusters of trees, and animals grazing far in the distance, cause the vision to reach away and wonder to build upon the mind. The sun follows a longer course in the day, and the sky is immense beyond all comparison. The great billowing clouds that sail upon it are shadows that move upon the grain like water, dividing light. Farther down, in the land of the Crows and Blackfeet, the plain is yellow. Sweet clover takes hold of the hills and bends upon itself to cover and seal the soil. There the Kiowas paused on their way; they had come to the place where they must change their lives. The sun is at home on the plains. Precisely there does it have the certain character of a god. When the Kiowas came to the land of the Crows, they could see the dark lees of the hills at dawn across the Bighorn River, the profusion of light on

RETELL

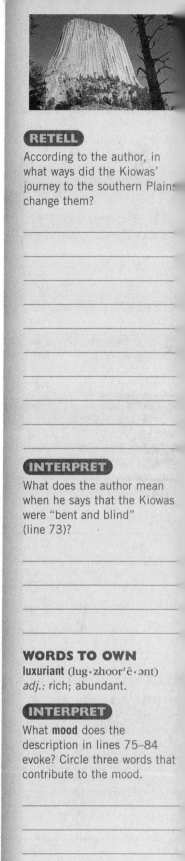

According to the author, in what ways did the Kiowas' journey to the southern Plains change them?

INTERPRET

What does the author mean when he says that the Kiowas were "bent and blind" (line 73)?

WORDS TO OWN

luxuriant (lug·zhoor′ē·ənt) *adj.:* rich; abundant.

INTERPRET

What **mood** does the description in lines 75–84 evoke? Circle three words that contribute to the mood.

the grain shelves, the oldest deity ranging after the solstices.[1] Not yet would they veer southward to the caldron of the land that lay below; they must wean their blood from the northern winter and hold the mountains a while longer in their view. They bore Tai-me in procession to the east.

A dark mist lay over the Black Hills, and the land was like iron. At the top of a ridge I caught sight of Devils Tower upthrust against the gray sky as if in the birth of time the core of the earth had broken through its crust and the motion of the world was begun. There are things in nature that engender an awful quiet in the heart of man; Devils Tower is one of them. Two centuries ago, because they could not do otherwise, the Kiowas made a legend at the base of the rock. My grandmother said:

Eight children were there at play, seven sisters and their brother. Suddenly the boy was struck dumb; he trembled and began to run upon his hands and feet. His fingers became claws, and his body was covered with fur. Directly there was a bear where the boy had been. The sisters were terrified; they ran, and the bear after them. They came to the stump of a great tree, and the tree spoke to them. It bade them climb upon it, and as they did so it began to rise into the air. The bear came to kill them, but they were just beyond its reach. It reared against the tree and scored the bark all around with its claws. The seven sisters were borne into the sky, and they became the stars of the Big Dipper.

From that moment, and so long as the legend lives, the Kiowas have kinsmen in the night sky. Whatever they were in the mountains, they could be no more. However tenuous their well-being, however much they had suffered and would suffer again, they had found a way out of the wilderness.

My grandmother had a reverence for the sun, a holy regard that now is all but gone out of mankind. There was a wariness in her, and an ancient awe. She was a Christian in her later years, but she had come a long way about, and she never forgot her birthright. As a child she had been to the Sun Dances; she had taken part in those annual rites, and by them she had learned the restoration of her people in the presence of Tai-me. She was about seven when the last Kiowa Sun Dance was held in 1887 on the Washita River above Rainy Mountain Creek. The buffalo were gone. In order to consummate the ancient sacrifice—to impale the head of a buffalo bull upon the medicine tree—a delegation of old men journeyed into Texas, there to beg and barter for an animal from the Goodnight herd. She was ten when the Kiowas came together for the last time as a

NTERPRET

the legend, seven Kiowa sters become the stars in the g Dipper. Why do you think is legend would be important the Kiowas?

VORDS TO OWN

enuous (ten′yo͞o·əs) *adj.:* ight; insubstantial; not firm.

ariness (wer′ē·nis) *n.:* aution; carefulness.

1. **solstices:** The solstices are the points where the sun is farthest north and farthest south of the celestial equator, creating the longest day (June 21) and the shortest day (December 21) of sunlight in the Northern Hemisphere.

living Sun Dance culture. They could find no buffalo; they had to hang an old hide from the sacred tree. Before the dance could begin, a company of soldiers rode out from Fort Sill under orders to disperse the tribe. Forbidden without cause the essential act of their faith, having seen the wild herds slaughtered and left to rot upon the ground, the Kiowas backed away forever from the medicine tree. That was July 20, 1890, at the great bend of the Washita. My grandmother was there. Without bitterness, and for as long as she lived, she bore a vision of deicide.[2]

Now that I can have her only in memory, I see my grandmother in the several postures that were peculiar to her: standing at the wood stove on a winter morning and turning meat in a great iron skillet; sitting at the south window, bent above her beadwork, and afterwards, when her vision failed, looking down for a long time into the fold of her hands; going out upon a cane, very slowly as she did when the weight of age came upon her; praying. I remember her most often at prayer. She made long, rambling prayers out of suffering and hope, having seen many things. I was never sure that I had the right to hear, so exclusive were they of all mere custom and company. The last time I saw her she prayed standing by the side of her bed at night, naked to the waist, the light of a kerosene lamp moving upon her dark skin. Her long, black hair, always drawn and braided in the day, lay upon her shoulders and against her breasts like a shawl. I do not speak Kiowa, and I never understood her prayers, but there was something inherently sad in the sound, some merest hesitation upon the syllables of sorrow. She began in a high and descending pitch, exhausting her breath to silence; then again and again—and always the same intensity of effort, of something that is, and is not, like urgency in the human voice. Transported so in the dancing light among the shadows of her room, she seemed beyond the reach of time. But that was illusion; I think I knew then that I should not see her again.

Houses are like sentinels in the plain, old keepers of the weather watch. There, in a very little while, wood takes on the appearance of great age. All colors wear soon away in the wind and rain, and then the wood is burned gray and the grain appears and the nails turn red with rust. The windowpanes are black and opaque; you imagine there is nothing within, and indeed there are many ghosts, bones given up to the land. They stand here and there against the sky, and you approach them for a longer time than you expect. They belong in the distance; it is their domain.

Once there was a lot of sound in my grandmother's house, a lot of coming and going, feasting and talk. The summers there were full of excitement and reunion. The Kiowas are a summer people; they abide the cold and keep to themselves, but when the season turns and the land becomes warm and vital they cannot hold still; an old love of going returns upon them. The aged visitors who came to my grandmother's

2. **deicide** (dē′ə·sīd′): murder of a god.

WORDS TO OWN
disperse (di·spurs′) *v.:* to scatter.

IDENTIFY
A **main idea** may be expressec after the details that support it. What details support the idea in lines 134–135?

RETELL
This paragraph marks a shift i narrative time. What new focu does this paragraph mark?

IDENTIFY
An **elegy** is a poetic lament. Underline **images** in lines 136–156 that contribute to an elegiac tone.

WORDS TO OWN
opaque (ō·pāk′) *adj.:* not transparent; not letting light pass through.

IDENTIFY
Find and underline two supporting details for the statement in lines 165–166.

WORDS TO OWN
vital (vīt′'l) *adj.:* filled with life.

ORDS TO OWN

mities (en′mə·tēz) *n. pl.:* treds.

lulge (in·dulj′) *v.:* to satisfy; ease; humor.

NTERPRET

ow is the image of a icket filling the moon nes 199–200) connected the narrator's view of his andmother?

BUILD FLUENCY

ead the passage aloud as xpressively as you can. Focus n the elements of pacing, mphasis, and tone.

INTERPRET

Vhat is the author's **tone** in ne concluding paragraph?

house when I was a child were made of lean and leather, and they bore themselves upright. They wore great black hats and bright ample shirts that shook in the wind. They rubbed fat upon their hair and wound their braids with strips of colored cloth. Some of them painted their faces and carried the scars of old and cherished enmities. They were an old council of warlords, come to remind and be reminded of who they were. Their wives and daughters served them well. The women might indulge themselves; gossip was at once the mark and compensation of their servitude. They made loud and elaborate talk among themselves, full of jest and gesture, fright and false alarm. They went abroad in fringed and flowered shawls, bright beadwork and German silver. They were at home in the kitchen, and they prepared meals that were banquets.

There were frequent prayer meetings, and great nocturnal feasts. When I was a child I played with my cousins outside, where the lamplight fell upon the ground and the singing of the old people rose up around us and carried away into the darkness. There were a lot of good things to eat, a lot of laughter and surprise. And afterwards, when the quiet returned, I lay down with my grandmother and could hear the frogs away by the river and feel the motion of the air.

Now there is a funeral silence in the rooms, the endless wake of some final word. The walls have closed in upon my grandmother's house. When I returned to it in mourning, I saw for the first time in my life how small it was. It was late at night, and there was a white moon, nearly full. I sat for a long time on the stone steps by the kitchen door. From there I could see out across the land; I could see the long row of trees by the creek, the low light upon the rolling plains, and the stars of the Big Dipper. Once I looked at the moon and caught sight of a strange thing. A cricket had perched upon the handrail, only a few inches away from me. My line of vision was such that the creature filled the moon like a fossil.[3] It had gone there, I thought, to live and die, for there, of all places, was its small definition made whole and eternal. A warm wind rose up and purled[4] like the longing within me.

The next morning I awoke at dawn and went out on the dirt road to Rainy Mountain. It was already hot, and the grasshoppers began to fill the air. Still, it was early in the morning, and the birds sang out of the shadows. The long yellow grass on the mountain shone in the bright light, and a scissortail[5] hied above the land. There, where it ought to be, at the end of a long and legendary way, was my grandmother's grave. Here and there on the dark stones were ancestral names. Looking back once, I saw the mountain and came away.

---

3. **fossil:** hardened remains of plant or animal life from a previous geological time period.
4. **purled** (purld): moved in ripples.
5. **scissortail:** a species of flycatcher bird. The bird's distinctive tail is an average of thirteen inches long and is divided like scissors near its end.

Setting

Setting is the time and location in which events occur or in which characters are placed. In his memoir, Momaday ranges over a variety of settings, skillfully using well-chosen images to create mood and atmosphere.

Explore Momaday's handling of setting in the memoir by filling out the chart below. In the top half of each box, write down an image the writer uses to describe the appearance of each place listed. In the bottom half of each box, describe either the Kiowas' reaction or Momaday's own personal reaction to the place. Then, answer the questions that follow the chart.

Rainy Mountain	The Land of the Crows
Yellowstone	**The Black Hills**

1. What images from the selection seem especially striking or poetic to you? Why?

____

____

____

2. How are the places that Momaday describes significant to the Kiowas?

____

____

____

Vocabulary: How to Own a Word

Word Bank
infirm
preeminently
luxuriant
tenuous
wariness
disperse
opaque
vital
enmities
indulge

Question and Answer

Answer the following questions, using context clues to show that you understand the meaning of the italicized Word to Own.

EXAMPLE: When grass becomes *brittle*, does it crumble easily? Yes

Explanation: Brittle grass is dry and fragile, and it crumbles when you step on it.

1. When Aho became *infirm*, was she physically strong? ____________
   Explanation: ____________

2. If an item is featured *preeminently* in a list, is it given a place of importance? ____________
   Explanation: ____________

3. When the Rockies are *luxuriant* with flowers, are there only a few of them in the area? ____________
   Explanation: ____________

4. When Momaday's grandmother demonstrates *wariness*, is she showing her recklessness? ____________
   Explanation: ____________

5. Would those who wanted them to *disperse* be happy if the Kiowas were not able to gather together? ____________
   Explanation: ____________

6. If Momaday were to *indulge* the reader with more stories, would he stop writing? ____________
   Explanation: ____________

7. When Momaday says the Kiowas' position was *tenuous*, does he mean that their position was secure? ____________

Explanation:

____

____

8. Is it difficult to see through a windowpane that is *opaque*? ____________

Explanation:

____

____

9. When the plains become *vital*, are they full of life? ____________

Explanation:

____

____

10. Do the Kiowas who bear the scars of past *enmities* carry only peaceful memories? ____________

Explanation:

____

____

From Rules of the Game

Make the Connection

Game Theory

This story focuses on a Chinese American girl who stumbles into the forbidding world of championship chess. But presently we come to understand that the story is really about an issue that is far more familiar: the clash between a mother's authority over her children and her ambition for them, and a child's need to find his or her own way.

Think about the rules of chess or of another game you know. Then, write down some ways in which a game's rules might be similar to rules of human relationships, especially between parents and children. What do you think the title of this story might mean? (Might the title have more than one meaning?)

FROM RULES OF THE GAME

FROM The Joy Luck Club

Amy Tan

My older brother Vincent was the one who actually got the chess set. We had gone to the annual Christmas party held at the First Chinese Baptist Church at the end of the alley. The missionary ladies had put together a Santa bag of gifts donated by members of another church. None of the gifts had names on them. There were separate sacks for boys and girls of different ages.

One of the Chinese parishioners had donned a Santa Claus costume and a stiff paper beard with cotton balls glued to it. I think the only children who thought he was the real thing were too young to know that Santa Claus was not Chinese. When my turn came up, the Santa man asked me how old I was. I thought it was a trick question; I was seven according to the American formula and eight by the Chinese calendar. I said I was born on March 17, 1951. That seemed to satisfy him. He then solemnly asked if I had been a very, very good girl this year and did I believe in Jesus Christ and obey my parents. I knew the only answer to that. I nodded back with equal solemnity.

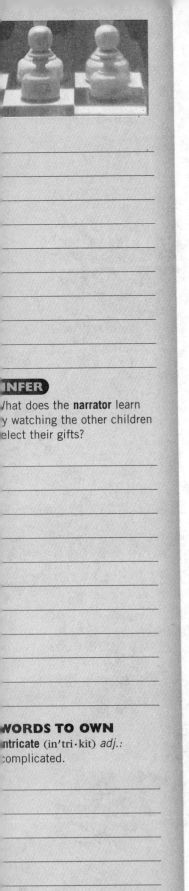

INFER
/hat does the **narrator** learn y watching the other children elect their gifts?

Having watched the other children opening their gifts, I already knew that the big gifts were not necessarily the nicest ones. One girl my age got a large coloring book of biblical characters, while a less greedy girl who selected a smaller box received a glass vial of lavender toilet water.[1] The sound of the box was also important. A ten-year-old boy had chosen a box that jangled when he shook it. It was a tin globe of the world with a slit for inserting money. He must have thought it was full of dimes and nickels, because when he saw that it had just ten pennies, his face fell with such undisguised disappointment that his mother slapped the side of his head and led him out of the church hall, apologizing to the crowd for her son who had such bad manners he couldn't appreciate such a fine gift.

WORDS TO OWN
ntricate (in′tri·kit) *adj.:* :omplicated.

As I peered into the sack, I quickly fingered the remaining presents, testing their weight, imagining what they contained. I chose a heavy, compact one that was wrapped in shiny silver foil and a red satin ribbon. It was a twelve-pack of Life Savers and I spent the rest of the party arranging and rearranging the candy tubes in the order of my favorites. My brother Winston chose wisely as well. His present turned out to be a box of intricate plastic parts; the instructions on the box proclaimed that when they were properly assembled he would have an authentic miniature replica of a World War II submarine.

Vincent got the chess set, which would have been a very decent present to get at a church Christmas party, except it was obviously used and, as we discovered later, it was missing a black pawn and a white knight. My mother graciously thanked the unknown benefactor, saying, "Too good. Cost too much." At which point, an old lady with fine white,

1. **toilet water:** perfumed after-bath skin freshener.

wispy hair nodded toward our family and said with a whistling whisper, "Merry, merry Christmas."

When we got home, my mother told Vincent to throw the chess set away. "She not want it. We not want it," she said, tossing her head stiffly to the side with a tight, proud smile. My brothers had deaf ears. They were already lining up the chess pieces and reading from the dog-eared instruction book.

I watched Vincent and Winston play during Christmas week. The chess board seemed to hold elaborate secrets waiting to be untangled. The chessmen were more powerful than Old Li's magic herbs that cured ancestral curses. And my brothers wore such serious faces that I was sure something was at stake that was greater than avoiding the tradesmen's door to Hong Sing's.

"Let me! Let me!" I begged between games when one brother or the other would sit back with a deep sigh of relief and victory, the other annoyed, unable to let go of the outcome. Vincent at first refused to let me play, but when I offered my Life Savers as replacements for the buttons that filled in for the missing pieces, he relented. He chose the flavors: wild cherry for the black pawn and peppermint for the white knight. Winner could eat both.

As our mother sprinkled flour and rolled out small doughy circles for the steamed dumplings that would be our dinner that night, Vincent explained the rules, pointing to each piece. "You have sixteen pieces and so do I. One king and queen, two bishops, two knights, two castles, and eight pawns. The pawns can only move forward one step, except on the first move. Then they can move two. But they can only take men by moving crossways like this, except in the beginning, when you can move ahead and take another pawn."

"Why?" I asked as I moved my pawn. "Why can't they move more steps?"

"Because they're pawns," he said.

"But why do they go crossways to take other men. Why aren't there any women and children?"

"Why is the sky blue? Why must you always ask stupid questions?" asked Vincent. "This is a game. These are the rules. I didn't make them up. See. Here. In the book." He jabbed a page with a pawn in his hand. "Pawn. P-A-W-N. Pawn. Read it yourself."

My mother patted the flour off her hands. "Let me see book," she said quietly. She scanned the pages quickly, not reading the foreign English symbols, seeming to search deliberately for nothing in particular.

"This American rules," she concluded at last. "Every time people come out from foreign country, must know rules. You not know, judge say, Too bad, go back. They not telling you why so you can use their

INFER

What is the mother's **motivati** for telling the boys to throw away the chess set?

WORDS TO OWN

ancestral (an·ses′trəl) *adj.:* inherited.

INFER

Why is the **narrator** intrigued by the chess set?

ETELL

e your own words to raphrase what the mother saying about rules (lines –86).

way go forward. They say, Don't know why, you find out yourself. But they knowing all the time. Better you take it, find out why yourself." She tossed her head back with a satisfied smile.

I found out about all the whys later. I read the rules and looked up all the big words in a dictionary. I borrowed books from the Chinatown library. I studied each chess piece, trying to absorb the power each contained.

I learned about opening moves and why it's important to control the center early on; the shortest distance between two points is straight down the middle. I learned about the middle game and why tactics between two adversaries are like clashing ideas; the one who plays better has the clearest plans for both attacking and getting out of traps. I learned why it is essential in the endgame to have foresight, a mathematical understanding of all possible moves, and patience; all weaknesses and advantages become evident to a strong adversary and are obscured to a tiring opponent. I discovered that for the whole game one must gather invisible strengths and see the endgame before the game begins.

ORDS TO OWN

scured (əb·skyoord′) *v.:* ncealed.

I also found out why I should never reveal "why" to others. A little knowledge withheld is a great advantage one should store for future use. That is the power of chess. It is a game of secrets in which one must show and never tell.

I loved the secrets I found within the sixty-four black and white squares. I carefully drew a handmade chessboard and pinned it to the wall next to my bed, where at night I would stare for hours at imaginary battles. Soon I no longer lost any games or Life Savers, but I lost my adversaries. Winston and Vincent decided they were more interested in roaming the streets after school in their Hopalong Cassidy[2] cowboy hats.

On a cold spring afternoon, while walking home from school, I detoured through the playground at the end of our alley. I saw a group of old men, two seated across a folding table playing a game of chess, others smoking pipes, eating peanuts, and watching. I ran home and grabbed Vincent's chess set, which was bound in a cardboard box with rubber bands. I also carefully selected two prized rolls of Life Savers. I came back to the park and approached a man who was observing the game.

"Want to play?" I asked him. His face widened with surprise and he grinned as he looked at the box under my arm.

"Little sister, been a long time since I play with dolls," he said, smiling benevolently. I quickly put the box down next to him on the bench and displayed my retort.

ORDS TO OWN

etort (ri·tôrt′) *n.:* quick nswer.

2. **Hopalong Cassidy:** cowboy hero of movies and television from the 1930s through the early 1950s.

Lau Po, as he allowed me to call him, turned out to be a much better player than my brothers. I lost many games and many Life Savers. But over the weeks, with each diminishing roll of candies, I added new secrets. Lau Po gave me the names. The Double Attack from the East and West Shores. Throwing Stones on the Drowning Man. The Sudden Meeting of the Clan. The Surprise from the Sleeping Guard. The Humble Servant Who Kills the King. Sand in the Eyes of Advancing Forces. A Double Killing Without Blood.

There were also the fine points of chess etiquette. Keep captured men in neat rows, as well-tended prisoners. Never announce "Check" with vanity, lest someone with an unseen sword slit your throat. Never hurl pieces into the sandbox after you have lost a game, because then you must find them again, by yourself, after apologizing to all around you. By the end of the summer, Lau Po had taught me all he knew, and I had become a better chess player.

A small weekend crowd of Chinese people and tourists would gather as I played and defeated my opponents one by one. My mother would join the crowds during these outdoor exhibition games. She sat proudly on the bench, telling my admirers with proper Chinese humility, "Is luck."

A man who watched me play in the park suggested that my mother allow me to play in local chess tournaments. My mother smiled graciously, an answer that meant nothing. I desperately wanted to go, but I bit back my tongue. I knew she would not let me play among strangers. So as we walked home I said in a small voice that I didn't want to play in the local tournament. They would have American rules. If I lost, I would bring shame on my family.

"Is shame you fall down nobody push you," said my mother.

During my first tournament, my mother sat with me in the front row as I waited for my turn. I frequently bounced my legs to unstick them from the cold metal seat of the folding chair. When my name was called, I leapt up. My mother unwrapped something in her lap. It was her *chang*, a small tablet of red jade which held the sun's fire. "Is luck," she whispered, and tucked it into my dress pocket. I turned to my opponent, a fifteen-year-old boy from Oakland. He looked at me, wrinkling his nose.

As I began to play, the boy disappeared, the color ran out of the room, and I saw only my white pieces and his black ones waiting on the other side. A light wind began blowing past my ears. It whispered secrets only I could hear.

"Blow from the South," it murmured. "The wind leaves no trail." I saw a clear path, the traps to avoid. The crowd rustled. "Shhh! Shhh!" said the corners of the room. The wind blew stronger. "Throw sand from the East to distract him." The knight came forward ready for the sacrifice. The wind hissed, louder and louder. "Blow, blow, blow. He

INFER

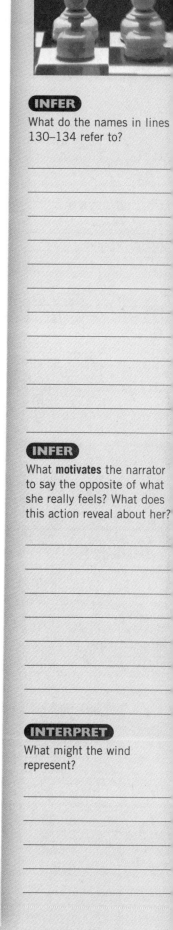

What do the names in lines 130–134 refer to?

INFER

What **motivates** the narrator to say the opposite of what she really feels? What does this action reveal about her?

INTERPRET

What might the wind represent?

ORDS TO OWN

ted (tout′id) *v.:* highly
ised.

digy (präd′ə·jē) *n.:*
remely gifted person.

lodorous (mal·ō′dər·əs)
j.: bad-smelling.

NFER/IDENTIFY

e the definition of the word
alodorous to infer the
eaning of the prefix *mal–*.
entify some other words
med with the same prefix.

cannot see. He is blind now. Make him lean away from the wind so he is easier to knock down."

"Check," I said, as the wind roared with laughter. The wind died down to little puffs, my own breath.

My mother placed my first trophy next to a new plastic chess set that the neighborhood Tao society had given to me. As she wiped each piece with a soft cloth, she said, "Next time win more, lose less."

"Ma, it's not how many pieces you lose," I said. "Sometimes you need to lose pieces to get ahead."

"Better to lose less, see if you really need."

At the next tournament, I won again, but it was my mother who wore the triumphant grin.

"Lost eight piece this time. Last time was eleven. What I tell you? Better off lose less!" I was annoyed, but I couldn't say anything.

I attended more tournaments, each one farther away from home. I won all games, in all divisions. The Chinese bakery downstairs from our flat displayed my growing collection of trophies in its window, amidst the dust-covered cakes that were never picked up. The day after I won an important regional tournament, the window encased a fresh sheet cake with whipped-cream frosting and red script saying, "Congratulations, Waverly Jong, Chinatown Chess Champion." Soon after that, a flower shop, headstone engraver, and funeral parlor offered to sponsor me in national tournaments. That's when my mother decided I no longer had to do the dishes. Winston and Vincent had to do my chores.

"Why does she get to play and we do all the work," complained Vincent.

"Is new American rules," said my mother. "Meimei[3] play, squeeze all her brains out for win chess. You play, worth squeeze towel."

By my ninth birthday, I was a national chess champion. I was still some 429 points away from grand-master status,[4] but I was touted as the Great American Hope, a child prodigy and a girl to boot. They ran a photo of me in *Life* magazine next to a quote in which Bobby Fischer said, "There will never be a woman grand master." "Your move, Bobby," said the caption.

The day they took the magazine picture I wore neatly plaited braids clipped with plastic barrettes trimmed with rhinestones. I was playing in a large high school auditorium that echoed with phlegmy coughs and the squeaky rubber knobs of chair legs sliding across freshly waxed wooden floors. Seated across from me was an American man, about the same age as Lau Po, maybe fifty. I remember that his sweaty brow seemed to weep at my every move. He wore a dark, malodorous suit. One of his pockets

3. **Meimei** (mā′mā′): Chinese for "little sister."
4. **grand-master status:** top rank in international chess competition.

was stuffed with a great white kerchief on which he wiped his palm before sweeping his hand over the chosen chess piece with great flourish.

In my crisp pink-and-white dress with scratchy lace at the neck, one of two my mother had sewn for these special occasions, I would clasp my hands under my chin, the delicate points of my elbows poised lightly on the table in the manner my mother had shown me for posing for the press. I would swing my patent leather shoes back and forth like an impatient child riding on a school bus. Then I would pause, suck in my lips, twirl my chosen piece in midair as if undecided, and then firmly plant it in its new threatening place, with a triumphant smile thrown back at my opponent for good measure.

I no longer played in the alley of Waverly Place. I never visited the playground where the pigeons and old men gathered. I went to school, then directly home to learn new chess secrets, cleverly concealed advantages, more escape routes.

But I found it difficult to concentrate at home. My mother had a habit of standing over me while I plotted out my games. I think she thought of herself as my protective ally. Her lips would be sealed tight, and after each move I made, a soft "Hmmmmph" would escape from her nose.

"Ma, I can't practice when you stand there like that," I said one day. She retreated to the kitchen and made loud noises with the pots and pans. When the crashing stopped, I could see out of the corner of my eye that she was standing in the doorway. "Hmmmph!" Only this one came out of her tight throat.

My parents made many concessions to allow me to practice. One time I complained that the bedroom I shared was so noisy that I couldn't think. Thereafter, my brothers slept in a bed in the living room facing the street. I said I couldn't finish my rice; my head didn't work right when my stomach was too full. I left the table with half-finished bowls and nobody complained. But there was one duty I couldn't avoid. I had to accompany my mother on Saturday market days when I had no tournament to play. My mother would proudly walk with me, visiting many shops, buying very little. "This my daughter Wave-ly Jong," she said to whoever looked her way.

One day, after we left a shop I said under my breath, "I wish you wouldn't do that, telling everybody I'm your daughter." My mother stopped walking. Crowds of people with heavy bags pushed past us on the sidewalk, bumping into first one shoulder, then another.

"Aiii-ya. So shame be with mother?" She grasped my hand even tighter as she glared at me.

I looked down. "It's not that, it's just so obvious. It's just so embarrassing."

INTERPRET

What does the mother's attention to Waverly's cloth and mannerisms reveal abo her?

WORDS TO OWN

concessions (kən·sesh′ənz) *n. pl.:* acts of giving in.

INTERPRET

What does this passage suggest about the difference between the **motivations** of Waverly and those of her mother?

"Embarrass you be my daughter?" Her voice was cracking with anger.

"That's not what I meant. That's not what I said."

"What you say?"

I knew it was a mistake to say anything more, but I heard my voice speaking. "Why do you have to use me to show off? If you want to show off, then why don't you learn to play chess."

My mother's eyes turned into dangerous black slits. She had no words for me, just sharp silence.

I felt the wind rushing around my hot ears. I jerked my hand out of my mother's tight grasp and spun around, knocking into an old woman. Her bag of groceries spilled to the ground.

"Aii-ya! Stupid girl!" my mother and the woman cried. Oranges and tin cans careened down the sidewalk. As my mother stooped to help the old woman pick up the escaping food, I took off.

I raced down the street, dashing between people, not looking back as my mother screamed shrilly, "Meimei! Meimei!" I fled down an alley, past dark curtained shops and merchants washing the grime off their windows. I sped into the sunlight, into a large street crowded with tourists examining trinkets and souvenirs. I ducked into another dark alley, down another street, up another alley. I ran until it hurt and I realized I had nowhere to go, that I was not running from anything. The alleys contained no escape routes.

My breath came out like angry smoke. It was cold. I sat down on an upturned plastic pail next to a stack of empty boxes, cupping my chin with my hands, thinking hard. I imagined my mother, first walking briskly down one street or another looking for me, then giving up and returning home to await my arrival. After two hours, I stood up on creaking legs and slowly walked home.

The alley was quiet and I could see the yellow lights shining from our flat like two tiger's eyes in the night. I climbed the sixteen steps to the door, advancing quietly up each so as not to make any warning sounds. I turned the knob; the door was locked. I heard a chair moving, quick steps, the locks turning—click! click! click!—and then the door opened.

"About time you got home," said Vincent. "Boy, are you in trouble."

He slid back to the dinner table. On a platter were the remains of a large fish, its fleshy head still connected to bones swimming upstream in vain escape. Standing there waiting for my punishment, I heard my mother speak in a dry voice.

"We are not concerning this girl. This girl not have concerning for us."

Nobody looked at me. Bone chopsticks clinked against the insides of bowls being emptied into hungry mouths.

I walked into my room, closed the door, and lay down on my bed. The room was dark, the ceiling filled with shadows from the dinnertime lights of neighboring flats.

ORDS TO OWN

eened (kə·rēnd′) *v.:* lurched ways.

NTERPRET

at does the comment in e 293 reveal about the ther's feelings?

In my head, I saw a chessboard with sixty-four black and white squares. Opposite me was my opponent, two angry black slits. She wore a triumphant smile. "Strongest wind cannot be seen," she said.

Her black men advanced across the plane, slowly marching to each successive level as a single unit. My white pieces screamed as they scurried and fell off the board one by one. As her men drew closer to my edge, I felt myself growing light. I rose up into the air and flew out the window. Higher and higher, above the alley, over the tops of tiled roofs, where I was gathered up by the wind and pushed up toward the night sky until everything below me disappeared and I was alone.

I closed my eyes and pondered my next move.

WORDS TO OWN

successive (sək·ses′iv) *adj.:* consecutive.

BUILD FLUENCY

Read this passage aloud as expressively as you can. Foc on the elements of **tone** and emphasis.

PREDICT

Tan uses the **imagery** of a chessboard to represent the **conflict** between daughter ar mother. What does the imag suggest about the probable **resolution** of the conflict between Waverly and her mother?

Conflict

Conflict is a struggle or clash between opposing forces or characters. **External conflicts** can exist between two people, between a person and nature or a machine, or between a person and a whole society. **Internal conflicts** involve opposing forces within a person's mind.

Explore Amy Tan's use of external and internal conflicts in "Rules of the Game" by filling out the chart below.

	External Conflicts	**Internal Conflicts**
Waverly		
Mrs. Jong		

Vocabulary: How to Own a Word

Word Bank
intricate
ancestral
obscured
retort
touted
prodigy
malodorous
concessions
careened
successive

Connotations

The words *slow* and *methodical* have similar denotations. However, in most contexts, being slow has a negative connotation, whereas being methodical is considered positive. Other words, such as *chair,* do not evoke any emotion and are considered neutral.

For the following Words to Own, decide which has a positive (**P**), negative (**N**), or neutral (**O**) connotation, and write the appropriate letter in the space provided before the number for that word. Then, explain your answer on the lines provided by using examples or personal experiences.

_____ **1.** intricate ______________________________

____

_____ **2.** ancestral ______________________________

____

_____ **3.** obscured ______________________________

____

_____ **4.** retort ______________________________

____

_____ **5.** touted ______________________________

____

_____ **6.** prodigy ______________________________

____

_____ **7.** malodorous ______________________________

____

_____ **8.** concessions ______________________________

____

_____ **9.** careened ______________________________

____

_____ **10.** successive ______________________________

____

Autobiographical Notes

Make the Connection

Know Thyself

The ancient Greek philosopher Socrates once said,"The unexamined life is not worth living." What exactly do you think it means to live an *examined* life? Might it mean stepping back from the world of everyday activities and gaining some perspective on who you are? on where you have been and where you are heading? Perhaps living an examined life means creating new angles of vision, asking questions, and proposing answers.

Suppose you were to create a set of autobiographical notes assessing your own development. What would you include? Use the space below to jot down your notes.

James Baldwin

Autobiographical Notes

RDS TO OWN
k (blēk) *adj.:* cheerless.

ORDS TO OWN
sored (sen′sərd) *v.:* cut or
anged to remove material
emed objectionable.

NTERPRET
w were Baldwin's gifts
vious in his childhood?

I was born in Harlem thirty-one years ago. I began plotting novels at about the time I learned to read. The story of my childhood is the usual bleak fantasy, and we can dismiss it with the restrained observation that I certainly would not consider living it again. In those days my mother was given to the exasperating and mysterious habit of having babies. As they were born, I took them over with one hand and held a book with the other. The children probably suffered, though they have since been kind enough to deny it, and in this way I read *Uncle Tom's Cabin* and *A Tale of Two Cities* over and over and over again; in this way, in fact, I read just about everything I could get my hands on—except the Bible, probably because it was the only book I was encouraged to read. I must also confess that I wrote—a great deal—and my first professional triumph, in any case, the first effort of mine to be seen in print, occurred at the age of twelve or thereabouts, when a short story I had written about the Spanish revolution won some sort of a prize in an extremely short-lived church newspaper. I remember the story was censored by the lady editor, though I don't remember why, and I was outraged.

Also wrote plays, and songs, for one of which I received a letter of congratulations from Mayor La Guardia,[1] and poetry, about which the less said, the better. My mother was delighted by all these goings-on, but my father wasn't; he wanted me to be a preacher. When I was fourteen I became a preacher, and when I was seventeen I stopped. Very shortly thereafter I left home. For God knows how long I struggled with the world of commerce and industry—I guess they would say they struggled with *me*—and when I was about twenty-one I had enough done of a novel to get a Saxton Fellowship. When I was twenty-two the fellowship was over, the novel turned out to be unsalable, and I started waiting on tables in a Village[2] restaurant and writing book reviews—mostly, as it turned out, about the Negro problem, concerning which the color of my skin made me automatically an expert. Did another book, in company with photographer Theodore Pelatowski, about the store-front churches in Harlem. This book met exactly the same fate as my first—fellowship, but no sale. (It was a Rosenwald Fellowship.) By the time I was twenty-four I had decided to stop reviewing books about the Negro problem—which, by this time, was only slightly less horrible in print than it was in life—and I packed my bags and went to France, where I finished, God knows how, *Go Tell It on the Mountain*.

Any writer, I suppose, feels that the world into which he was born is nothing less than a conspiracy against the cultivation of his talent—which attitude certainly has a great deal to support it. On the other hand, it is only because the world looks on his talent with such a frightening

1. **Mayor La Guardia:** Fiorello La Guardia, mayor of New York City from 1934 to 1945.
2. **Village:** Greenwich Village, a section of Manhattan noted as a center for writers and other artists.

indifference that the artist is compelled to make his talent important. So that any writer, looking back over even so short a span of time as I am here forced to assess, finds that the things which hurt him and the things which helped him cannot be divorced from each other; he could be helped in a certain way only because he was hurt in a certain way; and his help is simply to be enabled to move from one conundrum to the next—one is tempted to say that he moves from one disaster to the next. When one begins looking for influences one finds them by the score. I haven't thought much about my own, not enough anyway; I hazard that the King James Bible, the rhetoric of the store-front church, something ironic and violent and perpetually understated in Negro speech—and something of Dickens' love for bravura[3]—have something to do with me today; but I wouldn't stake my life on it. Likewise, innumerable people have helped me in many ways; but finally, I suppose, the most difficult (and most rewarding) thing in my life has been the fact that I was born a Negro and was forced, therefore, to effect some kind of truce with this reality. (Truce, by the way, is the best one can hope for.)

One of the difficulties about being a Negro writer (and this is not special pleading, since I don't mean to suggest that he has it worse than anybody else) is that the Negro problem is written about so widely. The bookshelves groan under the weight of information, and everyone therefore considers himself informed. And this information, furthermore, operates usually (generally, popularly) to reinforce traditional attitudes. Of traditional attitudes there are only two—For or Against—and I, personally, find it difficult to say which attitude has caused me the most pain. I am speaking as a writer; from a social point of view I am perfectly aware that the change from ill-will to good-will, however motivated, however imperfect, however expressed, is better than no change at all.

But it is part of the business of the writer—as I see it—to examine attitudes, to go beneath the surface, to tap the source. From this point of view the Negro problem is nearly inaccessible. It is not only written about so widely; it is written about so badly. It is quite possible to say that the price a Negro pays for becoming articulate is to find himself, at length, with nothing to be articulate about. ("You taught me language," says Caliban to Prospero,[4] "and my profit on't is I know how to curse.") Consider: the tremendous social activity that this problem generates imposes on whites and Negroes alike the necessity of looking forward, of working to bring about a better day. This is fine, it keeps the waters

3. **bravura** (brə·vyoor′ə): florid, brilliant style.
4. **Caliban to Prospero:** Caliban, a rough creature, is Prospero's slave, whom Prospero tries to civilize in *The Tempest* by William Shakespeare. The quotation is from Act I, Scene 2.

WORDS TO OWN

assess (ə·ses′) *v.:* to evaluat judge the value of.
conundrum (kə·nun′drəm) *n.* riddle.

INTERPRET

What does Baldwin mean by this "truce" (line 58)? What he saying about the status o African American identity?

INTERPRET

Why might Baldwin wish to avoid the impression of "special pleading" in his wor

BUILD FLUENCY

Read this paragraph aloud, focusing on the **main idea** and supporting details.

troubled; it is all, indeed, that has made possible the Negro's progress. Nevertheless, social affairs are not generally speaking the writer's prime concern, whether they ought to be or not; it is absolutely necessary that he establish between himself and these affairs a distance which will allow, at least, for clarity, so that before he can look forward in any meaningful sense, he must first be allowed to take a long look back. In the context of the Negro problem neither whites nor blacks, for excellent reasons of their own, have the faintest desire to look back; but I think that the past is all that makes the present coherent, and further, that the past will remain horrible for exactly as long as we refuse to assess it honestly.

ORDS TO OWN
erent (kō·hir′ənt) *adj.:* ar, logical, and consistent.

VALUATE
you agree with what dwin says about the effect not facing up to history? y or why not?

I know, in any case, that the most crucial time in my own development came when I was forced to recognize that I was a kind of bastard of the West; when I followed the line of my past I did not find myself in Europe but in Africa. And this meant that in some subtle way, in a really profound way, I brought to Shakespeare, Bach, Rembrandt, to the stones of Paris, to the cathedral at Chartres, and to the Empire State Building, a special attitude. These were not really my creations, they did not contain my history; I might search in them in vain forever for any reflection of myself. I was an interloper; this was not my heritage. At the same time I had no other heritage which I could possibly hope to use—I had certainly been unfitted for the jungle or the tribe. I would have to appropriate these white centuries, I would have to make them mine—I would have to accept my special attitude, my special place in this scheme—otherwise I would have no place in *any* scheme. What was the most difficult was the fact that I was forced to admit something I had always hidden from myself, which the American Negro has had to hide from himself as the price of his public progress; that I hated and feared white people. This did not mean that I loved black people; on the contrary, I despised them, possibly because they failed to produce Rembrandt. In effect, I hated and feared the world. And this meant, not only that I thus gave the world an altogether murderous power over me, but also that in such a self-destroying limbo[5] I could never hope to write.

'ORDS TO OWN
ucial (kroo′shəl) *adj.:* itical; decisive.
terloper (in′tər·lō′pər) *n.:* truder; meddler.
propriate (ə·prō′prē·āt′) : to take over.

One writes out of one thing only—one's own experience. Everything depends on how relentlessly one forces from this experience the last drop, sweet or bitter, it can possibly give. This is the only real concern of the artist, to recreate out of the disorder of life that order which is art. The difficulty then, for me, of being a Negro writer was the fact that I was, in effect, prohibited from examining my own experience too closely by the tremendous demands and the very real dangers of my social situation.

DENTIFY
nderline the **main idea** this paragraph.

I don't think the dilemma outlined above is uncommon. I do think, since writers work in the disastrously explicit medium of language, that it goes a little way toward explaining why, out of the enormous resources

VORDS TO OWN
xplicit (eks·plis′it) *adj.:* clear; efinite.

5. **limbo:** borderland state of uncertainty and oblivion.

of Negro speech and life, and despite the example of Negro music, prose written by Negroes has been generally speaking so pallid and so harsh. I have not written about being a Negro at such length because I expect that to be my only subject, but only because it was the gate I had to unlock before I could hope to write about anything else. I don't think that the Negro problem in America can be even discussed coherently without bearing in mind its context; its context being the history, traditions, customs, the moral assumptions and preoccupations of the country; in short, the general social fabric. Appearances to the contrary, no one in America escapes its effects and everyone in America bears some responsibility for it. I believe this the more firmly because it is the overwhelming tendency to speak of this problem as though it were a thing apart. But in the work of Faulkner, in the general attitude and certain specific passages in Robert Penn Warren, and, most significantly, in the advent of Ralph Ellison, one sees the beginnings—at least—of a more genuinely penetrating search. Mr. Ellison, by the way, is the first Negro novelist I have ever read to utilize in language, and brilliantly, some of the ambiguity and irony of Negro life.

About my interests: I don't know if I have any, unless the morbid desire to own a sixteen millimeter camera and make experimental movies can be so classified. Otherwise, I love to eat and drink—it's my melancholy conviction that I've scarcely ever had enough to eat (this is because it's *impossible* to eat enough if you're worried about the next meal)—and I love to argue with people who do not disagree with me too profoundly, and I love to laugh. I do *not* like bohemia,[6] or bohemians, I do not like people whose principal aim is pleasure, and I do not like people who are *earnest* about anything. I don't like people who like me because I'm a Negro; neither do I like people who find in the same accident grounds for contempt. I love America more than any other country in the world, and, exactly for this reason, I insist on the right to criticize her perpetually. I think all theories are suspect, that the finest principles may have to be modified, or may even be pulverized by the demands of life, and that one must find, therefore, one's own moral center and move through the world hoping that this center will guide one aright. I consider that I have many responsibilities, but none greater than this: to last, as Hemingway says, and get my work done.

I want to be an honest man and a good writer.

---

6. **bohemia:** any nonconformist, unconventional community, often made up of writers and other artists.

IDENTIFY

What is Baldwin's assessme of most prose written by African Americans? Underlir the statement.

INFER

Why does Baldwin admire the work of Ralph Ellison?

WORDS TO OWN

pulverized (pul'vər·īzd') *v.:* crushed; destroyed.

RETELL

In this long paragraph, Baldwin condenses his "note on his own character into a series of polished, concise observations. Choose one of these observations to paraphrase in your own words

Autobiography

In an **autobiography,** a writer offers an account of his or her own life. In "Autobiographical Notes," James Baldwin presents an abbreviated account of his development as a writer and thinker. Baldwin concludes this account with a statement of his personal goals.

In a **biography,** we usually look for factual accuracy and **objectivity.** In an **autobiography,** we look for **subjectivity.** We want the writer to get personal.

Select examples from Baldwin's essay that reveal the kind of personal, internal knowledge that only the writer could reveal, and write them on the lines provided.

Vocabulary: How to Own a Word

Connotations

Word Bank
bleak
censored
assess
conundrum
coherent
crucial
interloper
appropriate
explicit
pulverized

The words *eager* and *anxious* have similar denotations. However, in most contexts, being anxious has a negative connotation, whereas being eager is considered positive. Other words, such as *desk,* do not evoke any emotion and are considered neutral.

For the following Words to Own, decide which has a positive (**P**), negative (**N**), or neutral (**O**) connotation, and write the appropriate letter in the space provided before the number for that word. Then, explain your answer on the lines provided by using examples or personal experiences.

_____ **1.** bleak _______________

_____ **2.** censored _______________

_____ **3.** assess _______________

_____ **4.** conundrum _______________

_____ **5.** coherent _______________

_____ **6.** crucial _______________

_____ **7.** interloper _______________

_____ **8.** appropriate _______________

_____ **9.** explicit _______________

_____ **10.** pulverized _______________

Mirror

Make the Connection

Reflections

We all do it. We check our appearance in a mirror, partly to make sure we are appropriately groomed, partly in order to discover and polish our self-image.

If a mirror could talk, what might it say about the concerns of the people who pass before it or who gaze into it? In the space below, write down a few observations that a "talking" mirror might make.

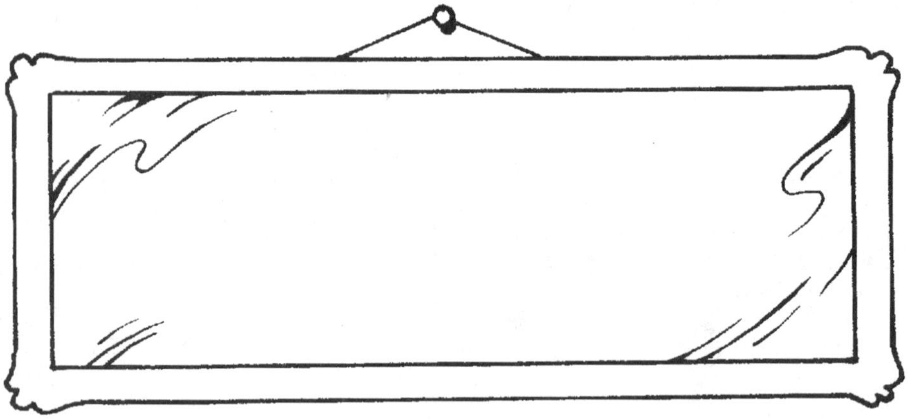

Sylvia Plath

Mirror

DENTIFY

ɿo or what is the **speaker** in e poem? What self-portrait es the speaker offer?

NTERPRET

xplain the meaning of lines 0–12.

NTERPRET

ow does the woman "reward" ɿe mirror?

BUILD FLUENCY

Read the poem aloud, oncentrating on tone, mphasis, and coherent nits of meaning.

I am silver and exact. I have no preconceptions.
Whatever I see I swallow immediately
Just as it is, unmisted by love or dislike.
I am not cruel, only truthful—
The eye of a little god, four-cornered.
Most of the time I meditate on the opposite wall.
It is pink, with speckles. I have looked at it so long
I think it is a part of my heart. But it flickers.
Faces and darkness separate us over and over.
Now I am a lake. A woman bends over me,
Searching my reaches for what she really is.
Then she turns to those liars, the candles or the moon.
I see her back, and reflect it faithfully.
She rewards me with tears and an agitation of hands.
I am important to her. She comes and goes.
Each morning it is her face that replaces the darkness.
In me she has drowned a young girl, and in me an old woman
Rises toward her day after day, like a terrible fish.

Speaker

The **speaker** is the person or object that voices the words of a poem. The speaker may be the poet, but more often the speaker is a character invented by the poet.

1. Who is the speaker in "Mirror"?

____

2. What feelings and attitudes does the speaker have?

____

____

3. Describe the qualities that the speaker claims to possess. What does the speaker imply in the phrase "eye of a little god" (line 5)?

____

____

____

____

4. What is the woman's attitude toward the speaker? Why do you think she feels this way?

____

____

____

____

5. What do you think of the speaker's attitude toward the woman? Is it as neutral as the speaker claims?

____

____

____

____

The Latin Deli: An Ars Poetica

Make the Connection

Native Tongue

Language is one of our most important tools of self-expression. Hidden in the words we say, beneath their literal meanings on the surface, are layers of personal associations, complex social implications, and cultural overtones. This is especially true of immigrants who try to adjust to a new country, but who are still drawn to their former homelands. You may be acquainted with recent immigrants who intermix words of their native language with English.

In the space below, write some of the things an immigrant might remember with fondness about his or her native country. Be as precise as possible.

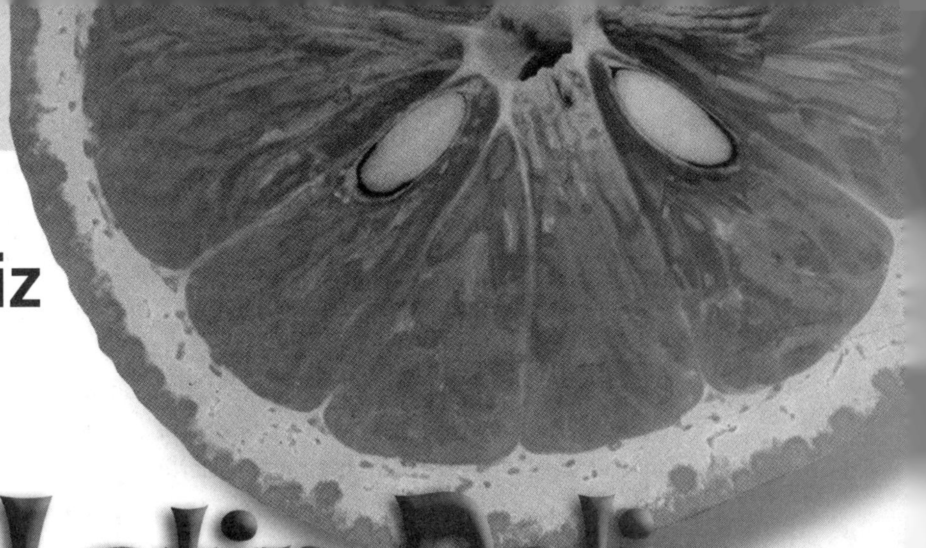

Judith Ortiz Cofer

The Latin Deli: An Ars Poetica

NFER

nat is meant by the **epithet** atroness of Exiles" (line 7)?

NTERPRET

hat do you think the "canned emories" (line 9) consist of?

NTERPRET

ne description of a ham-and-neese sandwich leads to a more ɔstract conclusion about the nmigrants. What is that ɔnclusion?

BUILD FLUENCY

ead the whole poem aloud, ɔcusing on rhythm, emphasis, ɔne, and coherent units of neaning.

INTERPRET

rs poetica is Latin for "the art f poetry." What might the uthor be saying about the ature of good poetry?

Presiding over a formica counter,
plastic Mother and Child magnetized
to the top of an ancient register,
the heady mix of smells from the open bins
of dried codfish, the green plantains[1]
hanging in stalks like votive offerings,[2]
she is the Patroness of Exiles,
a woman of no-age who was never pretty,
who spends her days selling canned memories
while listening to the Puerto Ricans complain
that it would be cheaper to fly to San Juan
than to buy a pound of Bustelo coffee here,
and to Cubans perfecting their speech
of a "glorious return" to Havana—where no one
has been allowed to die and nothing to change until then;
to Mexicans who pass through, talking lyrically
of *dólares* to be made in El Norte—
all wanting the comfort
of spoken Spanish, to gaze upon the family portrait
of her plain wide face, her ample bosom
resting on her plump arms, her look of maternal interest
as they speak to her and each other
of their dreams and their disillusions—
how she smiles understanding,
when they walk down the narrow aisles of her store
reading the labels of packages aloud, as if
they were the names of lost lovers: *Suspiros,*[3]
Merengues,[4] the stale candy of everyone's childhood.
She spends her days
slicing *jamón y queso*[5] and wrapping it in wax paper
tied with string: plain ham and cheese
that would cost less at the A&P, but it would not satisfy
the hunger of the fragile old man lost in the folds
of his winter coat, who brings her lists of items
that he reads to her like poetry, or the others,
whose needs she must divine, conjuring up products
from places that now exist only in their hearts—
closed ports she must trade with.

1. **plantains:** type of banana.
2. **votive offerings:** sacrifices made to fulfill a vow or offered in devotion.
3. ***Suspiros*** (sōōs·pē′rōs): type of small spongecake.
4. ***Merengues*** (mā·rān′gās): candy made of meringue (mixture of egg whites and sugar).
5. ***jamón y queso*** (khä·mōn′ ē kā′sō): Spanish for "ham and cheese."

Concrete and Abstract Language

In a literary work, **concrete language** involves the use of well-chosen sensory details to evoke and describe a particular subject. In contrast, **abstract language** deals with a subject in general terms and emphasizes intangible concepts like qualities and values. In abstract language, there are few sensory words, and details do not play a large role.

In the spaces provided, classify each word or phrase in the list below. If the item is concrete, write **C.** If it is abstract, write **A.**

__________ **1.** formica counter

__________ **2.** dried codfish

__________ **3.** memories

__________ **4.** a glorious return

__________ **5.** a pound of Bustelo coffee

__________ **6.** maternal interest

__________ **7.** plump arms

__________ **8.** the names of lost lovers

__________ **9.** wax paper

__________ **10.** comfort

PART 2 Standardized Test Practice

Literary Period Tests

Comparing Literature

DIRECTIONS

Read the following passage. Then, circle the lettered answer that best completes each numbered item.

from "What Is an American?" *Letters from an American Farmer*

Michel-Guillaume Jean de Crèvecoeur

This work is a famous tribute to America by a widely traveled French writer named Michel-Guillaume Jean de Crèvecoeur. He confirms the hopes of people disillusioned and burdened by history.

I wish I could be acquainted with the feelings and thoughts which must agitate the heart and present themselves to the mind of an enlightened Englishman when he first lands on this continent. He must greatly rejoice that he lived at a time to see this fair country discovered and settled; he must necessarily feel a share of national pride when he views the chain of settlements which embellishes these extended shores. When he says to himself, this is the work of my countrymen, who, when convulsed by factions, afflicted by a variety of miseries and wants, restless and impatient, took refuge here. They brought along with them their national genius, to which they principally owe what liberty they enjoy and what substance they possess. Here he sees the industry of his native country displayed in a new manner, and traces in their works the embryos of all the arts, sciences, and ingenuity which flourish in Europe. Here he beholds fair cities, substantial villages, extensive fields, an immense country filled with decent houses, good roads, orchards, meadows, and bridges, where a hundred years ago all was wild, woody, and uncultivated!

What a train of pleasing ideas this fair spectacle must suggest! It is a prospect which must inspire a good citizen with the most heartfelt pleasure. The difficulty consists in the manner of viewing so extensive a scene. He is arrived on a new continent; a modern society offers itself to his contemplation, different from what he had hitherto seen. It is not composed, as in Europe, of great lords who possess everything, and of a herd of people who have nothing. Here are no aristocratical families, no courts, no kings, no bishops, no ecclesiastical dominion, no invisible power giving to a few a very visible one, no great manufacturers employing thousands, no great refinements of luxury. The rich and the poor are not so far removed from each other as they are in Europe.

Some few towns excepted, we are all tillers of the earth, from Nova Scotia to West Florida. We are a people of cultivators, scattered over an immense territory, communicating with each other by means of good roads and navigable rivers, united by the silken bands of mild government, all respecting the laws without dreading their power, because they are equitable. We are all animated with the spirit of industry, which is unfettered and unrestrained, because each person works for himself. If he travels through our rural districts, he views not the hostile castle and the haughty mansion, contrasted with the clay-built hut and miserable cabin, where cattle and men help to keep each other warm, and dwell in meanness, smoke, and indigence. A pleasing uniformity of decent competence appears throughout our habitations. The meanest of our log houses is a dry and comfortable habitation.

Lawyer or merchant are the fairest titles our towns afford; that of a farmer is the only appellation of the rural inhabitants of our country. It must take some time before he can reconcile himself to our dictionary, which is but short in words of dignity and names of honor. There, on a Sunday, he sees a congregation of respectable farmers and their wives, all clad in neat homespun, well mounted, or riding their own humble wagons. There is not among them an esquire, saving the unlettered magistrate. There he sees a parson as simple as his flock, a farmer who does not riot on the labor of others. We have no princes for whom we toil, starve, and bleed; we are the most perfect society now existing in the world. Here man is free as he ought to be; nor is this pleasing equality so transitory as many others are. Many ages will not see the shores of our great lakes replenished with inland nations, nor the unknown bounds of North America entirely peopled. Who can tell how far it extends? Who can tell the millions of men whom it will feed and contain? For no European foot has as yet traveled half the extent of this mighty continent!

---

1. Crèvecoeur believes an English traveler to North America would probably feel —

A envy
B pride
C hostility
D anger

2. The "national genius" that Crèvecoeur believes the Americans inherited from the British lies in their —

F artistic taste
G literary ability
H industriousness
J sense of humor

3. According to Crèvecoeur, most people in America during this period —

A were wealthy landowners
B experienced abject poverty
C traveled constantly
D lived modestly and comfortably

4. Crèvecoeur describes the North American continent as —

F wildly beautiful and rugged
G vast and unexplored
H crowded and overpopulated
J artistically inspiring

5. According to Crèvecoeur, an important difference between Europe and North America is that the latter lacks —

A humble farmers
B aristocratic families
C lawyers or merchants
D religious leaders

DIRECTIONS

Read the following poem. Then, circle the lettered answer that best completes each numbered item.

Inscription for the Entrance to a Wood

William Cullen Bryant

Stranger, if thou hast learned a truth which needs
No school of long experience, that the world
Is full of guilt and misery, and hast seen
Enough of all its sorrows, crimes, and cares
To tire thee of it, enter this wild wood
And view the haunts of Nature. The calm shade
Shall bring a kindred calm, and the sweet breeze
That makes the green leaves dance, shall waft a balm
To thy sick heart. Thou wilt find nothing here
Of all that pained thee in the haunts of men,
And made thee loathe thy life. The primal curse
Fell, it is true, upon the unsinning earth,
But not in vengeance. God hath yoked to guilt
Her pale tormentor, misery. Hence, these shades
Are still the abodes of gladness; the thick roof
Of green and stirring branches is alive
And musical with birds, that sing and sport
In wantonness of spirit; while below
The squirrel, with raised paws and form erect,
Chirps merrily. Throngs of insects in the shade
Try their thin wings and dance in the warm beam
That waked them into life. Even the green trees
Partake the deep contentment; as they bend
To the soft winds, the sun from the blue sky
Looks in and sheds a blessing on the scene.
Scarce less the cleft-born wildflower seems to enjoy
Existence, than the wingèd plunderer
That sucks its sweet. The mossy rocks themselves,
And the old and ponderous trunks of prostrate trees
That lead from knoll to knoll a causey rude
Or bridge the sunken brook, and their dark roots,
With all their earth upon them, twisting high,
Breathe fixed tranquility. The rivulet
Sends forth glad sounds, and tripping o'er its bed
Of pebbly sands, or leaping down the rocks,
Seems, with continuous laughter, to rejoice
In its own being. Softly tread the marge,
Lest from her midway perch thou scare the wren
That dips her bill in water. The cool wind,
That stirs the stream in play, shall come to thee,
Like one that loves thee nor will let thee pass
Ungreeted, and shall give its light embrace.

1. "Inscription for the Entrance to a Wood" focuses primarily on —

A the premature death of heroes
B the comfort of nature
C ambition as the highest human goal
D guilt as the cause of human misery

2. At the end of the poem, the stranger is welcomed into the world of nature through —

F religious teachings
G riddles
H reason
J love

3. The poem portrays various elements of nature as —

A living in a fragile state of coexistence with each other
B part of a cyclical pattern of life and death
C rejoicing in the comfort of their existence
D constantly battling the human world in order to survive

4. The insects in the poem are described as —

F a marginal part of the natural world
G the lowest form of living beings
H annoying but hardworking creatures
J reflections of sublime beauty and grace

5. The **speaker** suggests that human beings should approach nature —

A with fear and caution
B with total abandon
C with a rational mind
D with openness and optimism

DIRECTIONS

Read the following selection. Then, circle the lettered answer that best completes each numbered item.

Pap Starts in on a New Life

Mark Twain

The following selection comes from the early part of Mark Twain's novel Adventures of Huckleberry Finn. *At this point in the novel (Chapter 5), Huck has been taken away from his irresponsible, drunken father and placed with a pious widow who is attempting to "civilize" him. Huck's father has heard that Huck has received some money, and the old man comes creeping into Huck's room one night in search of it. When Huck goes to his room and lights his candle, "there sat Pap—his own self!"*

I had shut the door to. Then I turned around, and there he was. I used to be scared of him all the time, he tanned[1] me so much. I reckoned I was scared now, too; but in a minute I see I was mistaken—that is, after the first jolt, as you may say, when my breath sort of hitched, he being so unexpected; but right away after I see I warn't scared of him worth bothering about.

He was most fifty, and he looked it. His hair was long and tangled and greasy, and hung down, and you could see his eyes shining through like he was behind vines. It was all black, no gray; so was his long, mixed-up whiskers. There warn't no color in his face, where his face showed; it was white; not like another man's white, but a white to make a body sick, a white to make a body's flesh crawl—a tree-toad white, a fish-belly white. As for his clothes—just rags, that was all. He had one ankle resting on t'other knee; the boot on that foot was busted, and two of his toes stuck through, and he worked them now and then. His hat was laying on the floor—an old black slouch with the top caved in, like a lid.

I stood a-looking at him; he set there a-looking at me, with his chair tilted back a little. I set the candle down. I noticed the window was up; so he had clumb in by the shed. He kept a-looking me all over. By and by he says:

"Starchy clothes—very. You think you're a good deal of a big-bug, *don't* you?"

"May I am, maybe I ain't," I says.

"Don't give me none o' your lip," says he. "You've put on considerable many frills since I been away. I'll take you down a peg before I get done with you. You're educated, too, they say—can read and write. You think you're better'n your father, now don't you, because he can't? *I'll* take it out of you. Who told you you might meddle with such hi-falut'n foolishness, hey?—who told you you could?"

"The widow. She told me."

"The widow, hey?—and who told the widow she could put in her shovel about a thing that ain't none of her business?"

"Nobody told her."

"Well, I'll learn her how to meddle. And looky here—you drop that school, you hear? I'll learn people to bring up a boy to put on airs over his own father and let on to be better'n

1. **tanned:** whipped.

what *he* is. You lemme catch you fooling around that school again, you hear? Your mother couldn't read, and she couldn't write, nuther, bother she died. None of the family couldn't before *they* died. I can't, and here you're a-swelling yourself up like this. I ain't the man to stand it—you hear? Say, lemme hear you read."

I took up a book and begun something about General Washington and the wars. When I'd read about a half a minute, he fetched the book a whack with his hand and knocked it across the house. He says:

"It's so. You can do it. I had my doubts when you told me. Now looky here; you stop that putting on frills. I won't have it. I'll lay for you, my smarty; and if I catch you about that school I'll tan you good. First you know you'll get religion, too. I never see such a son."

He took up a little blue and yaller picture of some cows and a boy, and says:

"What's this?"

"It's something they give me for learning my lessons good."

He tore it up, and says:

"I'll give you something better—I'll give you a cowhide."

He set there a-mumbling and a-growling a minute, and then he says:

Ain't you a sweet-scented dandy, though? A bed; and bed-clothes; and a look'n'-glass; and a piece of carpet on the floor—and your own father got to sleep with the hogs in the tanyard. I never see such a son. I bet I'll take some o' these frills out o' you before I'm done with you. Why, there ain't no end to your airs—they say you're rich. Hey?—how's that?"

"They lie—that's how."

"Looky here—mind how you talk to me; I'm a-standing about all I can stand now—so don't gimme no sass. I've been in town two days, and I hain't heard nothing but about you bein' rich. I heard about it away down the river, too. That's why I come. You git me that money tomorrow—I want it."

"I hain't got no money."

"It's a lie. Judge Thatcher's got it. You git it. I want it."

"I hain't got no money, I tell you. You ask Judge Thatcher; he'll tell you the same."

"All right. I'll ask him; and I'll make him pungle,[2] too, or I'll know the reason why. Say, how much you got in your pocket? I want it."

"I hain't got only a dollar, and want that to—"

"It don't make no difference what you want it for—you just shell it out."

He took it and bit it to see if it was good, and then he said he was going downtown to get some whiskey, said he hadn't had a drink all day. When he had got out on the shed he put his head in again, and cussed me for putting on frills and trying to do better than him; and when I reckoned he was gone he came back and put his head in again, and told me to mind about that school, because he was going to lay for me and lick me if I didn't drop that.

Next day he was drunk, and he went to Judge Thatcher's and bullyragged him, and tried to make him give up the money; but he couldn't, and then he swore he'd make the law force him.

The judge and the widow went to law to get the court to take me away from him and let one of them be my guardian; but it was a new judge that had just come, and he didn't know the old man; so he said courts mustn't interfere and separate families if they could help it; said he'd

2. pungle: pay the money.

druther not take a child away from its father. So Judge Thatcher and the widow had to quit on the business.

That pleased the old man till he couldn't rest. He said he'd cowhide me till I was black and blue if I didn't raise some money for him. I borrowed three dollars from Judge Thatcher, and Pap took it and got drunk, and went a-blowing around and cussing and whooping and carrying on; and he kept it up all over town, with a tin pan, till most midnight; then they jailed him, and the next day they had him before the court, and jailed him again for a week. But he said *he* was satisfied; said he was boss of his son, and he'd make it warm for *him*.

When he got out the new judge said he was a-going to make a man of him. So he took him to his own house, and dressed him up clean and nice, and had him to breakfast and dinner and supper with the family, and was just old pie to him, so to speak. And after supper he talked to him about temperance and such things till the old man cried, and said he'd been a fool, and fooled away his life; but now he was a-going to turn over a new leaf and be a man nobody wouldn't be ashamed of, and he hoped the judge would help him and not look down on him. The judge said he could hug him for them words; so *he* cried, and his wife she cried again; Pap said he'd been a man that had always been misunderstood before, and the judge said he believed it. The old man said that what a man wanted that was down was sympathy, and the judge said it was so; so they cried again. And when it was bedtime the old man rose up and held out his hand, and says:

"Look at it, gentleman and ladies all; take a-hold of it; shake it. There's a hand that was the hand of a hog; but it ain't so no more; it's the hand of a man that's started in on a new life, and'll die before he'll go back. You mark them words—don't forget I said them. It's a clean hand now; shake it—don't be afeared."

So they shook it, one after the other, all around, and cried. The judge's wife she kissed it. Then the old man he signed a pledge—made his mark. The judge said it was the holiest time on record, or something like that. Then they tucked the old man into a beautiful room, which was the spare room, and in the night some time he got powerful thirsty and clumb out on to the porch roof and slid down a stanchion and traded his new coat for a jug of forty-rod, and clumb back again and had a good old time; and toward daylight he crawled out again, drunk as a fiddler, and rolled off the porch and broke his left arm in two places, and was most froze to death when somebody found him after sun-up. And when they come to look at that spare room they had to take soundings before they could navigate it.

The judge felt kind of sore. He said he reckoned a body could reform the old man with a shotgun, maybe, but he didn't know no other way.

1. What is Huck's initial reaction to his father's unexpected appearance?

A He is furious.
B He panics and calls for help.
C He is scared.
D He does not care one way or another.

2. The primary reason Pap has come to see his son is that he —

F is concerned about Huck's well-being
G has heard that Huck is rich
H wants to warn Huck about becoming a dandy
J wants to give Huck a tanning for attending school

3. What does Pap think about Huck's ability to read?

A He is proud of his son and wants Huck to teach him how to read.
B He accuses Huck of trying to better himself.
C He tries to prove that Huck cannot really read.
D He says he will approve of it if Huck will give him money.

4. Which of the following statements about Pap's conversion is *not* true?

F Pap cries openly and proclaims that he is going to change.
G Pap signs a temperance pledge.
H Pap trades his new coat for a jug of whiskey.
J Pap becomes a church member and gets a job.

5. When Pap is found with a broken arm and the judge sees the condition of his room —

A the judge is mad because he has been fooled
B the judge and his wife invite Pap to work for them
C Huck feels sorry for him and gives him more money
D the court awards custody of Huck to Judge Thatcher

DIRECTIONS

Read the following poems. Then, circle the lettered answer that best completes each numbered item.

Daybreak in Alabama

Langston Hughes

When I get to be a composer
I'm gonna write me some music about
Daybreak in Alabama
And I'm gonna put the purtiest songs in it
Rising out of the ground like a swamp mist
And falling out of heaven like soft dew.
I'm gonna put some tall tall trees in it
And the scent of pine needles
And the smell of red clay after rain
And long red necks
And poppy colored faces
And big brown eyes
Of black and white black white black people
And I'm gonna put white hands
And black hands and brown hands and
    yellow hands
And red clay earth hands in it
Touching everybody with kind fingers
And touching each other natural as dew
In that dawn of music when I
Get to be a composer
And write about daybreak
In Alabama.

The Planet on the Table

Wallace Stevens

Ariel was glad he had written
    his poems.
They were of a remembered time
Or of something seen that he liked.
Other makings of the sun
Were waste and welter
And the ripe shrub writhed.
His self and the sun were one
And his poems, although makings of
    his self,
Were no less makings of the sun.
It was not important that they survive.
What mattered was that they should
    bear
Some lineament or character,
Some affluence, if only half-perceived
In the poverty of their words,
Of the planet of which they were part.

1. In Hughes's poem, which of the following things is *not* something the composer says he is going to put into his music?

A Tall trees
B Swamp mist
C The smell of red clay after rain
D The scent of pine needles

2. To what does Hughes compare the color of people's faces?

F Daybreak
G Music
H Clay
J Poppies

3. In Hughes's poem, to what could "daybreak in Alabama" refer?

A A beautiful sunset
B Westward migration
C A natural disaster
D Change for the better

4. The subject of Stevens's poem is the —

F writing of poetry
G solar system
H speaker's disillusionment
J richness of language

5. In "The Planet on the Table," which of the following statements is *not* true about the poems that Ariel writes?

A It is not essential that they survive.
B They were of a forgotten time.
C Ariel is happy that he wrote them.
D They were creations of the sun.

DIRECTIONS

Read the following passage. Then, circle the lettered answer that best completes each numbered item.

from The Glass Menagerie

Tennessee Williams

Scene 1

The characters appearing in this scene are as follows: Amanda Wingfield; her daughter, Laura Wingfield, who survived a childhood illness which left one of her legs shorter than the other; and Amanda's son, Tom Wingfield, who narrates the play.

The Wingfield apartment is in the rear of the building, one of those vast hive-like conglomerations of cellular living-units that flower at warty growths in overcrowded urban centers of lower middle-class population and are symptomatic of the impulse of this largest and fundamentally enslaved section of American society to avoid fluidity and differentiation and to exist and function as one interfused mass of automatism.

The apartment faces an alley and is entered by a fire escape, a structure whose name is a touch of accidental poetic truth, for all of these huge buildings are always burning with the slow and implacable fires of human desperation. The fire escape is part of what we see—that is, the landing of it and steps descending from it.

The scene is memory and is therefore nonrealistic. Memory takes a lot of poetic license. It omits some details; others are exaggerated, according to the emotional value of the articles it touches, for memory is seated predominantly in the heart. The interior is therefore rather dim and poetic.

At the rise of the curtain, the audience is faced with the dark, grim rear wall of the Wingfield tenement. This building is flanked on both sides by dark, narrow alleys which run into murky canyons of tangled clotheslines, garbage cans, and the sinister latticework of neighboring fire escapes. It is up and down these side alleys that exterior entrances and exits are made during the play. At the end of TOM'S *opening commentary, the dark tenement wall slowly becomes transparent and reveals the interior of the ground-floor Wingfield apartment.*

Nearest the audience is the living room, which also serves as a sleeping room for LAURA, *the sofa unfolding to make her bed. Just beyond, separated from the living room by a wide arch or second proscenium with transparent faded portieres[1] (or second curtain), is the dining room. In an old-fashioned whatnot[2] in the living room are seen scores of transparent glass animals. A blown-up photograph of the father hangs on the wall of the living room, to the left of the archway. It is the face of a very handsome young man in a doughboy's First World War cap. He is gallantly smiling, ineluctably smiling, as if to say "I will be smiling forever."*

Also hanging on the wall, near the photograph, are a typewriter keyboard chart and a Gregg shorthand diagram. An upright typewriter on a small table stands beneath the charts.

1. **portieres** (pôr·tyerz′): curtains covering a doorway, used instead of a door.
2. **whatnot:** set of open shelves for holding small objects ("whatnots").

The audience hears and sees the opening scene in the dining room through both the transparent fourth wall of the building and the transparent gauze portieres of the dining-room arch. It is during this revealing scene that the fourth wall slowly ascends, out of sight. This transparent exterior wall is not brought down again until the very end of the play, during TOM'S *final speech.*

The narrator is an undisguised convention of the play. He takes whatever license with dramatic convention is convenient to his purposes.

[TOM *enters, dressed as a merchant sailor, and strolls across to the fire escape. There he stops and lights a cigarette. He addresses the audience.*]

Tom. Yes, I have tricks in my pocket, I have things up my sleeve. But I am the opposite of a stage magician. He gives you illusion that has the appearance of truth. I give you truth in the pleasant disguise of illusion. To begin with, I turn back time. I reverse it to that quaint period, the thirties, when the huge middle class of America was matriculating in a school for the blind. Their eyes had failed them, or they had failed their eyes, and so they were having their fingers pressed forcibly down on the fiery Braille alphabet of a dissolving economy. In Spain there was revolution. Here there was only shouting and confusion. In Spain there was Guernica. Here there were disturbances of labor, sometimes pretty violent, in otherwise peaceful cities such as Chicago, Cleveland, Saint Louis . . . This is the social background of the play.

[*Music begins to play.*]

The play is memory. Being a memory play, it is dimly lighted, it is sentimental, it is not realistic. In memory everything seems to happen to music. That explains the fiddle in the wings. I am the narrator of the play, and also a character in it. The other characters are my mother, Amanda, my sister, Laura, and a gentleman caller who appears in the final scenes. He is the most realistic character in the play, being an emissary from a world of reality that we were somehow set apart from. But since I have a poet's weakness for symbols, I am using this character also as a symbol; he is the long delayed but always expected something that we live for. There is a fifth character in the play who doesn't appear except in this larger-than-life-size photograph over the mantel. This is our father who left us a long time ago. He was a telephone man who fell in love with long distances; he gave up his job with the telephone company and skipped the light fantastic out of town . . . The last we heard of him was a picture postcard from Mazatlán, on the Pacific coast of Mexico, containing a message of two words: "Hello—Goodbye!" and no address. I think the rest of the play will explain itself. . . .

[AMANDA'S *voice becomes audible through the portieres.*]

[*Legend on screen:* "Où sont les neiges?"[3]]

[TOM *divides the portieres and enters the upstage area.* AMANDA *and* LAURA *are seated at a drop-leaf table. Eating is indicated by gestures without food or utensils.* AMANDA *faces the audience.* TOM *and* LAURA *are seated in profile.*

---

3. **"Où sont les neiges?":** French for "Where are the snows?" This is a reference to a famous line by the fifteenth-century French poet François Villon. The complete line "Mais où sont les neiges d'antan?" is a sad question about the passing of time: "But where are the snows of yesteryear?"

The interior has lit up softly and through the screen we see AMANDA *and* LAURA *seated at the table.*]

Amanda (*calling*). Tom?

Tom. Yes, Mother.

Amanda. We can't say grace until you come to the table!

Tom. Coming, Mother. (*He bows slightly and withdraws, reappearing a few moments later in his place at the table.*)

Amanda (*to her son*). Honey, don't *push* with your *fingers.* If you have to push with something, the thing to push with is a crust of bread. And chew—chew! Animals have secretions in their stomachs which enable them to digest food without mastication, but human beings are supposed to chew their food before they swallow it down. Eat food leisurely, son, and really enjoy it. A well-cooked meal has lots of delicate flavors that have to be held in the mouth for appreciation. So chew your food and give your salivary glands a chance to function!

[TOM *deliberately lays his imaginary fork down and pushes his chair back from the table.*]

Tom. I haven't enjoyed one bite of this dinner because of your constant directions on how to eat it. It's you that make me rush through meals with your hawklike attention to every bite I take. Sickening—spoils my appetite—all this discussion of animals' secretion—salivary glands—mastication!

Amanda (*lightly*). Temperament like a Metropolitan star! [TOM *rises and walks toward the living room.*]

You're not excused from the table.

Tom. I'm getting a cigarette.

Amanda. You smoke too much.

[LAURA *rises.*]

Laura. I'll bring in the blanc mange.[4]

[TOM *remains standing with his cigarette by the portieres.*]

Amanda (*rising*). No, sister—you be the lady this time and I'll be the servant.

Laura. I'm already up.

Amanda. Resume your seat, little sister—I want you to stay fresh and pretty—for gentlemen callers!

Laura (*sitting down*). I'm not expecting any gentlemen callers.

Amanda (*crossing out to the kitchenette, airily*). Sometimes they come when they are least expected! Why, I remember one Sunday afternoon in Blue Mountain—

[*She enters the kitchenette.*]

Tom. I know what's coming!

Laura. Yes. But let her tell it.

Tom. Again?

Laura. She loves to tell it.

[AMANDA *returns with a bowl of dessert.*]

Amanda. One Sunday afternoon in Blue Mountain—your mother received—*seventeen*—gentlemen callers! Why, sometimes there weren't chairs enough to accommodate them all. We had to send the servant over to bring in folding chairs from the parish house.

Tom (*remaining at the portieres*). How did you entertain those gentlemen callers?

Amanda. I understood the art of conversation!

Tom. I bet you could talk.

Amanda. Girls in those days *knew* how to talk, I can tell you.

Tom. Yes?

[*Image on screen:* AMANDA *as a girl on a porch, greeting callers.*]

4. **blanc mange** (blə mônzh'): a dessert shaped in a mold.

Amanda. They knew how to entertain their gentlemen callers. It wasn't enough for a girl to be possessed of a pretty face and a graceful figure—although I wasn't slighted in either respect. She also needed to have a nimble wit and a tongue to meet all occasions.

Tom. What did you talk about?

Amanda. Things of importance going on in the world! Never anything coarse or common or vulgar. [*She addresses* TOM *as though he were seated in the vacant chair at the table though he remains by the portieres. He plays this scene as though reading from a script.*] My callers were gentlemen—all! Among my callers were some of the most prominent young planters of the Mississippi Delta—planters and sons of planters!

[TOM *motions for music and a spot of light on* AMANDA. *Her eyes lift, her face glows, her voice becomes rich and elegiac.*]

[*Screen legend:* "Où sont les neiges d'antan?"]

There was young Champ Laughlin who later became vice-president of the Delta Planters Bank. Hadley Stevenson who was drowned in Moon Lake and left his widow one hundred and fifty thousand in Government bonds. There were the Cutrere brothers, Wesley and Bates. Bates was one of my bright particular beaux! He got in a quarrel with that wild Wainwright boy. They shot it out on the floor of Moon Lake Casino. Bates was shot through the stomach. Died in the ambulance on the way to Memphis. His widow was also well-provided for, came into eight or ten thousand acres, that's all. She married him on the rebound—never loved her—carried my picture on him the night he died! And there was that boy that every girl in the Delta had set her cap for! That beautiful, brilliant young Fitzhugh boy from Greene County!

Tom. What did he leave his widow?

Amanda. He never married! Gracious, you talk as though all of my old admirers had turned up their toes to the daisies!

Tom. Isn't this the first you've mentioned that still survives?

Amanda. That Fitzhugh boy went North and made a fortune—came to be known as the Wolf of Wall Street! He had the Midas touch, whatever he touched turned to gold! And I could have been Mrs. Duncan J. Fitzhugh, mind you! But—I picked your *father!*

Laura (*rising*). Mother, let me clear the table.

Amanda. No, dear, you go in front and study your typewriter chart. Or practice your shorthand a little. Stay fresh and pretty!—It's almost time for your gentlemen callers to start arriving. [*She flounces girlishly toward the kitchenette.*] How many do you suppose we're going to entertain this afternoon?

[TOM *throws down the paper and jumps up with a groan.*]

Laura (*alone in the dining room*). I don't believe we're going to receive any, Mother.

Amanda (*reappearing, airily*). What? No one—not one? You must be joking!

[LAURA *nervously echoes her laugh. She slips in a fugitive manner through the half-open portieres and draws them gently behind her. A shaft of very clear light is thrown on her face against the faded tapestry of the curtains. Faintly the music of "The Glass Menagerie" is heard as she continues lightly:*]

Not one gentleman caller? It can't be true! There must be a flood, there must have been a tornado!

Laura. It isn't a flood, it's not a tornado, Mother. I'm just not popular like you were in Blue Mountain. . . .

[TOM *utters another groan.* LAURA *glances at him with a faint, apologetic smile. Her voice catches a little.*] Mother's afraid I'm going to be an old maid.

[*The scene dims out with "The Glass Menagerie" music.*]

---

1. The Wingfield family lives in a —

A wealthy neighborhood
B poverty-stricken community
C lower middle-class urban area
D secluded rural area

2. Amanda does not want Laura to clear the table or get dessert because she —

F wants Laura to recover from her illness
G wants Laura to look fresh for male visitors
H thinks Laura is superior to the rest of the family
J believes that Laura is an incompetent person

3. Tom says that he cannot enjoy his dinner because —

A he is suffering from indigestion
B his knife and spoon are only imaginary
C his mother's health worries him
D his mother criticizes his eating habits

4. Which of the following statements *best* describes Tom's attitude toward the story of Amanda's seventeen gentlemen callers?

F He doesn't want to hear her tell it again, but listens anyway.
G He is shocked by Amanda's past behavior, but hides his surprise.
H He openly admires his mother's unique gift for storytelling.
J He refuses to listen to Amanda's constant lies and exaggerations.

5. The **dialogue** involving Tom, Laura, and Amanda suggests that —

A Amanda's husband will probably reunite with his family
B Amanda wants to relive her past through her daughter
C Laura has a number of admirers
D Laura is withholding a secret from her mother

DIRECTIONS

Read the following passage. Then, circle the lettered answer that best completes each numbered item.

from Bone

Fae Myenne Ng

Everything had an alert quality. Brisk wind, white light. I turned down Sacramento and walked down the hill at a snap-quick pace toward Mah's Baby Store.

Mason was the one who started calling it the Baby Store, and the name just stuck. The old sign with the characters for "Herb Shop" still hangs precariously above the door. I've offered to take it down for Mah, but she's said No every time. Mason thinks she wants to hide.

An old carousel pony with a gouged eye and chipped tail stands in front of the store like a guard looking out onto Grant Avenue. I tapped it as I walked past, my quick good-luck stroke. A string of bells jingled as I pushed through the double doors.

A bitter ginseng odor and a honeysuckle balminess greeted me. Younger, more Americanized mothers complain that the baby clothes have absorbed these old world odors. They must complain about how old the place looks, too, with the custom-made drawers that line the wall from floor to ceiling, the factory lighting. Leon wanted to tear down the wall of mahogany drawers and build a new storage unit. But Mah doesn't want him touching anything in her store, and I was glad, too, because I love the tuck-perfect fit of the drawers, and the *tock!* sound the brass handles make against the hard wood.

Mah was showing off her newest stock of jackets to a woman and her child. I gave a quick nod and went straight to the back, where the boxes were stacked two-high. The fluorescent lights glowed, commercial bright.

The woman tried to bargain the price down but Mah wouldn't budge; she changed the subject. "Your girl is very pretty. How about I don't charge tax?"

Hearing that gave me courage. Mah was in a generous, no-tax mood, and that gave me high hopes for some kind of big discount, too. I knew I'd be tongue-tied soon, so I tried to press my worry down by telling myself what Grandpa Leong used to tell me, that the best way to conquer fear is to act.

Open the mouth and tell.

As soon as the woman and her child walked out the door, I went up to Mah and started out in Chinese, "I want to tell you something."

Mah looked up, wide-eyed, expectant.

I switched to English, "Time was right, so Mason and I just went to City Hall. We got married there."

Mah's expression didn't change.

"In New York," I said.

No answer.

"You know I never liked banquets, all that noise and trouble. And such a waste of so much money."

She still didn't say anything. Suddenly I realized how quiet it was, and that we were completely alone in the store. I heard the hum of the lights.

"Mah?" I said. "Say something."

She didn't even look at me, she just walked away. She went to the back of the store and ripped open a box. I followed and watched her bend the flaps back and pull out armfuls of baby clothes. I waited. She started stacking little mounds. She smoothed out sleeves on top of sleeves, zipped zippers, and cupped the colored hoods, one into another. All around our feet were tangles of white hangers.

"Nina was my witness." My voice was whispery, strange.

Mah grunted, a huumph sound that came out like a curse. My translation was: Disgust, anger. There's power behind her sounds. Over the years I've listened and rendered her Chinese grunts into English words.

She threw the empty box on the floor and gave it a quick kick.

"Just like that.
Did it and didn't tell.
Mother Who Raised You.
Years of work, years of worry.
Didn't! Even! Tell!"

What could I say? Using Chinese was my undoing. She had a world of words that were beyond me.

Mah reached down and picked up a tangle of hangers. She poked them into the baby down coats, baby overalls, baby sleepers. Her wrists whipped back and forth in a way that reminded me of how she used to butcher birds on Salmon Alley. Chickens, pheasants, and pigeons, once a frog. The time with the frog was terrible. Mah skinned it and then stopped. She held the twitching muscle out toward us; she wanted us to see its pink heart. Her voice was spooky, breathless: "Look how the heart keeps beating!" Then the frog sprang out of her hand, still vigorous.

Now I said in English, "It was no big deal."

"It is!"

Mah was using her sewing-factory voice, and I remembered her impatience whenever I tried to talk to her while she was sewing on a deadline.

She rapped a hanger on the counter. "Marriage is for a lifetime, and it should be celebrated! Why sneak around, why act like a thief in the dark?"

I wanted to say: I didn't marry in shame. I didn't marry like you. Your marriages are not my fault. Don't blame me.

Just then the bells jingled and I looked up and saw two sewing ladies coming through the door. I recognized the round hair, the hawk eyes.

"What?" I was too upset to stop. "What?" I demanded again. "You don't like Mason, is that it?"

"Mason," Mah spoke his name soft, "I love."

For love, she used a Chinese word: to embrace, to hug.

I stepped around the boxes, opened my arms and hugged Mah. I held her and took a deep breath and smelled the dried honeysuckle stems, the bitter ginseng root. Above us, the lights beamed bright.

I heard the bells jingle, the latch click, and looked up to see the broad backs of the ladies going out the door toward Grant Avenue. They were going to Portsmouth Square, and I knew they were talking up everything they heard, not stopping when they passed their husbands by the chess tables, not stopping until they found their sewing-lady friends on the benches of the lower level. And that's when they'd tell, tell their long-stitched version of the story, from beginning to end.

Let them make it up, I thought. Let them talk.

1. When the **narrator** comes into the store —

- **A** two women come in behind her
- **B** she finds that her mother has sold the business
- **C** she immediately begins talking to her mother
- **D** her mother is doing business with a customer

2. In the excerpt, we learn all of the following things about Mah *except* that she —

- **F** used to butcher birds
- **G** eloped when she was her daughter's age
- **H** normally does not bargain with customers
- **J** has been married more than once

3. What seems to reconcile the mother and daughter?

- **A** The daughter helps her mother fold baby clothes.
- **B** The daughter reminds her mother of past problems.
- **C** The mother says she adores Mason.
- **D** The mother gives her daughter advice.

4. How does the narrator's mood at the end of the selection differ from her mood at its beginning?

- **F** She has become preoccupied.
- **G** She is more relaxed.
- **H** She seems depressed.
- **J** She regrets her action.

DIRECTIONS

Read the following poems. Then, circle the lettered answer that best completes each numbered item.

The following two poems share certain qualities; they also show differences that can be attributed in part to the period in which each poem was written. "To My Dear and Loving Husband," by Puritan poet Anne Bradstreet (1612–1672), was published in 1678, six years after her death. Edna St. Vincent Millay (1892–1950), a famous poet from the modern period, published "Love is not all" in 1931.

To My Dear and Loving Husband

Anne Bradstreet

If ever two were one, then surely we.
If ever man were loved by wife, then thee;
If ever wife was happy in a man,
Compare with me, ye women, if you can.
I prize thy love more than whole mines of gold
Or all the riches that the East doth hold.
My love is such that rivers cannot quench,
Nor ought[1] but love from thee, give recompense.[2]
Thy love is such I can no way repay,
The heavens reward thee manifold,[3] I pray.
Then while we live, in love let's so persevere[4]
That when we live no more, we may live ever.

Love is not all

Edna St. Vincent Millay

Love is not all: it is not meat nor drink
Nor slumber nor a roof against the rain;
Nor yet a floating spar to men that sink
And rise and sink and rise and sink again;
Love can not fill the thickened lung with breath,
Nor clean the blood, nor set the fractured bone;
Yet many a man is making friends with death
Even as I speak, for lack of love alone.
It well may be that in a difficult hour,
Pinned down by pain and moaning for release,
Or nagged by want past resolution's power,
I might be driven to sell your love for peace,
Or trade the memory of this night for food.
It well may be. I do not think I would.

---

1. **ought:** archaic word meaning "anything."
2. **recompense** *n.:* repayment.
3. **manifold** *adv.:* in many ways.
4. **persevere** *v.:* pronounced so last two syllables rhyme with *ever*.

1. In “To My Dear and Loving Husband,” the **speaker** describes her love for her husband using **imagery** relating to —

- **A** wealth and nature
- **B** thirst and hunger
- **C** water and air
- **D** gold and diamonds

2. The speaker in Bradstreet’s poem states that her love for her husband is —

- **F** less than her love of wealth and comfort
- **G** greater than her love for God
- **H** less than the love other women feel for their husbands
- **J** as strong, if not stronger, than any other woman’s love

3. Bradstreet’s poem ends with a **paradox**—an apparent contradiction that reveals a truth. Which of the following items explains this paradox?

- **A** People who are no longer alive on earth can be alive forever in heaven.
- **B** People who don’t love each other on earth will love each other in heaven.
- **C** People should love each other while they’re alive because life is short.
- **D** People who don’t love each other will not live forever.

4. In “Love is not all,” the speaker compares love to what it is not and what it cannot do. Which of these points does the speaker make in lines 1–6?

- **F** Love cannot let you down.
- **G** Love cannot fill material needs or cure sickness.
- **H** Love is less important than friendship.
- **J** Love cannot last forever.

5. What **paradox** does the speaker in “Love is not all” point out in lines 1–8?

- **A** Love is painful, yet it makes us happy.
- **B** Loving oneself is more important than loving other people.
- **C** Love cannot save lives, yet people can die without it.
- **D** It is more important to love people than to heal them.

6. In Millay’s poem, which statement best describes the speaker’s **attitude** toward love?

- **F** The speaker believes that love will not let a person down.
- **G** The speaker thinks peace is more important than love.
- **H** The speaker thinks love fills an essential need.
- **J** The speaker thinks love isn’t worth the trouble.

7. A major stylistic difference between the two poems is —

- **A** Bradstreet’s poem rhymes and Millay’s poem does not
- **B** Millay uses more religious imagery than Bradstreet
- **C** Millay’s language is more contemporary than Bradstreet’s
- **D** only Bradstreet’s poem is addressed to a “you”

8. Which statement *best* describes the contrast in **tone** between the two poems?

- **F** Bradstreet's tone is spiritual, and Millay's tone is playful.
- **G** Bradstreet's tone is loving, and Millay's tone is regretful.
- **H** Bradstreet's tone is pessimistic, and Millay's tone is optimistic.
- **J** Bradstreet's tone is devoted, and Millay's tone is spiteful.

9. Which of the following statements *best* expresses the shared **theme** of the two poems?

- **A** Love makes life easier to bear.
- **B** Love is always painful.
- **C** Women love men more than men love women.
- **D** Love cures everything.

10. What is one way that each poem reflects the time period in which it was written?

- **F** Bradstreet's poem reveals her Puritan devotion to God, while Millay's poem addresses earthbound concerns.
- **G** Bradstreet's poem questions a woman's place in society, while Millay's poem uses romantic imagery.
- **H** Bradstreet's poem uses elaborate figures of speech, while Millay's poem does not.
- **J** Bradstreet's poem praises love, but Millay sees it only as troublesome.

DIRECTIONS

Read the following selections. Then, circle the lettered answer that best completes each numbered item.

The following two pieces of literature, which deal with the horror of war, were written about a hundred years apart. Stephen Crane (1871–1900) was born after the Civil War, but he wrote his best-known work, The Red Badge of Courage, *about the experiences of a young soldier facing battle in the Civil War. The poet Yusef Komunyakaa (1947–) won the Pulitzer Prize in 1994 for his poetry collection* Neon Vernacular. *"Camouflaging the Chimera" is based on his experiences in the Vietnam War, where he served as an information specialist.*

from The Red Badge of Courage

Stephen Crane

This excerpt from The Red Badge of Courage *describes a column of soldiers headed into battle. The "youth" is Henry Fleming, Crane's protagonist in the novel.*

Presently the calm head of a forward-going column of infantry[1] appeared in the road. It came swiftly on. Avoiding the obstructions gave it the sinuous movement of a serpent. The men at the head butted mules with their musket stocks. They prodded teamsters[2] indifferent to all howls. The men forced their way through parts of the dense mass by strength. The blunt head of the column pushed. The raving teamsters swore many strange oaths.

The commands to make way had the ring of a great importance in them. The men were going forward to the heart of the din. They were to confront the eager rush of the enemy. They felt the pride of their onward movement when the remainder of the army seemed trying to dribble down this road. They tumbled teams about with a fine feeling that it was no matter so long as their column got to the front in time. This importance made their faces grave and stern. And the backs of the officers were very rigid.

As the youth looked at them the black weight of his woe returned to him. He felt that he was regarding a procession of chosen beings. The separation was as great to him as if they had marched with weapons of flame and banners of sunlight. He could never be like them. He could have wept in his longings.

He searched about in his mind for an adequate malediction[3] for the indefinite cause, the thing upon which men turn the words of final blame. It—whatever it was—was responsible for him, he said. There lay the fault.

The haste of the column to reach the battle seemed to the forlorn young man to be something much finer than stout fighting. Heroes, he thought, could find excuses in that long seething lane. They could retire with perfect self-respect and make excuses to the stars.

---

1. **infantry** *n.:* foot soldiers.
2. **teamsters** *n. pl.:* drivers of teams of horses used for hauling.
3. **malediction** *n.:* curse.

He wondered what those men had eaten that they could be in such haste to force their way to grim chances of death. As he watched his envy grew until he thought that he wished to change lives with one of them. He would have liked to have used a tremendous force, he said, throw off himself and become a better. Swift pictures of himself, apart, yet in himself, came to him—a blue desperate figure leading lurid charges with one knee forward and a broken blade high—a blue, determined figure standing before a crimson and steel assault, getting calmly killed on a high place before the eyes of all. He thought of the magnificent pathos[4] of his dead body.

These thoughts uplifted him. He felt the quiver of war desire. In his ears, he heard the ring of victory. He knew the frenzy of a rapid successful charge. The music of the trampling feet, the sharp voices, the clanking arms of the column near him made him soar on the red wings of war. For a few moments he was sublime.[5]

4. **pathos** *n.:* the quality in something experienced or observed that arouses a sense of sorrow or pity.
5. **sublime** *adj.:* noble; majestic.

Camouflaging the Chimera[1]

Yusef Komunyakaa

We tied branches to our helmets.
We painted our faces & rifles
with mud from a riverbank,

blades of grass hung from the pockets
of our tiger suits.[2] We wove
ourselves into the terrain,
content to be a hummingbird's target.

We hugged bamboo & leaned
against a breeze off the river,
slow-dragging with ghosts
from Saigon to Bangkok,

with women left in doorways
reaching in from America.
We aimed at dark-hearted songbirds.

In our way station of shadows
rock apes[3] tried to blow our cover,
throwing stones at the sunset.
Chameleons

crawled our spines, changing from day
to night: green to gold,
gold to black. But we waited
till the moon touched metal,
till something almost broke
inside us. VC[4] struggled
with the hillside, like black silk[5]

1. **Chimera** (kī·mir′ə): a monster in Greek mythology. The word today also refers to a fanciful creation of the imagination.
2. **tiger suits:** black-and-green camouflage uniforms with stripes.
3. **rock apes:** apes or tailless monkeys known to throw rocks at humans, often scaring soldiers in Vietnam into thinking they were being attacked by the enemy.
4. **VC:** The Viet Cong were Communist forces that opposed the U.S. and South Vietnamese governments during the Vietnam War.
5. **black silk:** The Viet Cong wore black silk to camouflage themselves at night.

wrestling iron through grass.
We weren't there. The river ran
through our bones. Small animals took
refuge
against our bodies; we held our breath,
ready to spring the L-shaped
ambush, as a world revolved
under each man's eyelid.

---

1. Which of the following statements is *not* true, based on *The Red Badge of Courage* excerpt?

- **A** The soldiers are proud to go to battle.
- **B** The youth feels alienated from the soldiers leading the march.
- **C** The soldiers are delaying their charge into battle.
- **D** The youth imagines his own heroic death.

2. Which statement *best* represents the **situational irony** in the Crane excerpt?

- **F** Although the youth is fearless, he does not look forward to the battle.
- **G** The youth feels pride when looking at the enemy rather than when looking at his fellow soldiers.
- **H** The youth feels ecstatic when he fantasizes about his death.
- **J** Although he does not want to be a hero, the youth fights bravely.

3. Which of the animals mentioned in the Komunyakaa poem *best* **symbolizes** the soldiers?

- **A** Hummingbirds
- **B** Songbirds
- **C** Rock apes
- **D** Chameleons

4. The words that *best* describe the **tone** of Komunyakaa's poem are —

- **F** judgmental and condemning
- **G** adoring and extravagant
- **H** tense and apprehensive
- **J** bitter and sarcastic

5. Which statement accurately describes a contrast between the two selections?

- **A** Crane's piece is bitter, whereas Komunyakaa's poem is uplifting.
- **B** Crane's piece is written from one man's viewpoint, whereas Komunyakaa's poem uses the collective voice of a group of soldiers.
- **C** Crane's piece focuses on events the narrator remembers from the past, whereas Komunyakaa's poem takes place in the present.
- **D** Crane's piece emphasizes the loud sounds of the battle, whereas Komunyakaa's poem focuses on the smells of war.

6. Which of the following statements expresses a shared **theme** of these two selections?

- **F** Peace can be obtained only through bloodshed.
- **G** War requires ordinary people to perform extraordinary tasks.
- **H** Soldiers are incapable of true heroism.
- **J** Nature is ultimately ruined by war.

DIRECTIONS

Read the following poems. Then, circle the lettered answer that best completes each numbered item.

Some poets claim that all poetry is about other poetry. Certainly it is true that many poems are written to imitate or respond to other poems. The following poems were written by two poets who lived in very different times.

The first poem is by Walt Whitman (1819–1892). Whitman wrote poetry that was considered radical in its time because, for one thing, it sang of things that were not usually considered "poetic." For another thing it was written without any care for perfect rhymes.

The second poem was written by Jimmy Santiago Baca (1957–) nearly a hundred years after Whitman's death. Clearly, Baca was thinking of Whitman's Song of Myself *when he wrote* his *poem about* himself. *Evident in this poem is the fact that Baca had a troubled childhood. In his young adulthood he even spent time in prison.*

from Song of Myself

Walt Whitman

1.

I celebrate myself, and sing myself,
And what I assume you shall assume,
For every atom belonging to me as good belongs to you.

I loaf[1] and invite my soul,
I lean and loaf at my ease observing a spear of summer grass.

My tongue, every atom of my blood, form'd from this soil, this air,
Born here of parents born here from parents the same, and their
  parents the same,
I, now thirty-seven years old in perfect health begin,
Hoping to cease not till death.

Creeds and schools in abeyance,[2]
Retiring back a while sufficed at what they are, but never forgotten,
I harbor for good or bad, I permit to speak at every hazard,
Nature without check with original energy.

---

1. **loaf** *v.:* spend time idly; lounge about.
2. **abeyance** *n.:* temporary suspension; inactivity.

Who Understands Me but Me

Jimmy Santiago Baca

They turn the water off, so I live without water,
they build walls higher, so I live without treetops,
they paint the windows black, so I live without sunshine,
they lock my cage, so I live without going anywhere,
they take each last tear I have, I live without tears,
they take my heart and rip it open, I live without heart,
they take my life and crush it, so I live without a future,
they say I am beastly and fiendish, so I have no friends,
they stop up each hope, so I have no passage out of hell,
they give me pain, so I live with pain,
they give me hate, so I live with my hate,
they have changed me, and I am not the same man,
they give me no shower, so I live with my smell,
they separate me from my brothers, so I live without brothers,
who understands me when I say this is beautiful?
who understands me when I say I have found other freedoms?

I cannot fly or make something appear in my hand,
I cannot make the heavens open or the earth tremble,
I can live with myself, and I am amazed at myself, my love, my beauty,
I am taken by my failures, astounded by my fears,
I am stubborn and childish,
in the midst of this wreckage of life they incurred,
I practice being myself,
and I have found parts of myself never dreamed of by me,
they were goaded out from under rocks in my heart
when the walls were built higher,
when the water was turned off and the windows painted black.
I followed these signs
like an old tracker and followed the tracks deep into myself,
followed the blood-spotted path,
deeper into dangerous regions, and found so many parts of myself,
who taught me water is not everything,
and gave me new eyes to see through walls,
and when they spoke, sunlight came out of their mouths,
and I was laughing at me with them,
we laughed like children and made pacts to always be loyal,
who understands me when I say this is beautiful?

1. In *Song of Myself* 1, the speaker's **attitude** toward himself is *best* described as —

A self-hatred
B mild curiosity
C joyful wonder
D pessimism

2. Which of the following lines in *Song of Myself* 1 gives the *best* example of the speaker's love of life?

F "And what I assume you shall assume"
G "I celebrate myself, and sing myself"
H "I harbor for good or bad"
J "I lean and loaf at my ease"

3. Which statement *best* expresses the speaker's relationship with other people in *Song of Myself* 1?

A The speaker and other people are one and the same.
B The speaker feels alienated from other people.
C The speaker feels angry at other people.
D The speaker wants to control other people.

4. In line 1 of "Who Understands Me but Me," "they" most likely refers to —

F the speaker's best friends
G an oppressive society
H irresponsible teachers
J a loving family

5. At the end of Baca's poem, the speaker's **attitude** is *best* described as —

A hopeless
B remorseful
C triumphant
D exhausted

6. Which of the following statements *best* expresses the **contrast** in **tone** between the two poems?

F Whitman's tone is humorless, and Baca's tone is playful.
G Whitman's tone is judgmental, and Baca's tone is joyous.
H Whitman's tone is joyous, and Baca's tone is determined.
J Whitman's tone is loving, and Baca's tone is dreary.

7. Which of the following statements expresses a shared **theme** of these two poems?

A Technology has damaged the natural world.
B The speakers celebrate the miracle of one's self.
C Society cannot dominate the individual.
D Not all people are worthy of respect.

8. Which statement accurately describes a **contrast** between the two selections?

F Whitman's poem condemns society; Baca's poem does not.
G Whitman's speaker identifies himself with the world of nature; Baca's speaker does not.
H Whitman's poem is written in free verse; Baca's poem is not.
J Whitman's poem celebrates the human spirit; Baca's poem does not.

DIRECTIONS

Read the following poems. Then, circle the lettered answer that best completes each numbered item.

The following two poems are about a woman in Greek mythology—Helen of Troy—but they depict her in starkly different tones. The wife of King Menelaus of Sparta (one of the great city-states of ancient Greece), Helen was said to be the most beautiful woman in the world. After she ran off with (or in some versions was abducted by) Paris, a handsome prince from the city of Troy in Asia Minor, Menelaus and other Greek warriors attacked Troy to get her back. The resulting Trojan War lasted ten years. Edgar Allan Poe (1809–1849) first published "To Helen" *in 1831 and then again, slightly revised, in 1845. The poet H. D. (1886–1961) published* "Helen" *in 1924.*

To Helen

Edgar Allan Poe

Poe's poem is filled with many ***allusions,*** *or references, to classical mythology. Though Poe claimed he was describing the mother of a school friend, he is clearly alluding to Helen of Troy, the classical ideal of feminine beauty. Poe also alludes to another figure from classical mythology, Psyche, a mortal woman whose name means "soul." Psyche's great beauty captured the heart of Cupid, the god of love, who took her to live in the realm of the gods. Like Helen, Psyche is often used to represent ideal beauty.*

Helen, thy beauty is to me
Like those Nicéan barks of yore,
That gently, o'er a perfumed sea,
The weary, way-worn wanderer bore
To his own native shore.[1]

On desperate seas long wont to roam,
Thy hyacinth[2] hair, thy classic face,
Thy Naiad[3] airs have brought me home
To the glory that was Greece,
And the grandeur that was Rome.

Lo! in yon brilliant window-niche
How statuelike I see thee stand,
The agate lamp[4] within thy hand!
Ah, Psyche, from the regions which
Are Holy Land!

1. **Nicéan . . . shore:** Nicaea was a Greek colony; "barks" are ships. The "wanderer" is Odysseus from Homer's epic poem the *Odyssey*. Poe scholars have never found an adequate explanation for "Nicéan" (since Odysseus traveled home by ships from Phaeacia) and think Poe used the word to contribute to the musical quality of the poem.
2. **hyacinth** (hī'ə·sinth') *n.* used as *adj.*: an adjective used often in classical poems to describe hair that was hyacinthine, or wavy, like the petals on a hyacinth flower.
3. **Naiad** (nā'ad'): nymphlike. In Greek and Roman mythology, the Naiads were water nymphs believed to have healing powers.
4. **agate** (ag'it) **lamp:** a lamp made of agate, a semiprecious stone associated with immortality.

Helen

H. D.

All Greece hates
the still eyes in the white face,
the luster as of olives
where she stands,
and the white hands.

All Greece reviles
the wan face when she smiles,
hating it deeper still
when it grows wan and white,
remembering past enchantments
and past ills.

Greece sees unmoved,
God's daughter,[1] born of love,
the beauty of cool feet
and slenderest knees,
could love indeed the maid,
only if she were laid,
white ash amid funereal cypresses.

---

1. **God's daughter:** Helen was a daughter of Zeus, the king of the gods. She was conceived when Zeus (in the form of a swan) seduced the mortal Leda.

---

1. In the first two lines of Poe's poem, the main poetic device is —

A personification
B simile
C onomatopoeia
D metaphor

2. In Poe's first two stanzas the **speaker** is saying that Helen's beauty —

F makes him feel weary and desperate
G makes him long to travel by sea
H makes him feel intimidated
J makes him feel as if he is returning home

3. In the third stanza of Poe's poem, to what is Helen compared?

A A lamp
B Greece
C A statue
D Rome

4. In H. D.'s poem "Helen," what can be inferred about the cause of the Greek people's attitude toward Helen?

F They pity her because she is a victim.
G They condemn her for her role in the Trojan War.
H They forgive her for her past misdeeds.
J They are jealous of her beauty.

5. In the second stanza of H. D.'s poem, Helen grows increasingly pale because —

- **A** she knows she is growing old
- **B** she is angry at the Greeks' attitude toward her
- **C** she thinks she will be murdered and buried among cypresses
- **D** she is troubled by memories of her past

6. In the third stanza of "Helen," the speaker is saying that the people of Greece can love Helen —

- **F** despite the trouble she has caused
- **G** because they feel sorry for her
- **H** only when she is dead
- **J** because she is "God's daughter"

7. In contrast to Poe's poem, the overall **tone** in H. D.'s poem is —

- **A** bitter while Poe's tone is romantic
- **B** adoring while Poe's tone is bitter
- **C** envious while Poe's tone is ironic
- **D** reserved while Poe's tone is humorous

8. Unlike Poe's poem, H. D.'s poem depicts Helen as —

- **F** a symbol of classic beauty
- **G** a victim of male domination
- **H** the object of societal hatred
- **J** an ordinary woman

ACKNOWLEDGMENTS

For permission to reprint copyrighted material, grateful acknowledgment is made to the following sources:

Arte Público Press: "The Latin Deli: An Ars Poetica" by Judith Ortiz Cofer from *The Americas Review,* vol. 19, no. 1. Copyright © 1991 by Judith Ortiz Cofer. Published by Arte Público Press-University of Houston, 1991.

Elizabeth Barnett, Literary Executor: "Sonnet XXX" *of Fatal Interview* from *Collected Poems* by Edna St. Vincent Millay. Copyright © 1931, 1958 by Edna St. Vincent Millay and Norma Millay Ellis. Published by HarperCollins. All rights reserved.

Beacon Press, Boston: "Autobiographical Notes" from *Notes of a Native Son* by James Baldwin. Copyright © 1955 and renewed © 1983 by James Baldwin.

Estate of Gwendolyn Brooks: "of De Witt Williams on his way to Lincoln Cemetery" from *Blacks* by Gwendolyn Brooks. Copyright © 1991 by Gwendolyn Brooks. Published by Third World Press, Chicago, 60619, 1991.

Curbstone Press: "Who Understands Me but Me" from *What's Happening* by Jimmy Santiago Baca. Copyright © 1982 by Jimmy Santiago Baca. Distributed by Consortium.

Farrar, Straus & Giroux, LLC: "The Fish" from *The Complete Poems 1927–1979* by Elizabeth Bishop. Copyright © 1979, 1983 by Alice Helen Methfessel. "The Magic Barrel" from *The Magic Barrel* by Bernard Malamud. Copyright © 1950, 1958 and renewed © 1977, 1986 by Bernard Malamud.

Harcourt, Inc.: "The Jilting of Granny Weatherall" from *Flowering Judas and Other Stories* by Katherine Anne Porter. Copyright 1930 and renewed © 1958 by Katherine Anne Porter. "A Worn Path" from *A Curtain of Green and Other Stories* by Eudora Welty. Copyright 1941 and renewed © 1969 by Eudora Welty.

HarperCollins Publishers, Inc.: "Mirror" from *Crossing the Water* by Sylvia Plath. Copyright © 1963 by Ted Hughes. Originally appeared in *The New Yorker.* From *Black Boy* by Richard Wright. Copyright 1937, 1942, 1944, 1945 by Richard Wright; copyright renewed © 1973 by Ellen Wright.

Harvard University Press and the Trustees of Amherst College: "Because I could not stop for Death" and "The Soul selects her own Society" from *The Poems of Emily Dickinson,* edited by Thomas H. Johnson. Copyright © 1951, 1955, 1979, 1983 by the President and Fellows of Harvard College. Published by The Belknap Press of Harvard University Press, Cambridge, Mass.

Henry Holt and Company, LLC: "Design" and "Once by the Pacific" from *The Poetry of Robert Frost,* edited by Edward Connery Lathem. Copyright © 1956 by Robert Frost; copyright 1928, © 1969 by Henry Holt and Company, LLC; copyright © 1997 by Edward Connery Lathem.

Hyperion, a division of Disney Book Publishing, Inc.: From *Bone* by Fae Myenne Ng. Copyright © 1993 by Fae Myenne Ng.

Alfred A. Knopf, a division of Random House, Inc.: "Daybreak in Alabama" and "The Weary Blues" from *The Collected Poems of Langston Hughes* by Langston Hughes. Copyright © 1994 by The Estate of Langston Hughes. "The Planet on the Table" from *Collected Poems* by Wallace Stevens. Copyright 1954 by Wallace Stevens.

Liveright Publishing Corporation: "what if a much of a which of a wind" from *Complete Poems: 1904–1962* by E. E. Cummings, edited by George J. Firmage. Copyright 1944, © 1972, 1991 by the Trustees for the E. E. Cummings Trust.

New Directions Publishing Corporation: "Helen" from *Collected Poems 1912–1944* by H. D. Doolittle. Copyright © 1982 by The Estate of Hilda Doolittle. "The Red Wheelbarrow" from *Collected Poems: 1909–1939,* vol. I by William Carlos Williams. Copyright © 1938 by New Directions Publishing Corp.

G. P. Putnam's Sons, a division of Penguin Putnam Inc.: "Rules of the Game" from *The Joy Luck Club* by Amy Tan. Copyright © 1989 by Amy Tan.

Random House, Inc.: "Upon Receiving the Nobel Prize for Literature, 1950" from *Essays, Speeches and Public Letters* by William Faulkner, edited by James B. Meriwether. Copyright 1950 by William Faulkner. From *The Glass Menagerie* by Tennessee Williams. Copyright © 1945 by Tennessee Williams and Edwina D. Williams; copyright renewed © 1973 by Tennessee Williams.

Scribner, an imprint of Simon & Schuster Adult Publishing Group: "Soldier's Home" from *In Our Time* by Ernest Hemingway. Copyright 1925 by Charles Scribner's Sons; copyright renewed 1953 by Ernest Hemingway.

Rosemary A. Thurber and The Barbara Hogenson Agency: "The Secret Life of Walter Mitty" from *My World—And Welcome to It* by James Thurber. Copyright © 1942 by James Thurber; copyright renewed © 1971 by Helen Thurber and Rosemary A. Thurber. All rights reserved.

The University of New Mexico Press: From Introduction from *The Way to Rainy Mountain* by N. Scott Momaday. Copyright © 1969 by The University of New Mexico Press. First published in *The Reporter,* January 26, 1967.

Viking Penguin, a division of Penguin Putnam Inc.: From Act IV from *The Crucible* by Arthur Miller. Copyright 1952, 1953, 1954, copyright renewed © 1980, 1981, 1982 by Arthur Miller.

Wesleyan University Press: "Camouflaging the Chimera" from *Neon Vernacular: New and Selected Poems* by Yusef Komunyakaa. Copyright © 1993 by Yusef Komunyakaa.

PHOTO CREDITS

Abbreviations used: (tl) top left, (tc) top center, (tr) top right, (l) left, (lc) left center, (c) center, (rc) right center, (r) right, (bl) bottom left, (bc) bottom center, (br) bottom right, (bkgd) background.

Pages 18, 19, 20, 21, 22, 23, 24, 25, Comstock IMAGES; 27, Reproduced by kind permission of the vicar and church wardens of St. Botolph's Church, Boston, England; 17, *The Progress of Sin* (detail) (1744) by Benjamin Keach. Woodcut/Sinclair Hamilton Collection no. 21. Graphic Arts Collections. Visual Materials Division. Department of Rare Books and Special Collections. Princeton University Libraries; 24, *Benjamin Franklin Drawing Electricity from the Sky* (c.1805) by Benjamin West (1738–1820). Oil on paper on canvas (13 1/4" x 10"). Philadelphia Museum of Art: Mr. and Mrs. Wharton Sinkler Collection (PI98423); 37, (lc), John Henley/Corbis Stock Market, (bkgd), Image Copyright ©2003 Photodisc Inc.; 45, (c), National Archives, (bc), Joe Viesti/Viesti Associates, (br), Independence National Historical Park, Philadelphia, Pennsylvania; 72, 73, 74, 75, 76, 77, CORBIS Images/HRW; 63, Gray Braasch/Getty Images/Stone; 73, Kirchoff/Wohlberg, (bkgd), Image Copyright ©2003 Photodisc Inc.; 79, Image Copyright ©2003 Photodisc Inc.; 83, Image Copyright ©2003 Photodisc Inc.; 104, 105, 106, 107, 108, 109, CORBIS Images/HRW; 95, (c), Image Copyright ©2003 Photodisc Inc., (bkgd), HRW Photo; 101, Robert Essel/Corbis Stock Market; 111, Illustrations by Arvis Stewart for "The Raven"; 119, Getty Images/Eyewire Inc.; 134, 135, CORBIS Images/HRW; 137, University of Virginia Library, Charlottesville, Courtesy NGS; 147, (l), Reprinted by permission of the publishers and the Trustees of Amherst College from The Poems of Emily Dickinson, Thomas H. Johnson, ed., Cambridge, Mass.: The Belknap Press of Harvard University Press, Copyright ©1951, 1955, 1979, 1983 by the President and Fellows of Harvard College. Manuscript image courtesy of the Amherst College Library, (lc), Amherst College Library, Amherst, Massachusetts. (bl), Culver Pictures; 152, 153, 154, 155, 156, 157, Image Copyright ©2003 Photodisc Inc.; 159, Chester County Historical Society, West Chester, Pennsylvania; 159, (c), Image Copyright ©2003 Photodisc Inc. (bkgd), Kirchoff/Wohlberg; 177, Museum of the City of New York. Scala/Art Resource, NY; 193, Image Copyright ©2003 Photodisc Inc.; 205, (tl), Michael DeYoung/Alaska Stock Images, (bkgd), Alaska Stock Images; 222, 223, 224, 225, 226, 227, 228, 229, CORBIS Images/HRW; 247, Image Copyright ©2003 Photodisc Inc.; 235, Barry O'Rourke/The Stock Market, (bkgd), Image Copyright ©2003 Photodisc Inc.; 239, Ron Thomas/Getty Images/FPG; 245, (tl), (bl), (br), Liberty Collection/Getty Images/The Image Bank, (tr), Kirchoff/Wohlberg; 269, (tl), (br), (bkgd), Photofest; 279, (c), Eudora Welty Collection, Mississippi Department of Archives and History, (bkgd), Marco Polo/Phototake; 291, (tl), John F. Kennedy Library, Boston, Massachusetts, (tr), Department of Rare Books and Special Collections/Princeton University Libraries, (bl), Department of Rare Books and Special Collections/ Princeton University Libraries, (bc), Kirchoff/Wohlberg, (br), Leib Image Archives; 301, Image Copyright ©2003 Photodisc Inc.; 309, Kirchoff/Wohlberg, (bkgd), Image Copyright ©2003 Photodisc Inc.; 321, (c), AP/Wide World Photos, (bkgd), Image Copyright ©2003 Photodisc Inc.; 325, Image Copyright ©2003 Photodisc Inc.; 329, Getty Images/Eyewire Inc.; 333, HRW Photo Library; 338, 339, 340, 341, 342, 343, CORBIS Images/HRW; 345, Photofest; 356, 357, 358, 359, 360, 361, Getty Images/Eyewire Inc.; 363, Image Copyright ©2003 Photodisc Inc.; 381, Mississippi Valley Collection, University of Memphis Libraries; 397, Image Copyright ©2003 Photodisc Inc.; 403, James Barnett/Corbis Stock Market, (bkgd), Archives and Manuscripts Division of the Oklahoma Historical Society; 413, John Banagan/ Getty Images/The Image Bank; 425, Steve Schapiro/ Black Star; 433, Image Copyright ©2003 Photodisc Inc.; 437, Dennis Lisl/Getty Images/The Image Bank, (tr), Image Copyright ©2003 Photodisc Inc.

AUTHOR AND TITLE INDEX